FINANCE COMMISSION
AND
CENTRE-STATE FISCAL RELATIONS
History, Recommendations and Implications

B.M. JOSHI

ANAMIKA PUBLISHERS & DISTRIBUTORS (P) LTD.
4697/3, 21-A, Ansari Road, Daryaganj, New Delhi 110 002
Phones: 011-2328 1655, 011-2327 0239
Fax : 011-2786 8035
E-mali: anamikapublishers@yahoo.co.in

First Published 2013

ISBN 978-81-7975-429-0

PRINTED IN INDIA

Published by Anamika Publishers & Distributors (P) Ltd., 4697/3, 21A, Ansari Road, Daryaganj, New Delhi 110 002. Typeset by Aadil Printographics, Delhi 110 092 and Printed at Nagri Printers, Delhi 110 032

Contents

Contents

Foreword

I have gone through the manuscript "Finance Commission and Centre State Fiscal Relations—History, Recommendations and Implications", by Dr. B.M. Joshi, with great interest. His presentation does full justice to the title of the book. The interested reader can find all the basic material relevant to the subject at one place—right from the constitutional provisions relating to the Finance Commission to the Action Taken Report (ATR) by the government on the recommendations made by each of the thirteen Finance Commissions. The book is comprehensive and at the same time concise and readable. The treatment of the subject is informative, analytical, critical where necessary, objective and balanced. The book would be useful as reference material for a variety of readers—students and teachers, policy makers and professionals on the subject. It is also up-to-date because of the inclusion of the discussion on the Report of the 13th Finance Commission.

Dr. Joshi has been able to produce such a solid work because of his profound interest in the subject and protracted experience of sustained and dedicated work in a responsible position with the government of Uttar Pradesh. The publication of the book is also timely because the debate on Centre-State Fiscal Relations can be expected to be in full swing again with the constitution of the 14th

Finance Commission. The book can serve as a useful reference work for all those concerned, including the state governments.

Happily, I find myself in agreement with the position taken by the author on many issues, including the untenability of making the population of 1971 as the basis for devolution even beyond 2001, as it would penalize the poorer states for no fault of theirs; proliferation of Centrally Sponsored Schemes considerably erodes the states' freedom in decision-making, quite apart from distorting the allocation of resources; and the diminishing role of the Finance Commission vis-a-vis Planning Commission at a time when the role of the market and decentralized decision-making are expected to increase manifold.

The central question in the Centre-State financial relations is how to redress the imbalances in the availability of resources between the centre and states, on the one hand, and between the better-off and the poorer states, on the other. Thanks to the successful working of the institutions of Finance Commission and Planning Commission, the country has been able to achieve a high degree of economic integration. But economic integration so achieved can be strengthened further and sustained only if the regional imbalances in the availability of basic infrastructure are redressed and long-run comparative advantage enjoyed by the less developed states is fully exploited in the overall national interest. The role of the Finance Commission is unique in achieving this goal. I have no doubt that the book by Dr. B.M. Joshi would contribute fruitfully to the on-going debate on this vital issue.

C.H. Hanumantha Rao
Honorary Professor
Institute of Economic Growth
University of Delhi, Delhi

Preface

The subject of Centre-State relations, specially, the fiscal relations have always been at the forefront. Though many attempts had been made during the British rule through deliberations in many Committees and Commissions, culminating in Government of India Act 1919 and then, further, refined by Government of India Act 1935, but the friction has all along been there in the Centre-Provinces fiscal relations, because of the strong centralising tendency of the legislation.

The Constitution of India adopted, after great deliberations, had, by and large, the centralised tendency built into it, as was the case with Government of India Act. The distribution of sources of revenue and expenditure responsibilities was the basic cause of conflict, because of the mismatch between sources of revenue and expenditure responsibilities of Centre and the States. The system worked well, because of the one party rule both at the Centre and States. But, the areas as well as occurrence of friction increased with the change in the political spectrum. With the emergence of the regional parties and their taking over the reigns at the State level, the frequency of occurrence of friction has now increased.

Visualising the mismatch and the likely friction, the framers of our Constitution provided for an appropriate institution to deal with such a situation at a regular interval. As a result, the institution of Finance Commission emerged, which has been assigned with the task of minimising the non correspondence of sources of revenue and expenditure responsibilities—both of Centre and States—by recommending a scheme of devolution of central taxes and grants-in-aid to States in need of assistance.

In the beginning, only Income Tax was compulsorily shareable and Union Excise Duty sharing was permissive, but with the Constitution amendment, now all the central taxes are shareable. At the same time, the responsibilities have also increased over the years.

Since its inception, thirteen Finance Commissions have been constituted, which after deliberations with Centre and States, have given their recommendations leading to the minimisation of the mismatch. Many new developments have also taken place, which have enhanced the role of Finance Commission. From Income Tax and Union Excise Duty, the Commission today considers all the taxes for sharing their proceeds with the States. It has also been entrusted with the responsibility of helping the Local Bodies by transferring a certain portion of Central tax revenues.

Over the years, the role of Finance Commission has also changed. From the role of "arbitrator" between the Centre and the States in the matter of sharing of taxes and grants-in-aid, the Commission has now assumed the role of "facilitator" of reform measures mainly at the States level. The linking of FRBM Act with release of grants-in-aid and debt write off has greatly guided the States in thinking and initiating reforms measures which have ultimately had the States towards fiscal consolidation; and as a result, most of the States are in revenue surplus position and fall within the prescribed ceiling of GFD:GSDP ratio.

The book deals with the whole gamut of Central-States

fiscal relations. Starting with historical back ground of evolution of Centre Provinces (States) fiscal relations, the book mainly discusses the thirteen reports of the Finance Commissions constituted so far.

The whole book is divided into thirteen chapters, starting with the evolution of Central Province Relations during the British Rule. The first chapter narrates the various committees and commissions constituted during the pre-independence period including the Government of India Act 1919 and 1935. The second chapter discusses the Constitutional provisions relating to the provision of Finance Commission and related provisions affecting the working of the Finance Commission. The Third chapter examines the Composition, Terms of Reference (ToR) and the considerations given to the Finance Commission.

Against the background of Constitutional provisions and the terms of references, the fourth chapter analyses the issues enunciated by various Commissions and the approach adopted to deal with these issues. Chapters Five to Nine discuss the ToR wise recommendations made by the Finance Commissions. Chapter ten presents the general observations made by the Commission based on their experiences, while formalizing their recommendations.

Chapter Eleven briefly, discusses the Action Taken Reports (ATRs) as presented, along with the recommendations by the Government of India, before the Parliament. Based on the reports of thirteen Commissions and the emergence of National Development Council (NDC) and Planning Commission and Inter-State Council, emerging trends in the sphere of Centre-State Fiscal Relations have been discussed in the Twelfth Chapter. The last chapter is a critique of the Thirteenth Finance Commission report, which came up during the preparation of the book.

A separate part of the book consists of the various

annexures including relevant extracts from Constitution of India, composition and ATRs of Commissions, relevant portion of GOI Act, 1935. A proper reference of these has been made in the main text of the book.

It is added that the entire book is mainly based on the reports of all the thirteen Finance Commissions and wherever quotations have been taken, these have been clearly mentioned. Quotations from sources, other than the Finance Commissions reports, have also been properly mentioned.

It is, further, clarified that the work does not claim to be a technical and theoretical analysis of the reports of the Commissions. Many experts have done excellent studies on various aspects of the reports and there is a long list of such studies and many of them have been incorporated in the suggested readings appended at the end of the book. However, some analysis, wherever required, has been done in various chapters.

The inspiration of collecting the reports of Commissions and putting them together was drawn by me when one research scholar doing his Ph.D. on Centre-State Fiscal Relations came to me for helping him to get the relevant documents required, which is very difficult and time consuming. Though, it has become much easier now with the introduction of Computer Technology, to get everything at one place, yet this book will help the students to get entire gamut of documents and information regarding Finance Commissions at one place.

During the course of preparation of the book, the Finance Commission division of the State's Finance Department helped me immensely by providing published and unpublished data, reports along with ATRs of the Commissions and other relevant material. The list is too long to mention everyone by name. I am grateful to them all.

The major burden of typing the various drafts of the

manuscript was borne by Sri A.P. Sasi Kumar. Sri. R.M. Dalela, Retired Joint Director, helped me in going through the draft again and again. I am thankful to them for their efficient and ungrudging assistance.

Finally, my wife Sadhana's silent contribution in sparing me from the household responsibilities and providing a congenial and peaceful environment to enable me to concentrate on my work has now resulted in the form of this book. My children Paritosh, Tripti, Richa and grandson Aditya, also deserve the mention as they inspired me to complete this task.

I would specially like to thank Prof. C.H. Hanumantha Rao, Honorary Professor, Institute of Economic Growth, University of Delhi who went through the manuscript and gave valuable suggestions which helped me considerably in revising the manuscript for publication. Prof. Rao has also been kind enough to write the foreword of the book amidst his extremely busy schedule for which I am deeply beholden to him.

I am thankful to the Government of Uttar Pradesh in the Finance Department for giving me the permission to publish the study.

During my stay in the Finance Department, I had the occasion to oversee the work relating to preparation of State's memorandum, process voluminous data for Finance Commission and finally implement the recommendations of Five Finance Commission from Ninth to Thirteenth. Hence, the twenty years experience has gone into this study which has given me immense pleasure and satisfaction. The study will help the people and particularly the students who are interested in the subject of Centre-State Fiscal relations and I hope the efforts will not go in vain.

Gulistan Colony
Lucknow

B.M. Joshi

List of Abbreviations

ARC : Administrative Reforms Commission
AG : Accountant General
ATR : Action Taken Report
CSRC : Centre-States Reforms Commission
CSRC II : Centre-States Relations Commission II
CSS : Centrally Sponsored Scheme
CST : Central Sales Tax
CAG : Comtroller and Auditor General
CRF : Calamity Relief Fund
DCRF : Debt Consolidation and Relief Facility
DMA : Disaster Management Act
FC : Finance Commission
FRBML : Fiscal Responsibility and Budget Management Legislation
FRL : Fiscal Reform Legislation
GOI : Government of India
GDP : Gross Domestic Product
GFD : Gross Fiscal Deficit
GSDP : Gross State Domestic Product
GST : Goods and Services Tax
ISC : Inter State Council
NCCF : National Calamity Contingency Fund
NCCM : National Centre for Calamity Management

NCRF	:	National Calamity Relief Fund
NDC	:	National Development Council
NDMA	:	National Disaster Management Authority
NDRF	:	National Disaster Relief Fund
NEC	:	National Executive Committee
NPRD	:	Non Plan Revenue Deficit
NSSF	:	National Small Savings Fund
PC	:	Planning Commission
PRI	:	Panchahati Raj Institutions
RBI	:	Reserve Bank of India
RD	:	Revenue Deficit
SDMA	:	State Disaster Management Authority
SDRF	:	State Disaster Relief Fund
SEC	:	State Executive Committee
SFC	:	State Finance Commission
ToR	:	Terms of Reference
TGS	:	Technical and General Supervision
ULB	:	Urban Local Bodies
VAT	:	Value Added Tax

1. Evolution of the Centre-State Fiscal Relations: Historical Perspective

The history of evolution of Centre-State financial relations dates back to the days of East India Company. Though there was some control of Governor-General, but it was uncoordinated. After the assumption of sovereignty over the territories of India by the crown in 1858, some system started developing. Two things happened, one was the creation of the post of Secretary of State for India and the second was the addition of a Finance Member in Governor-General's Executive Council.

For the sake of understanding the developments leading to the formation of Constitution of India in 1950, the whole period can be divided into four time spans. One from 1858 to 1919 when the Government of India Act 1919 came into being. The Second time span related to 1919 to 1935, when the GOI Act 1935 was passed. The Third time span relates to 1935 to independence of country in 1947 and the Fourth time span relates to 1947 to 1950, when the Constitution came into being. The discussion on evolution of Centre-States fiscal relations has been done in that order.

Time Span—I (1858-1919)

During this period, a concept of fixed grants to each

province was introduced for their expenses of local services. Though the determination of grant amount had no sound basis, yet this was a beginning of the process of devolution of resources and delegation of financial authority to the provinces.

The major development took place in 1871, when a **"Scheme of Provincial Financial Settlements"** was introduced. This, to some extent, rationalised the financial arrangements by assigning to the provinces in stages the proceeds of the whole or part of the specified heads of revenue for general administrative purposes. For the first time, the sources of revenue and income generated from them were divided between the Centre and the provinces and the distribution was done on the basis of needs. A five yearly adjustment also started, though periodical increase was on the ad hoc basis.

In 1904, an amendment was made in this scheme by awarding to the provinces definite percentage of certain revenues. These arrangements were reviewed every five years and made quasi permanent in 1904 and then permanent in 1912. This division of revenues was further rationalized in 1919. Revenues from salt, customs, opium and receipts from commercial activities were retained wholly by the centre and revenues from civil departments, provincial works and provincial rates were handed over to the provinces. All other revenues, the more important of which were land revenue, income tax, excise, etc., were made divided heads of revenues.

Before the Govt. of India Act 1919 came into being, a Financial Relations committee under the chairmanship of Lord Meston was formed to advise on the contributions, which the provinces should make to the centre and the principles, on which, contributions should be computed. The committee recommended that 'stamps' in their entirety should be transferred to the provinces both on financial and administrative considerations. The Committee also said that there should be no departure from the principle that both the Centre and the provinces should have their own distinct and separate heads of revenues and advised against income tax being made a divisible head of revenue. Because of the severe criticism by the provinces regarding their contribution to centre, this was not implemented.

Time Span—II (1919-1935)

The Montague-Chemsford Report on Constitutional reforms led to the passing of GOI Act 1919. This Act sought to secure for the provinces a greater measure of financial autonomy by abolishing the divided heads and effecting a complete separation between the Central and the Provincial heads of revenue.

The main purport of the Government of India Act of 1919 was: (i) to make a beginning in responsible Government; (ii) to associate the Indian Princes (rulers of the India Native States under the British paramountcy) with the administration of India, especially in matters affecting the Indian Native States, and (iii) devolution of authority to Provincial Governments and the introduction of partial responsibility in the provinces by dividing the Provincial Governments into two parts, one responsible to the Secretary of State for India, and the other to the voters in the provinces. This system was known as Dyarchy.

The salient features of GOI Act 1919 were as follows:

I. Division of whole gamut of subjects of administration into two parts: (i) Central, and (ii) Provincial.

(a) Central Heads of Administration

Among the Central subjects, the most important were:

Defence–Navy, Territorial Army, and Air Forces, other than Police; Railways (with certain exceptions); communications of military importance and Posts and Telegraphs: Currency and Coinage; Public Debt: Sources of Imperial Revenue; Civil and Criminal Law and Procedure; Ecclesiastical Administration and All India Services: Central Institution of Scientific and Industrial Research: and all matters not specially declared to the provincial subjects[1].

(b) Provincial Heads of Administration

In the list of the provincial subjects, the most important of them were: Local Self-Government; Education (with certain exceptions); Medical Administration; Sanitation and Public Health; Public Works—such as Roads, Buildings and Light Railways; Agriculture; Development of Industries; Excise; Civil Veterinary Department, Fisheries, and Co-operative Societies; Famine Relief; Land Revenue Administration; Irrigation; Forests; Administration of Justice, Police, and Prisons; Inspection of Factories and Labour questions; Provincial borrowing; and Agency functions.

(c) Sources of Revenue of the Central and Provincial Governments

With the system of divided heads of administration, the question of the sources of revenue for the Central and Provincial Governments had been also spelt out. The system of the "divided heads", which was in operation, was abolished, but, in order to meet the deficit of the Central Government, a system of provincial contributions was laid down, which was to cease as soon as the Government of India was able to develop its resources to meet its entire

1 Foreign relations and relations with the Native States were not included in the list of the Central subjects.

expenditure.

The following were the sources of revenues of the Central Government: customs, Income-Tax, Railways, Posts and Telegraphs, and Salt and Opium.

Revenue accruing from land, and income from Excise (Spirits and Drugs), Irrigation, Forests, Stamps and Registration fees were assigned to the provinces. To meet the objections of the Governments of Bombay and Bengal, provision was made to assign 25% of the increase in the income-tax collected from the provinces to the provincial governments.

(d) Powers to the Legislature in regard to the Financial Statement

The Governor-General and his Council had to present the financial statement every year to both the Houses. Proposals for the appropriation of revenue, in the form of demands, were to be submitted by the Government on the recommendation of the Governor-General alone to the vote of the Legislative Assembly, except those relating to the following heads of expenditure:

(a) Interest and sinking fund charges on loans; (b) expenditure of which, the amount was prescribed by or under any law; (c) salaries and pensions of persons appointed by or with the approval of His Majesty or by the Secretary of State-in-Council; (d) salaries of Chief Commissioners and Judicial Commissioners; and (e) expenditure classified by the order of the Governor-General-in-Council as: (i) Ecclesiastical; (ii) Political; and (iii) Defence. Even any discussion in either of the Houses could not take place on these items, unless the Governor-General otherwise directed.

The Legislative Assembly had the power to assent or refuse its assent to any demand, except those demands, which have been referred to above, or reduce the amount of any demand by reducing the whole grant, but, the Governor-General was empowered, if he declared that he was satisfied that any demand, which was refused by the Legislative Assembly, was essential to the discharge of his responsibilities, to act as if, it had been assented to by the Legislative Assembly, notwithstanding the withholding of the assent or the reduction of the amount thereof by the Legislative Assembly.

In addition, in cases of emergency, the Governor-General was given the power to authorize such expenditure, as he deemed necessary to maintain the safety or tranquility of British India or any part thereof.

(e) Financial Powers of the Legislature

The Financial Statement, according to the Act of 1919, was to be presented to the Provincial Legislature every year and the proposals were made for the appropriation of money in the form of demand for grants. The Legislature had the power to assent, or refuse its assent to a demand, or reduce the amount of the demand. The financial powers of the Legislatures, like the powers of legislation, were also circumscribed by the Act. The Act laid down the following limitations: (i) the local Government had the power to restore any item of the demand in regard to a reserved subject even if it was refused or its amount was reduced by the Legislature, if the Governor of the province certified that the expenditure was essential to the discharge of his responsibility for the subject; (ii) in case of emergency, the Governor was empowered to authorise such expenditure, which he considered necessary for maintaining the safety or tranquility of the province, or for carrying on the administration of any department; and (iii) all proposals for the appropriation of money were to be made on the recommendation of the

Governor alone, whether related to the Reserved Transferred subjects.

In addition, there were other restrictions too. The proposals relating to the following heads of expenditure were not to be submitted to the Legislatures: (i) contributions payable by the Provincial Governments to the Governor-General-in-Council; (ii) interest and sinking fund charges on loans; (iii) expenditure, the amount of which was prescribed by or under any law; (iv) salaries and pensions of persons appointed by or with the approval of His Majesty, or by the Secretary of State for India-in-Council; and (v) salaries of the Judges of the High Courts of the provinces and of the Advocates-General.

The Joint Committee of Parliament drafted the rules under the GOI Act of 1919. These rules were promulgated in December 1920. The salient features were "The formula prescribed for determining the growth of revenue from income tax and the distribution of part of it to the provinces, where they originated, was complicated. The share given to the provinces was also small, being about 1.5 per cent of the increased yield. Secondly, as collection was not a true index of the province's contribution to the growth, a further adjustment was incorporated in the formula to take account of the fact that a part of the tax would be collected in the province other than the one, in which, income arose".

The Government of India Act 1919 and the Rules made thereunder gave the provinces considerable latitude in financial matters. They, now, had freedom to adjust the levies on transferred heads of revenue; they, similarly, had the right to spend whatever they liked on the transferred subjects. Expenditure on reserved subjects alone continued to be subject to regulation and control by the central government. The provinces were also given the power to float loans both in India and abroad on the security of their revenues, but there were restrictions on the exercise of this power. Loans could only be raised for financing projects of lasting public utility and only if the expenditure could not be reasonably met from current revenue. Loans raised in India had to have the prior approval of the Government of India and loans raised abroad the sanction of the Secretary of State. Both internal and external borrowings had to be on behalf, and in the name, of the Secretary of State.

Despite this liberalization, there was no separation of cash balances of the Centre and the provinces. There was a single "public account", on which, both operated. The provinces were given unlimited right to overdraw their accounts but they had to reimburse the account with the amount overdrawn before the close of the financial year. The provision of "ways and means", thus, continued to be a central responsibility. Though, the sources of revenue of the Centre and the provinces had been separated with freedom to them to exploit or adjust the levies, the provinces had, yet, to gain control over audit and accounts, borrowing and allied matters. It was a halfway house between control and autonomy.

Though, the financial relations between the Centre and the State were in existence based on Government of India Act 1919 and the rules made but they were not working satisfactorily. Hence, this subject was always under scrutiny and debate to find out a more rational and acceptable distribution. Further, the activities of both the Central and the Provincial governments were expanding and as a sequal to this their larger financial needs could no longer be met within the resources of existing taxation.

A high powered Taxation Enquiry Committee was constituted in 1924 to conduct a thorough enquiry into the whole field of taxation. The committee, therefore, recommended that general stamp duty, excise duty on "foreign" liquor, manufactured in the country and the revenue from opium should be transferred wholly to the Centre. This involved a sacrifice on the part of the provinces, but even then, the committee did not support the idea that the proceeds of certain taxes should be shared by the Centre with the provinces. The committee also rejected the suggestion that provinces should be given the power to levy an income tax or that the Centre should impose a surcharge on income tax for the benefit of the provinces. They, however, realized that as a result of their rather radical recommendations, weighted in favour of the Centre, the provinces would be in financial difficulties. They reconciled themselves to the continued use of income tax as a balancing factor. It was more rational, in their view, to give the provinces a share in this tax, rather than give them power to levy an income tax or to empower the Centre to impose a surcharge for distribution to the provinces. With regard to distribution formula, the committee suggested "Under this formula, the provinces would receive the proceeds of a basic rate on personal incomes. Taxes collected on incomes not pertaining to the residents in a particular province, such as tax on undistributed dividends of companies or on incomes of persons resident outside the province or the country and the whole of super tax should be retained by the Centre". In addition to the allotment made on the basis of personal incomes, the allocation of which would be based entirely on domicile, the committee also recommended that the principle of origin should be recognized by assigning to each province a small portion of the receipts of the corporation profits tax. This distribution was to be on the basis of collection in each province, subject to an adjustment in such cases, where incomes assessed in one province originated in another.

Another committee "Reform Enquiry Committee"

under the chairmanship of Sir Alexander Muddiman was constituted to enquire into the difficulty arising from, or defects inherent in, the working of the Government of India Act, 1919. The Committee came to the conclusion that separation was desirable as the autonomy granted to provincial governments would be rudimentary, until they exercised some control over the agency maintaining their accounts. But, later on, this scheme was abandoned.

The Simon Commission on Constitutional Reforms re-examined the question and recommended that the provincial governments should be made responsible for keeping their accounts at their own expense; audit should be separated from the keeping of accounts and the audit of provincial transactions should remain under the Auditor General of India as central charge. But, the joint select committee of British Parliament did not endorse this view; instead, recommended that "Central audit and accounts should apply as, at present, to the provinces for a period of five years; but provinces should be empowered to take over their own accounts or audit as well as accounts, on giving three years notice, the earliest date for such notice being two years after the establishment of provincial autonomy".

Time Span—III (1935-1947)

Another and the most important milestone in the evolution of financial relations was Government of India Act of 1935. But, before its enactment, there were intense deliberations. The Indian Statutory Commission 1930 discussed the issue and reports made public in 1930. It was Lord Walter Layfon, who worked as Financial Advisor to the Commission. The Round Table Conference appointed a Federal Structures Committee. This Committee appointed a sub committee **under Lord Peel in 1931**. This committee suggested that "at the very inception of the federation, the entire proceeds of income tax should be assigned to the provinces, but in the interests of uniformity and administrative convenience, its levy and collection should remain with the federal government".

Another expert Committee was constituted under **Lord Percy** to give practical shape to the principles of devolution enunciated by the Peel Committee.

In the meantime, British Government issued a **White Paper in December 1931,** embodying their proposals for Indian Constitutional Reforms including financial proposals. The White Paper made two recommendations on the division of resources. First, it proposed that the federal legislature should be empowered to assign to the provinces the whole or a part of the yield of salt duty, excise duties on commodities in the central list and export duties. Secondly, it proposed that though the levy and collection of terminal taxes and death duties should be in the hands of the federation, the entire net proceeds of both these levies should be distributed to the provinces. The federation should, however, have the right to impose a surcharge under both heads for its own purposes and retain the proceeds.

The **Percy Committee** made detailed recommendations. The committee advocated that "the provinces should receive an estimated amount of personal income tax of local incidence, personal super tax on the basis of collection from their residents, a share of the tax on non-residents and undistributed profits of companies on the basis of population. The amounts, thus, separately computed for each province should be added and expressed as a percentage of total collection as its share". It, further, suggested that the provincial shares should not be calculated every year, but once every five years to give stability to provincial estimates. Each revision should be on the basis of figures of personal income tax for the previous quinquennium.

After great deliberations as discussed above, the Govt. of India Act came into the statute book. The Act of 1935 was quite a lengthy and a detailed document. In spite of its many weaknesses, the Act had its own significance. It marked a second milestone on the road to full responsible Government, the first being the Act of 1919. The new grant of features were the suggestion to form the Federation and grant of autonomy to the provinces.

A provision was made in the Act to appoint a Financial Advisor to Governor General to assist him in safeguarding the financial stability and credit of the federal government.

A detailed procedure was laid in the Act for dealing with the financial matters, including presentation of annual financial statement before both the chambers of Federal Legislature. A detailed list of charged expenditure was also incorporated. A provision of supplementary statement of expenditure was also provided.

A new chapter was added for provincial executives. A similar procedure was added for dealing with the financial matters at the provinces level.

The Act clearly divided the subjects into three categories, viz. Federal List, consisting of 59 subjects, Provincial list, consisting of 54 subjects and concurrent list, consisting of 36 subjects. The subjects, which were of all India interest and demanded uniform treatment, were put on the federal list. Subjects, mainly of local interest, were placed in the Provincial list. The concurrent list included those subjects, which were primarily of provincial interest but, at the same time, required uniformity of treatment all over the country.

Chapter I of the Part VII of the Act 1935 dealt with the finances of the federation and the provinces. It clearly defined the "Revenues of Federation" and "Revenues of the Provinces". Apart from this, the Act clearly defined certain taxes and duties to be levied by the Federation and to be wholly or partly distributed among provinces also. Duties in respect of succession to property other than agricultural land, estate duty, stamp duty as mentioned in federal list, terminal taxes on goods or passengers carried by railway or air and taxes on railway fares were to be levied and collected by federation was not to form part of federation excepted collections Chief Commissioners' provinces, but were to be assigned to the provinces and distributed in accordance with such principles of distribution as may be formulated by the Act of Federal Legislature.

In case of taxes on Income other than agricultural income were to be levied and collected by the federation, but a prescribed percentage of net proceeds in any financial year was to be assigned to the Provinces in a manner as may be presented.

The Act talked about the corporation tax and said that it was not to be levied in any federal state until ten years had elapsed from the establishment of the federation.

There was a specific provision of salt duties, excise duties and export duties to be levied and collected by the federation and if the Act so provided were to be distributed among provinces, where the duty was imposed and the distribution was to be done as might be prescribed.

The Act also provided for giving grants-in-aid to certain provinces as his Majesty might determine to be in need of assistance and different sums might be provided for different States. The Act also refered to taxes on professions, traders, callings and employment for the benefit of a province, municipality district board, local board or other local authority. There was ceiling on the total amount payable in respect of any one person.

The Federal Structures Committee of the third Round Table Conference had before them the reports of both Peel and Percy committees and the White Paper of His Majesty's government but they still considered that the question of financial allocations should be reviewed afresh. The committee constituted for the purpose of sub-committee, naming Lord Peel who had headed the earlier sub-committee once again as chairman. The allocation of resources came under yet another examination in 1933-34 that of the Joint Parliamentary Committee on Indian Constitutional Reforms. After long deliberations, the Government of India Act 1935 was embodied in the Statute book.

The basic features of Government of India Act of 1935 were as under:

The financial provisions of the Government of India Act 1935 strengthened further, though indirectly, central control over the provinces even in the demarcated field of their political authority. Being largely dependent on the centre for financial support even in the administration of subjects assigned to them, the provinces could always be persuaded to put it euphemistically to listen to the Centre in the evolution of policies. Even, had the provinces been given co-ordinate or larger political authority, the financial provision of the Act, unless substantially modified, would have by themselves, frustrated the exercise of this authority. The extracts of Govt. of India Act 1935 relating to finance are given in **Annexure I.1.**

As a prelude to the introduction of Government of India Act 1935, Sir Otto Niemeyer made the following recommendations:

1. He adopted the minimum mentioned in the White Paper as the maximum possible.
2. He came to the conclusion that substantial justice

would be done by working out the percentage for each province based partly on residence and partly on population.

3. Sir Otto Niemeyer adopted "population", as the basis of distribution.
4. In regard to the distribution of the export duty on jute and jute goods, he suggested that the share of the provinces should be raised from 50% to 62½% of the net proceeds of the duty.
5. In addition to these assignments, he also recommended grants-in-aid for a limited period to the United Provinces, Assam, North-West Frontier Province, Sind and Orissa.
6. In regard to the outstanding debts of the provinces to the Centre, he recommended that all debts contracted prior to April 1, 1936 by Bengal, Bihar, Assam, Orissa and the North-West Frontier Province should be wholly cancelled and that the outstanding debt of the Central Province should be substantially reduced.

The recommendations of Sir Otto Niemeyer were accepted fully and embodied in the Government of India (Distribution of Revenues) order 1936. This order continued to regulate the distribution till 1940.

Thus, the Government of India Act of 1935 was one of the major milestones in the evolution of Centre-State financial relations. The Act of 1935 had, thus, not only embodied the basic principles of federal finance, but had also endowed the provinces with financial powers and authority which constituents units in a federation, normally, enjoyed.

Time Span—IV (1947-1950)

Though the Constituent Assembly was considering the

draft of the Constitution largely based on the Government of India Act 1935, yet it thought it necessary to assign the financial provisions relating to the union and the constituent units to an expert committee headed by Mr. N.R. Sankar. The Committee, largely, followed the concept of shared revenues, but considered the specific aspect of division of Income tax and Jute duty. This expert committee did not consider it fit to include export or import duty for distribution purposes, but recommended grant in aid as a temporary measure.

In case of Income tax, the committee recommended that the entire yield of the tax should be brought into divisible pool, except the amount realised from centrally administered areas. The States should get 60% share. This 60% should be distributed on the basis of collection (35%), population (20%) and marginal adjustments (5%). Further, 50% of Excise duty on Tobacco should be distributed among States on the basis of consumption.

The Expert Committee also recommended setting up of an independent Finance Commission to deal with these matters, specially dealing with the sharing of revenue. It, further, recommended that this commission should periodically review the subject of sharing of tax proceeds.

The Constituent Assembly did not fully accept the recommendations—it did not define the provincial share on the basis of distribution. It left this to be decided by the Finance Commission. Till such time as these issues had been decided by the order of President the acceptance of the recomendations had been held in abeyance by the Constituent Assembly.

Pending the Constitution of the Finance Commission (FC), a committee headed by Sir Chintamani Deshmukh was appointed in December 1949 to suggest the sharing formula only. The factors, which had influenced the reallocation in 1947, were reviewed by Sir Chintamani Deshmukh. They were mainly two: (a) the provinces of the Punjab and Bengal had lost large territories on partition: Assam had, similarly, lost an area. There should, therefore, be a partial resumption of the allocations previously made to these provinces for redistribution to others; and (b) the shares of Sind and the North-West Frontier Province had lapsed on the formation of Pakistan. Their shares should be redistributed and the percentage of the provincial share given to each province, including those partitioned should be re-fixed.

In view of this limited charter, Sir Chintamani Deshmukh merely attempted to calculate the share, which the territories of the Punjab and Bengal lost to Pakistan would have received had they existed as separate provinces at the time of Sir Otto Niemeyer's examination. Having determined their shares on the Niemeyer formula, he added to the resulting figure, the shares of Sind and the North-West Frontier Province to arrive at the total amount available for redistribution to the States of the Union in addition to their shares previously fixed. He corrected the percentages adopting population as the basis and made a few minor adjustments to give some weightage to the weaker States.

In regard to grants-in-aid in lieu of a share of jute export duty, Sir Chintamani Deshmukh considered that though these have been treated as "compensation payments", they were basically financial assistance to the four provinces. He recommended that this assistance should be continued for the period covered by his award but as fixed grants unrelated to the yield of the duty. Deshmukh award remained in force for the two financial years of 1950-51 and 1951-52.

A Committee named as "Indian States Finances Enquiry Committee" was, accordingly, constituted in

October 1948 under the chairmanship of Sir V.T. Krishnamachari to consider the question of federal financial integration of the erstwhile Indian States. The purpose was to find a settlement, which would make both the political and financial provisions of the Constitution equally applicable to all the constituent States of the Union.

The committee, therefore, recommended that the Centre should make good to these States, for a transitional period, the surplus from federal subjects computed on the basis of actual revenue and expenditure during an agreed basic period immediately preceding integration. The payments so made to the Part B States were called "revenue gap grants". These were guaranteed in full for the first five years and on a gradually diminishing scale for a further period of five years to reach approximately 60 per cent of the original grant. These States were given a share in the proceeds of income tax on the same basis as Part A States, but this was to be in lieu of the "revenue gap grant". The States received either the share of income tax or the grant, whichever was larger.

The acceptance of the recommendation of the Krishnamachari Committee with the agreement of the erstwhile princely States to be placed in Part B, prepared the ground for the drafting of a common financial code for all the States. Towards the end of 1949, Sri C.D. Deshmukh was requested to look into the matters which the States' had raised specially regarding sharing of Income Tax and Jute Export Duty. Sri Deshmukh gave his recommendation, which was popularly known as Deshmukh award, was effective from 1st April, 1950 and remained in force for 2 years till 31st March 1952. In the meantime, the First Finance Commission was constituted on 22nd November, 1951.

2. Indian Constitution and Centre-State Fiscal Relations

On July 18, 1947, the British Parliament passed the Independence Act of 1947, which set up in India two Independent Dominions—India and Pakistan—from August 15, 1947. On January 26, 1950, a new Constitution of an independent Republic came into operation.

Although Government of India Act 1935 formed the basis of deliberations of the Constituent Assembly, yet many new things were added in the Constitution of India, in general and in the areas of Centre-State fiscal relations, in particular. The basic objective of incorporating the financial principles and procedures was to ensure supremacy of the Parliament and a common financial code for centre as well as States.

(I) Division of Functions

So far as the legislative relations between Union and States are concerned, Article 246 provides for subject-matter of laws made by Parliament and subject-matter of laws made by Legislation of States and it provides for three lists of subjects to be divided between Union and States and a concurrent list. The Union list consists of 97 subjects, State list of 66 subjects and Concurrent list of 47 subjects. With the passage of time all the three lists have expanded. Under the Government of India Act 1935, the federal list consisted of 59 subjects, Provinces list of 54 subjects and the concurrent list of 36 subjects.

As will be evident from the perusal of those lists, it will be evident that the major sources of revenues are in the Union list and the major expenditure responsibilities are with the States. There is a clear-cut non correspondence between revenue sources and expenditure responsibilities. This mismatch between sources of revenue and expenditure responsibility can be gauged from the fact that the share of Centre in the combined revenue receipts is around 63% during Twelfth Finance Commission period against 37% of States, whereas the Central share in combined expenditure is 44% against 56% of States. In order to minimise this mismatch, a provision has been made under Article 280 of the Constitution for establishment of Finance Commission at five yearly intervals for recommending devolution of funds from the Centre to the States.

As per requirement of Article 280(2) of the Constitution, Government of India enacted a legislation "The Finance Commission (Miscellaneous Provisions) Act 1951" to determine the qualifications requisite for the appointment as members of Finance Commission and the manner, in which, they shall be selected and to prescribe their powers.

Consequent upon the Constitution (seventy third) and (seventy fourth) Amendment Acts, Para IX and IX-A was added relating to the Panchayats and Municipalities. These Local Bodies were given Constitutional status and further, a provision for constitution of Finance Commission, to review their financial position, was also added under article 243(1) and 243(y) of the Constitution. This was done on the same lines as in case of constitution of Finance

Commission under Article 280 of the Constitution.

In order to enable the local bodies to stand on their own with regard to resources, two new provisions 280(3)(bb) and 280(3)(c) were added by the Constitution (Seventy Third) and (Seventy Fourth Amendment) Acts. These provisions are:

280 (3)[1] [75]**[(bb)** the measures needed to augment the Consolidated Fund of a State to supplement the resources of the Panchayats in the State on the basis of the recommendations made by the Finance Commission of the State;]

280 (3)[1] [76]**[(c)** the measures needed to augment the Consolidated Fund of a State to supplement the resources of the Municipalities in the State on the basis of the recommendations made by the Finance Commission of the State;]

Thus, the Finance Commission was required to recommend measures to augment the Consolidated Fund of the State on the basis of recommendations of the State Finance Commission. These two items were added in the terms of reference of Eleventh and Twelfth Finance Commissions and these Commissions have, therefore, made specific recommendations on these two terms. But, the Tenth Finance Commission had felt that the development of these institutions would be impaired, if they were not given funds at their inception. Hence, even though, the terms of reference did not require the Commission to go into this aspect, yet the Tenth Finance Commission had provided grants to all States for this purpose.

---

1 Inserted by the Constitution (Seventy-third Amendment) Act, 1992, S.3 (w.e.f. 24.4.1993)

2 Inserted by the Constitution (Seventy-fourth Amendment) Act, 1992, S.3. (w.e.f. 1.6.1993.

So far as the distribution of revenues between the Union and States is concerned, there were clear provisions in the Constitution in the form of Articles 268, 269, 270, 271 and 272 of the Constitution.

Article 268 refers to such stamp duties and such duties of excise on medicinal and toilet preparations, as are mentioned in the union list, shall be levied by the union, but shall be collected by the States. ... which such duties are bivable and the proceeds shall be fully assigned to the State. Similarly, Article 269 list duties and taxes, which shall be levied and collected by Government of India, but shall be assigned to the States. These are:

(a) Duties in respect of succession of property other than agricultural land.
(b) Estate duty in respect of property other than agricultural land.
(c) Terminal taxes in respect of goods or passengers carried by railway, sea or air.
(d) Taxes on railway fares and freights.
(e) Taxes other than stamp duty or transactions in stock exchanges and futures market.
(f) Taxes on the sale & purchase of newspapers and on advertisements published thereon.
(g) Taxes on sale or purchase of goods other than newspapers, where such sale or purchase takes place in the course of inter-state trade or commerce. This was added by the Sixth amendment of the Constitution.
(h) Taxes on the consignment of goods, where such consignment takes place in the course of inter-state trade or commerce.

The net proceeds of these taxes shall not form part of the Consolidated Fund of India and shall be assigned to the

States, in which this tax is leviable and shall be distributed in accordance with such principles as may be formulated by Parliament by law.

Article 269 was amended by the Constitution (Eighth Amendment) Act 2000 and it stands as follows:

269. Taxes levied and collected by the Union but assigned to the States: [1][(1) Taxes on the sales or purchase of goods and taxes on the consignment of goods shall be levied and collected by the Government of India but shall be assigned, and shall be deemed to have been assigned, to the States on or after the 1st day of April, 1996 in the matter provided in clause (2).

Explanation: For the purposes of this clause,

(a) the expression "taxes on the sale or purchase of goods" shall mean taxes on sale or purchase of goods other than newspapers, where such sale or purchase takes place in the course of inter-state trade or commerce;

(b) the expression "taxes on the consignment of goods" shall mean taxes on the consignment of goods (whether the consignment is to the person making it or to any other person), where such consignment takes place in the course of inter-state trade or commerce.

(2) The net proceeds in any financial year of any such tax, except in so far as those proceeds represent proceeds attributable to Union territories, shall not form part of the Consolidated Fund of India, but shall be assigned to the States within which that tax is leviable in that year, and shall be distributed

1 Substituted by the Constitution (Eightieth Amendment) Act, 2000, S.2, for Cls.(1) and (2) (w.e.f. 9-6-2000).

among those States in accordance with such principles of distribution as may be formulated by Parliament by law.]

[6 61][(3) Parliament may by law formulate principles for determining when a [6 72][sale of purchase of, or consignment of goods] takes place in the course of inter-State trade or commerce.]

A new article 268-A has been added by Constitution (Eighty Eighth Amendment Act 2003 as below:

[6 43]**[268-A Service tax levied by Union, collected and appropriated by the Union and the States.**—(1) Taxes on services shall be levied by the Government of India and such tax shall be collected and appropriated by the Government of India and the States in the manner provided in clause (2).

(2) The proceeds in any financial year of any such tax levied in accordance with the provisions of clause (1) shall be—

(a) collected by the Government of India and the States;
(b) appropriated by the Government of India and the States,

in accordance with such principles of collection and appropriation as may be formulated by Parliament by law.]

Earlier Article 270(1) reads as "Taxes on Income, otherthan agricultural Income, shall be levied and collected by Government of India and distributed between the union and the States in the manner prescribed in clause (2).

---

1 Inserted by the Constitution (Sixth amendment) Act,1956, S.3.
2 Substituted by the Constitution (Forty Six amendments) Act,1982 S.2. for "sale or purchase of goods" (w.e.f. 2-2-1983).
3 Inserted by the Constitution (Eighty-eighth Amendment) Act,2003 S.2 (yet to be enforced.

Article 272 provided for the permissible division of Union Excise duties. But with the Constitution (Eightieth amendment) Act 2000, this Article was completely omitted and Article 270 was amended as under:

[6][81][270. **Taxes levied and distributed between the Union and the States**—(1) All taxes and duties referred to in the Union List, except the duties and taxes referred to in [articles 268, 268-A and 269], respectively, surcharge on taxes and duties referred to in article 271 and any cess levied for specific purposes under any law made by Parliament shall be levied and collected by the Government of India and shall be distributed between the Union and the States in the manner provided in clause (2).

(2) such percentage, as may be prescribed, of the net proceeds of any such tax or duty in any financial year shall not form part of the Consolidated Fund of India, but shall be assigned to the States within which that tax or duty is leviable in that year, and shall be distributed among those States in such manner and from such time as may be prescribed in the manner provided in clause (3);

(3) In this Article, "prescribed" means,

(a) until a Finance Commission has been constituted, prescribed by the President by order; and

(b) after a Finance Commission has been constituted, prescribed by the President by order after considering the recommendations of the Finance Commission.]

Thus with the Eightieth amendment, all Central taxes excepting taxes under Article 268, 268-A and 269 were made compulsorily divisible.

---

1 Substituted by the Constitution (Forty-sixth amendment) act, 1982, S.2, for "sale or purchase of goods" (w.e.f. 2.2.1983)

Thus before the Eightieth Amendment to the Constitution, there had been four categories of taxes and duties viz. (i) taxes the proceeds of which are wholly retained by the Union (ii) taxes the net proceeds of which are wholly assigned to the States (iii) the taxes the net proceeds of which are compulsorily shared with the States and (iv) taxes the proceeds of which may be shared with the States if parliament so desires.

The process of pooling of Central Taxes receipt was started by the Tenth Finance Commission and advocated the pooling of all taxes for devolution to States. The Commission accordingly recommended amendment to the Constitution. This amendment took place in June 2000.

With the Constitution (Eightieth Amendment) Act, there are only two types of taxes and duties (i) as defined in Article 270 of the Constitution, wherein all taxes are compulsorily shareable (ii) taxes defined in Article 268, 268-A and 269, which are to be levied by the Centre and then assigned to the States.

There has been longstanding demand of the States that, because of the rising expenditure responsibilities, there is a need to share more central taxes with the States and with this amendment, the longstanding demand of the States has been fulfilled. The Twelfth Finance Commission was, thus, the first Commission, which made recommendation regarding share of all taxes levied by Centre.

There are two other Articles namely 275 and 282 of the Constitution, which deal with the grants in aid by Union to certain States. Article 275 states that grants-in-aid may be given by union to States, which are in need of assistance and different sums may be fixed for different States.

There is a proviso also which says that after a Finance Commission has been constituted, no order shall be made under this clause by the President except after considering the recommendations of the Finance Commission.

A proviso to Article 275(1) has been added to the Article which makes it obligatory to make grants-in-aid towards the costs of the schemes undertaken by the States with the approval of the Central Government for promoting the welfare of Scheduled tribes and for raising the level of administration of scheduled areas to the generally prevailing in the State concerned. The determination of principles which should be observed in making grants-in-aid as also the actual amounts made available to individual States are also statutorily reserved for examination and recommendation by Finance Commission.

There is another Article 282 which says that the union or a State may make grants for any public purpose, notwithstanding that the purpose is not one with respect to which Parliament or the Legislature of the State, as the case may be, may make laws.

Though this Article appears under section "miscellaneous Financial Provisions" intended to be no more than a permissive provision to meet a situation not otherwise provided, but as the experience shows, the provisions of this Article are extensively used by the Planning Commission for giving Central Assistance for funding of State plans as well as central share as matching contribution for Centrally Sponsored Schemes. As will be evident in later chapters, the grants under Article 282 of the Constitution are many times higher than the share in central taxes and grants under article 275 put together. In this way, the role of Finance Commission seems to have been diluted.

There has been a good amount of debate regarding the scope of Article 275 and 282 of the Constitution and, in turn, the role of the Finance Commission and its exclusion in the matter of grants-in-aid under Article 282 of the

Constitution. Some of the Finance Commissions have dealt with this subject in their reports in great detail but nothing concrete seems to have been done in this matter.

Apart from these Constitutional provisions affecting central state relations especially fiscal relations, the emergence of Planning Commission as a permanent body has also greatly affected the relations between centre and states.

The Constitution makers had not envisaged any institution other than Finance commission for deciding the transfer of funds to States. They had seen merit in one single authority for transfer of powers from Centre to States. **Hence, there is no mention of Planning Commission anywhere in the Indian Constitution.** It came into being hardly about 90 days of promulgation of the Constitution on March 15, 1950 by an executive order. This had a great impact on the constitutional responsibility of the Finance Commission. The Planning Commission was made an independent body with an advisory role. As the planning was attached a very important role in the development process, the Prime Minister became the chairman of the Commission. The Commission worked as the secretariat of the National Development Council. Gradually, the Commission extended the scope of planning to embrace both physical and financial planning and, in fact, the Planning Commission became the supreme arbiter of future development in all the fields of planning and development.

The Planning Commission required the States to prepare and present the five yearly projections of revenues and expenditure to assess the availability of funds for funding of the plans. These projections included forecasts of capital receipts and expenditures also specially on the non-plan side. On the basis of these projections of receipt and expenditure, the Planning Commission started assessing the quantum of Central Assistance to be given to individual States. The Article 282 came to the rescue of the Planning Commission for making grants to the States for plan purposes.

In order to avoid adhocism in the allocations of Central Assistance, a Committee under the chairmanship of Dr. D.R. Gadgil, then Dy. Chairman of Planning Commission, recommended a formula for transfer of Central Assistance to States. This was known as "Gadgil Formula". With the passage of time, the formula was modified by the Committee under the chairmanship of Sri Pranab Mukerjee. Since then, it is known as "modified Mukerjee-Gadgil Formula".

But the emergence of Planning Commission (PC) as a supreme economic authority defeated the intentions of the Constitution makers and created an overlap of functions. Later on, there appeared an overlap on the award period of Finance Commission and Five Year Plan Period also. This mismatch created problems for the States in preparing the budgets and reflecting the plans in the budgetary provisions and making separate forecasts for the Finance Commission for deciding the needs of the States.

This matter of overlapping roles of Finance Commission and Planning Commission was raised, for the first time, by the Third Finance Commission in its Chapter on "General Observations". It observed that the role and functions of Finance Commission, as provided in the Constitution, can no longer be realised fully due to the emergence of the Planning Commission. After discussing the entire issue, the Commission had to observe that "the role of Finance Commission comes to be, at best, that of an agency to review the forecasts and acceptance of the revenue element of the plan as indicated by Planning Commission after determining the quantum of devolution and grants-in-aid to be made and, **at worst,** its function is merely to undertake an arithmetical exercise of devolution." Gradually, this was accepted as fait accompli and hence did not find mention in later reports. Instead, the Finance Commission talked of better coordination between the two bodies and the synchronization of the periods of award of Finance Commission and the Five year plan.

Another major development, which affected the relations between the Union and the State, was the initiation and proliferation of centrally sponsored schemes of various central ministries, specially dealing with the subjects in the State list. These schemes are known as Centrally Sponsored Schemes with varying shares of the Centre and the States. The assistance is, normally, given in the form of grants. These schemes are approved by the Planning Commission, funded by the central ministries and executed by the State agencies. This assistance is over and above the assistance given by the Planning Commission for funding of annual plans.

The States have, regularly, protested against these schemes and it is still a bone of contention between the Centre and the States. One, the States are not consulted in the formulation of these schemes. The same scheme is sought to be implemented by all the States, though the States differ with each other on many counts. Secondly, the schemes are sponsored on such subjects, which are in the State list. The schemes require creation of large number of posts separately for each scheme and after the expiry of the specified period the entire burden is placed on the State exchequer.

Many committees of Planning Commission (PC) have gone into these questions and have recommended closure of these schemes and also transfer of these to the States alongwith funds with the flexibility of suitable changes as per the needs of the States. Even with the acceptance of these reports by National Development Council (NDC), very few of such schemes have either been transferred or closed down. Most of the schemes in one form or the other are still continuing. But the central ministries are thriving on the funds of these schemes. As a result, there has been no change in the situation instead the number of schemes has gone up.

The assistance going to the States through Planning Commission and Central Ministries is quite substantial and is sometimes much higher than the amount transferred through Finance Commission. Thus many a time, the role of Finance Commission, which is a constitutional body, is diluted in favour of an executive institution and also by the Central Ministries. In such a situation, it becomes difficult for the State to take a holistic view of the total assistance flowing from the centre through these institutions because of the different norms, quantum and timeframe of the flow of assistance, requirements to be fulfilled and the institutional mechanism. Maybe because of these reasons, that the Constitution makers had conceived of a single Constitutional body to deal with the matters relating to transfer of funds from the Centre to the States, which would result in smooth Centre-State fiscal relations.

After the adoption of Constitution of India in 1950, the subject of Central-State relationship was visited for the first time in 1969. The subject included the various aspects of fiscal relations as well as the roles of Finance Commission and Planning Commission. The Government of India constituted "Administrative Reforms Commission (ARC)" under the chairmanship of Mr. K. Hanumanthaiya. The thirteenth report of the Commission dealt with Centre-State relations. The Commission submitted its report on June 19, 1969. In its report, the Commission covered all subjects affecting Centre-States relationship including allocation of sources of revenues and functions between the Centre and the States, the role of Governor, Inter-State Council, problem of law and order and other institutions having a bearing on Centre-State relations.

The Commission reviewed all the Constitutional provisions affecting Centre-State relations and solicited the views of Chief Ministers, Governors and eminent leaders of political parties. After deliberating on the subject, the Commission came to the conclusion that "No Constitutional amendment is necessary for ensuring proper and harmonious relations between the Centre and the States, inasmuch as, the provisions of the Constitution governing Centre-State relations are adequate for the purpose of meeting any situation or resolving any problems that may arise in this field." (Recommendation No. 1, p. 7).

On the allocation of functions, the Commission felt that, "without prejudice to the unity, integrity and security of the country, the fullest possible discretion should be given to the States to order their policies and measures according to their ideologies and programmes within the resources available to them in the areas falling within the State list (page 8)." Hence, the Commission recommended that the role of Central Ministries with regard to the State list should normally be handled by the States; otherwise those items of work which do not fulfill the criteria laid down by the Commission should be transferred to the States. "The Commission has categorically stated that the number of CSS should be kept to the minimum and criteria laid down for determining, which projects should be Centrally Sponsored should strictly be applied" (para 4.iv. page 10) In spite of ARC recommendations and also by many of the committees, the list of such items of work, where Central Ministries are venturing, is expanding. As has been discussed earlier, this has constantly been the big irritant in the Central-State relations and will remain so till the concept of Centrally Sponsored Schemes (CSS) is there.

So far as the distribution of financial powers between the centre and the States is concerned, the Commission had mainly dealt with grants-in-aid under Article 282 of the Constitution. The ARC has nothing to say about the provisions under Article 275 but it discussed Article 282 only. The ARC received the memorandum from the States showing great dissatisfaction about the procedure involved. The ARC made the following recommendations in this regard.

(i) The amount of total Central Assistance to be given to a State should first be determined. The amount to be given in the form of loans should then be worked out. The balance of the total assistance left after deducting the quantum of loans will be available for distribution of grants.

(j) A certain portion of the amount available as grant assistance should be "tied" to schemes or groups of schemes of basic national importance. The remainder should then be distributed *pro rata* over other schemes or groups of schemes, which are eligible for central assistance.

(k) The grants tied to schemes or groups of schemes of basic national importance will not be available for re-appropriation. Grants originally allocated to untied schemes or groups of schemes may, however, be re-appropriated to other schemes qualifying for Central Assistance.

(l) If there is a shortfall in implementation of State Plan taken as a whole and, as a result, the Central Assistance utilized by the State is more than what would be proportionate to the expenditure met by the State out of its own resources (the correct proportion being one which was initially settled at the time of the finalisation of the Plan), there should be a corresponding reduction in the Central assistance. Necessary adjustment in this regard should be made after the close of the relevant financial year.

(m) "Miscellaneous Development Loans" should be abolished after the introduction of the scheme of Central Assistance in the manner prescribed above.

(n) The number of Centrally Sponsored Schemes should be kept to the minimum and the criteria laid down for determining which projects should be Centrally Sponsored should strictly be applied. (para 4, pp. 10-11).

Majority of the above recommendations were accepted by the Government of India.

The ARC discussed two other measures (a) the steps to be taken to deal with the problem of mounting debts of the States to the Centre and (b) the need for pre-determination of the principles on the basis of which grants should be given for plan schemes.

So far as the Government of India loans to States are concerned, the Commission made the following recommendations (Recommendation p 15):

1. Loan for Plan schemes should be given only when they are of a productive type. Whether a scheme is productive or not, should be decided by the Planning Commission in consultation with the Finance Ministry and other Central Ministries concerned.
2. The repayment of productive loans should be made over a period of time, the State endeavouring to maximise the return on the investments and building up sinking funds for amortization of loans. The timely payment of a proper rate of interest

should be insisted upon.

3. Assistance for non-productive capital schemes should be in the form of capital grants.
4. The problem of dealing with outstanding Central loans to the States for plan schemes, as also the question of setting up of sinking fund for the amortization of debt, should be referred to a committee of experts.

As the experience has shown, these recommendations have not been implemented. First, plan loan is part of central assistance. Seventy per cent of the central assistance is given as "block loan" without going into the viability of schemes to be funded by these loans. In fact, these are untied loans. Secondly, there is a mismatch between the period of Finance Commission and period of five year plan. Thirdly, subject of central loans always forms part of the ToR of Finance Commission. Thus, the allocation, quantum, conditions of loans including interest and repayment always are in the focus of central state relations.

"The ARC feels that when the Constitution was framed recourse to Article 282 for the purpose of making grants for the five year plan schemes could not have been contemplated. It was urged before the ARC that the principles allocating grants should be enumerated by a different body created by law and Parliament and Finance Commission was suggested in this connection. The Commission felt that neither an amendment of the Constitution nor the passing of the special law is necessary. Article 282 of the Constitution lays down that it shall be the duty of the Finance Commission to make recommendations to the President as to "any other matter referred to the Commission by the President in the interest of sound finance."

The Commission has dealt with separately plan loans

and plan assistance and has come out with the following recommendations:

1. The Finance Commission may be asked to make recommendations on the principles which should govern the distribution of plan grants to the States. The appointment of the Finance Commission may be so timed that when making its recommendations, it will have before it an outline of the 5 year plan as prepared by the Planning Commission.
2. The application of the principles governing the distribution of plan grants from year to year will be left to the Planning Commission.
3. In order to secure effective coordination of the Finance Commission's recommendations and the Plan, a member of the Planning Commission may be appointed to the Finance Commission.
4. The Finance Commission should include two persons, one having experience of financial administration at the Centre and the other having such experience in a State.
5. The Unit of the Plan Finance Division of the Ministry of Finance at the centre may be strengthened. It should form the nucleus of the Finance Commission's secretariat from time to time (para 4, page 17).

As the practice has been, the Finance Commission enumerates the principles of grants-in-aid under Article 275 and not under Article 282 of the Constitution. So far as the grants-in-aid under Article 275 and Article 282 are concerned, this matter has always been hotly debated and in such discussions, the role of Planning Commission—an executive body—and the Finance Commission—a

Constitutional body is the central point. Many of the Finance Commissions have deliberated on this issue while dealing with the role and scope of the Finance Commission.

Thus, the Administrative Reforms Commission recommended the maintenance of status quo. Instead, it recommended that there should be greater coordination between the two bodies; one member of Planning Commission should be nominated as member of Finance Commission.

The subject of Central-State Relations (CSRC) was received by another Commission appointed in 1983 under the chairmanship of R.S. Sarkaria, a retired Judge of the Supreme Court. The mandate of the Commission among other subjects was to review the existing arrangements between the Centre and the States and to recommend such changes or other measures as may be appropriate. The Commission was asked to keep in view "the social and economic developments that have taken place over the years and have due regard to the scheme and framework of the Constitution.

Like ARC, the Sarkaria Commission also went into the whole gamut of issues affecting the Centre-State relations including the Constitutional provisions, role of Planning and Finance Commission, debt relief, calamity relief and operational issues including procedure of release of grants from Government of India. In finalizing its recommendations, the Commission prepared a detailed questionnaire on each subject and asked the views of the States. It also held discussions with eminent persons and initiated various studies.

When the Commission asked for the views of the States, the States represented on the transfer scheme, borrowings and issues relating to financial matters. There were clear-cut two view-points which emerged. The majority view was that there has been over centralization in legislature, administrative and financial powers of the Centre. It was felt that the resources of the States have not grown at a rate commensurate with the increase in their responsibilities. Further, with the emergence of Planning Commission, the concentration of powers in the hands of centre has gone up.

The Commission dealt with the matters relating to financial relations in Chapter X and have made detailed recommendations, but so far as the constitutional provisions are concerned, it came to the following broad conclusions:

(a) The basic scheme of the Constitution dividing the field of taxation between the Union and the States and incorporating adequate arrangements for sharing of resources between them is sound and no major modifications in it are called for.
(b) The scheme of Constitution earmarking certain taxes for the exclusive use of the Union is sound. While there is no particular advantage in bringing all tax receipts into the divisible pool, it may, on the other hand, place the Union at a disadvantage.
(c) Corporation tax should be permissively shareable with the States and distributed among them on the authority of law passed by Parliament.
(d) The present division of responsibilities between the Finance Commission and the Planning Commission may continue. The present arrangement has also not given rise to any serious problems to necessitate any changes.

In para 10.8.16, the Sarkaria Commission gives the rationale for the continuing of the present system. "As the Finance Commission is constituted periodically and works for a short period while planning being a dynamic process, hence a static five year framework would not meet the requirements of planning. The Planning Commission reviews annually the resources and plan needs of the States and recommends plan assistance. It will not be possible for the Finance Commission to perform such functions."

The Sarkaria Commission recommended that the member in charge of resources division of Planning Commission should "automatically" be a common member and remain in this charge even after the report is submitted. This arrangement would enable the adoption of an integrated approach in the assessment of financial resources and needs of the States by the two Commissions. But this recommendation of ARC and Sarkaria Commission was not accepted. It was in case of Thirteenth Commission that the member of Planning Commission was appointed as the member of Finance Commission.

The Sarkaria Commission had also emphasized the need for synchronization of Five Year Plan period with the reference period of Finance Commission. The Commission has observed that "there is an impression that once the Finance Commission report is submitted, it is not of much consequence beyond determining major parameters. A planned economy presupposes utmost financial discipline. The entire system of resource transfer built on the basis of the recommendations of a semi-judicial body of expert would crumble in case there is scant regard for the norms entered by it (para 10.8.19)". Till date no serious attempt has been made in this direction by the Central Govt. In the same vein, the Commission has emphasized that each Finance Commission should view with great concern the violation of the regiment given by the preceding Commission and thus try to enforce a stricter discipline in checking wasteful expenditure (para 10.8.22).

After 1983, another Commission was constituted in April, 2007 under Justice M.M. Punchi, a former Chief

Justice of India as chairman and four other members. The Commission was asked to review the working of the existing arrangement between the Union and the States as per the Constitution of India. The ToR among other items of Centre-State relations, financial resources and sharing of resources were also included for review and recommendations. In this examination, the fiscal relations and the role of Finance Commission was also included. Para 8(iii)(g) specifically stated that the Commission shall have particular regard to the impact of the recommendations made by the 8th to 12th Finance Commission on the fiscal relations between the Centre and the States, specially the greater dependence of the States on devolution of funds from the Centre. The Volume III of the report exclusively deals with "Centre-State Financial Relations and Planning".

The Punchi CSRC II, before making its recommendations, has, in great detail, reviewed the development since the submission of reports by Sarkaria Commission in 1983. The CSRC II mainly highlights the economic reforms initiated during this period as well as changes in tax sharing (80th amendment) introduction of tax on services, 73rd and 74th amendment to the Constitution, tax reform including VAT, Fiscal Reforms Legislation, fixing a yearly borrowing ceiling, changes in the plan assistance to States. The Commission also highlighted the growing inter-state disparities during a span of roughly twenty seven years.

Further, the Commission has reviewed trends in fiscal transfers to States and in the process highlighted the dependence of States on central transfers. The review shows that the share of central transfers in the aggregate revenue receipts of the States has remained stable at around 40%. Within the total transfers from the Centre, dependence on share in central taxes was more visible as compared with grants from the Centre.

The Commission has identified some important and contentious issues raised by States and other stake holders, and issues, which have come to the fore following the economic liberalization and other policy changes in the areas of Central-State fiscal relations. The issues relating to the role of Planning Commission and Finance Commission have also been dealt with extensively. The issues identified are:

(i) **Vertical imbalance in resource raising**—As per States' complaint, the resource transfers to them have not been commensurate with their growing responsibilities. Because of the inclusive growth as objective, the State's responsibilities have increased manifold, for services and programmes, which are at the core of a more equitable social order, come within the purview of States under the Constitution.

(ii) **Growing Central Expenditure on functions of State list**—The Commission has observed that a fifth of the expenditure incurred by Centre was on subjects, which were in the domain of States as per Twelfth Finance Commission report. With the introduction of new Central Plan Schemes and new Centrally Sponsored Schemes (CSS), this proportion will further go up. The Commission has, further, observed that these are discretionary transfers and these have severely constrained the States in drawing and implementing schemes according to their priorities and felt needs of people. Hence, the Punchi Commission has recommended a comprehensive review of all transfers to States with a view to minimising the component of discretionary transfers, particularly those channeled through CSS.

(iii) **Growing regional imbalances**—These are causes of concern. The Commission suggested improvement in infrastructure facilities, maintenance of assets already created in backward areas, multi pronged strategy for development, improve the quality of governance and service delivery, access to banking services and institutional finances.

(iv) **Compliance and Enforcement cost of Central Legislation**—There are a number of Central Legislations like Environment Protection Act, Wildlife Protection Act, Forest Conservation Act the Bio-diversity Conservation Act, the Tribal Conservation Act for which the States are not compensated, though the recently enacted Right to Education Act has some cost sharing with the States. Food Security Act is yet to come. The Commission has recommended that the additional expenditure liabilities on States on the above count should be suitably compensated for which an institutional mechanism needs to be emphasized and the institution of Finance Commission is best suited for it.

(v) Impact of pay revision by Central Govt. on State Finances is another issue, where States have to, willy nilly, revise the scales of State Govt. employees. The Commission has recommended that the ToR of future Finance Commissions should be formulated in such a way that the additional commitments of States on account of pay revision are fully taken into account.

(vi) **Revision of Royalty Rates on Major Minerals**—The Commission has recommended that the royalty rates should be reviewed at least every three years without any delay, and the States should be properly compensated for any delay in the revision of royalty beyond three years.

(vii) The Commission has also recommended the sharing of off-shore royalty and sale proceeds of spectrum with States for expenditure on infrastructure items.

(viii) The Commission has also talked about professional tax, taxes under Article 268 and 269 of the Constitution. In case of professional tax, the Commission has recommended that the current ceiling on professional tax should be completely done away with by a Constitutional amendment.

With the 88th amendment to the Constitution, the scope of raising more revenue from taxes under Article 269 is now almost non-existent with the reduction in the number of taxes leviable and imminent abolition of Central Sales Tax (CST). The Commission has recommended that the scope of raising more revenue from the taxes mentioned in Article 268 should be examined afresh.

(ix) **Fiscal Responsibility and Budget Management (FRBM) Legislation**—The Commission considered the legislation as a game changing development ushering in an act of rule based management of public finances. It attributed the all-round improvement in public Finance to FRBM legislation.

The Commission has recommended that:

(a) "one size fits all" approach has to be amended and State specific targets of fiscal deficit should be fixed.

(b) Quality of fiscal adjustment should be built into the FRBM targets. The specification of target with regard to maintaining certain levels of expenditure on social services, maintenance and creation of capital assets should be built into the legislation.

(c) The off budget borrowings should be accounted for.

(d) The FRBMA should be amended to clearly specify

the circumstances which should warrant the deviation from the targets.

(e) To bring greater accountability, all fiscal legislations should provide for an annual assessment by an independent body and its report to be tabled in Parliament/State Legislature.

(x) The Commission has agreed with the present scheme of fixing overall borrowing limits.

(xi) The Commission has recommended a change in the interest rate on National Small Savings Fund (NSSF) loans to States but no change in the repayment period.

(xii) States should be fully compensated for any additional expenditure they bear or revenue loss they suffer on account of measures taken by the Union to maintain macro-economic stability.

The Commission has gone through the basic ToRs and the "considerations" given to Finance Commission. It has also taken note of the States' contention that these considerations are ever expanding and are loaded in favour of Centre and have been restricting the working of the Finance Commission. The Commission found merit in the contention of States and hence recommended that the considerations in the ToR of the Finance Commission should be even handed as between Centre and States. There should be an effective mechanism to involve the States in the finalisation of ToR of the Finance Commission.

The Commission also examined the issues of levies and surcharges. It has observed that the revenue through levies and surcharges has increased. The Commission has, therefore, recommended that the Central Govt. should review all the existing cesses and surcharges, with a view to bringing down their share in the gross tax revenue.

On the issue of plan and non-plan conundrum, the

Commission has recommended that an expert committee may be appointed to look into the issue of distinction between the plan and the non-plan expenditure.

Without going into the role of Finance Commission v/s Planning Commission and difficulty being pointed out by few Finance Commissions, this Commission has talked about much better coordination between the two. The synchronization of periods of Five Year Plan and award period of Finance Commission should be attempted again.

The Commission has strongly endorsed the recommendation of the Twelfth Finance Commission that the Finance Commission division in the Ministry of Finance should be converted into a full fledged department serving as the permanent secretariat for the Finance Commission.

While discussing Finance Commission transfers, the Commission has observed that these transfers were not much helpful in reducing inequalities. The Commission has recommended the use of more sophisticated methods to assess the needs of backward areas/States and providing with higher transfers. With regard to relative position of share and grants, the Commission has said that this matter should better be left to the judgment of the Finance Commission.

The Commission highlighted the problems arising out of the non-synchronization of the award periods of the State Finance Commission and the Central Finance Commission.

It is evident from the above narration that the Punchi Commission has tried to discuss all those burning issues, which directly or indirectly affect the Central-States Fiscal relations. Without disturbing the basic structure, the Commission has tried to find out solutions outside the frame work of the Constitution and have made practical recommendations, which can be easily implemented provided there is will to do so.

3. Composition, ToR and Considerations of Finance Commission

Article 280 of the Constitution provides for the constitution of a Finance Commission (FC) within 2 years from the commencement of the Constitution and thereafter at intervals of every fifth year or such earlier times as the President may consider necessary. The constitutional provisions relating to Finance Commission are given in Annexure III.1.

Originally, the Constitution required the Finance Commission to make the recommendations on the following issues:

(a) The distribution between the Union and the States of the net proceeds of taxes, which are to be or may be divided between them and the allocations between the States of the respective shares of such proceeds;

(b) The principles which should govern the grants-in-aid of the revenues of the States out of the Consolidated Fund of India;

(c) Any other matter referred to the Commission by the President in the interest of sound finance.

Later on, with the Constitution 73rd and 74th amendment Acts, the following issues were added:

280 (3)[751] [(bb) the measures needed to augment the Consolidated Fund of a State to supplement the resources of the Panchayats in the State on the basis of the recommendations made by the Finance Commission of the State;]

280 (3) [762][(c) the measures needed to augment the Consolidated Fund of a State to supplement the resources of the Municipalities in the State on the basis of the recommendations made by the Finance Commission of the State;]

Article 280 of the Constitution, which provides for the constitution of the Finance Commission, authorized Parliament to determine the qualification required for appointment as members of the Commission, the manner, in which, they should be selected and to prescribe the powers of the Commission for the performance of their functions.

The Finance Commission (Miscellaneous Provisions) Act, **(Annexure III.2)** was, accordingly, enacted in 1951 to deal with these questions to make it possible to assemble the Commission by 1952 as required by the Constitution. The Act prescribes that the chairman of the Commission should be selected from among those persons, who have experience in public affairs and four other members should be selected from among persons, who (a) are, or have been, or are qualified to be appointed as judges of a High Court; or (b) have special knowledge of the finances and accounts of the government; or (c) have had wide experience in financial matters and in administration; or (d) have special knowledge of economics.

The Commission is authorized to determine their own

---

1 Inserted by the Constitution (Seventy-third Amendment) Act,1992, S.3 w.e.f. 24.4.1993.

2 Inserted by the Constitution (Seventy-fourth Amendment) Act,1992, S.3. w.e.f. 1.6.1993.

procedure of business, and has been given the powers of a civil court in the matter of summoning and enforcing the attendance of witnesses, requiring the production of any documents and requisitioning and public record from any court of office. The Commission is also authorized to require any person to furnish information on such points or matters as in the opinion of the Commission may be useful for, or relevant to the matter under their consideration. Any person so required is legally bound to furnish such information within the meaning of Section 176 of the Indian Penal Code.

The first Finance Commission was appointed by an order dated 22nd November, 1951 under the chairmanship of Sri K.C. Neogy. Three other members, alongwith one member secretary were also appointed. One of the members of the Commission was retired Justice of the High Court. Since then thirteen Finance Commissions have been constituted and the composition and award period of each Commission is given in **Annexure III.3.**

A glance at the composition of thirteen Finance Commissions, show that the prescribed strength, requisite specialisations and background of their members and time limit in their constitution is duly adhered to. In some cases, the member of the Planning Commission, in charge of financial resources, was appointed as ex-officio member of the Finance Commission as recommended by the Administrative Reforms Commission and also by the Sarkaria Commission, but it was not followed consistently. This suggestion was made to have a proper and better co-ordination between the two institutions. After a long gap, the Thirteenth Finance Commission has one member from the Planning Commission.

The composition of Finance Commission was one of the matters before Sarkaria Commission, in which, some of the State Governments suggested that State Government representative should also be a member of the Finance Commission. But the Sarkaria Commission did not find favour with this suggestion and viewed that there is no need for any changes in the present arrangement in regard to the constitution of Finance Commission.

Althouth the Finance Commissions have been appointed at regular intervals, as envisaged in the Constitution, but the Five Year Plans have not been formulated with regular intervals **(Annexure III.4)**. This overlap and mismatch in the award period of Finance Commission and the Five Year Plan period have created difficulties not only for the Commission but for the States also in taking into account the States requirements on the one hand, and recommendations of the Finance Commission on the other, while preparing the annual budget.

As has been discussed earlier, this difficulty of non-synchronization of award period of Finance Commission and the Five Year plan period has been mentioned by various Finance Commissions. Sarkaria Commission and Punchi Commission on Centre-State financial relations have extensively discussed this issue and have recommended that attempts should be made to synchronize these two periods.

Terms of Reference and Considerations

A detailed list of "Terms of Reference" **(Annexure III.5)** and "Considerations" of all the Finance Commissions constituted so far is given in **Annexure III.6.**

Though the ToR and the duties of the Finance Commission are given in the Article 280 of the Constitution, yet some "Considerations" came to be included in the Presidential order. The notification constituting the First Commission did not contain any "consideration" other than those included in Article 280 of the Constitution. The Second Commission was asked to give its recommendations on some "additional matters" but no "Considerations" were there in the notification. In fact, the system of adding "Considerations" originally stemmed from the Fifth Finance Commission and ever since the list of considerations has expanded Commission after Commission. In all the notifications, the word "in making its recommendations the Commission shall take into considerations" has been written.

Many issues have been raised during the debates immediately after the constitution of every Commission and also after the presentation of the report. The common argument put up by the States was that these have conditioned the approach and methodology of the Commission. Secondly, these considerations are heavily loaded against the States. The notification of constitution of Ninth Finance Commission binds the Commission to follow the "normative approach". Similarly, since the Eighth Commission, it has been made mandatory for the Commission to adopt population figures of 1971 as the basis.

So far as these issues are concerned, the Government of India in the Ministry of Finance drafts the Presidential order. There is no set and regular system of consultations with the State Governments. While formulating ToR for Seventh and Eighth Finance Commission, there was some consultations between the Chief Ministers and the Union Finance Minister. Then, there was consultation between the Union Expenditure Secretary and some of the selected States' finance secretaries in case of Ninth Commission. But in case of later Commissions, no consultation at any level was done except asking for written suggestions from the States and the considerations are unilaterally determined by the Government of India.

With regard to second issue of "binding" on the Finance Commission, it was also debated before the Sarkaria Commission on Centre-State Relations. As has been mentioned in para 10.8.39 of the report, "the Government of India reported to the Commission that these considerations are, therefore, to be viewed as "an illustrative list of the factors considered by the Government germane to the task of the Finance Commissions".

The Sarkaria Commission has clearly stated that "we are not convinced that any reference to Finance Commission unless constituting a term of reference vide Article 280(3) of the Constitution, can bind or delimit its approach. However, it will only be appropriate and befitting the statutory and high status of the Finance Commission that any considerations suggested to it, besides its terms of reference under Article 280(3), are put in a language which does not give an impression of formally binding it to adhere to a given approach or methodology (para 10.8.40).

As has been discussed earlier, this issue was raised by the States before the Punchi Commission also and the Commission found merit in the contention of States and said that the considerations should be even handed as between the Centre and the States. There should be an effective mechanism to involve the States in the finalisation of the ToR of Finance Commissions (para 6.2.05).

Thus, it is apparent that the observations and recommendations made by the Sarkaria Commission in 1983 were not considered by the Govt. of India; otherwise the Punchi Commission would not have been compelled to make the above observations and recommendations. It is profoundly hoped that when Fourteenth Commission will be constituted in November 2012, the Govt. of India would have established an effective mechanism involving the States in the finalisation of ToR as well as including considerations on even keel.

Some of the important considerations, which the various Finance Commissions religiously followed in shaping their recommendations, can be cited as below:

(a) The efforts to be made by those States to raise additional revenues from the sources available to them; **(FC III)**

(b) (i) The requirements on revenue account of those States to meet the expenditure on administration, interest charges in respect of their debt, maintenance and upkeep of plan schemes completed by the end of 1968-69, transfer of funds to local bodies and aided institutions and other committed expenditure. **(FC IV).**

(ii) The scope for better fiscal management as also for economy consistent with efficiency which may be effected by the States in their administrative, maintenance, developmental and other expenditure **(FC V).**

(c) (i) The requirements of States which are backward in standards of general administration for upgrading the administration, with a view to bringing it to the levels obtaining in the more advanced States over a period of ten years; **(FC VI).**

(ii) The scope for better fiscal management and economy consistent with efficiency which may be affected by the States in their administrative, maintenance, developmental and other expenditure; **(FC VI).**

(iii) The Commission may make an assessment of the non-plan capital gap of the States on a uniform and comparable basis for the five years ending with 1978-79. In the light of such an assessment, the Commission may undertake a general review of the States' debt position with particular reference to the Central loans advanced to them and likely to be outstanding at the end of 1973 and suggest changes in the existing terms of repayment having regard *inter-alia* to the overall non-plan gap of the States, their relative position and the purpose for which the loans have been utilised, and the requirements of the Centre **(FC VI).**

(iv) The Commission may review the policy and arrangements in regard to the financing of relief expenditure by the States affected by natural calamites and examine inter-alia the feasibility of establishing a National Fund to which the Central and State Governments may contribute a percentage of their revenue receipts **(FC VI).**

(d) (i) Adequate maintenance and upkeep of capital assets and maintenance of plan schemes completed by the end of 1978-79, the norms, if any, on the basis of which specified amounts are allowed for the maintenance of different categories of capital assets and the manner in which such maintenance expenditure could be monitored being indicated by the Commission; **(FC VII).**

(ii) In making its recommendations on the various matters aforesaid, the Commission shall adopt the population figures of 1971 as the basis in all cases where population is regarded as a factor for determination of devolution of taxes and duties and grants-in-aid. **(FC VII, VIII, IX, X, XI,XII,XIII).**

(e) The scope for better fiscal management and economy in expenditure consistent with efficiency; **(FC VII).**

(f) (i) Adopt a normative approach in assessing the receipts and expenditure on the revenue account of the States and the centre and, in doing so, keep in view the special problems of each States, if any, and the special requirements of the Centre such as defence, security, debt-servicing and other committed expenditure or liabilities **(FC IX).**

(ii) Have due regard to the need for providing adequate incentives for better resource mobilisation and financial discipline as well as closer linking of expenditure and revenue raising decisions **(FC IX).**

(iii) Keep in view the objective of not only balancing the receipts and expenditure on revenue account of both the States and the Centre, but also generating surpluses for capital investment **(FC IX).**

(g) (i) The requirements of the States for meeting the non-plan revenue expenditure also keeping in view the potential for raising additional taxes **(FC X).**

(ii) The need for ensuring reasonable returns on investment by the States in irrigation projects, power projects, state transport undertakings, departmental commercial undertakings, public sector enterprises etc. **(FC X).**

(h) The Commission may, after making an assessment of the debt position of the States as on the 31st March 2004, suggest such corrective measures as are deemed necessary, consistent with macro-economic stability and debt sustainability. Such measures recommended will give weightage to the performance of the States in the fields of human development and investment climate **(FC X).**

(i) The need to improve the quality of public expenditure to obtain better outputs and outcomes **(FC XIII).**

(j) The need to manage ecology, environment and climate change consistent with sustainable development **(FC XIII).**

Going through the reports of the Finance Commissions, the following conclusions can be drawn.

(i) All the notifications clearly mention that the Commission "shall take into account" the considerations mentioned in the notification. Therefore, these have become bindings for the Commission to follow and these have been religiously followed by all the Commissions. The Commissions have dealt each and every consideration, in detail, and have taken them into account while making their recommendations.

(ii) The considerations are heavily loaded against the States. Excepting one or two, which have to be looked into in case of Government of India, all other considerations are to be applied in case of States. A thorough scrutiny of the State's finances has to be done before recommending share in central taxes, debt relief and calamity relief and grants-in-aid.

(iii) One of the important considerations was to take the population of 1971 into consideration wherever population is regarded as a factor for determination of grants-in-aid. Though, the reference to Parliament's resolution was referred to as basis of including this in the list of consideration, but it is also a fact that the period of validity of resolution expired in 2001 and there was no further extension beyond 2001. As this was included in the list of considerations and in spite of protests from States, the Finance Commission could not do anything about it.

Thus in spite of this clear position, the successive Finance Commissions have followed the considerations both in letter and spirit as will be evident when the approach, methodology and recommendations are discussed at length in the later chapters.

Recommendations and Notes of Dissent

Out of Thirteen Commissions constituted so far, in case of five Commissions notes of Dissent were recorded. In case of Third Commission, the dissenting note was recorded by the member Mr. G.R. Kamat. Sri Mohan Lal Gautam recorded the dissenting note in Fourth Commission. Prof. Raj Krishna wrote a dissenting note in Eighth Commission and Justice A.S. Qureshi dissented in Ninth Commission.

Separate notes were also appended (not dissenting) by member Sri. R. Kaushalendar Rao (First Commission), by 2 members of Fourth Commission, one by Fifth Commission member, Sri. N.C. Jain, and Dr. A. Baghchi wrote a note and a note of observation in Eleventh Finance Commission **(Annexure III.7)**.

Excepting Five Commissions (Third, Eighth, Eleventh, Twelfth and Thirteenth) the recommendations of all other Commissions were unanimous. By and large, the recommendations made by the Finance Commissions have been accepted by the Government of India. However, there have been instances when the recommendations of the Finance Commissions were not accepted. These have been briefly discussed below:

(i) The Third Finance Commission's recommendation for devolution as part of Article 275 grants towards 75 per cent of the revenue component of the Third

Five Year Plan was not accepted. The reason given by the Government was that no real advantage was seen in channelising grants for the same purpose from two different sources.

(ii) Two recommendations made by the Seventh Finance Commission were not accepted. They were:

(a) The loss equal to the difference between the amount of excise revenue realised on sale of potable liquor and that assumed by the Commission may be compensated by the Centre to the full extent.

(b) The small savings loan should be treated as "loans in perpetuity".

The former recommendation was not accepted on the ground that as prohibition was among the Directive Principles of State Policy, the State should also bear the loss. The Union Government's contribution was fixed at 50 per cent. In the case of the latter recommendation, the Government was not convinced of the logic given by the Commission and did not accept the recommendation. However, a decision was subsequently taken to postpone the recovery of these loans from the States for the period of the Finance Commission (1979-1984).

(iii) The final recommendations of the Eighth Finance Commission were not implemented during 1984-85, i.e. the first year of the Commission's period of reference, during which its Interim recommendations remained in force.

It is, indeed, unfortunate that the Eighth Finance Commission's final recommendations were not implemented in 1984-85, which caused serious financial problems to some States.

4. Approaches and Issues of Finance Commission

This chapter deals with the approach adopted by the Commissions while finalising their recommendations. The background, in which the Commissions were set up, also influenced the approach of the Commissions. The fiscal situation prevailing at that time affecting the finances of the Centre and the States also influenced the shaping of recommendations. The discussion of the approach adopted by First to Thirteenth Finance Commission will show a common theme running through all the Commissions.

As it was the first of its kind, the First Finance Commission did not have any guidelines or considerations before it to follow. **The Commission had before it three committees' reports viz. Sir Otto Niemeyer Committee, N.R. Sankar Committee and the Deshmukh award 1950.** Based on these reports, the First Commission had to decide on its own approach and guidelines.

The Commission, in deciding about its course of action, has observed that "we had, however, to take into account not merely the needs of the States, but the ability of the Centre as well to assist the States by the transfer of a larger portion of its revenues" (**FC I** - para 7 page 19).

The Commission has, further, said that "In drawing

up the scheme of assistance, we have kept three main considerations in view. Firstly, the additional transfer of resources from the Centre must be such as the Centre could bear without undue strain on its resources, taking into account its responsibility for such vital matters as the defence of the country and the stability of its economy. Secondly, the principles for the distribution of revenues between the States and the determination of grants-in-aid must be uniformly applied to all the States. Lastly, the scheme of distribution should attempt to lessen the inequalities between States" (**FCI** - para 8, page 22).

The plan of assistance, which the Commission drew up after setting up above three guidelines, includes both devolution of taxes and grants-in-aid but relying more on devolution of revenues. In the words of Commission, "The plan of assistance which we have drawn up envisages a substantial transfer of resources from the Centre to the States. We have used the methods both of devolution of revenue and grants-in-aid, but have relied substantially on the devolution of revenue for securing this transfer. In doing so, we believe we are meeting the general desire of the States themselves. The method has also the advantage of linking the revenues of the States directly with those of the Centre, so that both share in whatever elasticity the revenue that is divided between them possesses. In our proposals for the devolution of revenue, we have widened the field of division by recommending the division of a few excises in addition to increasing somewhat the States' share in the divisible pool of income-tax. An increase in the number of divisible taxes also makes it possible to diversify the basis of distribution and achieve a balanced scheme which would benefit all the States. We have recommended general grants-in-aid to such of the States to whom our scheme for the devolution of revenue does not provide adequate resources.

We have also recommended grants-in-aid to some of the less developed States to enable them to make some progress in one of the important social services of national interest (**FC I** - p 8, para 20)."

Another important decision, which the Commission took, was that the Commission will not make any recommendation in regard to grants for meeting the capital requirements of the States, which should be met largely from borrowed funds. This approach set by the first Commission is still being followed by successive Commissions (**FC I** - p 8, para 23).

Thus, the First Finance Commission looked into three considerations (i) Centre's ability to raise additional resources (ii) Centre's responsibility for vital matters (iii) principles of distribution to be applied equally to all States. These are very important considerations, which later Commissions took as guiding principles and ToR included these considerations also.

Like the First Finance Commission, no guidelines were issued to the Second Finance Commission (SFC) apart from the one, which contained in the Article 280 and 275 of the Constitution. At that time, the States entered with the Government of India a tax rental agreement, which says that an additional duty of Excise should be levied on mill-made textiles, sugar and tobacco, including manufactured tobacco, in replacement of the sales taxes now levied by the State Governments the net proceeds being distributed among the States, subject to the present income derived by each of the States, being assured to it. This was given as an additional ToR to the Commission. Further, another ToR was also given to SFC to make recommendations as to the principles which should govern the distribution under article 269 of the Constitution of the net proceeds in any financial year of the tax on railway fares proposed to be levied by the Railway Passenger fares bill 1957.

The Commission sought clarification regarding exact scope of the reference made under Article 275 of the Constitution. The majority of the Commission felt that clause (2) of Article 275 covered not only the substantive portion of clause (1) but also the two provisos appended to it. If we accordingly wrote to the Secretary to the President suggesting that if this interpretation was acceptable to the President, he might be pleased to issue necessary orders to enable the Commission to make recommendations regarding grants under the provisos. We were informed in reply that the President had been advised that as the duty of the Commission to make recommendations was only in respect of grants-in-aid as to which Parliament could make a law under clause (1) of article 275 and as the provisos constituted exceptions to the main provision and there was no mention in them of Parliament making any law, the power of the Commission to make recommendations under clause (2) of article 275 did not extend to the grants under the two provisos. The President, accordingly, decided that no order needs to be issued asking for the Commission's recommendations regarding the grants under the provisos to article 275 (**FC II** - para 8, page 5).

The Finance Commission was required to make recommendations for grants-in-aid to the States, keeping in view the requirements of the II Five Year Plan (F.Y.P.); hence, the second Finance Commission took the view that "the Commission will take into account the "basic" as well as "developmental" needs of the States. So far as the developmental needs are concerned, the Commission made it clear that the plan, as a whole, has been approved by the National Development Council and Parliament. We did not, therefore, consider it proper to assume the role of a revising body. We, accordingly, made it clear that, while it was open to the States to move the Planning Commission for any modification of the plan or for increase in the provision made in it for any scheme, we would accept the allocation as finally made by the Planning Commission" (**FC II** - Para 20, page 10).

The Second Finance Commission has in its general observations indicated some difficulties in the functioning of two Commissions viz. Planning Commission and Finance Commission. Some anomalies inevitably arise where the functions of the two Commissions—the Finance Commission and Planning Commission—overlap. The former is a statutory body with limited functions, while the later has to deal comprehensively with the finances of the Union and the States in the widest sense of the term. So long as both these Commissions have to function, there appears to be a real need for effectively coordinating their work. It will be an advantage if, in future, the period covered by the recommendations of a Finance Commission coincides with that of a five year plan. Further, it is desirable to eliminate the necessity of making two separate assessments of the needs of the States" (**FC II** - para 27, page 13).

This problem is being faced by all the successive Commissions. The matter was raised before the Sarkaria Commission and also before the Punchi Commission, but no attempt seems to have been made to synchronise the award period of Finance Commission and the five year plan period. The approach of the Second Finance Commission with regard to grants-in-aid was "The principles formulated by the previous Finance Commission for regulating grants-in-aid of the revenues of the States are, if we may say so, unexceptionable. They suggested that the budgetary needs of the States should be the starting point for determining the assistance required by the States, but that the needs thus disclosed should be adjusted with regard to certain other considerations. First, the budgets of the States should be reduced to a comparable basis by making adjustments in respect of abnormal, unusual and non-recurring items of revenue and expenditure. Secondly, due allowances should be made for "clear cases" of failure of States to maximise tax effort. Thirdly, in order not to place a premium upon extravagance, the States endeavour to secure reasonable economies in expenditure should be taken into consideration. Fourthly, where standards of social services in any State are significantly lower than in others, it should qualify for special assistance. Fifthly, special disabilities of States due to abnormal conditions beyond their control should be provided for. Lastly, grants may be made to certain States in furtherance of broad purposes of national importance, such as primary education, in respect of which they may be specially backward" (**FC II** - para 62, page 23).

"We see no reason for departing from this basic approach to the problem of grants-in-aid, although our emphasis on the various principles laid down by our predecessors has been influenced by subsequent developments. We endorse the pri ple of fiscal need and interpret fiscal need comprehensively by taking into account the impact of the completion of the first five year plan and the needs of the second. We have, as in the past, taken an integrated view of the finances of the Union and the States and the financial capacity of the Union to assist the States, after meeting its own essential commitments. We have sought to formulate a scheme of grants-in-aid which should under normal conditions, enable the States to balance their budgets after meeting their normal revenue expenditure as well as the revenue expenditure incidental to the execution of the second five year plan. We have, as far as possible, reduced the State budgets to a comparable basis. We have also made allowance for the various factors by which the computation of budgetary needs has to be adjusted and have treated grants-in-aid as residuary assistance to the States after taking into account devolution of revenue in other forms." (**FC II** - page 63)

"Our predecessors thought that, while considering the eligibility of a State for a grants-in-aid and the amount of such aid, due weight should be given to tax effort, so that the States, which raise adequate resources through taxation, are not penalised and no premium is put upon lack of self-help. The principle of tax effort is unexceptionable, but, as they themselves admitted, "It is only in clear cases of inadequate taxation" that it should effect the quantum of assistance which the States may be otherwise qualified to get. "Clear cases" of inadequate taxation are difficult to determine. Low per capita taxation in poor States may simply be evidence of low taxable capacity. An agricultural State with a low level of purchasing power has to maintain a comparatively high level of per capita expenditure to sustain a reasonable standard of public services. An industrial State can raise much larger per capita revenue than an agricultural State, even though the kinds and rates of taxes are the same in both. It is, therefore, difficult to decide whether a State is taxing its people adequately in relation to their income and taxable capacity. Some kind of empirical judgment is inevitable. In our assessment of tax effort, we have assumed that if a State raised additional revenue which it has promised for the plan, it will have done its part." (**FC II**- page 22, para 64)

"Another consideration, which weighed with the previous Commission, is the function of grants-in-aid in reducing inequalities in the standards of basic social services in the States. We recognize that maintenance of certain important services at a minimum national level may justify giving special grants-in-aid. Since total resources are limited, this can be achieved only by stages. We have taken the view that it is the function of the Planning Commission and the National Development Council to ensure the equalisation, as far as practicable, of the standard of essential social services in the various States of the Union. To the extent that plan expenditure incurred on raising the level of social services has become committed expenditure, we have taken it into account. For our scheme of devolution, we have accepted the plan as ensuring in equitable development in the field of social services. There is, therefore, now no room for any grants in this field, such as the grant for expansion of primary education recommended by the last Commission." (**FC II** - page 25, para 65)

After discussing the pros and cons of the approach of previous Commission, the Second Commission recommended three principles of grants-in-aid (i) The eligibility and amount should depend on the comprehensive needs of State (ii) The gap should be met by share in taxes and (iii) grants for broad purposes may also be given. The principles enunciated by the Second Commission, in a way, became guiding principles for future Commissions.

Third Finance Commission

In the scheme of the report, the Third Finance Commission (TFC) did not have any chapter on "Issues and Approach" to be adopted by the Commission in dealing with the ToR. Instead, the Commission straightway went into each ToR. While making its recommendations, the Commission deliberated on the issues pertaining to each ToR and gave its rationale of making recommendations.

With regard to assessing budgetary needs of the State, the Commission adopted the procedure followed by the Second Commission in regard to (a) expenditure on natural calamities (b) no assessment of loss due to prohibition (c) excluded from the forecasts the provision of redemption of debt (d) included grants from Central Road Fund (e) taken into consideration the liability arising out of the changed pattern of central assistance for some specific items.

The Third Commission also stressed that "in our schemes of affording assistance, we have adhered to the principle that the budgetary needs of the States, as assessed, should be met as far as possible by the devolution of taxes and grants-in-aid should be made to provide residuary fiscal aid (**FC III** - page 12, para 18).

The Commission followed the principles laid down by Second Commission with regard to distribution of assigned taxes. With regard to sharing of Income Tax, the Commission argued that while population should remain as main factor of distribution, the factor of contribution should receive adequate attention. With regard to Union Excise Duty, the Commission stressed that a larger devolution of Union Excise Duties will keep the States to meet their expanding responsibilities. As a result, a number of commodities were included in the list.

Fourth Finance Commission

The fourth Finance Commission has devoted a full chapter (chapter 2) to the basic approach by the Finance Commission. As per the Commission, there are two main issues involved viz. what part of divisible revenues should go to the States and what should be the distribution interse. The Commission observed that "whatever principles are laid down with regard to these issues have, however, to be based upon economic realities of the country and formulated within the framework of the provisions of the Constitution". (**FC IV** - page 7 para 12)

The Commission has considered the role of Planning

Commission and the consequent distinction that has evolved between plan and non-plan expenditure. Finally, the Commission came to the conclusion that it should be desirable to leave all plan expenditures out of its considerations. The decision is based not on grounds of Constitutional limitations of the power of Finance Commission but on practical considerations consequent on institutional arrangements relating to the Five year plans" (**FC IV** - para 13, page 8). The Commission has, further, stated that the Commission has been specifically, asked to take into account the committed expenditure on the maintenance and upkeep of the completed third plan schemes may be taken to imply that new outlays on fourth plan schemes are not expected to enter into its estimates (**FC IV** - para 15, page 9). The Commission, therefore, confined itself to the non-plan expenditure vis-a-vis revenue receipts.

The Finance Commission also made it clear that "we have not, however, taken the view that the function of the Finance Commission is simply to recommend such devolution and grants-in-aid as would merely fill up the non-plan revenue deficit as reported by the States because such an approach will be extremely mechanical. We have reassessed the States' estimates and we have not taken budgetary deficits as a criterion for distribution in case of divisible taxes and duties." (**FC IV** - para 17, page 9)

The Commission, further, clarified that the budgetary deficits as a criterion for distribution in case of divisible taxes and duties has not been taken into account. The Commission has observed that "the Constitution does not say that it should be distributed on the basis of budgetary needs. In case of Union Excise Duty also, the provisions are similar. The same is the case with Estate Duty because it is a State tax collected by the Centre and, therefore, budgetary needs do not enter the distribution criteria. The additional duty of excise in lieu of sales tax, is again a state tax in substance and the distribution should logically be based on the principles of compensation for loss of revenue **(FC IV - page 9, para 18)**.

The obvious implication of Article 275 for grants-in-aid is that if any State is in need of assistance after the taxes to be compulsorily or optionally shared with the States have been distributed on the basis of the principles uniformly applicable to all States such assistance has to be granted under Article 275. Corrective action for residuary deficits can be taken only under the authority of the Article **(FC IV - page 10, para 19)**.

The Fourth Commission did not consider the criteria of "relative financial weakness of the States" as the criteria for determining the shares of taxes as recommended by Third Commission. The Commission argued that if any State is in need of financial assistance because of large deficits that cannot be covered by uniformly applied principles of tax sharing should appear explicitly as grant rather than being disguised as shares of taxes **(FC IV - page 10, para 20)**.

Fifth Finance Commission

The Commission has devoted chapter 2 of the report in highlighting the problems of Central-State financial relations and their approach to tackle these issues.

While describing the Constitutional provisions regarding Central-State financial relations, the Commission has observed that there is in built imbalance between the functional responsibilities assigned to the States and the financial resources allocated to them. There is a chronic gap between the State's own revenues and their expenditure commitments and consequently there is persistent and growing need for larger transfers of funds to States.

The Commission has come out with a scheme of federal finance with the two broad purposes. First, it should augment the State's own resources so as to help them meet their expenditure needs as far as can be done from the surplus of the Union (**FC V** - para 2.7, page 11). Secondly, it is desirable to see that the transfer of funds is so designed as to assist adequately the States with comparatively less capacity to raise resources. Insofar as the question of grants-in-aid under Article 275 of Constitution is concerned, the Commission has observed that the Article 275 is designed to help the States, which are less developed and have less capacity to raise resources of their own (**FC V** - Para 2.8, page 11).

With regard to the question of considering plan and non-plan expenditure, the Fourth Finance Commission was not specifically asked to take into account the requirement of plan, the Commission did not do so because it considered it desirable that the Planning Commission having been specifically constituted for this purpose, should have unhampered authority in this domain. The Fifth Commission was, specifically, asked not to take into consideration requirements of the plan for the purpose of recommending sums to be given as grants under Article 275. The Finance Commission was of the view that to deal with plan expenditure again would blur the entire division of functions between the Finance Commission and the Planning Commission.

Sixth Finance Commission

Like the Fifth Finance Commission, the Sixth Finance Commission has also devoted a full chapter on the "Approach" to be followed by the Commission. In adopting its approach, the Finance Commission, in the very beginning, clearly mentioned that "we feel it would be more purposeful if we confine ourselves to delineating certain directions in which, in our judgment, new initiatives need to be attempted, without, of course, disturbing too violently the delicate framework that has been painstakingly evolved in the last 25 years" **(FC VI** - para 1, page 5). Thus, the Sixth Finance Commission (SFC), by and large, followed the previous Finance Commissions in dealing with the issues relating to ToR.

With regard to the increasing role of Planning Commission in the flow of funds from Centre, the Sixth Finance Commission had to say the following: "The fact that Planning Commission has come into prominence in the last two decades as another channel for resource transfers does not in anyway detract from the efficacy of the provisions embodied in the Constitution. The advent of economic planning has only further strengthened the bonds of financial kinship between the Centre and the States and has underlined, even in a more pronounced manner than envisaged in the Constitution, the common stake that the Centre and the States have in the proper utilisation of the resources of the nation as a whole. It may be stated that the Planning Commission has emerged as an effective instrument for raising the scale of transfer of resources from the Centre to the States" **(FC VI** - page 6).

The Finance Commission has for the first time raised the issue of exploitation of potential of resource rising. It said that "in our view the difficulties, which have been experienced from time to time in the field of Centre-State financial relations, are not due primarily to the particular pattern of distribution of resources as laid down in the Constitution. The root cause for dissatisfaction among the States is to be found in the fact that the rate of growth of our economy has not been fast enough to meet the rising expectations of our people. We have also not exploited fully our potential for resource mobilization. We would, therefore, urge that attention should be focused on how best the various instruments in the fiscal armoury of the Central and State Governments can be further "sharpened" and adequate resources raised for social and economic development". **(FC VI** - para 8)

In the same vein, the Commission has also, for the first time, raised the issues of tax evasion, tax avoidance and waste and extravagance in public expenditure. The Commission also talked of efficient deployment of public funds, in particular, investment in productive enterprises in the public sector. The concept of "sound fiscal management" was introduced for the first time by the Commission. In fact, the Commission has devoted the whole chapter on this subject.

While elaborating the role of Finance Commission in the context of social and economic planning, the Finance Commission has earmarked the task of settling the optimal distribution of the resources of the public sector between the Centre & States.

While referring to distinction between plan and non-plan, the Commission has observed that "In the sphere of planning, there is a growing realisation that the Central and State Plans reinforce each other and together subserve certain widely shared economic and social objectives. But unfortunately, and presumably because of the present unrealistic distinction between Plan and non-Plan, a similar healthy approach is not being brought to bear upon the allocation of resources between the Centre and the States when it comes to assessing the non-plan requirements." **(FC VI** - para 14, page 7)

Dealing with the Approach to Fifth Plan, the Finance Commission has clearly indicated that "When the emphasis is on social justice, there is no escape from a realignment of resources in favour of the States, because services and programmes, which are at the core of a more equitable social order, come within the purview of the States under the Constitution." **(FC VI** - para 16, page 8)

The Commission has touched upon inter-state variations in levels of administrative and social services and has said that we have sought to raise the provisions for some of the administrative and social services upto the national average in the backward States. We hope that we have broken new grounds in the Indian Federal Finance". **(FC VI** - para 20, page 8)

From the review of the approach followed by the Sixth Finance Commission, it clearly emerges that the Commission has definitely broken new grounds in the matters of fiscal relations. The questions like tax potential, tax evasion, tax avoidance, unproductive expenditure and return on capital investment were never approached by the earlier Commissions. The question of regional disparities in the matter of standards of administration and social services was, for the first time, looked by the Finance Commission and recommended some grants-in-aid to backward States. As will be seen later, these questions formed the "other considerations" for future Commissions.

Seventh Finance Commission

The Commission has discussed the general issues with regard to centre and State fiscal relations and their views on various issues are given in Chapter IX of the report.

The first issue is the addition of "considerations" which the Commission has to take into account while framing their recommendations. As this paragraph was added for the first time, many of the States argued that these were constraints on the Commission which has to hold the balance between the Centre and States and, therefore, the

Centre ought not to indicate what considerations should be kept in mind by the Commission. After discussing the issue at length the Commission concluded that "it is, therefore, reasonable to take the view that the "considerations" were not constraints on the Commission in anyway". **(FC VII** - para 4, page 59)

The Seventh Commission, for the first time, clearly formulated the principles of grants in aid under Article 275 of the Constitution. These have been narrated in para 5 of Chapter 9 of the report, which in later years, formed the essential basis for setting the guidelines for successive Finance Commissions. These have been discussed, in detail, in the chapter on grants-in-aid.

The Seventh Finance Commission, for the first time, introduced the new dimensions in forecasting receipts and expenditures of the States.

"In the course of our work, we have taken into account the tax effort of the States and the returns which prudent management of public enterprises should fetch to the State Governments. We have also projected expenditure requirements on the revenue account in such a manner as to induce States to improve efficiency and to regulate expenditure carefully. While providing for upgradation of emoluments, we have gone by objective tests and discounted larger expenditure which some of the States had proposed. In the matter of narrowing disparities in the standards of services between the less developed and the advanced States, we have decided that the required amounts should be provided by way of specific grants-in-aid. We have taken prohibition as a national policy, and are recommending grants from the Centre to States to cover losses of excise revenue. We have also recommended that the net interest liability devolving on the States in each year for the period covered by our Report on account of their fresh borrowings and lendings should be made good by grants to be calculated and paid by the Central Government." **(FC VII** - para 6, page 59).

The issues, relating to the overlap of functions of Finance Commission and Planning Commission, specially with regard to transfer of funds to States, were again cropped up before the Seventh Finance Commission also through memoranda submitted by various States. The Commission did discuss these issues and devoted a few paras of its report and finally reconciled to the existing situation by saying that "Whatever may have been the position in the past in the matter of the size of discretionary Central transfers, the freedom of a Finance Commission to evolve its own scheme of transfer the period covered by its Report is in no way limited. The only constraints on it are firstly, that it has to operate within the four corners of the constitutional provisions and secondly, that it should leave the area of Plan investment and Central Assistance for State Plans to the Planning Commission. The later is not, in any real sense, a constraint on the Finance Commission. The Central assistance for State Plans is not decided independently of the situation of the State resulting from the Finance Commission awards, for, to the extent that the States' resources are improved *vis-a-vis* their requirements for their plans, the proportion of Central assistance for the plan in the total transfer can be smaller" **(FC VII** - para 10, page 60).

With regard to minimising the inter-State disparities, the Finance Commission showed greater concern than the previous Finance Commissions. The Commission observed that "Our focus should, therefore be specifically on how to place the financially weaker States in a position from where, with the guidance of the Planning Commission, they could get a better start than has been the case in the past, in absolute terms as well as relative to the advanced States. There is no other way of achieving this objective than to ensure that our fiscal transfer scheme leaves, as many of the poorer States as possible, with surpluses on the revenue account, which could be ploughed back for fresh development. In our view the role of a Finance Commission should not be negative, of filling in the revenue gaps only, but positive in that its scheme of devolution gives a better start for developmental outlay" **(FC VII** - para 18, page 62).

Eighth Finance Commission

The Eighth Finance Commission in Chapter II has very briefly discussed the approach adopted by them in dealing with the issues of transfer of funds.

The Commission has, while dealing with the competing claims of the Centre and the States and further of different States, taken the national interest as a whole in view.

The Commission has tried to strike a balance with regard to share of the States and the Centre's needs as well as in allocation between States. The basic question in the mind of the Commission was "how to reconcile the need to accelerate the development of backward States without hindering the further development of more advanced States".

With regard to grants-in-aid under Article 275 of the Constitution, which were fixed for five years by earlier Commissions, the Eighth Finance Commission built flexibility by giving a measure of buoyancy by providing 5% rate of growth during the forecast period.

Justifying the adoption of gap filling approach, the Commission has argued it on two grounds. First the Commission reassesses the forecasts and applies certain norms. The approach has been objective both on the revenue and expenditure side. Secondly, the requirements of the

States on account of developmental needs should, according to practice, be estimated and generally met by the Planning Commission. Consequently, even if fiscal needs are to be taken into account, they would have to be limited to the needs on non-plan accounts.

The Finance Commission has attempted to reduce regional imbalances between States in addition to covering revenue gap. This objective has been attempted by recommending grants-in-aid for upgradation of standards of administration. As per Finance Commission, the scheme of devolution as recommended has also a distributive role in that it provides additional resources to the less developed States.

Ninth Finance Commission

Ninth Finance Commission submitted two reports, one relating to year 1989-90 and another for 1990-95. The reasons for submitting two reports are enumerated in para 1.4 of the report and there is no need to discuss them herein.

There appeared certain new features in the notification constituting the Finance Commission and detailing the Terms of Reference and other considerations. First, the word "shall" has been added for other considerations giving an impression that these are mandatory to follow. Secondly, the Commission was asked to follow "normative" approach. The other considerations were loaded in favour of the Centre and against the States. These matters were raised by various Chief Ministers in their memoranda and the Commission tried to clear the doubts of the States.

The Commission emphasized the need to identify the reasons for rising trend of revenue deficit both at the Centre and the States. Hence, the Ninth Finance Commission talked of rising of revenues as the main priority area. In case of revenue expenditure, the Commission talked of the rising subsidies and interest payments. In the light of these two trends, the adoption of normative approach assumed significance.

As per the Commission, though adequate volume of resources must be made available to the States for fulfilling their constitutional requirements, the manner of transfer should not be such as to weaken the fiscal responsibility and must leave scope, at least at the margin, for linking revenue rising and expenditure decisions.

The Ninth Finance Commission enunciated two principles (a) maintenance of fiscal responsibility and uncompromising commitment to economy and efficiency, and (b) inter-State equality. The Commission felt that once assistance is granted on the basis of these two principles, it would clearly be the responsibility of each Government (including the Centre) to balance the revenue budget.

The Commission touched upon the respective roles of Finance Commission and Planning Commission, when the questions of Plan and non-Plan sides of revenue account were considered. In the first report, the Commission only mentioned that it will come out with its views in the main report of the Commission. However, it mentioned that the Finance Commission shall not disturb or weaken the planning process and economic planning must continue to be the prerogative of Planning Commission.

Ninth Finance Commission—Second Report

The Commission started with the observation that "The federal transfers must be adequate in the context of legitimate budgetary needs of the States while being just and fair to minimise the vertical and horizontal imbalance within the confines of available resources." **(FC IX** - para 2.1)

In the second report also, the Finance Commission had kept in view two basic principles (a) a fair apportionment of revenue resources given their constitutional responsibilities and overall limitation of resources, (b) the manner of transfer of resources be such that to preserve fiscal autonomy of the States and to promote fiscal responsibility on the part of both Centre and States. These same principles were enunciated by the Commission in its first report also.

The Commission took serious note of the deteriorating fiscal scenario in the country. The area of concern was rising revenue deficit of Centre and States put together. The implications of rising revenue deficit are large, diversion of all savings and borrowing for filling this gap without any return to service the debt taken. As a consequence, the interest payments also rise. As per the Finance Commission, this vicious circle must be broken.

In the final analysis, the Commission underlined its approach and methodology (**FC IX** - para 2.9) and stated that (a) phasing out of revenue deficits of the Centre and the States in such a manner that the deficits are reduced to zero or a relatively small figure by March 31, 1995. (b) Equity in the distribution of fiscal resources both vertically and horizontally and (c) promotion of fiscal discipline and efficiency in the utilization of resources.

In order to implement these principles, the Commission adopted a normative approach. In this connection, the Finance Commission adopted the same approach, which it did in the first report.

Tenth Finance Commission

The Commission's approach was guided by the "paramount need to restore fiscal equilibrium in the economy". While making the recommendations, the Commission had in its mind the budgetary scenario of the Centre and States, the emerging issues in federal finance and the evolving macro economic policy environment.

Like other Finance Commissions, the Tenth Finance Commission also dealt with the question of plan and non-plan outlay and expenditure. According to the Commission, the clubbing of the revenue and the capital components in one category termed as plan outlay has generated a tendency to use borrowings to finance revenue expenditure. It is imperative to match the revenue resources separately with the revenue component of the plan. Failure to appreciate this basic requirement of fiscal discipline is one of the main causes of the endemic fiscal disequilibrium.

The Commission focused its attention to the need to reduce the fiscal deficit and also to achieve the balance on the non-plan revenue account.

One of the major shifts in the approach of the Tenth Finance Commission was the view that "it would be in the interests of better Centre-State relations if all Central taxes are pooled together and a proportion devolved upon the States". The basic argument put forward was that it would make the vertical sharing simple and transparent. It will also give greater freedom to the Centre in choosing tax policy measures in an integrated manner. The Commission recommended an alternative scheme of devolution. This ultimately led to the amendment in the Constitution.

With regard to the persistant problem of accumulating debt, the Tenth Finance Commission has a different approach. As per the Commission, the solution to the debt problem lies in restoring the revenue account balance and generating surplus for investment. Hence, the Commission, for the first time, introduced two schemes of debt relief based on incentive, one related to improvement in the revenue account balance and second to debt retirement from the proceeds of disinvestments of equity in public sector enterprises.

Eleventh Finance Commission

The Eleventh Finance Commission, while deciding its approach, started with the identification of the problems being faced by the States. In doing so, the Commission went into the broad magnitudes and trends in the budget imbalance. The following points emerge after the overview of: (a) fiscal deficits are being driven more and more by deficits in the revenue account of the budget. This deterioration has been more acute in the later half of nineties (b) spurt in the post devolution deficits in States (c) the level of indebtedness has gone up significantly. The contingental liabilities have also gone up.

The FC-XI identified two main causes of fiscal deterioration (a) Fifth Pay Commission impact and (b) cyclical recession in economic activity retarding the growth of tax revenues.

On the expenditure side, apart from salary component, other items of revenue expenditure also showed an abnormal increase. Subsidies—direct and indirect—and pensions also showed an increase.

The FC-XI has approached the issues in terms of budget outcomes and the key budget variables viz. level of revenue, expenditure and deficits. The schemes seek to restore budget balance in the medium terms by reducing the fiscal deficits substantially and eliminating revenue deficit at the states level. The Commission has also suggested a change in the composition of expenditure.

The scheme of restructuring of the finances of the Govt. is designed to move the public finances of Indian economy way from chronic deficits and unsustainable debt and bring them on a course that will strengthen the foundations of growth consistent with stability. The restructuring plan has fixed the targets of RD and GFD to come down to a certain level over a five year period.

While determining the share of central taxes that may devolve on the States, the Commission has not departed too much from the pattern that has evolved in recent years. In order to strengthen the incentives for fiscal discipline, the Commission has suggested a scheme of debt relief linked to reduction of debt ratio.

The Commission also highlighted the difficulty in assessing the requirements under the plan. First, there was in earlier times, a common link between Finance Commission and Planning Commission through a member of Planning Commission being a member of Finance Commission also. This practice ended with the Tenth Finance Commission. The Second was the desynchronization of the reference periods of FC and PC. As per FC-XI, the restructuring towards fiscal balance is not possible unless the expenditure needs of the Centre and the States are looked into its totality and not segregated into compartments like plan and non-plan.

Twelfth Finance Commission

The Commission kept in mind the need to sustain the growth momentum with prevailing fiscal and macro economic situation.

As per the ToR, the Commission was asked to review the finances of the Centre and the States, and suggest a restructuring plan of public finances, with a view to resting budgetary balance and macro economic equity. In this process, the Commission had given explicit and implicit incentives for adoption of fiscal correction and restructuring plan. The Commission had recommended the enactment of FRBM legislation and had made it a part of the restructuring plan. This was to result in an institutional framework to encourage fiscal consolidation. Debt relief was also linked to monitorable achievement in regard to fiscal correction.

While talking of design of fiscal transfer the Finance Commission defined the objective of equity and efficiency and also the transfers were predictable and stable. The Commission was guided by three considerations of needs, cost disabilities and fiscal efficiency for tax devolution scheme. While designing the scheme of fiscal transfers, the Commission talked, in detail, about the correction of vertical and horizontal imbalances. The Commission was guided by the equalisation criteria determined on the basis of a normative approach, while determining the tax devolution and grants-in-aid. In case of tax devolution, the Commission thought of ensuring reasonable vertical transfers. The Commission also touched upon and laid accent on the need for removing deficiency in fiscal capacity and deficiency in revenue effort. In this process, the Commission was guided by these considerations viz. needs, cost disabilities and fiscal efficiency. For ensuring minimum level of services in the case of education and health, the normative approach was adopted for grants to these sectors as well as maintenance expenditures.

Thirteenth Finance Commission

The approach to fiscal correction starts with the determination of the feasible target for debt-GSDP ratio, consolidated for Centre and States put together and for States separately. This combined ratio has been fixed at 68% to be achieved by 2014-15 and 45% for the Central Government keeping in mind, the targets of elimination of revenue deficit and fixing ceiling of GFD. Another important point about this path of fiscal correction is that this will start with a time lag of one year. Year 2010-11, has been taken as an "adjustment year" and fiscal consolidation path to start from 2011-12. Another important aspect of this process is the recognition of the fact that one size does not fit all unlike previous FCs which fixed the uniform target for each and every State **(FC XIII** - para 3.24).

Thus, fiscal consolidation has been linked to incentives like the FC-XII, which linked it to DCRF facility. The incentives are linked to higher tax collections on the one hand and change in the type of expenditure on the other. Thus, the Commission has given directions for expenditure reforms. This is an important element in the approach to fiscal road map for the future. The expenditure reforms include improved supply of public goods which includes reduction of existing integrated and regressive subsidies and also improving the productivity of expenditure.

There is a fundamental change in the approach of the FC-XIII regarding principles of grants-in-aid. The grants have been designed in a "forward looking" manner and to areas beyond the FRBMA. Secondly, grants have a conditionality element, but in the words of FC-XIII, care has been taken that these conditions do not affect decision making by the State Government and Local Bodies. "Mere utilization" of grant is not good enough hence this has been linked to some measurable output targets. Three objectives have been cited in this regard (i) to ensure additionality of resources i.e. the grant will not substitute what the State Government was doing from its own resources but will do some additional public good with this fund (ii) Grants will help improve transparency and accountability, thus, enabling a feed back-route in improving public policy formulation and implementation and (iii) the conditions will help in better monitoring of expenditure.

In the words of Commission, "grants have been designed, with a view to incentivising improvements in accountability of transparency in, and innovation—at the cutting edge—of the public goods delivery process" **(FC**

XIII - para 3.26). This is a new way on focusing on outcome, instead of aiming at the utilization of grants without any reference to outcome, as has been the the system in vogue with the previous Commissions hitherto.

Keeping in mind environmental sustainability and environmental resources available to poor and vulnerable groups, the Commission has tried to incentivise fiscal policies that promote measures for energy conservation, renewable energy, soil conservation, aforestration and affordable access to safe drinking water. This is indeed all together a new approach which this Commission has adopted, keeping in view the "Consideration" given to Commission in para 6(viii) of the notification

Having discussed the Commission-wise issues raised and the approach followed in shaping the recommendations, one finds that these have been affected, on the one hand, by the ToRs and considerations handed out to the Commission and major changes, at that time, affecting specially the fiscal side of the economy on the other. Though the basic ToR have remained the same except the addition of Article 280(3)(bb) and (c) of the Constitution after the 73rd and 74th amendment of the Constitution, yet there have been additions in TORs, which were termed as "considerations".

Upto the Sixth Finance Commission, these considerations were part of TOR relating to grants-in-aid, where the Finance Commission was directed to decide the matter under Article 275 of the Constitution taking into considerations of those factors. The Commission was, thus, generally bound to consider the items referred therein, while finalising these recommendations.

From Seventh Commission onward, these were not part of the basic TOR, but were separately mentioned and this list of considerations went on increasing

Commission after Commission. Though, most of the items were common in the list of considerations of Commissions, but many new items were added to the list, which directly or indirectly reflected the fiscal and economic situation of the economy and which required due attention of the Commission.

When the matter of plan assistance was not clearly settled, then the need for financing the plan was part of the consideration of Third and Fourth Commission after that it was not there in the list of considerations. Whenever there was problem of unauthorised overdraft by the States, the matter was referred to fifth Finance Commission for solutions. After that this did not find place in later Commissions.

In a few Commissions' ToRs, the assessment of non-plan capital gaps of the States also finds mention but with the passage of time, the reference to capital gap is not there in TOR. Similarly, a separate TOR was there with regard to distribution of net proceeds of additional excise duty on textiles, tobacco and sugar till Ninth Finance Commission. The Ninth Commission was given to examine the feasibility of merger of additional duty of excise with the basic duty of excise.

After the 1990 economic crisis, the era of economic reforms started in the country, the concept of gross fiscal deficit (GFD) prominently figured in all discussions and the question of sustainability of fiscal deficit and its ratio to Gross Domestic Product (GDP) was hotly debated. The TORs of later Commissions were influenced by this debate. For the first time, the question of reducing fiscal deficit was referred to Tenth Finance Commission. This was specifically laid down in the TOR of Eleventh Commission. The question of raising Tax: GDP and Tax GSDP ratio was also added to Twelfth Finance Commission. The question of "macro economic stability", debt sustainability and "fiscal reforms facility" figured in the list of considerations of Twelfth Finance Commission.

The ToR of the Thirteenth Finance Commission talks of "measures for maintaining a stable and sustainable fiscal environment consistent with equitable growth", "need to improve the quality of public expenditure to obtain better output and outcomes", "need to manage ecology, environment and climate change consistent with sustainable development". Thus, with the changing times and emerging needs of the economy, the Commissions were assigned the additional tasks other than those referred to in the Constitution.

Other than the First Finance Commission, which had no past precedent except two committee reports and the Deshmukh award 1950, the approach of each Commission was guided by two factors. First, the Commission was guided by the list of considerations handed down to it from time to time. Though, these were not part of constitutional provisions and the States protested against them before the Sarkaria Commission and to Punchi Commission, and further adversely commented upon by these Commissions, yet not only these considerations have continued unabated; but neverthless, the list of considerations has been ever expanding. As the word "shall take into consideration" is conspicuously written in the notification hence, willy nilly, the Commissions have to take into account these considerations while making the recommendations. Thus, the approach to be followed by the Commission is hadged by these considerations which severe as conditionalities.

Secondly, all the Commissions have taken serious note of the treatment given by previous Commissions and formulated their approach and the methodology, considering the recommendations of past Commissions. All the Commissions have extensively referred to the guidelines and principles followed by earlier Commissions.

There is great commonality in the approach followed by Finance Commissions. In following the principles of horizontal and vertical distribution, all the Finance Commissions have followed the objective of equity and efficiency. All the Finance Commissions, while deciding the shares of the States, have adopted the criteria representing cost disability, need and efficiency. Various combinations of the criteria, representing these three objectives, have been followed by all the Finance Commissions with different weightage assigned to them. This is evident from the fact that share of States in taxes based on these criteria, by and large, has remained the same except a few exceptions.

So far as the grants-in-aid is concerned, it was the first Finance Commission, which set the tone for future Finance Commissions, though some refinement was done by each Commission. The first Commission decided the principles, which will decide need as well as quantum of grants-in-aid. Later Commissions followed and it was the Seventh Finance Commission, which again decided the principles but which were, by and large, the same as decided by first Finance Commission.

It was first Finance Commission, which decided that apart from general grants, specific grants can be given and conditions can also be imposed. In the earlier stages, mainly the general grants-in-aid was given which was untied and specific purpose grants-in-aid was far less, but gradually the share of specific grants grew and the system of imposing conditions on specific grants utilization became more prominent.

The First Commission also decided that the assessment of need will be budgetary needs. The methodology adopted by First Commission by reassessing the forecast of revenue and expenditure given by the States on some common criteria was the methodology adopted by all the successive Commissions. All the Commissions assess the needs on the basis of this methodology and find out the gap between revenue and expenditure.

This gap was filled by the share in Central Taxes and even after that if some gap remains, this will be filled by the grants-in-aid, was the principle followed by all the Commissions after First Finance Commission laid down this principle. This approach came to be known as gap filling approach and is still being followed.

It was also decided very early that the Commission will not assess the need for the plan side and this guideline was followed by all the Commissions, except the Third Commission. The member secretary of the Third Commission objected to it and his view was accepted and majority view was rejected.

The system of debt relief changed with the passage of time. The system of write off was gradually replaced by the debt consolidation and rescheduling of loan with interest, in terms of repayment period, as well as lowering of rates of interest. This was of great relief to the States in the form of reduction in quantum of repayment, interest amount and created a fiscal space, which, to some extent, was filled by development expenditure.

There are many such examples, which point out to the fact that there was consistency in the approach followed by the successive Finance Commissions with the changing times requiring new thinking; the approach has also changed but the basic objective of maintaining balance in the Central-State fiscal relations was always in the minds of Finance Commissions.

CHART I
Transfer of Funds from Centre to States

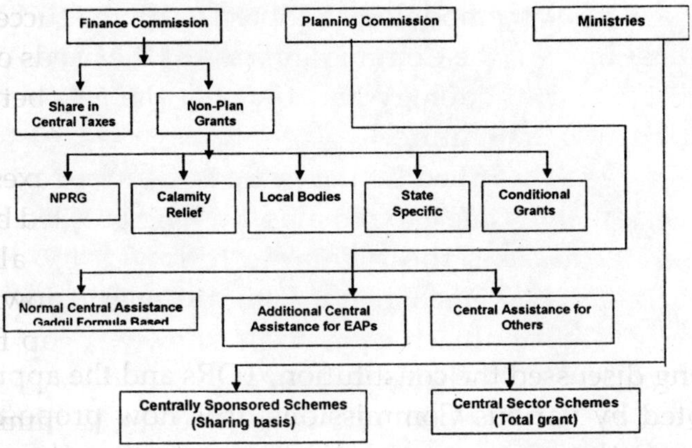

5. Sharing of Central Taxes (Recommendations)

Having discussed the constitution, TORs and the approach adopted by various Commissions, it is now proposed to discuss the recommendations made by the First Commission to Thirteen. Though, the recommendations are mainly confined to the TORs given to the Commissions, but the Commissions were also guided by the "Considerations" handed down to them. The TORs, as given in Article 280 of the Constitution, refer only to determination of divisible pool, horizontal distribution, determination of principles of grants-in-aid, their quantum, distribution among States and the conditions attached to the release of grants. After the 73rd and 74th amendments to the Constitution, the Commissions have been asked to make recommendations for Local Bodies and PRIs also. These are, therefore the constitutional requirements.

But going through the "considerations", one finds that the Commissions have been asked to give their recommendations on a variety of new issues in consonance with the developments in the economy, especially on the fiscal side. To mention a few like Goods and Services Tax (GST), Fiscal Reform Legislation (FRL), Debt Relief, Calamity Relief, Fiscal Consolidation Road Map etc. These are outside the TOR, but are to be "considered" by the

Commissions while making their recommendations.

The recommendations of the Finance Commission, against this background, are discussed under different sections like vertical transfers, which included the concept of divisible pool and overall ceiling, horizontal transfer including sharing formula, grants-in-aid and the conditionalities and other matters like debt and calamity relief and other measures including fiscal correction road map, accounting and budgeting.

Vertical Transfers

Much development has taken place since the First Finance Commission in the matter of fiscal transfers. The TOR of the First Commission mentioned that the Commission will recommend the distribution between the Union and the States of the net proceeds of taxes, which are to be or may be divided between them. Article 270 provided for compulsory sharing of Income Tax. Such proceeds assigned to States did not form part of the Consolidated Fund of Centre. Article 272 of the Constitution provided for sharing of Union Excise Duties, if the Parliament by law so provided. The shares to States were to be provided from the Consolidated Fund of India as Grants-in-aid.

This position continued till Tenth Finance Commission, which recommended sharing of all taxes with the States. The argument forwarded by the Commission was that this change will enable the States to derive the advantage of sharing the buoyancy of all taxes to ensure greater certainty in revenue flows to States and to facilitate increased flexibility in tax reforms. The Tenth Finance Commission, on its own, recommended an alternative scheme of devolution, which included all the central taxes for sharing with the States.

This resulted in the 80th amendment of the

Constitution, which provided for the sharing of the proceeds of all taxes and duties levied by the Govt. of India with the States, except the central sales tax, consignment tax, surcharge on central taxes and earmarked cesses. This heralded a new phase in devolution to States and with this the concept of "divisible pool" and the "overall ceiling of transfer from Centre" also came into being. The Eleventh Finance Commission was the first to use these new concepts in making their recommendations.

Till the Tenth Finance Commission, tax sharing was confined to Income Tax and Union Excise Duty and additional Excise duty on some items. In case of Income Tax, the share of States varied from Commission to Commission. A brief summary is given in the **Annexure V.1**. This will show that the First Commission recommended a share of 55% of the net proceeds of Income Tax, which rose to 85% in Ninth Finance Commission but the Tenth Finance Commission lowered it to 77.5% on ground that the authority that levied and administered the tax should have a significant and tangible interest in the yield.

After the Eightieth amendment, the concept of "divisible pool" came into being, where a certain percentage of gross tax revenue of all taxes levied by the Centre should be set apart for distribution among the States. The Eleventh Finance Commission was the first Commission to make recommendations on tax shares under the new dispensation. It recommended State's share in central taxes at 29%. The Commission observed that as a result of the 80th amendment, additional duties of excise on Tobacco, Textiles, Sugar cannot be passed on to States; hence there is need to review earlier arrangement pending that the Commission recommended that in addition to 28%, 1.50% should be allotted separately to States. The Twelfth Finance Commission increased this share to 30.5%. For the purpose of tax devolution, the proceeds of additional excise duties, in lieu of sales tax on Textiles, Tobacco and Sugar, were treated as part of the divisible pool of Central taxes.

The Thirteenth Finance Commission raised the share from 30.5% to 32% and it also said that the Commission is not earmarking any portion of recommended 32% share in shareable net central tax revenue as attributable to additional duties of excise, in lieu of Sales Tax, and the Commission is not recommending any reduction in the share of States in the event of levy of VAT on textiles, tobacco and sugar.

As far as the distribution of proceeds of Union Excise Duties was concerned, it varied from Commission to Commission till the Tenth Commission. Upto the Third Commission, the proceeds of excise duty on certain commodities were shared with the States. During the award period of the First Commission, 40% of the proceeds of the tax on three commodities were shared, in the second Commission the number of commodities increased to eight but the share was reduced to 25%, with enlargement of number of commodities to 35, the share was, further, reduced to 20%. The share of 20% remained static till Sixth Finance Commission. The Seventh Commission raised the share to 40%. The argument advanced was that the Union Excise Duties should have a predominant role in the financial resources to the States.

The Eighth Commission raised the State's share to 45%. Ninth and Tenth Commission continued with this share. This sharing formula changed with the 80th Constitution Amendment, when all the Central Taxes were made shareable and made part of the divisible pool.

Till the time of Tenth Finance Commission, many taxes were also shared with the States on the recommendations of the Finance Commission. The additional duty of excise on mill made textile, tobacco and sugar was one of them. This was given for the first time to the Second Finance Commission as an additional TOR and this continued upto Tenth Finance Commission.

The Second Finance Commission was also given an additional term of reference regarding distribution of net proceeds of Estate Duty in respect of property other than agricultural land levied by GoI in the States within which such duty is leviable. This continued till the Eighth Finance Commission and after that it does not find mention in the ToRs of later Commissions.

The question of merger of additional excise duty on textile, tobacco and sugar with the basic excise duty was considered by the Ninth and Tenth Finance Commission. But it did not form part of Eleventh, Twelfth and Thirteenth Finance Commissions as their receipt formed part of the divisible pool.

Another development in the realm of vertical transfer was the introduction of "overall ceiling" on total central transfers to States from all channels on the revenue account. This concept was introduced for the first time by the Eleventh Finance Commission. Based on the prevailing levels of transfers on revenue account, the Eleventh Finance Commission recommended an overall ceiling of 37.5% of the gross revenue receipt of the centre. This was raised to 38% by the Twelfth Finance Commission. The Thirteenth Finance Commission, further, raised it to 39.5%.

Different Finance Commissions have approached the question of vertical transfers differently. But the common theme running throughout was that due regard was given to the requirements of the Centre as well as the States. Upto Fourth Commission, though there was no reference to the assessment of needs of the Centre in their "considerations" yet the Commissions looked into them while apportioning the share of the States. The First Commission had clearly stated that "the transfer of resources from the Centre must be such as the Centre could bear without undue strain on its resources taking into account its responsibility for vital matters as defence of the country and stability of its economy".

After the Sixth Finance Commission, a specific "consideration" was added as "the resources of the Central Govt. and the demands thereon on account of the expenditure on civil administration, defence and border security, debt servicing and other committed expenditure or liabilities". Thus started the appreciation for need of applying, more or less, uniform norms for assessing the resources and requirements of the Centre and the States.

Thus, all the Finance Commissions reassessed the revenue and expenditure forecasts given by the Centre and the States on their own yardsticks, which the Ninth Commission termed as "Normative Approach". Most of the time, the norms, specially on the receipt side, were not based on past trends and capacity of States but on certain thumb rule. For example, each State must earn a dividend of 5% on the equity invested in State PSUs even though all PSUs were making losses. As a result, when actuals came from the Accountant General, the assessments of revenue and expenditure made both by the States and the Commission were nowhere near to the actuals. This will be evident when the data relating to U.P. is seen **(Annexure V.2).**

The Thirteenth Finance Commission has, further, to say in the matter. As per the Commission, there has to be long term stability in the relative shares of the Centre and States in combined revenue receipts and in combined revenue expenditure. The share of States after transfers will be constant only if their share in central taxes is increased by a margin by which the buoyancy of central taxes exceeds the buoyancy of State tax revenue. As per the Commission, the buoyancy of central taxes was higher than that of State taxes, hence there is a need for increasing the share of States. It is because of this reason that the divisible pool increased by the Thirteenth Finance Commission.

Further, the Thirteenth Finance Commission, while recommending vertical transfer, had many considerations in mind. The revenue raising capacity of the Centre and the States, emerging pressure on expenditure because of the initiatives of the Centre, impact of pay revision on States and also the increase in share of cesses and surcharge as well as non-tax revenue weighted heavily on Finance Commission while deciding the vertical transfer.

At the time of recommending vertical devolution, the Twelfth Finance Commission said that "While determining share of States in the divisible pool of Central taxes, it is necessary to look at the levels of overall transfers relative to Centre's gross revenue receipts, the relative balance between tax devolution and grants, and feasible redistribution that can be undertaken in the interse share of States in tax devolution. We consider that if the share of States is increased, the redistributive content in the interse distribution will have to be increased significantly by altering the weights among the distribution criteria, so as to be consistent with equalisation criteria. We have, therefore, used grants to a larger extent as an instrument of transfer." (para 7.22) "Having said that the Commission has increased the share from 29.5% to 30.5%. In fact, there was no increase as 1% was the share on additional duties of excise on textiles, tobacco and sugar, which was merged with the gross tax revenue. This will be evident that the approach of the Commission was, by and large, to maintain the overall stability in the vertical devolution.

In the end, it can be said that the first job of the Finance Commission was to remove or minimise vertical fiscal imbalance, originating from the division of functions and sources of revenue between the Centre and the States. Two approaches, based on constitutional provisions, are visible in vertical devolution recommendations. Upto the Ten Finance Commissions, the vertical devolution was based on individual tax sharing on a selective basis. Only Income Tax including Corporation Tax, Union Excise Duty, Additional Excise Duty, Estate Duty and the Tax on Railway Passenger fares were shared with the States. But it resulted in Centre neglecting the shared taxes and concentrating more on non shared taxes, cesses and duties and non-tax revenues. With the eightieth amendment, all the taxes are being compulsorily shared and with this the overall buoyancy or negative growth because of the economic slowdown are also being shared with the States.

Horizontal Devolution

After making recommendations regarding vertical distribution between Union and the States of the net proceeds of Central taxes which are/ can be divided, the next task, or more important task was to recommend allocations amonghst the States of the respective shares of the tax proceeds. This allocation, in normal parlance, is known as the horizontal devolution. The basic objective was to offset horizontal fiscal imbalances resulting from fiscal disadvantages of certain States to ensure provision of certain minimum levels of essential services in the States.

"Horizontal imbalance" refers to the mismatch between revenues and expenditures of States. This horizontal imbalance arises due to expenditure and revenue differences. The revenue differences may arise due to differences in fiscal capacity or in revenue raising effort.

Expenditure differences may arise due to differences in area, terrain, population resulting in differences in unit cost. Cost differences may, further, be beyond the control of the States. The horizontal differences are clearly visible when one looks to per capita incomes, poverty ratio, level of social and economic services etc.

Thus, the starting point of horizontal devolution was the equity rationale. There is vast literature on the subject which discusses the various aspects of inter governmental transfer. Fiscal equity argument is the most discussed rationale of transfers. All the Finance Commissions have tried to design horizontal transfers on the equity considerations but at later stage, the efficiency criteria was also added to the devolution criteria. As will be evident, inter governmental transfers have been designed in a variety of ways. Finally, it has boiled down to equity and efficiency considerations.

In designing the transfer formula, all the Commissions have tried to take three things in considerations. First, besides being equitable, the formula must be transparent and simple. Secondly; it should not allow fiscal laxity and thirdly the method of making transfers should not only be but also appear to be objective. The successive Finance Commissions have tried to design the system objectively so that the States have confidence in the transfer scheme and have generally accepted it.

According to Dr. Raja J Chelliah, the design of Central transfers must satisfy a few fundamental principles. First, the system should preserve the principle of autonomy. Secondly, the link between decision to spend and to raise resources must be kept intact at least at the margin. Thirdly, in order not to generate the wrong incentives and avoid interference with the State autonomy, the volume of transfers should not be determined on the basis of actual gaps or moderated gaps. Fourthly, the formula for transfers should remain stable for a reasonable period of time and finally in addition to transfers to close the vertical gap, there should be transfers to weaker States to equalise the fiscal capacity[1].

It is against this background that the formulae used by various Finance Commissions have been examined in detail. Different percentages of receipt and sharing formulae have been used by successive Commissions, which have been presented in **Annexure V.3, Annexure V.4** and **Annexure V.6**. A perusal of the formula used brings the whole Thirteen Finance Commissions period into three broad periods. First period can be from First Commission to Seventh Commission. The second period to Eighth, Ninth and Tenth Commission and the third period covers the Eleventh, Twelfth and Thirteenth Commission period.

In the first category, separate formulae were used for distribution of interse shares of States in income tax and Central Excise Duties. This approach was followed by the Commissions because there were separate constitutional provisions governing sharing of Income Tax and Union Excise Duties.

In case of second category, the Commission recommends a uniform formula for the inter-se distribution of Income Tax (excluding the percentage of proceeds earmarked for distribution on the basis of origin) and Union Excise Duties.

In the third category, came the recommendations of Eleventh, Twelfth and Thirteenth Commissions, where a single formula was recommended for interse distribution of all the Union Taxes and Duties, which became shareable with the States.

---

1. **Raja J Chelliah** : (2010) Political Economy of Poverty Eradication in India and Essays in Fiscal Reforms, Sage Publication p.76.

Going through the formulae used by various Finance Commissions, one finds that roughly fourteen indicators were used by the Commissions **(Annexure V.7)**. In case of Income Tax, population and contributions were used upto Seventh Commission. In case of Eighth, Ninth and Tenth, per capita interse ratio, income distance, poverty ratio, index of backwardness, area and tax effort were used.

In case of Union Excise Duties, apart from population, index of backwardness, per capita interse, income distance, IATP, Poverty Ratio, Revenue Equalisation, area and tax effort were used.

When the concept of divisible pool was introduced during the Eleventh Commission award period, apart from population and area, income distance, tax effort, fiscal capacity distance, fiscal discipline and index of infrastructure were used during Eleventh, Twelfth and Thirteenth Finance Commission award period.

All the Commissions have used these indicators in different combinations and have assigned different weightage to them and different reasons have been assigned for using a particular indicator. These indicators, in general, represent the needs, level of backwardness, cost disability and fiscal efficiency.

Instead of discussing the various combinations of indicators used by the successive Commissions, it is now proposed to discuss the individual indicators adopted by the various Commissions.

I. Population

As will be evident from **Annexure V.3, Annexure V.4** and **Annexure V.6** population has been used as one of the most important indicator by all the Finance Commissions. Till the Tenth Finance Commission, different weightages were given for distribution of Income Tax and different for Union

Excise Duty. In case of Income Tax, 90% weightage was given to population by First to Seventh Commission. Eighth Commission reduced the weightage to 22.5%, which the Ninth Commission also followed. The Tenth Finance Commission, further, reduced it to 20%.

In case of Union Excise Duty, First Commission gave 100% weightage, Second 90%, Forth and Fifth 80%, Sixth 75%, Seventh, Eighth and Ninth reduced to 25% and Tenth, further reduced to 20%.

When the divisible pool concept came, then single formula was used for devolution. In this formula also population was a major factor to be recknoed with throughout in varying proportions. The Eleventh Commission gave weightage of 10%, Twelfth raised it to 25% and Thirteenth Finance Commission continued with 25% weightage to population.

So far as the question of using population as an indicator is concerned, broadly, the census figures were taken into account. First Commission used 1951 census figures and subsequent Commissions used the latest available census figures. The Sixth Commission used 1971 census figures. But after that there was specific mention in the ToR of successive Commissions regarding use of census figures. It read as—"In making its recommendations on the various matters aforesaid, the Commission shall adopt the population figures of 1971 in all cases, where population is regarded as a factor for determination of devolution of taxes and duties and grants-in-aid".

This consideration was added on the basis of a Parliament resolution dated September 30, 1982. This reads as "In a federal system, the sharing of Central resources with the States is a matter of considerable importance. In all cases where population is a factor as in the allocation of Central Assistance to State Plans, devolution of taxes and duties, and grants-in-aid, the population figures of 1971 will continue to be followed till the year 2001. Family Planning and population control is a subject in the Concurrent List, yet the implementation of the Family Welfare Programme is very much the responsibility of State Governments. Assistance for the implementation of the programme is provided by the Central Government to the States on cent per cent basis. In order to ensure a purposeful implementation of the Family Welfare Programme, the principle of lining 8 per cent of Central Assistance to State Plans with their performance and success in Family Welfare Programme will be continued (Ministry of Health and Family Welfare D.O. Letter No. 23011/28/82/PLY dated 30 September, 1982)."

Though the validity of this resolution was till year 2001 and it was not extended further by any resolution of Parliament, yet it is still being followed. The reference to 1971 population still finds mention even in the Thirteenth Finance Commission when 1981, 1991, 2001 census are available. Many of the States protested against this on the ground that three more census figures have come and secondly, if population represents the "need" of the area and people, then assessing the need on the basis of 1971 population will not be realistic and will not do justice to the populous States, which are also backward States. But the Finance Commissions were bound by the ToRs and considerations; hence they could not do anything about it and just followed the directives.

But in case of additional duty of excise on textiles, tobacco and sugar, the Ninth and Tenth Commission argued that this consideration of 1971 population does not apply to additional duties of excise because the population factor of 1971 has to be applied to "devolution of taxes" and duties and grants-in-aid. The Commission further contended that the additional duty of excise fell on different categories and is distributed because of tax rental agreement, which cannot be equated with devolution, the Tenth Commission also agreed with Ninth Commission's contentions view points and applied the latest census figures.

The Thirteenth Finance Commission has to say this in favour of population as in indicator of interse devolution. "Population is an indicator of the expenditure needs of the State. It is simple, objective and transparent indicator that ensures predictability" (para 8.27)

The reasons forwarded for adopting population as an indicator of interse distribution are manifold. The first and foremost is that the population is an indicator of needs both on economic and social front of the citizens of the State. The State Govt., has to provide basic economic and social infrastructure facilities to each and every citizen of the country. Secondly, population reflects the backwardness also. Incidentally most populous States are backward States. Thirdly, the population criterion is a most objective criterion and has no statistical bias. Any substitute for population is not free from any bias.

Thus, population as an indicator in the devolution scheme to a great extent helped the most populous States, which are backwards also. Thus, indirectly backwardness always figured in the distribution formula though in varying proportions.

II. Area

Area an indicator of interse devolution was, for the first time, used by the Tenth Finance Commission, which gave a 5% weightage to it. The Eleventh Commission raised it to 7.5%, Twelfth Finance Commission further raised it to 10% and Thirteenth Finance Commission retained the 10%

weightage. The Tenth Commission used an adjustment factor, whereby no State received a share higher than 10% at the upper ends and less than 2% at the lower end. Eleventh Commission adjusted by minimum 2% and maximum of 10%. The Twelfth Finance Commission fixed a minimum ceiling of 2% and fixed no maximum ceiling. The Thirteenth Finance Commission followed the principle recommended by Twelfth Finance Commission.

The Tenth Finance Commission argued that a State, with a larger area, has to incur additional cost to deliver a comparable standard of service to its citizens. It, further, said that the differences in the costs of providing services may increase with the size of a State but only at a decreasing rate and that beyond a point incremental cost becomes negligible. The Commission, further, pointed out that the States with smaller areas have to incur certain minimum costs in establishing the framework of Government machinery and the cost of providing services may be higher because of terrain region. Hence, the adjustment factor was introduced, which was followed by the later three Commissions. This "Area" in a sense represented the cost disability factor.

III. Collection/ Contribution

Contribution or collection as an indicator was used in case of income tax only and was recommended by First to Ninth Finance Commissions. First four Commissions gave a weightage of 20% and Fifth to Ninth Commissions reduced the weightage to 10% and introduced other indicators also.

Though the First Commission opined that collection was by itself an inadequate index of contribution, yet taking a broad view of the position, the First Commission recommended that 20% of the proceeds should be distributed on the basis of the relative collections of the

States. The Second Commission felt that taking all factors into account, collection should be completely abandoned in favour of population as a basis of distribution. However, to prevent a sudden break in the continuity, it reduced the percentage share of contribution to 10%.

The contribution continued to be a factor till the Ninth Commission. The Tenth Commission dropped this factor giving following reasons.

"The country as a whole represents a common economic space and market and growing into dependence in economic activities has considerably weakened the case for locally originating incomes in the non-Agricultural sector. Hence there is no need to retain contribution as a criterion of distribution."

IV. Revenue Equalisation

This indicator was used for the first and last time by the Seventh Finance Commission and no other Commission used this indicator. Further, this was used only in case of interse distribution of proceeds of Central Excise duty. Twenty five per cent weightage was given by the Seventh Finance Commission.

"The revenue equalisation principle we have adopted is in recognition of the fact that States, which are less favourably placed in regard to their resource potential, should be specially helped in order to place them in a position, where they can also take steps more readily for the betterment of the people living in those States. We have computed the per capita revenue potential of each State with reference to the average per capita SDP for the triennium 1973-76. The per capita average of each State's own tax and non-tax revenue for 1975-76 and 1976-77, obtained from the Accounts, were regressed on the average per capita income, excluding the five atypical States of

Manipur, Meghalaya, Nagaland, Sikkim and Tripura. We thus, derived the estimated values of per capita revenue of each State. The distance of the per capita revenue, thus, estimated for each State from the maximum estimated per capita revenue among all the States—that of Punjab—has been multiplied by the estimated population of the State as on 1st March, 1976 obtained from the Registrar General of census. For the atypical States their own average per capita revenue for the years 1975-76 and 1976-77 has been adopted. The percentage of the product of the distance of the per capita revenue so estimated from that of Punjab and the population for each State in the total of these products for all the States gives us the share of each State in the 25 per cent component of the divisible pool of excise. In the process described, it will be noted that if a State has been lacking in effort to raise resources compatible with its resource potential, it will not be rewarded. Nor is any State penalised which has raised resources in excess of the estimated revenue consistent with its resource potential."

V. Income Adjusted to Total Population (IATP)

This indicator was adopted by the Seventh Finance Commission, which was followed by Eighth and Ninth Finance Commissions but later Commissions did not adopt this indicator in their scheme of horizontal distribution; further the indicator was used only for the distribution of proceeds of Union Excise Duties.

The Seventh Finance Commission gave a weightage of 25%, which was raised to 50% by the Eighth Commission but the Ninth Commission in its reports reduced it to 12.5%. The Commission adopted these criteria to represent backwardness of the State. Argument was also advanced that the State's population weighted by the inverse of the average per capita SDP termed the Income adjusted to total population has also been adopted by the Planning Commission for distribution of Central Plan assistance too.

The Tenth Finance Commission examined the Distance and IATP formula in greater detail **(Para 5.39 and Appendex-4)** and found that compared to distance formula, in the IATP formula, the middle income States have to bear a relatively higher burden of adjustment, which it interpreted as a deficiency of the formula.

VI. Poverty Ratio

The indicator was used by the Seventh and Ninth Finance Commissions only in its first report. The Seventh Finance Commission used these criteria for distribution of proceeds of Union Excise Duty only and gave a weightage of 25%. The argument put forward by the Commission was that "it should be recognised that the poverty problem of some of the States is partially the result of special factors on which the Govt. concerned have little control. We have, therefore, decided to give some weightage to this factor, with a view to taking account of such special factors (para 35)

The Ninth Finance Commission adopted these criteria for distribution of proceeds of Income Tax as well as Union Excise Duty, but gave different weightage. In case of Income Tax, it gave a weightage of 11.25% and 12.5% in case of Union Excise Duties. The poverty percentage in each State was the proportion of people living below the poverty line in the State to the aggregate poor population in all States.

But this indicator was challenged by many States including those States where persons living below poverty line were very high and was undoubtedly backward and poor. The opposition was mainly because of the reliability of data and the methodology used for estimation of the poverty ratios. The Ninth Commission itself rejected this indicator in its second report mainly because (a) Statewise data on the number of people below poverty line were not statistically reliable and (b) the methodology of measurement was not conceptually sound because it had assumed the same amount of calorie requirement in all place regardless of terrain and climate and had also ignored price variables. Hence, Eighth and Tenth Commission did not adopt this indicator, instead adopted well accepted indicator of relative backwardness of the States.

VII. Income Distance and Per capita Inverse

These are the two methods, which have been used by the Eighth and later Finance Commissions. These are treated more reliable indicators to measure the relative backwardness of the States.

Income Distance method measures the distance of per capita income of each State from the per capita income of the State, which has the highest per capita income. This value is then multiplied by the population of each State. Some adjustments are made to give weightage to the highest per capita income state. This was adopted by Sixth, Seventh, Eighth, Ninth and Tenth in case of Excise Duty transfers. Eighth, Ninth and Tenth Commissions used this for distribution of income tax proceeds also.

The weightage given to this indicator prior to Eleventh Finance Commission varied from Commission to Commission. In case of Income Tax, it varied from 45% in Seventh to Ninth and 60% in case of Tenth Commission. In case of Excise Duty it varied from 25% to 60%

The Eleventh Finance Commission also used this index and gave a very high weightage of 62.5%. The Twelfth Commission also adopted these criteria but reduced its weightage to 50%. The Thirteenth Finance Commission did not consider this indicator and explained that in the income distance criteria measured by per capita GSDP is a proxy for distance between States in taxable capacity. When the proxy is so applied, the procedure implicitly provides a single average tax to GSDP ratio to determine fiscal capacity, distance between States. Hence, the Commission used a separate criterion (Para 8.30/8.31).

The per capita inverse indicator was used for distribution of Income Tax by Eighth, Ninth and Tenth Finance Commissions

The Twelfth Finance Commission had given a weightage of 50% to distance criteria which the Thirteenth Commission reduced it to 47.5% and the reduced percentage of 2.5% was added to fiscal discipline and raised the share to 17.5% (Tax effort 7.5% + Fiscal Discipline 7.5% + 2.5% from Income Distance Criteria).

VIII. Index of Backwardness

The Ninth Finance Commission (second report) used the index of backwardness and gave a 11.25% weightage for distribution of proceeds of Income Tax, but this weightage was raised to 12.5% in case of Union Excise Duty. The successive Finance Commissions did not use this indicator.

The Ninth Commission worked out the composite index of backwardness—combining two indices i.e. (a) total population of scheduled castes and scheduled tribes and (b) the total number of agricultural labourers in different States. This indicator did not find favour with neither the States or the successive Finance Commissions. The basic question in adopting this indicator is the selection of the factors contributing to backwardness. The factors selected cannot be termed as apt and are not commonly accepted ones. Further, the interse weightage given also creates problems and built in to it an element of subjectivity.

IX. Index of Infrastructure

The Eleventh Finance Commission evolved an index of infrastructure as one of the criteria for distribution of divisible pool and it gave a weightage of 5%. The index consisted of five sub sectors for economic infrastructure i.e. agriculture, banking, electricity, transport and communication and two of social infrastructure consisting of education and health. The Eleventh Finance Commission gave it a weightage of 7.5%.

The composite index was prepared by the Eleventh Finance Commission using data for 18 States only and applied it to all the 23 States on the basis of ramdom sampling technique, which adequately satisfies the criterion for representative sample for the bulk.

X. Tax Effort

This criterion was, for the first time, used by the Tenth Finance Commission and gave it a weightage of 10%. Eleventh Finance Commission also used this criterion, but reduced the weightage to 5% only. Twelfth Finance Commission also used this criterion but raised the weightage to 7.5%.

Tax effort has been taken as an efficiency criterion and this is in confrontings with the "considerations" assigned to these Commissions regarding restructuring of State Finances. Though the Tenth Finance Commission has taken tax effort as a dominant factor, but it has also observed that the measurement of tax effort is not a straight forward exercise because tax effort must be related to tax potential and for detection, and there are differences in the nature and composition of tax basis among States. In spite of this observation, the this criterion was followed by the Eleventh and the Twelfth Finance Commission.

XI. Fiscal Discipline

The criterion was adopted by the Eleventh Finance Commission and a weightage of 7.5% was assigned to it. The Twelfth Finance Commission also continued with this criterion and also accorded a weightage of 7.5% to it. This index was defined as an improvement in the ratio of own revenue receipts of a State to its total revenue expenditure related to similar ratios for all States as a criterion of measurement.

This criterion was against the backdrop of the fiscal reforms programmes based on Fiscal Restructuring Policy followed by GoI and the Fiscal Reform Legislation (FRL) passed by many States even before the recommendations of the Twelfth Finance Commission's mandatory condition of enactment of FRL and achievement of RD and GFD targets as precondition of eligibility for debt relief. The Thirteenth Finance Commission did not recommend this criterion.

According to the Thirteenth Finance Commission, "The own revenue receipts of a State include own tax revenues and thus, the criterion of fiscal discipline also captures the tax efforts of States. We have, therefore, dropped the use of tax effort as separate criterion. There is a strong case to give an incentive to the States following fiscal prudence, particularly in the context of the need to return to the path of fiscal correction. We have, therefore, assigned a weightage of 17.5% to fiscal discipline which includes tax effort, too **(FC XIII** - para 8.36)

XII. Fiscal Capacity Index

This criterion was used by the Thirteenth Finance Commission and gave a weightage of 47.5%. In fact, this was a replacement of income distance criterion, which was used by the Twelfth and few other Commissions.

The argument put forward by the Thirteenth Finance Commission was that "Income Distance Criterion is a proxy for the distance between States in tax capacity. When the proxy is so applied, the procedure implicitly provides a single tax to GDP ratio to determine fiscal capacity distance amonghst States. This Commission recommended the use of separate averages for measuring taxable capacity—one for general category States and another for special category States. The justification is that between the two categories a single average applied to GSDP does not accurately capture the taxable base for two reasons. The first is the variation in sectoral composition of GSDP. The second reason is that GSDP estimates, at present are available as factor cost and, therefore, exclude income such as accruing in the form of remittances (para 8.31). The procedure has been defined in para 8.32 and 8.33 of the FC XIII.

A review of the indicators/criteria used by all the Thirteen Finance Commissions brings out the fact that different combinations of indicators were used. These indicators can be clubbed into three categories viz. indicators representing needs/backwardness of the State. Under this category, the most important was the population, the poverty ratio, Income distance criteria etc. Under the second category came the cost disability indicators which included area, index of backwardness, Index of infrastructure, revenue equalisation, IATP and the third category included the efficiency criteria like contribution, tax effort, fiscal discipline and fiscal capacity index.

As will be evident from the perusal of the formula, different combinations of indicators with relative weightage were used by the various Finance Commissions, on various priorities of equity and efficiency objectives. It is also evident that the equity objective was the most prevalent in the minds of Finance Commissions. As population reflected the equity considerations, it found prominent place in all the schemes. Its weightage varied from 90% upto seventh commission to 10% in Eleventh Commission. But whenever the population weightage was reduced, it was compensated by other indicators like distance of per capita income, poverty ratio, index of backwardness, IATP and equalisation principle. As a result, the need and backward indicators were allotted the highest weightage. The combined weightage of these two indicators hovered around 90% to 75%.

The cost disability factors like area and index of infrastructure got the second priority after the need factors. In the earlier Commissions, the efficiency factors got the least priority with indicators like tax effort and fiscal discipline entering the devolution scheme at a very late stage i.e. during the Tenth Commission, tax effort criterion was introduced. The fiscal discipline criteria were added during Eleventh Commission period. They put together constituted about 15% of the divisible amount. During the Thirteenth Commission period, the new efficiency criteria were added with an enhanced weight of 47.5%. Though, it is a debatable issue as to include these criterion as a criteria representing backwardness or efficiency one. Because, they replaced the income distance criteria, it will be proper and reasonable to use them as criteria representing backwardness.

In the light of above, it is to be seen whether the formula, used by various Finance Commissions, have served the twin objective of equity and efficiency, which had been the constant theme of all the Finance Commissions constituted hitherto. For the sake of analysis, Thirteen Finance Commissions have been divided into two groups. First group consists of First to Tenth Commission and second group consists of the last three Commissions i.e. Eleventh, Twelfth and Thirteenth Commissions. The basic reason for doing so is that during the first ten Commissions, there had been mainly four taxes, which had been shared with the States like Income Tax, Union Excise Duty, Additional duty of Excise and Textiles, Tobacco and Sugar and tax on Railway Passenger Fares. For few years Estate Duty had also been shared. Further, different formula had been used separately for these taxes where different indicators and weightages were given. In the second group, the concept of divisible pool was there and a single formula was used for interse distribution of gross tax receipts of the Centre. It is, further, to be noted that the number of States has increased over the years. During the First Commission award period the number of States was 14, which increased to 15 in Second ant Third Finance Commission and 17 in Fourth, 21 in Fifth and Sixth, 22 in seventh and Eighth, 25 in Ninth and Tenth, 26 in Eleventh, 28 in Twelfth and Thirteenth Finance Commission award period.

The share in Central taxes of different States for Thirteen Commission award periods has been given in **Annexure V.8**. This has been, further, split in three groups as discussed above. One group consists of backward States, the second group consists of the rest of the general category States and the third group consists of special category States and the relevant data are presented in **Table 5.1, Table 5.2 and Table 5.3.**

It is evident from the above **Tables** that the percentage share of developing States upto the Eighth Finance

Commission was less than the share of developed States in the total amount of taxes shared with the States. In the Second and Third Commission period the ratio between developing and developed States was 40 : 56 and 39 : 55 respectively. The share of developing States rose slowly from 29% in Fourth Commission to 44% in Eighth Commission period. But equal percentage about 44% was divided between these two categories during Ninth and Tenth Commission award period. This shows that at the aggregate level equal shares were allotted to these categories, which in general, shows that the equity considerations did not weigh higher than the other considerations.

Several reasons may be assigned to this treatment. First, upto ten Finance Commissions separate formulae were used for distribution of proceeds. **If one looks at separately the shares of income tax and central excise, one finds that the major share has gone to developing States because of the indicators used.** Upto Tenth Commission, the population, per capita income, Income distances, poverty ratio, index of backwardness were used, which represented the backwardness of States. The Tenth Commission used two new indicators like area, which represented cost disability and tax effort, which represented efficiency criteria but 85% weightage was given to backwardness indicators and only 15% to others.

In case of Union Excise Duty, in the earlier stages, excise duty on very few commodities was shared. Though the Fifth Commission onwards used various indicators representing backwardness, yet as the amount to be distributed was less in comparison to Income Tax; hence, it did not reflect the bias in favour of backward States.

Further, separate principles of distribution of receipts

TABLE 5.1
Percentage Share of States in the Divisible Pool

(%)

Item	*I-FC*	*II-FC*	*III-FC*	*IV-FC*	*V-FC*	*VI-FC*	*VII-FC*	*VIII-FC*	*IX(i)-FC*	*IX(ii)-FC*	*X-FC*
1	*2*	*3*	*4*	*5*	*6*	*7*	*8*	*9*	*10*	*11*	*12*
General Category States											
I. Developing States											
Bihar	10.9	8.7	9.3	9.1	11.0	10.4	11.2	11.2	11.6	11.0	11.3
Chattisgarh	—	—	—	—	—	—	—	—	—	—	—
Madhya Pradesh	7.6	6.6	7.0	6.8	7.5	7.7	8.0	7.8	7.7	7.4	7.4
Orissa	3.9	3.5	4.5	4.0	4.0	3.8	4.2	4.4	4.3	4.9	4.3
Rajasthan	3.9	4.2	4.6	4.4	4.6	4.7	4.6	4.3	4.9	5.3	5.0
Uttar Pradesh	17.5	16.6	13.9	14.9	16.8	16.2	16.7	16.6	17.4	15.8	16.2
Jharkhand	—	—	—	—	—	—	—	—	—	—	—
Total :	**43.8**	**39.6**	**39.3**	**39.2**	**43.9**	**42.8**	**44.7**	**44.3**	**45.9**	**44.4**	**44.2**
II. Developed States											
Andhra Pradesh	8.9	8.2	7.9	7.6	7.6	8.0	7.8	7.7	7.2	7.5	7.9
Gujarat	—	4.2	6.0	5.6	5.0	5.2	5.0	4.0	3.6	3.9	3.9
Haryana	—	—	—	1.6	1.6	1.7	1.6	1.2	1.2	1.3	1.2
Karnataka	1.0	5.1	5.1	5.1	5.0	5.4	5.2	4.8	4.8	4.5	4.9
Kerala	0.4	3.4	4.1	3.9	4.0	3.8	4.0	3.5	3.4	3.3	3.5
Maharashtra	17.4	12.9	11.2	11.9	10.6	10.0	8.9	7.3	7.3	6.9	6.2

Punjab	4.5	4.8	5.5	2.9	2.5	2.4	2.2	1.7	1.6	1.7	1.5
Tamil Nadu	10.6	8.6	7.5	7.9	7.6	7.6	7.7	6.8	7.1	6.8	6.1
West Bengal	11.1	9.3	8.8	8.9	8.2	8.3	8.2	7.9	7.2	7.1	6.8
Goa	—	—	—	—	—	—	—	—	0.2	0.4	0.3
Total :	**53.9**	**56.5**	**56.1**	**55.4**	**52.1**	**52.4**	**50.6**	**44.9**	**43.6**	**43.4**	**42.3**
III. Special Category States											
Assam	2.5	2.7	3.2	2.9	2.4	2.6	2.6	3.5	3.4	3.4	3.4
Himachal Pradesh	—	—	—	—	0.5	0.6	0.6	1.5	1.2	1.4	1.8
Jammu & Kashmir	—	1.1	1.3	1.5	0.9	0.8	0.8	2.1	2.0	2.5	2.9
Manipur	—	—	—	—	0.1	0.2	0.2	0.8	0.6	0.8	0.8
Meghalaya	—	—	—	—	0.2	0.2	0.2	0.7	0.5	0.6	0.7
Nagaland	—	—	—	1.1	0.1	0.1	0.1	0.9	0.6	0.9	1.1
Sikkim	—	—	—	—	—	—	0.5	0.2	0.1	0.2	0.3
Tripura	—	—	—	—	0.1	0.3	0.3	1.0	0.8	1.1	1.1
Uttrakhand	—	—	—	—	—	—	—	—	—	—	—
Arunachal Pradesh	—	—	—	—	—	—	—	—	0.6	0.6	0.7
Mizoram	—	—	—	—	—	—	—	—	0.6	0.7	0.7
Total :	**2.5**	**3.8**	**4.5**	**5.5**	**4.3**	**4.8**	**5.3**	**10.7**	**10.4**	**12.2**	**13.5**

Source : Report of various Finance Commissions.

of additional excise duties were adopted by various Finance Commissions (**Annexure V.1**). As is evident, in the first five Commissions, some guaranteed amount was distributed, which were mainly based on the sales tax collections for specified years, but after the Sixth Commission, concept of guaranteed amount was done away with and the net proceeds were distributed on the basis of a formula, which normally included population, production, sales tax collections and per capita SDP. Thus, all together a different criteria was adopted for sharing of proceeds of duties of additional excise on textiles, tobacco and sugar.

Because of the use of different formula for distribution of proceeds and also the different quantum of receipts, the overall distribution shows that on an average an equal percentage was distributed among developing and developed States. It is also to be noted that the share going to special category States grew slowly from 2.5% in First Commission to 5.3% in Seventh Finance Commission, but it doubled up in Eighth Finance Commission and then gradually rose to 13.5% in Tenth Finance Commission.

But if one looks to share of individual States, one finds that (a) Uttar Pradesh (17.5%) and Bihar (11%) cornered about 29% of the 43.8% share of developing States (b) the share of individual State has, generally, remained constant throughout the first ten Commissions like Bihar's share remained around 11%, Madhya Pradesh about 7%, Orissa about 4% and Rajasthan and Uttar Pradesh had shares about 4% and 16% respectively.

But the share of developed States does not show this trend. In the First Commission award period Andhra Pradesh (9%), Maharashtra (17%), Tamil Nadu (11%) and West Bengal (11%) cornered the major share. But this share has under gone a change over the years. The major decline is in case of Maharashtra, whose share went down from 17.4% in First Finance Commission to 6% in Tenth Finance Commission. Similar is the case with Tamil Nadu and West Bengal. Punjab has also seen a declining trend. Its share has gone down from 4.5% in First Finance Commission to 1.5% in Tenth Finance Commission. But other States share has, by and large, remained constant. The reasons narrated earlier can be attributed to this phenomenon as well.

But looking at the situation emerging out of the recommendations of Eleventh, Twelfth and Thirteenth Finance Commissions, it is quite different from the trends of first ten Commissions discussed above. The overall trend is given in **Table 5.2**

TABLE 5.2

Share in Central Taxes during XI, XII and XIII Finance Commissions

(%)

Item	*XI FC*	*XII FC*	*XIII FC*
(1) Developing States	53.2	53.7	53.7
(2) Developed States	38.3	38.8	36.7
II. Special Category States	8.0	8.0	9.6
III. Total	100.0	100.0	100.0

The following trends emerge from the **Table 5.2**. First, the share of developing States was much higher (53%) than the share of developed States (38%), which indicates that the backward States got higher share in the divisible pool. This is clear because of the formula used by these Commissions. More weightage has been given to indicators reflecting backwardness, and less to cost disability and efficiency indicators. Secondly, inspite of using different indicators by the Commissions, the total shares of developing and developed States has, by and large, remained constant over the three award periods.

This has been categirically brought out by the Thirteenth Finance Commission in their commentary that "the whole exercise was done, among other things, with the objective of maintaining the shares of the States." It has also tried to justify by comparing the shares of States with the assumed SDP, that the shares of States has, in fact, has gone up as per cent of GSDP but in actual percentage terms, it was a mixed bag as will be evident from **Table 5.3.** (b) By building up a Gross State Domestic Product on notional basis, these developing states have been able to garner a much larger share of the collected Central Taxes. These tendencies should be depreciated, as these can cause harm to the really developed states.

TABLE53
Share in Central Taxes during XI, XII and XIII Finance Commission

(%)

Item	XI FC	XII FC	XIII FC	Average
General Category				
I. Developing States				
Bihar	14.6	11.0	10.9	12.2
Chattisgarh	—	2.7	2.5	2.6
Madhya Pradesh	8.8	6.7	7.1	7.5
Orissa		5.1	5.2	4.8
5.0				
Rajasthan	5.5	5.6	5.9	5.7
Uttar Pradesh	19.1	19.3	19.7	19.4
Jharkhand	—	3.4	2.8	3.1
Total: 53.1	**53.9**	**53.7**	**53.6**	
II. Developed States				
Andhra Pradesh	7.7	7.4	6.9	7.3
Gujarat	2.8	3.6	3.0	3.1
Haryana	0.9	1.1	1.0	1.0

Karnataka	4.9	4.5	4.3	4.6
Kerala	3.1	2.7	2.3	2.7
Maharashtra	4.6	5.0	5.2	4.9
Punjab	1.1	1.3	1.4	1.3
Tamil Nadu	5.4	5.3	5.0	5.2
West Bengal	8.1	7.1	7.3	7.5
Goa	0.2	0.3	0.3	0.3
Total: 38.8	**38.3**	**36.7**	**37.9**	
III. Special Category States				
Assam	3.3	3.2	3.6	3.4
Himachal Pradesh	0.7	0.5	0.8	0.7
Jammu & Kashmir	1.3	1.2	1.4	1.3
Manipur	0.4	0.4	0.5	0.4
Meghalaya	0.3	0.4	0.4	0.4
Nagaland	0.2	0.3	0.3	0.3
Sikkim	0.2	0.2	0.2	0.2
Tripura	0.5	0.4	0.5	0.5
Uttrakhand	0.7	0.9	1.1	0.9
Arunachal Pradesh	0.2	0.3	0.3	0.3
Mizoram	0.2	0.2	0.3	0.2
Total: 8.0	**8.0**	**9.4**	**8.5**	

It is evident from the **Table V.3** that except Uttar Pradesh, the share of all the developing States has gone down. Bihar's share has gone down from 14.6% in Eleventh Finance Commission to 11% in Twelfth Finance Commission. Similarly, in case of Madhya Pradesh, it went down from 8.8% to 7.1% in Thirteenth Finance Commission. Same is the case with Chattisgarh, Orissa and Jharkhand. Though the overall share of developing States has remained around 54%, but individually, the shares of 5 States has gone down, share of 3 including Uttar Pradesh has, by an large, remained constant.

In case of developed States, the share of 6 out of ten States has remained, by and large, at the same level and the share of four States has gone down.

The synopsis of the salient feature of the overall

analysis is that, though all the three Finance Commissions tried to balance the equity and efficiency considerations in devising the formula for distribution of divisible pool, yet the ultimate outcome has been the maintenance of status quo of shares of the States but, neverthless it can be safely said—without any contradiction that, in overall terms, the major portion has gone to the developing States.

6. Grants-in-Aid (Recommendations)

Article 275 of the Constitution provides that "grants from the Union to certain States (1) such sums as Parliament may by law provide shall be charged on the Consolidated Fund of India, in each year, as grants-in-aid of the revenues of such States as Parliament may determine to be in need of assistance and different sums may be fixed for different States. "There are two provisos to the Article 275(i) which deal with Scheduled Tribes and Scheduled Areas and the State of Assam. Article 275(ii) says that "until provision is made by the Parliament under clause (1), the powers conferred on Parliament under that clause shall be exercisable by the President by order and any order made by the President under this clause shall have effect subject to any provision so made by Parliament:

"Provided that after a Finance Commission is constituted, no order shall be made under this clause by the President except after considering the recommendations of the Finance Commission."

Thus, as per requirement of the Article 275 (2) of the Constitution, Article 280(3) of the Constitution has become part of main ToR, which requires the Finance Commission to make recommendations to the President as to (b) the principles which should govern the grants-in-aid of the revenues of the States out of the Consolidated Fund of India.

This provision pursuant to the Article 280(3)(b), thus, forms part of the ToRs of all the Finance Commissions but many "considerations" were added in subsequent Commissions to enlarge upon the scope of the Commission's authority regarding recommendatio of grants-in-aid.

The *First Finance Commission* apart from the basic ToR, was given two additional ToRs. These were (a) The Commission will make recommendations in regard to the sums to be prescribed as grants-in-aid of the revenues of Assam, Bihar, Orissa and West Bengal, in lieu of assignment of any shares of the net proceeds in each year of the export duty on Jute and Jute products to these States in accordance with the provisions of Article 273 of the Constitution; and (b) the States in need of assistance and the sums payable to such States as grants-in-aid of their revenues under the substantive portion of clause (1) of Article 275 of the Constitution.

The ToR of the *Second Commission* required the Commission, apart from substantive provision, to consider the requirements of Second Five Year Plan and also the efforts made by those States to raise additional revenues from the sources available to them.

The same ToR was repeated for the Third Finance Commission, too. But in case of the Fourth Commission, besides the basic ToR on Grants-in-aid, the Commission was asked to consider (i) the revenue sources of those States for the five years ending with the Financial year 1970-71 on the basis of levels of taxation likely to be reached in Financial Year 1965-66; (ii) the requirements of those States to meet the committed expenditure on maintenance and up keep of plan schemes completed during the third plan; (iii) further, expenditure likely to devolve upon the States for the servicing of their debt; (iv) creation of a fund out of excess, if any, over a limit to be specified by the Commission of the net proceeds of estate duty on property, other than agricultural land accruing to a State in any financial year for the repayment of the State's debt to the Central Govt.; (v) the scope of economy consistent with efficiency, which may be effected by the States in their administrative expenditure.

In the Fifth Commission's ToR, three considerations were added to the basic ToR of grants-in-aid: (a) the revenue resources of those States for the five years ending with financial year 1973-74 (b) requirement on revenue account of those States to meet the expenditure on administration, interest charges in respect of their debt, maintenance and upkeep of plan schemes, transfer of funds to local bodies and aided institutions and other committed expenditure; and (c) scope for better fiscal management as also for economy consistent with efficiency, which may be effected by the States in their administrative, maintenance, developmental and other expenditure.

The *Sixth Finance Commission's* ToR on grants-in-aid had six considerations to be looked into while making recommendations on grants-in-aid: (i) the existing practice in regard to determination and distribution of Central assistance for financing State Plans; (ii) the revenue resources of those States for the five years ending with the financial year 1978-79 on the basis of the levels of taxation likely to be reached at the end of the financial year 1973-74; (iii) the requirements on revenue account of those States to meet the expenditure on administration taking also into account such provision for emoluments of Government employees, teachers and local body employees as obtaining on a specified date as the Commission deem it proper in the light of the States' capacity and needs, interest charges in respect of their debt, transfer of funds to local bodies and aided institutions and other committed expenditure;

(iv) adequate maintenance and upkeep of capital assets and maintenance of plan schemes completed by the end of 1973-74, the norms, if any, on the basis of which specified amounts are allowed for the maintenance of different categories of capital assets being indicated by the Commission; (v) the requirements of States, which are backward in standards of general administration for upgrading the administration, with a view to bringing it to the levels obtaining in the more advanced States over a period of ten years; and (vi) the scope for better fiscal management and economy consistent with efficiency, which may be effected by the States in their administrative, maintenance, developmental and other expenditure.

The ToR of *Seventh Finance Commission* on grants-in-aid did not have any considerations as part of grants-in-aid but had a long list of considerations which had an effect on the recommendations of the Commission. These were (iii) the revenue resources of those States for the five years ending with the financial year 1983-84 on the basis of the levels of taxation likely to be reached at the end of the financial year 1978-79 and the targets set for additional resource mobilisation for the plan; (iv) the requirements on revenue account of those States to meet the expenditure on administration and other non-plan commitments or liabilities, keeping, however, in view national policies and priorities. In assessing such requirements, the Commission shall take into account (a) such provision for emoluments of Government employees, teachers and local body employees as obtaining on a specified date as the Commission deem it proper and with reference to appropriate objective criteria rather than in terms of actual increases that may have been given effect to; and (b) commitments in regard to interest charges on their debt, transfer of funds to local bodies and aided institutions; (v) adequate maintenance and upkeep of capital assets and maintenance of Plan scheme completed by the end of 1978-79, the norms, if any, on the basis of which specified amounts are allowed for the maintenance of different categories of capital assets and the manner in which such maintenance expenditure could be monitored being indicated by the Commission; (vi) the requirements of States, which are backward in general administration for upgradation of standards in non-developmental sectors and services, with a view to bringing them to the levels obtaining in the more advanced States over the period covered by the Report of the Commission; the manner in which such expenditure could be monitored, being also indicated by the Commission.

The same considerations were accorded in the ToR of the *Eighth Finance Commission*. But the ToR of Ninth Finance Commission did not contain such a long list of considerations except—(i) the resources of the Central Government and the demands thereon, on account of the expenditure on civil administration, defence and border security, debt-servicing and other committed expenditure or liabilities; (ii) the existing practice in regard to determination and distribution of Central assistance for financing State Plans; (iii) the revenue resources of those States for the five years ending with the financial year 1988-89 on the basis of the levels of taxation likely to be reached at the end of the financial year 1983-84 and the targets set for additional resource mobilisation for the plan; (iv) the requirements on revenue account of those States to meet the expenditure on administration and other non-plan commitments or liabilities, keeping, however, in view national policies and priorities. In assessing such requirements, the Commission shall take into account (a) such provision for emoluments and terminal benefits of Government employees, teachers and employees of local bodies as obtaining on a specified date, as the Commission deems it proper and with reference to appropriate objective criteria, rather than in terms of actual increases that may have been given effect to; and (b) commitments in regard to interest charges on their debt, transfer of funds to local bodies and aided institutions;

The list of considerations included in the ToR of *Tenth Commission* included such items which had a bearing on the sanctioning and disbursement of grants-in-aid to States. The main considerations were (i) the objective of not only balancing the receipts and expenditure on revenue account of both the States and the Central Government, but also generating surplus for capital investment and reducing fiscal deficit; (iii) the maintenance and upkeep of capital assets and maintenance expenditure on plan schemes to be completed by 31st March, 1995 and the norms on the basis of which specified amounts are recommended for the maintenance of the capital assets and the manner of monitoring such expenditure; (iv) the requirements of States for modernization of administration, e.g. computerization of land records and providing faster channels of communication upto and above the district level, and for upgrading the standards in non-developmental sectors and services, and the manner in which the expenditure can be monitored (vi) the requirement of the States for meeting the Non-Plan revenue expenditure also keeping in view the potential for raising additional taxes.

Similarly, the *Eleventh Finance Commission's* list of considerations also included the points affecting the determination of grants-in-aid. These were (i) revenue resources of the States for the five years commencing on 1st April, 2000, on the basis of the levels of taxation likely to be reached in 1998-99, targets set for additional resources mobilisation for the Plan and the potential for raising additional taxes; (ii) the requirement of the States for meeting the Plan and non-Plan revenue expenditure, keeping in view the need for generating surplus for capital investment and reducing fiscal deficit; (iii) the maintenance and upkeep of capital assets and maintenance expenditure of plan schemes to be completed by 31st March, 2000 and the norms on the basis of which specified amounts are recommended for the maintenance of the capital assets and the manner of monitoring such expenditure; (iv) the requirements of States for upgradation of standards in non-developmental and social sectors and services, particularly of States, which are backward in general administration, with a view to modernising and with the object of rationalising the administrative set up in the interest of speed, efficiency and sound fiscal management; (v) such provisions for emoluments and terminal benefits of Government employees including teachers and other employees of aided institutions as obtaining on a specified date as the Commission deems it proper and with reference to appropriate objective criteria, rather than in terms of actual increases that may have been given effect to.

In case of *Twelfth Commission* ToR, considerations like (i) the resources of the State Governments, for the five years commencing from 1st April, 2005, on the basis of levels of taxation and non-tax revenues likely to be reached at the end of 2003-04 (ii) the objective of not only balancing the receipts and expenditure on revenue account of all the States and the Centre, but also generating surpluses for capital investment and reducing fiscal deficit; and (iii) taxation efforts of the Central Government and each State Government as against targets, if any, and the potential for additional resource mobilization, in order to improve the tax-Gross Domestic Product (GDP) and tax-Gross State Domestic Product (GSDP) ratios as the case may be had implications for grants-in-aid.

The *Thirteenth Finance Commission* had a wider list of considerations, which were to be kept in mind while recommending grants-in-aid to the States. These were (i) the objectives of not only balancing the receipts and expenditure on revenue account of all the States and the Union, but also generating surpluses for capital investment; (ii) the impact of the proposed implementation of Goods and Services Tax with effect from 1st April, 2010 including its impact on the country's foreign trade; (iii) the need to improve the quality of public expenditure to obtain better outputs and outcomes; (iv) the need to manage ecology, environment and climate change consistent with sustainable development; (v) the expenditure on the non-salary component of maintenance and upkeep of capital assets and the non-wage related maintenance expenditure on plan schemes to be completed by 31st March, 2010 and the norms on the basis of which specific amounts are recommended for the maintenance of the capital assets and the manner of monitoring such expenditure;

Thus, apart from the basic ToR on determination of the principles which should govern the grants-in-aid of the revenues of the States and the sums to be paid to those States, the Commission was given list of considerations which the Commission shall keep in mind while making its recommendations. Earlier these considerations were part of basic ToR on grants-in-aid but in later Commissions, these were given states independent of basic ToRs. As is evident the list went on increasing and new considerations were added as per the exigencies of the situation. Accordingly, the approach of the Commissions and the types of grants also went on changing.

Against the tasks to be performed by the Commissions, the basic approach of the Commissions changed from

Commission to Commission. But basically the Commission, while recommending the grants, dealt with the issues concerning approach, assessments of needs and their criteria, quantum of grants-in-aid and the tax; grant ratio and finally the very important issue relating to conditional or unconditional grants. To decide these issues, the Commissions evolved their own principles and guidelines.

The First Finance Commission had devoted a whole Chapter (VII) to the determination of the principles of grants-in-aid. In discussing the issue, the Commission had extensively dealt with the relevant provisions of the Govt. of India Act, 1935 and the provisions of the Constitution. In defining the term grants-in-aid, the Commission discussed section 142 and 150 of GOI Act. It, further, said that Article 275(1) in its substantive part was worded, similarly, to section 142 of GOI Act while Article 282, except for the substitution of "any public purpose" for "any purpose" also followed the wordings of section 150 of GOI Act.

In para 5 of Chapter VII, the Commission viewed that the scope of Article 275 or Article 280(3)(b) should not be limited solely to grants-in-aid, which are completely unconditional, grants directed to broad but well defined purposes could reasonably be considered as falling within their scope. Thus, the Commission distinguished between general grants, which may be of conditional nature.

The Commission, after discussing extensively the role of grants prior to independence and also the experiences of other countries, had come to the inavitable conclusion that "both the methods of conditional and unconditional grants should have their part to play in the scheme of assistance by the centre. Unconditional grants should reinforce the general resources of the State Govts. which they would be free to allocate among competing purposes, according to their best judgment. Grants for broad purposes might be given to stimulate the expansion of particular categories of services, rather than specified schemes under those categories" (Chapter VII para 16, pp. 95,96).

The First Finance Commission recommended the principles of grants in aid based on six parameters (a) Budgetary needs (b) tax effort (c) economy in expenditure (d) standard of social services (e) special obligations (f) broad purposes of national importance.

(a) **Budgetary needs**—This had been identified as the important criterion for determining eligibility of a State for grant-in-aid as well as for the assessment of the amount of the grants-in-aid. For this purpose, budget had been the starting point of an examination of needs. In the process of examination of budget, the first step was to normalise the estimates presented by the State to make them comparable. These adjustments were to be include any unusual, non-recurrent item of receipt and expenditure.

(b) **Tax Effort**—The extent of self-help should determine the eligibility criterion as well as the amount of help required from the Central Govt.

(c) **Economy in Expenditure**—Allowance should be made for possibilities of economy in expenditure. The method of extending financial assistance should be such as to avoid any suggestion that the Central Govt. had taken upon itself the responsibility for helping the States to balance their budget from year to year.

(d) **Standard of Social Services**—The object of grants-in-aid was to help the State in equalizing standards of basic social services. The standard of social service might be criterion of grant-in-aid.

(e) **Special Obligations**—Grants-in-aid might be given to help a State to meet special burdens or obligations of national concern though within a State sphere, if they involve an undue strain on expenditure.

(f) **Broad Purposes of National Importance**—Grants might be given to further any beneficent service of primary importance in regard to which, it was in the national interest to assist the less advanced States to go forward.

While recommending grants-in-aid and its quantum, the Commission had recommended the grants based on the normal budgetary needs of the State. This indirectly meant that the Commission tried to match the expenditure requirements after adjusting the receipts of the State. This was, normally, called the "gap filling approach", a nomenclature became popular in later years. Special problems and unforeseen factors also went into consideration. Apart from general purpose grant, the First Finance Commission had recommended grants-in-aid to States for advancement of such an important social service as primary education.

The Second Finance Commission observed that "the principles formulated by the previous Finance Commission are unexceptionable." So far as the budgetary needs were concerned, the Second Commission had, by and large, accepted the contention and had treated grants-in-aid as residuary assistance to the States, after taking into account devolution of resources in other forms. Though, the Second Commission accepted the factor of tax effort, it had assumed that if a State raised additional revenue, which it had promised for the plan, it would have done its part. In case of grants reducing inequalities in the standards of basic services, the Second Commission did not recommend any grant because this would be taken care by the plan.

The Second Finance Commission enunciated three broad principles such as "(i) the eligibility and the amount should depend on its fiscal need in a comprehensive sense. In a Union, in which, the centre and the States cooperate for planned development, grants-in-aid should subserve this end (ii) the gap between ordinary revenue of a State and its normal inescapable expenditure should, as far as possible, be met by sharing of taxes. Grants-in-aid should be largely a residuary form of assistance given in the form of general and unconditional grants; and (iii) grants for broad purposes may also be given. While they last, they should be grants-in-aid of revenues but the States would be under an obligation to spend the whole amount in furtherance of the broad purposes indicated. Where those purposes were provided for in a comprehensive plan there would be no scope for such grants" (**FC II** - p 25, para 66).

While recommending grants-in-aid, the Commission had observed that "we have, as far as possible, tried to meet the requirements of the States by giving them share of taxes. For most of them, however, this devolution, on the basis of common factor for all the States, falls short of their total needs and we have tried to make good the deficiency by grants-in-aid" (**FC II** - p 46, para 123). Thus, the Second Commission followed what came to be known as gap filling approach.

The Third Commission recommended that the total amount of the grants-in-aid should be of an order, which would enable the States alongwith any surplus out of the devolution to cover 75% of the revenue component of the plan. The member secretary of the Commission put up a note of dissent on this recommendation which the GoI accepted.

The Fourth Finance Commission did not consider the requirements on the plan side and recommended grants-in-aid after assessing the requirements on the budgetary side on the basis of several considerations. Thus, in a way, the Fourth Finance Commission adopted a gap filling approach and recommended general purpose grants without any conditions attached to it.

The Fifth Finance Commission had observed that "the emphasis must shift significantly from budgetary needs to broad fiscal needs as suggested by Second Finance Commission. We have, accordingly, tried to apply the principles laid down by the previous Commissions more extensively" (**FC V** - para 6.5). Extensive scrutiny of revenue and expenditure forecasts was done, with a view to placing them on a comparable footing as well as correcting errors of estimation. The Commission did not consider requirements on the plan side. Finally, the Commission recommended grants-in-aid only to those States, where gap arose after devolution of taxes. Thus, this Commission also adopted the gap filling approach in the matter of grants-in-aid for general revenues of the State and, hence, these were unconditional grants.

The Sixth Finance Commission, like all other earlier Commissions, has also taken the view that grants-in-aid of revenues of the States should be related to the fiscal needs of the States. A close and critical scrutiny of the forecasts of receipts and expenditures of State Govt. for the period covered by the award is an essential first step in the determination of fiscal needs. Based on this approach, the Commission, normatively, reassessed the revenue and expenditure forecasts made by the States. Many considerations were taken into account like fiscal discipline, reduction in arrears of taxes and also the liabilities of the States. The Commission clarified that "while we have made every effort to assure every State adequate resources to maintain budgetary equilibrium, we have not adopted the approach of mechanical filling up of the gap between receipts and expenditure on present levels of efficiency in the collection of revenue and management of public enterprises" **(FC VI -** page 67 para 3). All said and done, the Commission continued to follow the gap filling approach.

A significant departure has been made by the Sixth Finance Commission that it has recommended grants-in-aid to those States that are backward in standards of general administration to come up to a certain national minimum. For this purpose, the Commission has identified certain administrative and social services as to be of crucial importance and have proposed that the States, whose expenditure in per capita terms is below all States averages by the last year of the award period should be given grants-in-aid. Those services included primary education, medical and health welfare of scheduled castes and tribes and other backward classes. The Commission also proposed the safeguards to ensure that the funds are not diverted for other purposes. Thus, these grants have conditions to attach to them.

The Seventh Finance Commission formulated their own principles of grants-in-aid under Article 275 of the Constitution. These were:

(a) "Grants-in-aid may, in the first place, be given to States to enable them to cover fiscal gaps, if any, to enable them to maintain the levels of existing services in the manner considered desirable by us and built in their revenue forecasts. In this connection, consideration should be given to the tax effort made by the individual States in relation to targets for the plan, to economy in expenditure consistent with efficiency and to prudent management of public sector enterprises.

(b) Grants-in-aid may be made as correctives intended to narrow, as far as possible, disparities in the availability of various administrative and social services between the developed and the less developed States, the object being that every citizen, irrespective of the State boundaries within which he lives, is provided with certain basic national minimum standards of such services. While, the long term objective may be to provide to each citizen these services at the levels obtaining in the most advanced States, due regard should be had to the feasibility of upgrading these standards in the shorter term.

(c) Grants-in-aid may also be given to individual States to enable them to meet special burdens on their finances because of their peculiar circumstances of matters of national concern **(FC VII** - page 49 of the Report)

After this, the Commission, like other Commissions, formulated their own guidelines for assessment of revenues and the expenditure forecasts made by the States and in reassessing looked into the fiscal needs of the States on the expenditure side. The Commission had, further, observed that "the role of the Finance Commission should not be negative, of filling in the revenue gaps only but positive in that its scheme of devolution gives a better start for developmental outlay. The Commission had clearly stated that "the grants-in-aid element in the transfer scheme should as far as possible be residual item and attempts should be made to effect the bulk of the transfers through tax shares" **(FC VII** - p. 63, para 19).

The Seventh Finance Commission was specifically

asked to look into the requirements of backward States in general administration for upgradation of standards in non developmental services and the manner of monitoring. The Commission selected following areas for upgradation grants.

(i) Administration of taxes
(ii) Treasury and Accounts administration
(iii) Judicial administration
(iv) General administration, consisting of revenue, district as well as tribal administration and secretariat services.
(v) Police
(vi) Jails

In deciding the quantum of grants-in-aid, the Commission had decided some rules like—

(i) Grants-in-aid can be given for capital expenditure also.
(ii) Grants will not be given to those States who have surplus on revenue account on the basis of reassessment made by the Commission.
(iii) Where standards of administration needed upgradation, grants-in-aid be made equivalent to the revenue and capital provision which has been estimated.

Because these were specific purpose grants, the Commission had recommended a monitoring mechanism so that the grants-in-aid is actually utilised for the specified purposes and are not diverted. Another objective was to see that the desired results in physical terms are achieved by incurring expenditure. The financial and physical indicators were also stressed. The States must prepare physical plans of action and get them approved by the concerned Ministries of GoI. On the basis of recommendation of administrative Ministry, the Ministry of Finance should release the funds. The Commission gave indicative guidelines for preparation of the action plans, too.

Thus, such type of grants were recommended for the first time by the Seventh Finance Commission and linked the financial plan to physical plan of action and a strict monitoring mechanism was also evolved and pressed into service, which is still being followed by successive Commissions.

The Eighth Finance Commission followed the principles enumerated by the Seventh Finance Commission. The gap filling approach was adopted for general grants to States. After assessing the revenues and expenditure, the revenue surplus/deficit was arrived at and the grant was given to those states only which had revenue deficit in their account.

The Commission recommended grants-in-aid for special problems. The special problems were not clearly defined. The Commission, said simply, that there are some problems of special nature, even though purely within the States sphere of activities; and secondly, there are some problems of national importance. This grant was recommended to ten States only out of which 7 were special category States and three Madhya Pradesh, Punjab and Rajasthan were general category States. How these have been selected has been stated in the chapter on special problems in the report.

The Commission also recommended grants-in-aid as the Centre's contribution to "margin money" of the States. Further, the Commission has given grants-in-aid to selected States' requirements to meet the interest liability arising out of fresh borrowings by States during the forecast period. The Commission also recommended grants-in-aid for three other purposes viz, grant for meeting the cost of deployment of Central forces, committed expenditure of plan schemes and finally, for meeting additional installments of D.A.

Like Seventh Finance Commission, the Eighth Finance Commission recommended grants-in-aid for upgradation of standards of administration. For this purpose, the Commission selected the following sectors—

Police;
Education;
Jail Administration;
Tribal Administration;
Health;
Judicial Administration;
District and Revenue Administration;
Training; and
Treasury and Accounts Administration.

As these are specific purpose grants, the Commission desired to ensure that (a) the grants are utilised for the purpose for which, they are given and (b) the desired results are achieved in physical terms. For this purpose, the Commission recommended a detailed monitoring mechanism in para 12.73 of the report. The following institutional arrangement was also recommended:

(a) At Govt. of India level there should be an inter-ministerial empowered committee for monitoring the progress of utilisation. It was also expected that members will visit the States for on the spot verification of work.
(b) At State level similar Empowered Committee under the Chairmanship of Chief Secretary.

In order to expedite the utilisation of grants, the Ministry of Finance will release initially 10% of grant "on account" basis. After receiving the plan of action, 30% will be released. Rest of the grant will be based on physical progress in implementation.

The Ninth Finance Commission, in its first report, held

the view that grants should continue to be made largely on the basis of budgetary needs and, hence, it also followed the same approach of gap filling after reassessing the receipts and expenditure forecasts submitted by the States. Apart from the revenue gap grant, the Commission recommended grants-in-aid for upgradation of standards of administration as well as special problems.

The Commission argued that as the recommendations of Eighth Commission were rescheduled only for four years (1985-1989), hence, the Ninth Finance Commission decided to continue the upgradation grants so as to provide for, inter alia, fulfilling of the shortfall in the physical targets set by the Eighth Commission. Hence, it recommended grants-in-aid for those sectors including special problems, which were selected by the Eighth Commission. In case of special problems like drought loans, special loans to Punjab, Bhopal Gas leak tragedy and slum improvement, restoration and protection of Dal lake, Sri Lankan refugees were included. It also recommended grants-in-aid for balance work under special problems for which grants were recommended by the Eighth Finance Commission. The Commission recommended the same mechanism of monitoring as was recommended by Eighth Commission.

In its second report, the Ninth Finance Commission had recommended both non-plan deficit grant as well as plan deficit grant to States. The Commission had not recommended any other grant; hence, these two types of grants were unconditional in nature. With regard to the scope of Article 275 and 282, one of the members put up a dissenting note.

The Tenth Finance Commission assessed the need for assistance on the basis of reassessment of forecasts of revenues and expenditures estimates submitted by State

Govts. Because of the new consideration in ToR of the objective of reducing fiscal deficit, the Commission also considered the fiscal balance on revenue as well as on capital account. The Commission did not consider the plan outlay or non plan capital account. The Commission assumed that with the improvement in the non-plan revenue account of the Centre and the States, there will be reduction in fiscal deficit also.

According to the Commission, the difference between assessed needs and assessed post devolution resources availability on the non-plan revenue account is a resource gap. This gap is ideally estimated through the full fledged normative exercise. The Commission has, thus, recommended grants-in-aid to cover post devolution assessed deficit. In a way, the Tenth Commission also followed the gap filling approach, which was consistently followed by earlier Finance Commissions.

Apart from this deficit grant under Article 275, the Commission had to consider the requirements of States for modernization of administration, e.g. computerization of land records and providing faster channels of communication upto and above the district level and for upgrading the standards in non developmental sectors and services and the manner in which such expenditure can be monitored. This was specially mentioned in para 4(iv) of the notification.

In identifying areas of upgradation, the Commission was largely guided by such considerations as their relevance and importance to administration and society, neglect across States and the long term deleterious consequences, if no remedial action is taken soon. The Commission also considered State specific problems. The Commission, finally, selected following areas for upgradation.

A. District Administration

(i) Police
(ii) Fire Services
(iii) Jails
(iv) Record Rooms
(v) Treasuries and Accounts

(B) Education

(i) Promotion of Girls Education
(ii) Additional Facilities for Upper Primary Schools
(iii) Drinking water facilities in Primary Schools

(C) State Specific Problems

The Commission, further, decided not to recommend grants-in-aid to those States, which have been assessed to have an overall non-plan revenue surplus before devolution. It argued that it is not only desirable but also necessary and possible to these States to give from their own resources priority allocation to the areas needing upgradation. Furthermore, the Commission recommended the existing arrangement of monitoring so as to fall in line with the recommendations made, by the Eighth and Ninth Finance Commission.

Like the Tenth Finance Commission, *Eleventh Finance Commission* followed the same approach for determination of grants-in-aid to the States. The approach was that grants-in-aid may be given to the States to cover the assessed deficit on non-plan revenue account after devolution of taxes & duties.

The deficits are worked out after excluding any unusual or non-recurrent item of revenue or expenditure. The Commission also recommended grants-in-aid for the upgradation of standards of administration of the States.

The Commission identified twelve sectors.

(i) District Administration
(ii) Police Administration
(iii) Prison Administration
(iv) Fire Services
(v) Judicial Administration
(vi) Fiscal Administration
(vii) Health Services
(viii) Elementary Education
(ix) Computer Training for School Children
(x) Public Libraries
(xi) Heritage Protection
(xii) Augmentation of traditional water resources.

The Commission recommended State specific grants for special problems also. For sanction and disbursement of grants, the Commission recommended sanction by SLEC for the projects. The release of grants was as per the time schedule indicated in the project. The unutilised grant for a particular year may be carried forward for the next year but the grants that remain unutilized as on 31st March 2005 shall lapse. The Commission recommended the same mechanism for monitoring and evaluation as recommended by earlier Commissions.

The Twelfth Finance Commission also followed the lines taken by earlier Finance Commissions. The Commission also assessed the needs of the States on the basis of reassessment of receipts and expenditures and then recommended the grants-in-aid to those States only, which had revenue deficit after taking into account the devolution amount. The Commission said that this approach is different from a pure gap filling approach. The Commission distinguishes by saying that in case of pure gap filling approach, the deficits are assessed without making any corrections in the fiscal behavior of the States, while this Commission has followed a normative approach, which ensures that deficiency in the fiscal capacity is corrected, but inadequate revenue effort or excessive expenditure is not encouraged.

The Finance Commission had allowed higher role for grants-in-aid in overall Finance Commission transfers and three reasons have been assigned for adopting this approach. First, these are determined in absolute terms and amounts are known; secondly, these can be targeted better; and thirdly, in determining these, better appraisal can be done of cost disabilities and redistributive considerations that are not adequately reflected in the tax devolution formula. Based on these, the Commission has raised the share of grants, relative to devolution of taxes as compared to previous Commissions.

Apart from revenue deficit grant, the Commission had recommended grants-in-aid for education, health, maintenance of roads, maintenance of buildings and forests and heritage conservation. In addition to these special purpose grants, the Commission had recommended State specific grants also. For each specific grant, specific conditions were also set for release of grants.

The Thirteenth Finance Commission has observed that grants-in-aid is an important instrument, which enables the Commission to effect its scheme of transfers more comprehensively and address various issues. The Commission has ventured into new areas for grants-in-aid besides the usual non-plan revenue deficit grant to fill the gap in reassessed receipts and expenditure after taking into account the devolution of tax share.

The Commission took note of the introduction of Rights to Education Act (RTEA) and has recommended grant-in-aid in the primary education sector to help the States overcome their resource constraint in funding this sector.

Because of the two new "considerations" added in the ToR i.e. "need to improve the quality of public expenditure to obtain better outputs and outcomes" and "the need to manage ecology, environment and climate change consistent with sustainable development", the Commission designed these grants as "forward-looking" and have linked them to attainment of goals in future. In case of these grants, the conditionalities stipulate the release of incentive amounts on attainment of bench marked targets. The Commission has recommended a "performance grant" to those States, which have made sustained efforts to adhere to the fiscal reform path laid down by their FRBM legislations.

The Commission recommended grants-in-aid for maintenance of roads also with the hope that this will help in sustaining road connectivity. Thus, the Commission recommended following types of grants—

(i) Post Devolution Non-Plan Grants
(ii) Performance Incentive grants
(iii) Elementary Education Grant
(iv) Environment related Grant
  (a) Protection of Forests
  (b) Renewable sources of Energy
  (c) Water Sector Management
(v) Improving Outcomes
  (a) Reduction in IMR
  (b) Improvement in Delivery of Justice
  (c) Incentive for issuing UIDS
  (d) District Innovative Fund
  (e) Improvement of Statistical System at State and District level
  (f) Employees & Pension Data Base
(vi) Maintenance of Roads & Bridges.

Apart from the above, the Commission has recommended

State specific grants also and grant for implementation of GST by States.

The Commission, have prescribed specific conditionalities for grants-in-aid in all the above categories mentioned above. Apart from those, three general conditions have also been recommended by the Commission (a) No funds may be used for land requisition by the States (b) grants may be released in a phased manner; and (c) accounts shall be maintained and utilization certificate given as per financial rules.

But the most important condition of the release of State specific grant is the enactment/amendment of the FRL, incorporating the targets set out in Fiscal Correction Road Map. The Commission has recommended performance related grants from the second year of the award period and has termed the first year as "adjustment year" for the States to make adequate preparations at the ground level to make implementation smooth and successful in the succeeding years.

The resume of the treatment of grants-in-aid under Article 275(1) of the Constitution by different Finance Commissions highlights the development of system and types of grants-in-aid and in the process brings out the following issues:

(i) The terms of reference alongwith considerations under went changes Commission after Commission. In the earlier Commissions, the basic Constitutional provision under Article 275(1) contained a few points, which the Commission will take into account, while recommending grants-in-aid. After that many new considerations were added in the ToR, which had a bearing on the recommendations. The new considerations were like upgradation of standards of administration in non-development sectors, specific problems of the State etc. The list of considerations, further, widened in the Thirteenth Commission's besides the ToR and altogether new considerations were also added like need to improve quality of public expenditure to obtain better outputs and outcomes and need to manage ecology, environment and climate change consistent with sustainable development. With the enlargement of the scope of grants-in-aid, the quantum of grants-in-aid also changed and so also the distinction between plan and non-plan and development and non-development sectors, for grants-in-aid.

(ii) The First Finance Commission set out certain principles for determining grants-in-aid. The successive Commissions agreed with those principles with varying emphasis on principles. But in terms of general principles, overall guidelines stood at the back of every successive Finance Commission. It was the Seventh Finance Commission, which, further, enunciated principles, which were substantially on the similar lines as followed by earlier Commissions. Eighth and subsequent Commissions were in agreement with these principles, but these Commissions modified them as per their thinking and the ToRs given to them. The core of the principles adopted by all the Commissions was the need of the State based on budgetary requirements.

(iii) The method of assessment of needs as adopted by the First Finance Commission was followed by all the Finance Commissions. The Commissions took the "budgetary needs" of the States as the starting point. In this process, the Commissions reassessed the forecasts of receipts and expenditure based on certain norms fixed by them and also built in the additional requirements of the States, if any, in the expenditure and also eliminated abnormal types of expenditure from the assessment. The gap between the receipts and expenditure, thus, was treated as non plan gap which needed financial support. After devolution of taxes, the final gap, which arrived at, was treated as the need of the State for grant-in-aid. As is evident, all the Finance Commissions adopted this approach commonly called as "gap filling approach". Other types of grants-in-aid were recommended by the Commissions based on "other considerations" handed down to them in conjunction with the TORs.

(iv) All the States had pleaded before all the Commissions that major portion of devolution should come through share in Central taxes which is their legitimate claim and a "certain" amount, which the State should definitely get. Further, the States will also get the benefit of buoyancy of taxes through devolution. The grants-in-aid having built in uncertainty and in majority of cases are conditional. The Commission, it seems, accepted the contention of the States and as the **Table 6.1** will show major portion of devolution has come through share in Central taxes.

Frankly speaking, all along the Finance Commissions have treated grants-in-aid as residuary item meriting on the last priority. The table shows that major portion of transfer is through share in Central Taxes. In case of the First Commission, the share grant ratio was 88 : 12,

TABLE 6.1
Transfers by Finance Commission

(*₹ in Crore*)

Item	*Share*		*Grant*		*Total*
	Absolute	*Relative*	*Absolute*	*Relative*	*100%*
FC-I	* 361.61	***87.9%***	50.00	***12.1%***	**411.61**
FC-II	* 851.77	***81.2%***	197.20	***18.8%***	**1048.97**
FC-III	* 1066.76	***81.4%***	244.00	***18.6%***	**1310.76**
FC-IV	* 1323.19	***75.8%***	421.83	***24.2%***	**1745.02**
FC-V	* 4605.00	***86.6%***	710.99	***13.4%***	**5315.99**
FC-VI	* 7099.24	***73.9%***	2509.61	***26.1%***	**9608.85**
FC-VII	* 19233.05	***92.3%***	1609.92	***7.7%***	**20842.97**
FC-VIII	* 35682.58	***90.4%***	3769.43	***9.6%***	**39452.01**
FC-IX (i)	* 11785.64	***86.3%***	1876.78	***13.7%***	**13662.42**
FC-IX(ii)	* 87882.00	***82.9%***	18154.43	***17.1%***	**106036.43**
FC-X	* 206343.00	***91.0%***	20300.30	***9.0%***	**226643.30**
FC-XI	376318.01	***86.5%***	58587.39	***13.5%***	**434905.40**
FC-XII	613112.02	***81.1%***	142639.60	***18.9%***	**755751.62**
FC-XIII	1448096.40	***84.8%***	258580.30	***15.2%***	**1706676.70**

Note : * *The proceeds of share of Excise Duty and other taxes like Estate Duty, Additional Excise Duty and Taxes of Railway Passenger fares etc. are included.*
Source : Report of various Finance Commissions

which rose to 90 : 10 in Eighth F.C., then 91 : 9 in case of Tenth F.C. In case of 12th Commission, the ratio was only 81: 19. Looking into the grant side, the highest share of grant was during the Sixth Commission, when it was 26% after that it was 7.7% in the Seventh, 9.6% in the Eighth, then slightly rose in the Ninth Commission to the Twelfth Commission but it went down to 15% in the Thirteenth Commission period.

(v) A question, which was discussed by all the Finance Commissions, was whether grants-in-aid should be confined to non-plan revenue account or it should be extended to plan revenue account also.

CHART VI 1

Transfer by Finance Commission

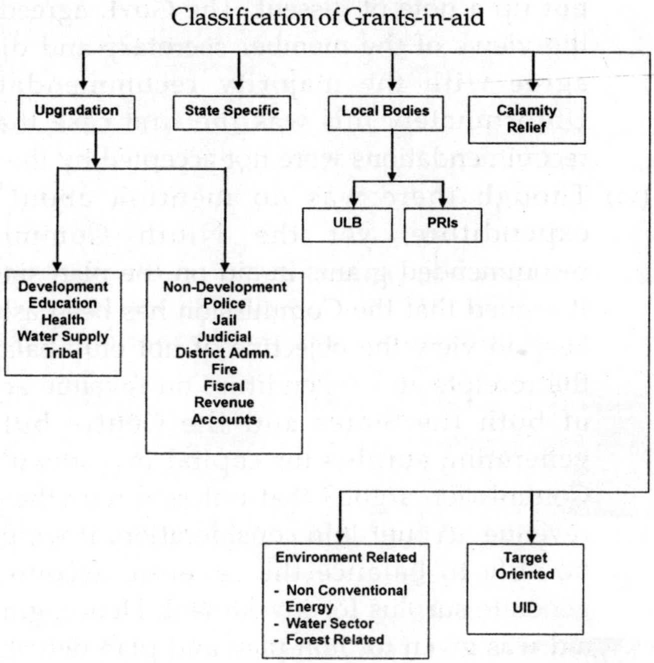

The ToRs of the Second, Third and the Eleventh Commissions were to be read and followed in conjunction with the considerations regarding State plans. Hence, these Commissions considered the plan needs of the States, but rest of the Commissions did not recommend any grant-in-aid on the plan side. Particular mention may be made of the Third Finance Commission, which felt that the fiscal needs of the plans should not be left out of consideration. It, therefore, recommended not unanimously that the total amount of grants-in-aid should be of an order which would enable the States alongwith any surplus out of the devolution, to cover 75% of the revenue component of their plans. The member secretary of the Commission put up a note of dissent. The Govt. agreed with the views of the member secretary and did not agree with the majority recommendations. Unfortunately this was the first case that the recommendations were not accepted by the Govt.

(vi) Though there was no mention about plan expenditure, yet the Ninth Commission recommended grants-in-aid on the plan side too. It argued that the Commission has been asked to keep in view the objective of not only balancing the receipts and expenditure on revenue account of both the States and the Centre but also generating surplus for capital investment. The Commission argued that unless it took the entire revenue account into consideration, it would not be able to balance the revenue account and generate surplus for investment. Hence, grant-in-aid was given for non-plan and plan deficits.

(vii) Another issue, which was strongly advocated by the States before the Finance Commission was that the grants under Article 275(1) of the Constitution are given after assessing the needs; hence no conditions should be attached to them. The First Finance Commission discussed this issue, in detail, and held the view that first there was scope for both general and special purpose grants being given under this Article. Grants for general purposes, which will enforce the general revenues of the States, will be unconditional and those given for broad purposes can have conditions attached to them. This principle, in general, was followed by all the subsequent Commissions. It is, generally, seen that the Finance Commission, which recommended grants-in-aid for specific purposes and for special problems did impose certain conditions for utilization of grants-in-aid. In a few cases like the Second and the Third Commissions, they did not prescribe any conditions of review. Because of the specific mention of "the manner in which such the expenditure could be reviewed, the Sixth, Seventh and Eighth Commissions, specifically, recommended the monitoring and release of grants mechanism.

The question of conditional grants became more pertinent in case of the Twelfth and the Thirteenth Finance Commissions. The Commissions recommended various types of grants, apart from the non-plan deficit grant. Each and every grant has specific conditions attached to them. The conditions are more stringent in case of the Thirteenth Commission, which has, inter alia, recommended enactment/amendment of the Fiscal Responsibility and Budget Management Act with certain targets as conditions precedent to the release of the State specific grants. Roughly, all the grants given under various heads by the Thirteenth Finance Commission have outcome targets and the release is linked to the achievement of those targets. Thus, the grants have been linked to outcome targets and physical targets. Similar is the case with the local body grants. Nine conditions, including some new enactments, have been laid down for release of grants. Thus, conditional grants have now become the rule, rather than the exceptions and are also becoming more stringent-requiring States to make extra efforts to fulfil the conditions to get the grants.

(viii) Though the Finance Commissions have recommended other types of grants apart from NPRD, yet NPRD forms a major component of total grants-in-aid as will be evident from **Table 6.2.**

TABLE 6.2
NPRD Grant as % of Total Grants-in-aid

Commission	*Total Grants*	*NPRD Grant*	*%ge*
I	80.00	50.00	62.5
II	197.20	37.55	19.0
III	244.00	109.25	44.8
IV	421.83	121.89	28.9
V	710.99	637.85	89.7
VI	2509.61	2509.61	100.0
VII	1609.92	1173.12	72.9
VIII	3769.42	1690.93	44.9
IX(I)	1876.78	984.06	52.4
IX(II)	18153.25	6016.35	33.1
X	20300.00	7582.68	37.4
XI	58587.00	35359.00	60.1
XII	142640.00	56856.00	39.9
XIII	318581.00	51800.00	16.3

Total grants included grants for excise and additional excise duty, Railway Passenger Fare, Margin Money, Local Bodies and Calamity Relief.
NPRD (Non-Plan Revenue Deficit).

In the earlier Commissions, the major portion of grants was given for non plan revenue deficit gap filling, but after the Seventh Commission, the percentage has varied. In the Seventh Commission it was 73%, which, gradually, went down and reached a lower of 37% in the Tenth Commission. In Eleventh, it rose to 60%, but again started declining and reached a lowest level of 16% in the Thirteenth Commission award period.

It seems that the fiscal reforms measures initiated

by the Twelfth Commission and making it compulsory to enact Fiscal Reform legislation with Revenue deficit and fiscal deficit reduction targets and linking them to release of grants has resulted in the improved fiscal position of the States. Most of the States, which were in revenue deficit regime, have come out of it and have entered the revenue surplus regime during the Twelfth Commission award period. As a result, there was reduction in the non-plan revenue gap grant after devolution and the amount decreased considerably.

(ix) Apart from recommending grants for upgradation of standards of administration, Commissions recommended grants-in-aid for special problems of the States and specific purpose grants to States. Different Commissions identified different problems of the State and the list went on increasing. Similarly, State specific grants were also recommended by the later Commissions. The Thirteenth Finance Commission recommended State Specific grants to the tune of ₹ 27,945 crore, which was 11% of the total grants-in-aid.

(x) The grant for relief expenditure was, for the first time, referred to the Sixth Finance Commission and after that it became a regular feature of the ToRs of successive Finance Commissions. Earlier, the Second Finance Commission introduced the concept of margin money and built it into the expenditure requirements of the State. This practice was followed upto the Fifth Commission. From the Ninth Commission onwards, a new scheme of Calamity Relief was introduced with the creation of Calamity Relief Fund with 75% contribution by the Centre and 25% by the States.

With the Disaster Management Act 2005 coming into force, the Thirteenth Finance Commission changed the earlier scheme of disaster management and created Disaster Management and Disaster Response Fund at the national & State level.

(xi) The Tenth Finance Commission was the first to recommend grant-in-aid to Urban Local Bodies and Panchayati Raj Institutions, in view of the coming of 73rd and 74th Constitution Amendment. After that, this is the regular ToR of successive Commissions. Eleventh and the Twelfth Commissions recommended grants-in-aid on some internal guidelines, but the Thirteenth Finance Commission recommended a certain percentage of gross tax revenue of the Centre and distributed the amount based on a formula making it a principled basis for horizontal distribution among the tiers of ULBs and Panchayats (PRIs).

(xii) The Commissions, which recommended specific purpose grant or upgradation grant, also emphatically pointed out the need for deployment of certain suggested the monitoring mechanism and the procedure for release of grants. The release was linked to utilization certificates and the achievement of physical targets fixed. The Commissions also talked of the evaluation of the schemes. But it was an enigma whether the full grant was utilized or not and whether the physical targets fixed were ever achieved or not. A few Commissions observed that the position of utilization of funds was not known to successive Commissions and also whether the targets were achieved or not. It would have been worthwhile if the Govt. of India had presented the status report on grants recommended by the predecessor Commission. This would have helped the successor Commission to suggest corrective measures, if any, while recommending grants in aid other than grant under substantive Article 275(1) of the Constitution.

7. Debt Position and Relief Measures (Recommendations)

The subject of borrowing was also one of the important considerations handed out to the Finance Commissions for review and remedial measures. This consideration covered the related question of interest payment. As most of the borrowings was done by the States from the Govt. of India, the debt-servicing of the Central loans also attracted the attention of the Finance Commissions. At the incipient stages, the Finance Commission was asked to consider the modifications in the rates of interest and terms of repayment of the loans made to the various States by the Govt. of India (Second Finance Commission-ToR 4(d)). But no reference was there in case of these loans and their repayment in the ToR of the Third and Fourth Finance Commissions.

The ToR of the Fifth Finance Commission had a mention about problem of unauthorized overdraft of certain States with RBI and the procedure to be observed for avoiding such over drafts (V-4(J)). The ToR (para 5) of the Sixth Finance Commission was required to make an assessment of non-plan capital gap of the States. In the light of such an assessment, the Commission may undertake a general review of the State's debt position with particular reference to Central loans advanced to them and likely to be outstanding as at the end of 1973-74 and suggest necessary changes in the existing terms of repayment having regard to inter alia the overall non-plan gap of the States, their relative position and specific purposes for which the loans have been utilized and the requirements of the Centre. Thus, the question of comprehensive review of the debt position was entrusted to the Sixth Finance Commission for the first time.

The ToR of the Seventh and the Eighth Finance Commission (para 6(8) and 6(9)) was, somewhat, similar to the ToR of the Sixth Finance Commission. There was slight change in the ToR of the Ninth Commission (p. 8). It was asked to make a review of debt position of States and suggest corrective measures. The same ToR was there in case of the Tenth, the Eleventh and the Twelfth Finance Commissions. The ToR of Thirteenth Finance Commission (para 5) was altogether different. The Commission was asked "to review the status of the finances of the Union and the States, keeping in view, in particular, the operation of the States' Debt Consolidation and Debt Relief Facility 2005-10 and suggest measures for maintaining a stable and sustainable fiscal environment, consistent with equitable growth."

Recommendations

The second Commission recommended two measures, one relating to rationalisation of rates and second, consolidation and rescheduling of loans, outstanding as on 31st March, 1957 relating to all loans given during the period between 15th August, 1947 and 31st March, 1956. In short, the scheme proposed by the Commission was (para 160, page 57):

(i) the balance of all loans carrying interest at 3% or more per annum and repayable on or after 1st April 1977, be consolidated into one loan @3% per annum payable on 31st March, 1987;

(ii) the balance of all loans carrying an interest at 3% or more per annum and repayable on or before 31st March, 1977 be consolidated into single loan at 3% repayable on 31st March 1982;

(iii) the balance of all loans carrying at interest less than 3% and repayable on or after 1st April 1977 be consolidated into single loan @ 2.5 % repayable on 31st March 1987; and

(iv) the balance of all loans carrying an interest at less than 3% and payable on or before 31st March 1977 be consolidated into one single loan @ 2.5% per annum repayable on 31st March, 1982.

The Commission expected a savings of about ₹ 5 crores, as a result of reduction in interest charges. Thus, there will be only four types of loans which will bring about a great deal of order and simplicity in this field. The Commission also suggested that this scheme should be considered for adoption for future years also. This will mean that each State will get only two loans in a year one medium term and another long term. Only ways and means loans can be given during the currency of the year.

The Fifth Finance Commission in its interim report dealt with the problem of unauthorized overdraft. It discussed the reasons leading to overdrafts by the States and made detailed recommendations regarding avoidance and non-recurring of such a situation. But it did not discuss the debt position of States.

The ToR of the Sixth Commission (para 5), for the first time, required the Commission to undertake a general review of the States' debt position with particular reference to central loans and suggest changes in the existing terms of repayment. It was also asked to make an assessment of the non-plan capital gap of the States on a uniform and comparable basis for five years ending 1978-79.

As the assessment of non-plan capital gap has been placed before the review of debt position, it has been treated as an essential prelude to the formulation of proposals for revision of terms of outstanding Central loans.

The Commission scrutinised all the capital transactions under various heads of the budget and decided to have the following receipt and disbursement on capital account heads (para 25).

(a) Capital Receipts	(b) Capital Disbursement
(i) Recoveries of Loans & Advances	(i) Repayment of loans to the Centre (excluding Small Savings loans)
(ii) State Provident Fund	(ii) Loans to Govt. servants for purchase of vehicles.
(iii) Civil Deposits	(iii) Compensation Bonds
(iv) Inter-State Debt Settlement	

On the basis of above, the Commission assessed a non-plan gap of ₹ 1994.62 crore during the Fifth Plan period. While formulating its scheme of debt relief, the Commission made it clear that relief cannot be on a uniform basis and that a degree of discrimination is inevitable. For the sake of analysis, the Commission drew a distinction between plan and non-plan loan. Though it has added that this distinction is made only for purpose of facilitating analysis only, yet the discrimination built into the analysis may invite criticism.

The Commission classified all non-plan loans into 13 categories and discussed each one of them, in greater detail, for their inclusion or exclusion for debt relief. By the process of elimination, the Commission selected the following loans for debt relief:

(i) loans for strengthening of police and provision of amenities.
(ii) loans for relief and rehabilitation.
(iii) Pre-autonomy debts for complete write off.
(iv) miscellaneous non-plan loans.

Plan loans were grouped into 16 categories and the Commission recommended that all the loans given for specific purposes as part of the State plans prior to 1669-70 and for Centrally Sponsored / Central Schemes upto and inclusive of 1973-74 be consolidated at the end of 1973-74 and a revised period of repayment was suggested.

Similarly, the Commission recommended the consolidation and rescheduling of loans for multi-purpose river valley schemes, major and medium irrigation and power development. The Commission revised the period of repayment of all loans given for clearance of over drafts. The loans for meeting cash gaps in resources were also rescheduled.

To recommend the discretionary debt relief, the Commission assessed the relative capacity of States to service outstanding debt. It related the burden of debt as reflected in the amount falling due for repayment to GSDP. On the basis of relative burden of debt, all the States were grouped into three categories as per the ratio. Group A consisted of those States whose ratio was less than 10%, group B consisted of those States, whose ratio was within 10 and 20% and group C comprised those States, whose ratio was above 20%.

For discretionary debt relief, the Commission selected, besides loans for irrigation and power projects, the loans for natural calamities, special accommodation loans, miscellaneous development loans and block loans. The total debt relief, thus, recommended was to the tune of ₹ 1969.62 crore. The Sixth Finance Commission treated small savings loan as a separate category and did not consider it for debt relief.

The ToR of the Seventh Finance Commission were similar to the Sixth Finance Commission, except with one difference. The Sixth Finance Commission was asked to suggest "changes in the existing terms of repayment", whereas Seventh Commission was asked to suggest "appropriate measures" to deal with non-plan capital gaps. The Seventh Finance Commission was further asked to take into consideration the purpose for which the loans have been utilised and the requirements of the Centre.

Like the Sixth Finance Commission, the Seventh Finance Commission also went into all transactions both on receipt and expenditure on capital account. In doing so, the Commission kept in mind the general considerations propounded by Sixth Finance Commission. The Seventh Commission scrutinized all the receipts and expenditure on the capital account and included some and dropped others in order to assess the non-plan capital gap. After analysing the various heads of account like capital outlay, compensation bonds, loans from GoI, contingency and Public Accounts items, the Commission assessed the non-plan capital gap for five years at ₹ 3512.18 crore.

After assessing the non-plan capital gap, the Commission reviewed the debt position of States. It observed that the States' indebtedness to the Centre constituted a predominant component of their total debt burden. A major part of the debt burden of the States to the Centre is attributable to the large loan assistance, being provided by the Centre to the States for financing the plan. The so called "Central Assistance" for funding the State's plan consisted of 70% of loan and 30% as grant component. Even the Central Assistance for Externally Aided Projects consisted of 70 : 30 loan: grant component.

The Commission was, further, asked to take into account the purpose for which the Central Govt. loans have been utilized by the States. The Commission observed that as bulk of plan loans as part of Central Assistance and were part of block assistance were not given for any specific purpose. Similar was the case with Small Savings loans. Other loans given for financing of plan also came into this category. Hence, as observed by the Commission, it was not possible to determine the purpose of loan and its utilization by the States.

In order to assess the utilization, the Commission saw the total capital funds available to the States and categorized into four groups in ascending order of cost involved to the States in procuring these funds on capital account (para 23).

Category (i)	no cost funds which include surplus on revenue account, recoveries of loans & advances and deposits and reserve funds not bearing any interest
Category (ii)	loans from GoI net of repayment
Category (iii)	market loans net of repayment
Category (iv)	loans from Financial Institutions, net accretion to provident fund etc.

Similarly, the Commission worked out capital outlays & loans and return advances made by the State Govt. during the same period of 12 years. The Commission classified them again into three categories:

(a) loans, which are not likely to give any return to State Budget and sufficient to cover interest charges, termed as non-productive purposes like outlay on public works, roads & bridges, education, social security and welfare.

(b) semi productive outlays, which give return to meet interest charges only like agricultural & allied services, multipurpose river projects etc. and loans for power projects.

(c) utilization towards productive purposes, where the States ought to be able to make recoveries sufficient to meet their interest and repayment liabilities.

On the above basis, the Commission, thus, estimated State wise loans into three categories. The percentage in each category has varied. As per the categorization, loans for non-productive purposes were confined to those States, which are categorized as non special category States. A small percentage of loans was used by Kerala (25%), Orissa (Odisha) (10%) and West Bengal (5%) for non productive proposes, Gujarat utilized 10% of loans for semi productive purposes whereas Punjab used 100% loans for productive purposes. Andhra Pradesh and Madhya Pradesh were the two States, which utilised only 10% of the loans for productive purposes. Majority of States used the loans for semi-productive purposes.

The case of small savings loan was treated on a separate footing by the Sixth and the Seventh Commissions and did not consider these loans for write off. The Seventh Commission treated them as loan in perpetuity, which was objected to by one member. The Central Govt. did not accept the recommendation to consider the small savings loan to States as loan in perpetuity.

The Terms of Reference of the Ninth Commission were similar to ToR of the Eighth Commission. As per the ToR, the Commission was asked (a) to make an assessment of the non-plan capital gap of the States on a uniform and comparable basis for 1984-89 (b) to undertake a general review of the States' debt position, particularly of Central loans outstanding as on 31.03.84 and (c) suggest appropriate measures to deal with the non-plan capital gap.

The Commission, by and large, adopted the same methodology for assessing the non-plan capital gap. This has been elaborated in para 14.3 and Annexure XIV of the report. On the basis of the exercise done by the Commission, a gap of ₹ 6806.19 crore has been estimated. The Commission then reviewed the States' debt position. While reviewing, the Commission made the following observations:

(a) The Central loans have doubled from ₹ 13,463 crore to ₹ 27,059 crore in the preceding five years.
(b) The indebtedness of the States testifies to the position of compulsion for financing the large part of plan outlays through borrowings. The revenue resources are inadequate to meet the ever growing development requirements, hence their dependence on central transfers. Therefore, the development outlays are financed through borrowings by the States of necessity.

While suggesting measures to deal with non-plan capital gaps, the commission's general approach to the problem of indebtedness was as follows:

(i) There is, basically, nothing wrong in the growth of public debt, but borrowed funds must be utilized for investment purposes and not for consumption.
(ii) The relationship between the Union and the State is one of the partnerships, in which loans constitute an important mechanism for transfer of resources. The loan funds constitute a pool of resources recycled between the Union and the States in accordance with their emerging requirements.
(iii) The Commission was not in favour of write off, as it would reduce the pool of resources.
(iv) The loan transactions between the Union and the States is not merely a Creditor-Debtor relationship, but an indication of partnership between the Union and the States in the common endeavour for future economic development.

(v) The Commission has assumed that there will be no default in overdraft payment and hence, no change has been incorporated in the terms of repayment of overdraft loans.

(vi) A separate treatment has been given to the small savings loan by the Commission and in the process fully concurred with the views originally expressed by the Sixth Finance Commission; hence, it left the small savings loans outside the scope of debt relief.

After taking out overdraft loans and small savings loans repayment, the Commission worked out the non-plan capital gap at ₹ 3852.64 crore.

The Commission categorized the States into four groups on the basis of a ratio of Central loans as per cent of GSDP.

Group A—States (6) with ratios upto 20%.
Group B—States (5) with ratios above 20% but less than 33%
Group C—States (4) with ratios above 33%
Group D—States (7) hill States with special problem.

Then, the Commission worked out non-plan capital gap as %ge of Revenue surplus. Again, the States were grouped into four categories. This grouping was slightly different from the earlier groups. The Commission made regrouping, in which, group A consisted of 6 States, B four, instead of 5, 'and group C comprised 5, instead of four, and group D remained as it is with 7 States.

On the basis of this classification, the Commission suggested the debt relief scheme.

(a) the maximum period of rescheduling should not exceed 30 years.

(b) States in group A & B may be given debt relief to the extent of not more than 35% and 55% respectively of their reassessed non-plan capital gaps.

(c) States in group C and D may be given relief of 75% and 85% respectively of their reassessed non plan capital gaps.

On the basis of above approach, a detailed scheme was presented in para 14.41. The total debt relief, thus, came to ₹2285.39. The Commission also recommended interest relief as given in para 14.43.

The ToRs of the Ninth Commission were different from the ToRs of earlier Commissions. Para 8 of the ToR says that "the Commission may make an assessment of the debt position of the States as on 31.03.1989 and suggest such corrective measures as deemed necessary, keeping in view the financial requirements of the Centre. The corrective measures will be with particular reference to investments made in infrastructure projects and shall have linkage with improvement in financial and management efficiency.

After estimating the outstanding debt of the States, the Commission went on examining the reasons of indebtedness. The major cause has been identified as financing of investments under the plans through borrowings. Further, some amount of borrowings, of late, has been diverted for current consumption expenditure. If it were only for investment purposes, the indebtedness should not cause any worry.

The Commission was of the view that the circle of first sanctioning loans and their rescheduling at regular intervals will neither speak of an orderly management of financial affairs nor be conducive to the appropriate application of funds. The Commission felt that this chain should be broken. In para 9.18, the Commission enunciated the principles of debt relief as under:

(i) Rescheduling of repayments and write off are undesirable.

(ii) A write off may be considered only under exceptional circumstances.

(iii) Conversion of debt into grants, except under special circumstances, would not be conducive to fiscal discipline.

(iv) Rescheduling of debt when the terms of repayment are unreasonable.

(v) Loans should be repaid out of amortization Fund.

Keeping in views the above principles, further the Commission made recommendations regarding debt relief as follows:

(a) The modified Gadgil formula as well as the ratio 70 : 30 will continue to operate, but part of the loan assistance would now be shifted to the market.

(b) The RBI should work out a suitable formula, according to which, the States would be required to maintain amortization funds to the extent considered necessary by the Bank.

(c) The maturity period of Central loans to States should have a maturity period of 20 years. Fifty per cent of these loans should be granted a five year initial grace period moratorium after which repayment spread to 15 years.

(d) No change in the terms and conditions relating to small savings loans.

(e) For externally aided projects, following recommendations have been made.

  (i) 100% of the assistance should be passed on to the States.

  (ii) The World Bank assistance should be passed on as of now.

(f) Outstanding loans for drought relief should be written off.

(g) Loans for relief work relating to Bhopal gas tragedy be adjusted against other payments due from Govt. of Madhya Pradesh.

(h) Special loans to Punjab, a two years moratorium on repayment of principal and interest should be given.

(i) according to General Debt Relief Scheme—

  (i) Link extend of relief to the performance of the States, in respect of their investments in two sectors, namely, power and road transport. After working out rate of return on investments in these two sectors, the States were divided in there categories:

    (a) The States, where the rate of return was more than 15%
    (b) Rate of return between 10% and 15%.
    (c) Rate of return less than 10%.

The relief recommended as—

(i) Relief in repayment of 1984-89 State plan loans during 1990-95 to the extent of 10% for first category of States, 7.5% for second category, 5% for third category, uniform relief of 10% for all special category of States.

The loan, which remains outstanding after that, should be made repayable in 10 equal installments. These loans should carry a rate of interest of 9%.

One of the members, Justice A.S. Qureshi did not agree with the scheme and put up a note of dissent.

Under para 8 of the TOR, the Tenth Commission was asked "to make an assessment of the debt position of the States as on 31st March, 1994 and suggest such corrective measures as are deemed necessary also keeping in view the financial requirements of the Centre." Apart from this, Commission has also been asked to consider the objective of not only balancing the receipts and expenditure on revenue account of both the States and Central Govt. but also generating surplus for capital investment and reducing fiscal deficit (para 4(1)).

Unlike other Commissions, the Tenth Commission was asked to consider over all debt position and not relating to Central loans only. Based on the review, the Commission observed that—

(a) The share of central loans in the total debt of States has been steadily declining and the share of higher cost resources is increasing.
(b) The high income States currently account for slightly more than a quarter of outstanding debt for all States.
(c) Financing plan outlays continues to constitute the core of the borrowing requirements of the States.

The Commission identified the disturbing features of the debt profile of States and its management and pointed out that—

(i) Diversion of borrowed funds for meeting revenue expenditure.
(ii) Use of loans in unproductive enterprises or enterprises, which are potentially productive but are beset by poor performance and currently yielding low or even negative returns.
(iii) Non provision for depreciation or amortisation funds in respect of Govt. owned assets leading to repayment out of fresh loans.

With growing repayment obligations, the net of repayment loans are getting lesser by lesser, year after year. But the gross market borrowings are so managed by the RBI as to ensure availability of predetermined amounts for the States net of repayments. It, further, said that the Debt: GSDP ratio has risen to about 69% in 1994-95.

The Finance Commission recommended debt relief measures keeping in view the following objectives:

(i) that the quantum of relief is limited;
(ii) that priority is given to the States under severe fiscal strain; and
(iii) that incentives are given for better fiscal management.

Having set the objective, the Commission considered plan loans, small savings loans and amortization of funds. **The Finance Commission did not favour small savings loans being treated as loans in perpetuity and did not recommend any change in their repayment.** Regarding amortization of loans, the Commission reiterated the Ninth Commission's recommendation and restated that the modalities should be worked out by the RBI expeditiously.

The debt relief recommended by the Commission has two parts—

(a) a scheme of debt relief for all States linked to fiscal performance; and
(b) specific relief for the States with high fiscal stress, special category States and the States ridden with debt problems, warranting special attention.

Apart from these, the Commission recommended a scheme for encouraging retirement of debt from the proceeds of disinvestment of equity holdings of the State Govt. (Chapter III, para 3.20)

In order to measure fiscal performance of States, a comparison of ratio of all revenue receipts to total revenue expenditure in a given year (r) with the average of corresponding ratios (r*) in the three years immediately preceding was made. Generalised debt relief may take the form of a certain percentage of repayment falling due in the award period.

Bihar, Uttar Pradesh and Orissa (Odisha), which were considered as highly fiscal stressed States and special category States were recommended writing off of 5% of repayment due during 1989-95 and outstanding on 31st March, 1995. High fiscal stress has been indicated by an average ratio of interest payments to revenue expenditure exceeding 17% during 1989-90 to 1993-94. Regarding special loans to Punjab, one third of the repayment of principal falling due during 1995-2000 on these term loans be waived.

The wording of ToR of Eleventh Finance Commission was slightly different from that of the Tenth Finance Commission. Para 8 says that "the Commission may make a review of debt position of the States as on 31st day of March 1999 and suggest such corrective measures as are deemed necessary, keeping in view the long term sustainability for both the Centre and the States.

While on the subject of restructuring public debt, the Commission discussed at length the question of sustainable debt and fiscal deficit. The Commission observed that the sustainability of fiscal deficit would depend on the expected rate of return on Govt. investment including expenditure on human capital and the efficiency of the revenue system to finance the resulting debt-servicing needs. Other things remaining the same, if the rate of return on investment, financed by deficit is lower than the interest rate at which, incremental debt to finance the deficit is incurred, then the debt and fiscal deficit will tend to spiral.

While discussing the debt position of the States, the Commission made the following conclusions:

(a) The share of the the Central loans in the total debt of the States has been continuously declining and the share of internal debt and public provident fund is increasing.

(b) The long term debt of the States has been gradually shifting to relatively costlier sources.

(c) Aggregate debt of the States as percentage of GSDP have gone up from 20.71% in 1996-97 to 23% in 1998-99.

(d) The burden of debt servicing has increased substantially due to gradual and steady increase in interest rates, among other things.

While discussing sustainability issue, the Commission tried to answer the following questions (p 11.11)

(i) At what level, should debt be stabilized as a percentage of GDP in case of the Centre, and GSDP in case of the States?

(ii) What are the conditions under which these can be sustained by respective Govts. ?

The Commission said that answers to these questions depend critically on the rate of growth (nominal) of GDP/GSDP the effective interest rate on borrowings, the rate of growth revenue receipts and the proportion of primary expenditure (Expenditure – Interest Payment) relative to GDP/GSDP that may be considered desirable. Given other things remaining the same, a State, which has a higher growth rate relative to interest rate, can sustain debt at higher level relative to GSDP.

In this context, the Commission looked into the relative position of the States' interest payment to revenue receipts. On the basis of this ratio the States have been divided into four categories, follows:

I Category	Interest Payment more than 25% of RR	Punjab, Orissa, Uttar Pradesh & West Bengal
II Category	Between 20-25%	Bihar, Rajasthan
III Category	Between 10-15%	9 States
IV Category States	Below 10%	4 special category

The Commission suggested three steps for reducing the debt burden of the States (para 11.14)

(i) Incremental Revenue Receipts should meet the incremental interest burden and incremental primary expenditure.
(ii) A surplus may be generated on revenue account to meet future repayment obligations. This surplus should be credited to the Sinking Fund for this purpose.
(iii) The State should have and maintain a balance in the revenue account.

Like the Tenth Commission, the Eleventh Finance Commission, too continued with the incentive scheme with slight modification. The Eleventh Commission increased the factor of 2 to 5 on the extent of improvement. It excluded share in Central Taxes and grants-in-aid from revenue receipts.

The Commission continued with the generalised debt relief scheme of the Tenth Commission for fresh loans during 1994-99 and outstanding as on 31.03.99 with slight modification.

(i) Instead of a factor of 2, a factor of 5 to be applied on the index of improvement on revenue balance.
(ii) The ceiling of stipulated relief is to be set at 25% of repayment due in any one year, instead of 10%; and

(iii) In the calculation of revenue receipt share in Central taxes and grants in aid to be excluded.

A very modest debt relief of ₹ 500.00 crore to ₹ 700.00 crore was expected from this scheme over a five year period. A separate treatment was done for special term loans to Punjab. The Eleventh Finance Commission had a detailed review of loans against small savings. The Commissions considered three issues:

(a) Treating small savings loans in perpetuity.
(b) Lowering rate of interest on these loans.
(c) Increasing the share of the States.

In issue (a), the Commission did not consider conversion of these loans into perpetuity. In this, it has agreed that the net collections cannot be disbursed as loans in perpetuity or grants for the reason that these are not the revenue receipts of the Govt., but are borrowings incurring liability which are to be repaid to the subscribers. The Commission did not agree to increase in shares of States and lower the rate of interest.

In case of assistance for externally aided projects, the Commission suggested that the issue of passing on external assistance on the terms and conditions different from original terms conditions be examined, in detail, and system recast to meet the requirements of equity, efficiency and transparency.

The Commission also recommended, for the first time, fixing a ceiling on giving guarantees by enacting suitable legislation and such limit should form part of the overall limits of borrowings under Articles 292 and 293. These recommendations are on the point of corrective measures. Apart from these, the Commission has recommended fixing limits on borrowings from the Public Account and other sources, which are not borne on the security or

Constitutional amendment may also be considered (11.46). Finally, the Commission reiterated the recommendation of earlier Commissions regarding the need for setting up a Sinking Fund in each State for amortization of debt.

The ToR of the *Twelfth Finance Commission* was much wider than all the earlier Commissions. Two separate but inter dependent with each other considerations were added. These are (1) The Commission shall review the Fiscal Reform Facility introduced by the Central Government on the basis of the recommendations of the Eleventh Finance Commission, and suggest measures for effective achievement of its objectives (2) The Commission may, after making all assessment of the debt position of the States on the 31st March, 2004, suggest such corrective measures as are deemed necessary, consistent with macro-economic stability and debt sustainability. Such measures recommended will give weightage to the performance of the States in the fields of human development and investment climate. (para 8 para 9.)

It is for the first time that a Commission in this case the Twelfthe Finance Commission has been asked to review the fiscal reform facility recommended by the previous Commission and suggest corrective measures. Para (iv) and 9 are the same as were in case of the Eleventh Commission.

As per clause 5 of ToR, the Commission discussed, in great detail, the plan of restructuring of public finances and in the process the objectives of debt reduction and equitable growth. While discussing growth of public debt, the Commission observed, a very high (76%) combined Debt-GDP ratio of the Centre and the States. This high level of ratio results in high interest payment relative to revenue receipt, resulting in further increase of revenue deficit. This inevitably leads to growings increased fiscal deficit. Thus, a vicious circle is created of rising FD, high debt, burden large interest payment libaility revenue deficit and back to increased laxity in fiscal deficit.

After discussing the issues of sustainability of fiscal deficit against the background of theoretical propositions propounded in the literature, the Commission put forword its recommendations as follows (para 4.45).

(i) The overall debt-GDP ratio on the combined account (with external debt measured at historical exchange rates) may be targeted to be brought down to 56 per cent of GDP over a period of time. Since the level is estimated to be as high as 81 per cent of GDP at the end of 2004-05, it should be brought down to at least 75 per cent by the end of 2009-10.

(ii) The level of combined interest payments relative to revenue receipts should be brought down from 34 percent in 2004-05 to 22 per cent in 2009-10, and eventually to about 17 per cent.

(iii) The system of on-lending by the Centre to the States should be phased out. The long term goal for the Centre and the State for the debt-GSDP ratio should be 28 per cent each. Their fiscal deficit to GDP ratio targets should be 3 per cent each.

The plan of debt restructuring recommended by the Twelfth Commission comprised the following:

(a) Loans to be repaid in a specified number of years.

(b) The centre should progressively reduce its intermediation in the State borrowings.

(c) The States should be allowed to borrow the repayment amount from the market, in addition to its net borrowing requirements according to the stipulated path of restructuring public finances.

The Commission in para 4.54 suggested restructuring of Centre and State finances. It has also detailed the dimensions of restructuring including restructuring of debt. The Commission prescribed limit of GFD at 3% of GSDP/GDP.

In the light of restructuring of finances, the Commission recommended the debt relief measures, which had two componeents.

(a) Consolidation of all State debt to the Centre outstanding at the end of 2004-05 at an interest rate of 7.5% to be paid in 20 years.

(b) Debt Relief scheme linked to achievement in reducing revenue deficit. It has a precondition attached to it. The benefit of this scheme will be available to those States, which enact a Fiscal Responsibility Legislation (FRL) that provides for eliminating revenue deficit and bringing fiscal deficit to 3% of GSDP, not later than 2008-09, incorporating annual targets for reduction of fiscal and revenue deficits and presenting a consolidated growth and fiscal strategy statement along with budget.

In its chapter on "Debt Position of States—Relief and Corrective Measures", the Commission examined the debt sustainability on two counts (a) Debt-GSDP ratio and (b) ratio of interest payment to total revenue receipts. The debt-GSDP ratio showed that Orissa (62.93%), Bihar (55.33%), Punjab (48.51%), Rajasthan (45.38%) and Uttar Pradesh (39.08%) had the highest GSDP-Debt ratio in that order.

In case of interest payment-receipt ratio, the States were grouped in five.

I. Category—above 35%	—	Orissa, Punjab & West Bengal.
II. Category—28-35%	—	Himachal Pradesh, Rajasthan & Uttar Pradesh
III. Category—22-28%	—	Andhra Pradesh, Bihar, Gujarat,

		Haryana, Kerala.
IV. Category—18-22%	—	Goa, Jharkhand, Karnataka, Madhya Pradesh, Maharashtra & Tamil Nadu
V. Category—10-18%	—	All special category States.

The above position reflected the deteriorating debt situation of States on both the counts. The position is grim in case of Bihar, Himachal Pradesh, Kerala, Orissa, Punjab, Rajasthan, Uttar Pradesh and West Bengal on the basis of both the indicators.

The Commission made a mention of the debt swap scheme introduced by GoI and its overall impact. The Commission recommended a debt consolidation and rescheduling scheme as follows:

(a) The central loans to States contracted till 31.03.04 and outstanding as on 31.03.05 (₹ 1,28,795 crore) may be consolidated and rescheduled for a fresh term of 20 years (resulting in repayment in 20 equal installments) and an interest rate of 7.5% be charged on them. The total relief worked out to ₹ 21276 crore in interest payment and ₹ 11929 crore in principal repayments.

This general debt relief shall be available to all the States with effect from the year they enact the FRL as indicated earlier.

(b) The Scheme of debt write off is based on fiscal performance. The States will be provided with tangible incentive, if a reduction of revenue deficit takes place, as desired. This will entitle them to a write off of debt. The quantum of write off of repayment will be linked to the absolute amount, by which, the revenue deficit is reduced in each successive year during the award period. If the revenue deficit is brought down to zero, the entire repayment during the period will be written off.

The manner of operation of the scheme has been detailed in para 12.44.

For future lending, the Commission recommended that the Central Govt. should not act as an intermediary and allow the States to approach the market directly, except in case of fiscally weak States, where it can resort to lending.

In case of external assistance, the Commission recommended that external assistance transferred to the States on the same terms and conditions as attached to such conditions by external funding agencies, Thereby making GoI a financial intermediary without any gain or loss. This assistance extended too States should be managed through a separate fund in the public account. The fund could also be utilised for taking care of foreign exchange fluctuation risk.

The Commission gave a separate treatment to loans to Punjab combating insurgency and loans to Gujarat for rehabilitation of earth quake victims.

The Commission recommended the setting up of Sinking Fund for amortisation of all loans including loans from banks, liabilities on account of NSSF. It also recommended for constitution of guarantee redemption fund through earmarked guarantee fees. Govt. guarantee should be provided by evaluating risk profile of guarantees.

There is no direct reference to review of debt position and debt relief in the ToR of the Thirteenth Finance Commission but there are two paras, which directly and indirectly refer to this subject. These are para 5 and para 8-A.

Para 8 was referred to FC on 25.08.2008 though original notification was dated 13.11.2007. These paras are (1) The Commission shall review the state of the finances of the Union and the States, keeping in view, in particular, the operation of the State's Debt Consolidation and Relief Facility (DCRF) 2005-2010 introduced by the Central Government on the basis of the recommendations of the Twelfth Finance Commission, and suggest measures for maintaining a stable and sustainable fiscal environment consistent with equitable growth. (2) The Commission may review the present arrangements as regards financing of Disaster Management with reference to the National Calamity Contingency Fund and the Calamity Relief Fund and the funds envisaged in the Disaster Management Act, 2005 (53 of 2005), and make appropriate recommendations thereon.

The above two issues were discussed by the Commission while recommending revised road map for fiscal consolidation (Chapter 9) and recommended debt relief within the contours of Fiscal Road Map. While reviewing the DCRF of Twelfth Finance Commission, the Commission considered two types of loans, which were left over by the Twelfth Finance Commission, the NSSF loan and loans against Centrally Sponsored Schemes. The Commission recommended a common rate of interest at 9% on the NSSF loans contracted till 2006-07 and outstanding at the end of 2009-10. It has recommended that there is need for more comprehensive reforms in the overall administration of NSSF.

In case of loans against CSS, the Commission thought that continuation of these loans is not consistent with the policy of discrimination recommended by Twelfth Finance Commission. Hence, it recommended that these loans as outstanding at the end of 2009-10 be written off. It also recommended that any further lending from the Centre to the States should be completely avoided.

The Commission extended the DCRF facility for the award period limited to those States, which could not avail of this facility during the Twelfth Finance Commission award period subject to enactment of FRL. Benefit of interest relief of NSSF and write off of CSS loans only was recommended if the States bring out a necessary amendment/ enactment of FRL.

A perusal of the history of recommendations made by the successive Commissions the changes in their approach and recommendations on debt relief makes an interesting reading and shows that recommendations made by the Commissions were in tune with the changing times requiring different treatment to the problem of indebtedness of the States. These can be summarised below:

(i) The First and Fifth Finance Commission did not have debt position review and relief measures as part of their ToR. Hence, these Commissions directly did not touch upon these subjects and, hence, made no recommendations.

(ii) All other Commissions had this subject on their ToR. It ranged from review of the Central loans and modification of terms of repayment and revision of rate of interest. In such a situation, the Commissions confined their recommendations on debt relief to changes in the repayment schedule and modifications of rates of interest.

(iii) From the Sixth Commission onwards, a comprehensive review of debt position of the States was the main ToR of Finance Commissions along with the suggestions regarding corrective measures. For giving effect to the corrective measures, the majority of Commissions relied on the rescheduling of principal and modifications of rates of interest. In a few cases, the measure of write off was also recommended, but by and large, all the Commissions did not agree with this measure of relief.

(iv) With the States fiscal position deteriorating and debt burden mounting and debt servicing becoming a serious problem, the Finance Commissions, specially Ninth Commission and onwards, started thinking in terms of linking relief to improvement in the fiscal situation of the States. For this, Commissions formulated performance/incentive based debt relief schemes. The incentive based schemes suggested were—linking relief to investment in power sector, relief linked to reduction of revenue and fiscal deficit, relief confined to fiscally stressed States only, category wise relief. The relief facility availability was also linked to enactment/amendment of FRL.

In a way, this conditional relief facility was good instead of generalised debt relief because in a conditional relief, States were forced willy nilly to Purse the reform measures like reduction of revenue deficit and fiscal deficit in order to avail of the debt relief facility and the results were encouraging. After the introduction of conditional relief scheme, many of the State's fiscal situation improved, achieved revenue surplus and nearly brought down the GFD:GSDP ratio within the prescribed ceiling.

(v) Most of the States had been pleading before the successive Finance Commissions about treating loans from NSSF as loans in perpetuity and include these loans in their relief schemes. But, these were not accepted by first Twelve Commissions. It was the Thirteenth Finance Commission, which examined this issue in greater detail and recommended a partial relief measure in the form of common rate of interest at 9%. For many of the issues discussed by the Finance Commission, it recommended a comprehensive reform in the overall administration of NSSF.

(vi) The Thirteenth Finance Commission also recommended that in future, no loans be given for centrally sponsored schemes and recommended a write off of the outstanding loans against centrally sponsored schemes given to the States.

(vii) It was for the first time that the Twelfth Commission recommended a new loan policy. It recommended that, in future, the Central Govt. should not act as an intermediary and all the States to approach the market directly. The Govt. of India accepted the recommendations and has stopped giving loans to the States now. As a result, in case of central assistance, the Govt. of India is giving only 30% of the Central Assistance and not the 70% of loan component, which has to be raised by the States from the market. This is a major change, which has come about on the basis of the Twelfth Commission's recommendations.

(viii) Another development, which has taken place, is the fixation of annual borrowings ceilings for each State. This was also one of the recommendations of the Finance Commission. Every year, the Govt. of India announces the borrowing ceiling, keeping in view the fiscal reform path recommended by the Finance Commission. This was in relation to reduction targets of Gross Fiscal Deficit.

(ix) A few of the Commissions recommended corrective measures in the form of creation of Sinking Fund, Guarantee Redemption Fund and guarantee ceilings also. The Reserve Bank of India (RBI) has also recommended Consolidated Sinking Fund, Guarantee Redemption Fund as well as Guarantee

Ceiling Act. Many of the States have created such funds and have kept them out of Public Account.

(x) The problem of unauthorized overdraft was referred to the Fifth Finance Commission. It also included procedure to be recommended to avoid such overdrafts. The Finance Commission recommended a periodical review of the limits by the RBI. The RBI has been doing such a periodical reviews regularly by the expert committee and has been making necessary change in the Ways and Means Advances and the Overdraft Regulation Scheme. As a result, the States have been following this scheme strictly and are avoiding a situation of stoppage of Govt. payments by the Banks. The avoidance of such a situation by the States has become an article of faith with the States. The States manage the cash position overdraft in such a way that they clear it on the last allowed day by suo motto stopping payments, collecting & depositing some balance with RBI and so on (resorting to window dressing). After a break, they again start the cycle all over again.

(xi) Thus, it can be concluded that the Finance Commissions with their recommendations, have helped the States in coming out of adverse fiscal situation, achieve revenue surplus and contain the GFD at reasonable level and help them in containing debt: GSDP ratio and helping the States in bringing out this ratio to a sustainable level.

8. Calamity Relief (Recommendations)

The arrangement regarding calamity relief started by the Second Finance Commission, on their own, without any reference in ToR, followed by successive three Commissions, was commonly called as "margin money" approach. In this approach, a specified sum was set apart by the States as margin for relief expenditure with Centre meeting excess requirements during this period. The concept of Calamity Relief Fund was also floated where surplus fund out of this margin money will be parked and used in case of Calamity without affecting the normal expenditure of the States. It was also suggested to invest these surplus funds in Govt. securities. The idea of sharing of relief expenditure between Centre (75%) and States (25%) was mooted during this period. This was, thus, the beginning of the Calamity Relief Scheme recommended by future Commissions, specially the Ninth Finance Commission.

Though there was no reference to calamity relief, the Third Finance Commission (para 17 page 11), while estimating budgetary gap of each State, maintained the same procedure in regard to assistance towards unforeseen expenditure on natural calamities such as floods, famine and droughts. The fourth Commission was also not given the subject of calamities in their ToR, but the Commission followed the same procedure as was adopted by the Second and the Third Finance Commission (para 109 p 4a). The Fifth Finance Commission, by and large, followed the earlier Finance Commission in the matter of calamity relief (page 51 para 6.15). The Commission in para 6.17 recommended for creation of Famine Relief Fund as recommended by Third Finance Commission. The Commission observed that though earlier Commissions recommended the creation of fund and investing surplus funds in the securities, but the State Govts. have not implemented it. The Commission, further, observed that "if this position continues and the annual appropriations are used to relieve the current ways and means position of the States, the provision allowed by us for calamity relief would not serve its real purpose." The Commission, further, recommended that 75% of the assistance should be given as grant. The remaining portion should be borne by the States.

The subject of Calamity Relief was formally referred to the Sixth Finance Commission, when this subject was specifically included in the ToR. Before that, the Second Finance Commission took this issue in Chapter XVII dealing with miscellaneous matters, which arose in the course of their work.

The VI Commission has observed that "we were struck by the dislocation caused to the finances of many of them (States) by unforeseen expenditure on natural calamities like famine, droughts and floods and we were impressed with the need for making some regular provision to meet this type of expenditure. In our estimates of committed expenditure of States, we have included a margin for enabling them to set apart annually from their revenue sizable sums to be accumulated in a fund for meeting expenditure on natural calamities" (para 184). The Commission decided the amount based on the annual average expenditure over the last decade.

In the same vein, the Commission suggested a creation of separate Fund and transfer of these amounts to such Fund. The balance of the Fund should be invested in readily marketable govt. securities so that they may be available when needed without the States having, except in very abnormal circumstances, to curtail their expenditure or approach the union for assistance.

Though, the Sixth Finance Commission was given a specific ToR regarding Calamity Relief, in the end, it again followed the margin money approach followed by the earlier Commissions. The Commission considered the establishment of a national fund period by the Central and the State contributions and ultimately came to the conclusion that the proposal is neither feasible nor desirable (para 10 page 65).

The Commission examined the expenditure, being incurred on a large scale on an ad hoc basis and came to the conclusion that, instead of spending on an ad hoc basis on schemes of relief of dubious nature, provision should be made on a large scale basis for development of drought prone and flood-prone areas in the Fifth Plan—both in the State and the Central sectors.

The Seventh Finance Commission's ToR was slightly larger in scope than the Sixth Commission. As the Sixth Finance Commission talked of wasteful expenditure on dubious schemes of Calamity Relief, the ToR of the Seventh Commission had a specific mention of "having regard to the need for avoidance of wasteful expenditure".

After the report of Sixth Finance Commission, the GOI modified its policy of assistance, wherein assistance given to a State for relief expenditure is to be adjusted within the ceiling of Central assistance for States plan.

After discussing the Central scheme of assistance towards relief expenditure, the Commission observed that the States should bear a significant share of the total relief expenditure burden. The Commission also felt that the burden of non-plan expenditure, which does not create any new asset, cannot be properly taken care in the present scheme. Secondly, it was also found difficult to adjust plan assistance for relief against the plan ceilings of the State. Hence, the Commission felt that it would be appropriate and necessary to introduce modifications. For doing so, the Commission distinguished between relief expenditure necessitated by drought on the one hand and floods, cyclones earth quakes and the like on the other.

The Commission, in short, recommended the following scheme:

(i) For expenditure in excess of margin, the State Govt. should make a contribution from its plan for providing relief employment mostly to mitigate the effects of drought.

(ii) The extent of assistance by the States should be assessed by Central team, but it should not exceed 5% of Annual Plan Outlay. This should be treated as State contribution.

(iii) This should be treated as an addition to the plan outlay and covered by advance plan assistance.

(iv) The adjustment of advance plan assistance should be adjusted within 5 years following the end of drought.

(v) This assistance should be made available half as grant and half as loan.

(vi) For repairs and restoration of public works, the Central Assistance should be given as non-plan grant, not adjustable against plan assistance to the extent of 75% of the total expenditure in excess of margin. The remaining 25% should be borne by the States.

The ToR of the *Eighth Commission* (para 10) was similar to the ToR of the Seventh Finance Commission. After ascertaining the views of the States, the Ministry of Agriculture, Ministry of Finance and the Planning Commission, the Commission came to the conclusion that having regard to all aspects of the problems, it is not easy to devise a better scheme. The Commission also came to the conclusion that the margin money is proving to be insufficient, because the relief expenditure, in many States, reached hitherto unprecedented proportions. Hence, the Commission revised the quantum of margin money.

The Commission made a departure in the manner of funding of the margin money. The Centre should contribute 50% of the margin money every year. A State will be entitled to draw the Central share after it has exhausted its own share. The balance of Central share, if not paid, should be carried forward for next year. The Commission did not suggest the surplus fund investment in securities. The Commission recommended present arrangements relating to central assistance for drought and floods, cyclone etc. It recommended Fire damage be treated on the same footing as floods etc.

The ToR of the *Ninth Commission* was similar to the Eighth Commission, but a new item was added to it. The Commission was asked to examine, inter alia, the feasibility of establishing a national insurance fund, to which the State Govts. may contribute a percentage of their revenue receipts. In its first report, the Commission continued with the margin money approach followed by earlier Commissions and made a detailed recommendation in its second report.

In para 6.7 of the second report, the Commission observed that the present system of grant-in-aid, by its very nature, would lead to dissatisfaction to the States, because of method of assessment followed by Central team at a short notice. There may be substantial under-assessment of the damage. Hence, the Commission went on for an alternative scheme.

After finding establishment of National Insurance Fund, as not feasible, the Commission cameup with an altogether new scheme of calamity relief. The main features were:

(i) A Calamity Relief Fund should be established, separate from the general revenues of the States.
(ii) Centre (75%) and State (25%) should contribute to this fund. Centre's contribution will be as non-plan grant.
(iii) Fund to be kept in a nationalised bank and administered by a committee. The committee will decide all matters connected with the financing of the relief expenditure.
(iv) The fund available at the end of fifth year will be available as resource for the plan.
(v) In case the State requires a higher amount, then, it can draw 25% as advance from the next year's Central contribution.

The ToR of the *Tenth Finance Commission* simply mentions about the review of the present scheme of Calamity Relief Fund and may make appropriate recommendations thereon. The Tenth Commission recommended the continuation of the current scheme of Calamity Relief Fund with some modifications. The changes proposed were the following:

(a) Before releasing the amount due in any year, Ministry of Finance shall ensure that the Central contributions, released in earlier years, have been credited to CRF.
(b) There should be flexibility in the choice of avenues

for investment subject to ensuring security & liquidity.

(c) A committee of experts and representatives of States may be set up by Ministry of Agriculture to draw up a list of items, the expenditure on which alone will be chargeable to CRF.

(d) The norms for the amounts that can be given or spent under each of the approved items be presented by the State level committee.

(e) The AGs should see that only expenditure on items approved by the Ministry of Agriculture is booked to the Head 2245—National Calamity.

The Commission recommended creation of National Calamity Relief Fund (NCRF) for calamities of severe nature. The Centre and the States will contribute. It will also be kept outside Public Account.

The ToR of the *Eleventh Finance Commission* was similar to that of Tenth Finance Commission. The Eleventh Finance recommended the continuance of the CRF with certain modifications which are as follows:

(a) Expenditure on restoration of infrastructure and other capital assets, except those which are intrinsically connected with relief operations and connectivity with the affected area and population should be met from the plan funds on priority.

(b) Medium and long-term measures be devised by the concerned Ministries of the Government of India, the State Governments and the Planning Commission to reduce and, if possible, eliminate the occurences of these calamities by undertaking developmental works.

(c) The release of the funds from the Centre to the

CRF of each State may be done in two installments, viz. on 1st of May and 1st of November, each year. The installment due on 1st May should be released only after receiving from the State Government a certificate indicating that the amount received during the preceding financial year has been credited to the CRF, accompanied by a statement giving the updated expenditure and the balance amount available in the CRF. This statement, itself, should be treated as utilisation certification.

(d) The scheme of NFCR should be discontinued, in view of the difficulty in evolving an unambiguous definition of calamity of rare nature, and the difficulty in providing adequate financial assistance to the States from the limited amount available in the Fund.

(e) A National Centre for Calamity Management (NCCM), under the Ministry of Agriculture, be established to monitor all types of natural calamities, including calamities of rare severity, without any specific reference from the Central Government or the State Governments. This Centre (NCCN) should be empowered to make recommendations to the Central Government also as to whether a calamity is of such severe nature as would call for financial assistance to the affected State over and above, what is available in the CRF or other plan/non-plan sources.

(f) Any financial assistance provided by the Central Government to the States, in this regard, should be recouped by levy of a special surcharge on Central taxes. Collections from such surcharge/ cess should be kept in a separate fund created in the public account of the Central Government, to which it should contribute ₹ 500 crore as the initial core amount. Outgo from this fund should be recouped by levy of the surcharge.

(g) This National Centre should also develop expertise for providing training to the States' manpower on a regular basis, keep an inventory of physical resources available at various places for meeting the calamities and undertake monitoring and documentation.

(h) Every State should develop an inter-disciplinary cadre under the Relief Commissioner, comprising 200 to 300 persons, who could be deployed for relief works on the occurrence of a natural calamity within the State or in any other part of the country.

The ToR of the *Twelfth Finance Commission* (p. 10) had a different wording as it referred to "The Commission may review the present arrangements as regards financing of Disaster Management with reference to the National Calamity Contingency Fund and the Calamity Relief Fund and make appropriate recommendations thereon".

The modifications, which the Commission, suggested in the existing scheme of Calamity Relief are briefly narrated below:

(a) Besides cyclone, drought, earthquake, fire, flood and hailstorm, the definition of natural calamity, as applicable at present, may be extended to cover land slides, avalanches, cloud burst and pest attacks.

(b) The provision for disaster preparedness and mitigation needs to be built into the State plans, and not as a part of calamity relief.

(c) A committee, consisting of scientists, flood control specialists and other experts, be set up to study and map the hazards to which several States are subject to.

(d) The scheme of NCCF may continue, in its present form, with core corpus of ₹ 500 crore. The outgo from the fund may continue to be replenished by way of collection of National Calamity Contingent Duty and levy of special surcharge.

The *Thirteenth Finance Commission's* ToR, in relation to treatment of Calamity Relief, is different from the ToRs of earlier Commissions. The ToR (para 8) is as follows:

"The Commission may review the present arrangements as regards financing of Disaster management with reference to the National Calamity Contingency Fund and the Calamity Relief Fund and the funds arranged in the Disaster Management Act, 2005 (53 of 2005) and make appropriate recommendations thereon."

Thus, the ToR talks of "disaster" instead of "calamity" and the National Calamity Fund (NCCF), Calamity Relief Fund and the funds envisaged in Disaster Management Act (DMA) 2005. The Commission was also asked to review the present arrangements.

With the Disaster Management Act, 2005 coming into force, the earlier scheme of Calamity Relief with CRF/NCCF and the arrangements have became irrelevant, because the DMA provides for separate funds and a separate mechanism for implementation. Hence, as per the Thirteenth Finance Commission "the entire spectrum of disaster management" will have to undergo a revamp in accordance with the provisions of the Act. The Finance Commission, thus, formulated a wholly new scheme of disaster management as per the requirements of the newly enacted Disaster Management Act, 2005.

The salient features of the DMA are—

(a) The word "disaster" has been used in place of "calamity".

(b) DMA provides for much wider definition of disaster as a catastrophe, mishap, calamity or grave occurence in an area arising from national or man made curses or by accident or negligence, which results in substantial loss of life or human suffering or damage to, and destruction of property or damage to or degradation of environment and is of such a nature or magnitude as to be beyond the coping capacity of the community of the affected area.

(c) A separate administrative mechanism has been provided in the Act. The act envisages the formation of National Disaster Management Authority (NDMA) at the apex level for disaster management. The Act also envisages a National Executive Committee (NEC) that shall provide execution assistance to NDMA.

(d) On the similar lines, the State Disaster Management Authority (SDMA) and the State Executive Committee (SEC) will be established.

(e) At the district level, there will be District Disaster Management Authority under the Chairmanship of D.M.

(f) The role and responsibilities of NDMA/NEC and SDMA/SEC and DDMA have been defined to be performed during the time of relief operations.

(g) The Act provides for the two funds at each national, state and district level.

(h) The national funds shall be credited with an amount which the Central Govt. may provide. However, there is no analogous provision for the State and the District level funds.

The Commission invited the views of the concerned Ministries of GOI viz. Home, Agriculture, Finance and the Planning Commission and the NDMA on the various aspects relating to operationalisation of the DMA. The views of the State Govt. were also obtained. The Commission went through the international experience of countries like Australia, the USA, Canada, South Africa, Japan and Brazil. It also reviewed the existing scheme of Calamity Relief.

On the basis of the above extensive review, the Thirteenth Finance Commission formulated its recommendations, which have been narrated in para 11.74 of the report. The recommendations cover areas like Financial Arrangements, Disaster Mitigation, allocations for SDRFs, list of calamities capacity building, Fund for pooled procurement, Risk pooling and insurance and finally administrative mechanism.

The summary of recommendations has been given in para 11.107 which is reproduced below:

(i) The CRF to be merged into the SDRFs of the respective States and the NCCF into the NDRF. Contribution to the SDRFs to be shared between the Centre and the States in the ratio of 75:25 for general category States and 90:10 for special category States. (paras 11.78, 11.79, and 11.82)

(ii) Balances as on 31 March, 2010 under NCCF and the State CRFs to be transferred to the NDRF and respective SDRFs (paras 11.78 and 11.93).

(iii) Budgetary provisions for the NDRF to be linked to expenditure of the previous year from the fund. With cesses being subsumed on introduction of the GST, alternative sources of financing to be identified (Para 11.78)

(iv) Total size of the SDRF has been worked out as ₹ 33,581 crore to be shared in the ratio given above (para 11.92)

(v) An additional grant of ₹ 525 crore provided for capacity building (para 11.102).

(vi) Assistance of ₹ 250 crore to National Disaster Response Force to maintain an inventory of items required for immediate relief (para 11.103).

(vii) Provisions relating to the DDRF in the DM Act may be reviewed and setting up of these funds left to the discretion of the States (para 11.96).

(viii) Mitigation and reconstruction activities to be kept out of the schemes funded through FC grants and be met out of overall development plan funds of the Centre and the States (para 11.83).

(ix) The list of disasters to be covered under the scheme financed through FC grants to remain as it exists currently. However, manmade disasters of high-intensity may be considered for NDRF funding once norms have been stipulated and requisite additional allocations made to the NDRF (para 11.100).

(x) The administrative mechanism for disaster relief to be as prescribed under the DM Act, i.e., the NDMA/NEC at the Centre and the SDMA/SEC at the State level. Financial matters to be dealt with by the Ministry of Finance as per the existing practice (paras 11.105 and 11.106).

(xi) Prescribed accounting norms to be adhered to for the continuance of Central assistance to the SDRFs (para 11.95).

9. Grants to Local Bodies (Recommendations)

The subject of grants-in-aid to Local Bodies—a word used both for Urban Local Bodies (ULBs) and Panchayati Raj Institutions (PRIs)—is of a recent origin in the long history of Finance Commissions. This system of grants-in-aid started with the 73rd and 74th Constitution Amendment. The Constitution amendment was far wide and comprehensive, making these bodies as third tier of Govt. The amendment provided for the three Fs to these institutions. These were functions, functionaries and the Finances. The amendment also provided for the constitution of two important bodies viz. State Election Commission and State Finance Commission. Amendment also provided for the grants-in-aid to these local bodies through State Govt. It is another matter that the status on the actions following the Constitutional amendment is far from satisfactory.

Though there was no mention in the ToR of the Tenth Commission about Local Bodies, yet as the amendment to the Constitution had become effective before finalisation of the report by the Tenth Finance Commission, the Commission made recommendations regarding measures to augment the Consolidated Fund of the State. The Commission has observed that it could recommend such measures only after ascertaining the needs for them and the primary basis for this would have been the State Finance Commissions (SFC's) reports which were not available. Hence, the Commission recommended grants-in-aid on an ad hoc basis.

While recommending grants-in-aid, the Commission had clearly put two conditions viz. the local bodies should be required to provide matching contribution by raising resources and secondly, the grant is not intended for expenditure on salaries and wages administrative expenditure

It was the Eleventh Finance Commission which was, for the first time, [after the 73rd and 74th Constitutional Amendment] given two specific ToRs—one relating to ULBs and the second relating to PRIs. The ToRs contained two basic elements:

(a) Measures needed to augment the Consolidated Fund of the State to supplement the resources of Local Bodies, on the basis of recommendations made by SFCs [3(c) and (d)]

(b) The Commission shall take into account the recommendations of the SFC and in case of the SFCs not being constituted or report not being finalised, the Commission shall make its own assessment about the manner and extent of such augmentation. In doing so, the Commission shall take into account the three factors (i) provision required to be made for emoluments and terminal benefits of employees including teachers of LBs (ii) review of existing powers of LBs to raise resources (iii) Powers, Authority and Responsibility transferred to ULBs and PRIs under Article 243 C and 243 W of the Constitution read in conjuction with Schedules Eleven and Twelve.

Regarding the SFCs reports as the essential basis of recommendations, the Eleventh Commission stated in unambiguous terms that the Commission could not do so in full measure for several reasons. These have been summarised below:

(a) Under the Constitutional provision, there is no synchronization of the periods covered by reports of SFCs and FCs. Though some reports of SFCs were available but were of different periods. The Eleventh Commission suggested a Constitutional amendment of Article 243(i) to enable a State to set up the SFC at the expiration of every fifth year or earlier akin to the provision under Article 280.

(b) Many of the reports have not addressed the specific terms listed in Article 243(i) and 243(y), nor have they provided a clear idea about the powers, authorities and responsibilities actually entrusted to local bodies. The principles of sharing of state taxes have not been clearly enunciated. In the light of these observations, the Commission suggested a detailed chapter scheme narrating approach, analysis of resources, the principles of distribution of State taxes between States and ULB (vertical) between ULBs and Panchayats of different tiers (horizontal). Separate chapter on measures to improve financial position of local bodies.

(c) Regarding no time limit for finalisation of ATR by the State Govt., six months limit has been recommended by the Eleventh Commission.

(d) No alternative approach has been suggested, where the SFCs reports are not available. The Commission recommended that suitable amendments may be made to the Constitution so that Central FCs do not get into such a predicament. Hence, it recommended deletion of words "on the basis of recommendations of SFCs" (para 10-11).

The Commission also recommended that States should by legislation, ensure that the chairpersons and members of SFCs may be drawn from among experts in specific discipline such as, economics, law, public administration and public finance (para 8.12).

Thus, the reports of SFCs were not very helpful to the Eleventh Finance Commission, which then made its own assessment on the basis of two studies conducted on ULBs and PRIs and the memoranda submitted by the State Governments and with extensive interaction on the State visits with representatives of Panchayats and Urban Local Bodies.

The Commission's recommendations relate to (a) augmentation of Consolidated Funds of the States (b) reforms in local taxes and rates [para 8.16] (c) maintenance of civic services [para 8.18], (c) audit and accounts [para 8.19 and 8.20] and (d) data base on the finances of the local bodies [para 8.21]. The Commission recommended statewise specific amounts for maintenance of accounts and database to the finances of local bodies.

The Commission laid special emphasis on account and audit of local bodies. In the light of colossal funds being transferred to these bodies, the Commission felt the need to evolve a system of maintenance of accounts by the local bodies that could be adopted by all the local bodies. According to the Commission, the area of accounts and audits needs to be set right under the close supervision of CAG and supported by specific earmarking of grants recommended to local bodies. Then, the Commission made specific suggestions regarding audit and account.

In para 8.22, the Commission recommended a total grant of ₹ 1600 crore for PRIs and ₹ 400 crore for ULBs keeping in view the availability of resources and overall limit of flow of funds from the Centre to the States. Inter se distribution was recommended on the basis of a formula [8.27] with following criteria and weightage.

1.	Population	40%
2.	Index of decentralisation	20%
3.	Distance from highest per capita Income	20%
4.	Revenue effort	10%
5.	Geographical area	10%

In the end, the Commission recommended administrative and legislative changes and, in some cases, further amendment to the Constitution. These have been enumerated in para 8.28.

The Commission listed the core civic services, which it would support including primary education, health, drinking water, street lighting and sanitation. It indicated that the funds released should be earmarked for operation and maintenance of these functions. The funds were other wise untied with the proviso that they should not be used for payment of salaries and wages.

The terms of reference of the Twelfth Commission were exactly the same as that of the Eleventh Finance Commission. Before finalising their recommendations, the Commission sought the views of the State Governments, Ministry of Rural Development, Ministry of Urban Development and poverty alleviation, CAG report on audit and account. The Commission also sponsored various studies conducted by NIRD and NIPFP, and also organized two seminars, one each for ULBs/PRIs, implementation status of the recommendations of Tenth and the Eleventh Finance Commissions, and utilization of grants-in-aid. The views of the State Governments helped the Commission in understanding the practical problems faced by the State Governments and Local Bodies in their functioning.

Some common points/suggestions have emerged out of the exercise conducted by the *Twelfth Finance Commission,* which can be summarised as below:

(1) Poor Revenue efforts by PRIs/State Government reluctance also
(2) Lack of administrative machinery to collect charges.
(3) Limited capacity of people in rural areas.
(4) Non-synchronization of periods of SFCs/FCs

Editorial Commentary

The cocerned Central Finance Commission should lay down pseicifc standard, in conformity with which the SFCs should present their reports.

(1) Partial acceptance of reports of SFCs
(2) Poor quality of SFC report and casual manner in which these are constituted.
(3) Implementation of recommendations of SFCs/FCs in a time bound manner.
(4) Accounting procedure should be modernized.
(5) Performance budgeting and social audit to be introduced.
(6) ULBs should recover full cost of providing services.
(7) Inter Govt. transfers including share in state taxes and grants in aid should be formula based and not amendable to negotiation.
(8) Levy of certain taxes and user charges should be

made obligatory—minimum revenue collection must be insisted upon.

(9) Incentive grants related to revenue collections beyond a prescribed minimum be introduced.

(10) Revenue transfers from States to Local Bodies be made statutory, all untied grants to Local Bodies should be made statutory in nature.

(11) SFC should be constituted for a period of 18 months and a time limit of six months be prescribed to act on SFC recommendations.

(12) Maintenance of accounts by panchayats be standardized the accounts of intermediate and District Panchayats be subjected to audit by C&AG.

(13) Very few revenue powers have been given to PRIs.

(14) Data deficiencies persist.

(15) The dependence of PRIs on State & GOI has increased.

(16) The system of grants has not been rationalised.

(17) Transfers from Central Finance Commission should be linked to effective fiscal decentralisation.

(18) Need for incentivising local revenue collection.

(19) Norms based close ended grants system.

The above list is illustrative. and not exhaustive. The views mainly related to constitution, functioning and implementation of recommendations of SFCs, incentive based system of grants in aid, more taxation powers to these bodies and the ARM efforts of these bodies.

The C&AG presented before the Commission a status report regarding "Accounts and Audit" of Local Bodies. These are related to 6 specific items. The status report says that (a) 19 States have entrusted the Technical Guidance & Supervision (TGS) to CAG(b) the CAG has already prepared the required formats for accounts & audit (c) 18 States have accepted those formats for PRIs and 6 States for ULBs (d) CAG is also conducting training programmes and (e) the C&AG has formulated draft standard formats for creation of a networked database on the finances of local bodies. The Status report, thus, shows that the work is in different stages in different States and in some States nothing has started.

The Commission also examined the role of State Finance Commission while renewing the working of past SFCs and has made recommendations covering their timely constitution, selection of members, quality of reports, their consideration, acceptance and ATRs.

Keeping all these factors into consideration, the Commission recommended a grant of ₹ 25000 crore for a five year period 2005-2010. This is equivalent to 1.24% of the sharable tax revenue and 0.9% of gross revenue receipts of the Centre. It further recommended a division of grants between ULBs and PRIs at 80 : 20 ratio.

After discussing inter se allocation among the various States, the Commission discussed, in great detail, the formula used by Eleventh Finance Commission and suggested a different criterion for allocation. A comparative picture of the formula used by the Eleventh and the Twelfth Finance Commissions will help in better understanding.

(%)

	XI FC	*XII FC*
1. Population	40	40
2. Geographical Area	10	10
3. Distance of Income	20	20
4. Index of Decentralization	20	—
5. Index of Deprivation	—	10
6. Revenue effort	10	20

Thus, there is only one major difference. Instead of index of decentralization, the index of deprivation was used. The deprivation index was prepared taking into account intra State disparities on the basis of data relating to certain minimum needs of the population. Two core services drinking water and sanitation were taken into account to prepare the index. Fetching water from a distance and households with no latrines within house premises and house holds with no drainage facilities for flow of waste water have been taken into account to construct the index.

Two disturbing factors have been observed by the Twelfth Finance Commission (a) Non/under utilization of grants recommended by the Eleventh Finance Commission (b) inability of States/LBs to raise matching contribution. Because of the lack of matching contribution depriving LBs of grants will not be a right approach. Hence, the Twelfth Finance Commission did not impose such condition but the Commission did not relax the first condition that grants will be released only if the amounts already released are fully utilized.

Another problem was brought to the notice of Finance Commission i.e. delay in release of Commissions grants to local bodies. The Commission observed that often the State Govt. was found to use them for their ways and means comfort and show no sense of urgency in passing them on to the rightful recipiants (LBs). This starts a vicious circle by delay in release of grants from GoI, then delay at the stage of the States and so on and so forth. To curb this undesirable practice, the Central Govt. should take a serious view of any delay beyond 15 days in passing on of these grants by States from the date of release of grants by the Centre. While issuing guidelines, the Central Govt. decided to impose penal interest per day beyond a period of 15 days in releasing grants in aid. This has deterred the States in withholding the grants at their level.

The *Thirteenth Finance Commission* followed the same

TABLE 9.1
Amounts Allocated by Previous FCs & Amounts Drawn

(' in Crore)

Commission	*Amount Allocated*		*Amount Drawn*		*Amount not Drawn*	
	PRIs	*ULBs*	*PRIs*	*ULBs*	*PRIs*	*ULBs*
FC-X (1995-2000)	4,380.93*	1,000	3576.35 (66.46%)	833.88 (83.39%)	804.58 (33.54%)	166.12 (16.61%
FC-XI (2000-05)	8,000	2,000	6601.85 (82.52%)	1751.89 (87.59%)	1398.15 (17.48%)	248.11 (12.41%)
FC-XII **(2005-09)	18,000	4,500	16664.77 (92.58%	4024.54 (89.43%)	1335.23 (7.42%)	475.46 (10.57%)

Note: * ' 100 per capita of rural population
** From 1 April, 2005 to 6 November, 2009

Source : *Ministry of Finance, Government of India.*

procedure for eliciting suggestions from different quarters including holding seminars before finalising their recommendations. In this process, the Thirteenth Finance Commission also reviewed the utilisation status of grants-in-aid recommended by the previous three commissions. This situation is given by the Commission in Table 9.1 which has been reproduced below for the sake of information—

The table makes interesting reading. In case of 10th Finance Commission amount not drawn was 33.5% in case of PRIs and 16.6% in case of ULBs. There is some improvement in case of Eleventh Finance Commission where amount not drawn has dropped to 17.48% and 12.41% respectively. The latest position of Twelfth Commissions grant shows further improvement. But not drawing a force amount of grant-in-aid is not a very satisfactory position. This is in spite of the fact that there is always a hue and cry for shortage of funds at local body level.

The Commission has identified the issues, on which, it has based its recommendations. These are as follows:

(a) Devolution related issues:
- (i) Use of Devolution Index
- (ii) Share in Divisible Pool
- (iii) Delay in sending Funds to Local Bodies

(b) Accounts of Local Bodies:
- (i) Audit and Accountability of Local Bodies

(c) Functioning of SFCs:
- (i) Synchronization with Central Finance Commissions
- (ii) Quality of SFC Reports
- (iii) Implementation of SFC reports
- (iv) Article 280(3)(bb) and (c)

(d) Role of Development Authorities

After discussing the above issues, the Commission formulated its recommendations. So far as the grants-in-aid are concerned, the Commission for the first tiem recommended a specific percentage of gross tax revenue as grants-in-aid to the States. Starting with 1.50% in 2010-11, the percentage goes on increasing to 2% in 2011-12, then to 2.5% in 2012-13, 2013-14 and 2014-15.

For assuring at this percentage, the volume of the divisible pool for the previous year be used as the basis of computing the grant eligibility for a particular year. After actuals of that year are determined, adjustments may be made in the second tranche of the two tranche system.

Further, the grant will have two components—basic component and a performance based component. The Commission has stipulated conditions for releasing performance grants. Nine conditions have been stipulated by the Commission, which have been detailed in para 10.61 of the report.

These two grants will be divided into urban and rural areas on the basis of 2001 census population. This 26.82% will go to urban bodies and 73.18% to rural bodies. Inter se distribution has been done on the basis of following formula (Table 9.2)

(%)

Criterion	*Weights Allotted (%)*	
	PRIs	*ULBs*
Population	50	50
Area	10	10
Distance from highest per capita Sectoral Income	10	20
Index of devolution	15	15
SC/STs proportion in the population	10	
FC local body grants utilisation index	5	5
Total	**100**	**100**

The process of release of grants has also been outlined by the Commission. First year installments will be released in two installments but future years grants will be released only when the nine conditions stipulated in the report are fulfilled. The Commission has recommended for continuance of the condition of release of grants to Local Bodies but has reduced the number of days to five. If the money is not passed on to the States, the penal interest per day will be charged. The Commission has made separate recommendations for the special areas.

10. General Observations by Commissions

The Finance Commissions constituted so far, barring a few, have a chapter titled "general observations". This chapter contained various issues and situations faced by the Commissions regarding general issues, including logistic arrangements to suggestions for future Commissions.

The First Finance Commission, in Chapter X "Miscellaneous", recommended a small organization preferably as part of Secretariat of President to make a continuous study of finances of States, so that whenever a Finance Commission is set up in future, they will have sufficient material available to them at their disposal, at the very commencement of their enquiry. The Commission suggested various types of studies to be undertaken by this organization.

The Commission felt the need for improving the available statistics in regard to income tax. In this process, the Commission suggested that the Finance Commission (Miscellaneous Provisions) Act, 1951 should be amended so as to include a provision similar in terms to that in section 6(1) of the taxation of Income (Investigation Commission) Act, 1947.

The Second Finance Commission in Chapter XVII "Miscellaneous" had following to say regarding the difficulties faced by the Commission in their smooth working. Two difficulties referred to in the report are:

(a) The first is related to accounting procedure followed by the States not being uniform. Many examples were citied by the Commission, where States adopted different system of projecting receipts and expenditure. Hence, the Commission recommended a uniform accounting procedure, which should be examined in consultation the with Controller and Auditor General (CAG).

(b) The second was the absence of reliable statistics, particularly those relating to consumption. It also noted that reliable figures of collection of Sales Tax on individual commodities are not available. The Commission suggested that a nucleus staff with the experience of the work of Finance Commission should be retained within the Finance Ministry and made available to future Commissions.

The Commission drew the attention to certain Constitutional implications of changing pattern of financial relations between Union and States. It observed that among the shared taxes, income tax is losing its dominant position. The proportion of excise revenue and even share of grants is going up with share of other taxes, becoming important sources of devolution. Hence, the Commission observed that it is for consideration whether the time is not ripe for a review of the constitutional provisions dealing with the financial relations between the Union and the States.

The Third Finance Commission in its Chapter VII "General Observations", observed that the Commission felt impelled to raise issues of general character, though not related to the ToRs. But these are relevant in the context of the recommendations, the Commission makes, which merit consideration in the interest of national economic growth and the introduction of a minimum acceptable standard of social services all over the States.

After the establishment of Planning Commission in 1950, it is the Third Finance Commission in 1961 (after about 11 years) for the first time observed that the Constitution provides for assessment of the needs of the States as well as the measures of assistance to be afforded and the form, in which, this should be given are determined by an independent Commission. But this role and function of FC, as provided in the Constitution can, no longer be realised fully due to the emergence of the Planning Commission as an apparatus for national planning. The conflict of role, function etc. between Finance Commission, a constitutional body and planning Commission, a statutory body surfaced for the first time. Though, this conflict was highlighted by the Second Commission, when it talked of overlap of the functions of Planning and Finance Commission and had urged the need for a real and effective coordination between the two.

In its general observations, the Finance Commission identified a few areas of conflict. Before finalising the plan, the Planning Commission assesses the requirements of resources needed and expenditure responsibilities on the plan side. *In this way, the forecast of revenue and expenditure is done by Planning Commission.* Against this background, the Commission observed that "the role of Finance Commission comes to be, at best, that of an agency to review the forecasts of revenue and expenditure submitted by the States and the acceptance of the revenue element of the plan as indicated by Planning Commission for determining the quantum of devolution and grants-in-aid to be made; and, at worst, its function is merely to undertake an arithmetical exercise of devolution, based on the amount of assistance for each State already settled by Planning

Commission, to be made under different heads on the basis of certain principles prescribed."

The Second Commission had urged that there was real need for effectively coordinating the work of Commission. The Third Commission suggested two alternatives (a) to enlarge the functions of Finance Commission to enforce total financial assistance to be afforded to the States. This would be in harmony with the spirit and even express provisions of our Constitution. The second is to transform the Planning Commission into Finance Commission at appropriate time.

The Commission also mentioned the complaint of the States that there is perceptible trend in centralisation of resources in addition to centralisation of State functions. The Commission also referred to the trend that the States are becoming more and more dependent on central assistance on an ever increasing scale. According to the Commission, this is diluting the accountability of the State cabinet to their legislature but also it is coming in the way of development of a greater sense of responsibility in their administration.

The Commission also observed that because of the gap filling approach followed by the Commission, the States are developing an allergy to tap resources. The Commission also talked of tax wars in neighbouring States. It also referred to lack of reliable data as observed by the earlier two Commissions. The Finance Commission also noted the tendency of States to inflate their resources to get a large Plan from the Planning Commission.

The Fourth Finance Commission highlighted the need for institutional arrangement for inter-governmental consultations in the matters of taxation and others to avoid misgiving. Like earlier Commissions, this commission also talked of the necessity of establishing a standing organization in the Ministry of Finance for continuing the

Finance Commissions work. The Commission also discussed the subject of borrowings by the States and observed that service and amortisation of funds stemming from the market borrowings must be part of revenue liability of the States. The Commission indicated a list of items on which the statistical data will be required by the Commission.

The Fifth and the Sixth Finance Commissions reports did not contain any chapter on general observations. The Seventh Finance Commission referred to the suggestions made regarding Finance Commission to be a permanent body. After discussing the logic behind this suggestion, the Commission was not in favour of a permanent body by saying that the advantage in the present system is that it allows for the induction of persons with fresh approach and unbiased minds as members. The Commission also favoured creation of an independent unit to continue with the work of the Finance Commission. In order to have a fruitful and competent research work in the field of public finance, the Commission recommended the easy accessibility of the data and research study undertaken by the Commission during the course of its work to the interested persons.

The Eighth Finance Commission talked of the problems faced by it, because of non-synchronization of the Finance Commission award period and five year plan period. The Commission observed that there are many important parameters in respect of which, there should be a similarity of approach by the two Commissions. This can be possible only if the two Commissions report for the same five year period. The Commission also felt the need of having a division so that it could continue to function during the period of interregnum between the two Commissions. The Commission recommended such a division at the State level, too. The Commission also recommended about the advance action taken prior to the constitution of the Commission. It recommended posting of an officer, as officer on special duty, who will be ready with all the necessary arrangements needed for the Commission to start functioning immediately on constitution and not waste time on logistics.

The Ninth Finance Commission talked of some policy changes with the objective of restoring fiscal equilibrium. The areas referred to by the the Commission relate to following the normative approach, availability of data. Restraining the growth of expenditure of Centre, reduction in growth of indebtedness, discipline on budgetary operations followed by the States, guidelines by RBI for permissible amount of RBI credit to the Government accessibility of funds linked to performance. The Commission in para 10.12 suggested specific steps for bringing down the rate of growth of revenue expenditure in the immediate future. Application of zero based budgeting, no increase in employment in Govt. sector, plug leakages, phasing out the revenue deficit and the revamping the public enterprises are some areas, where action can be taken for reduction of expenditure.

The Tenth Finance Commssion highlighted the need for fiscal discipline in the light of rapid deterioration in the financial position of the Central and State Governments. Consolidation the revenue deficit, economies in expenditure, selective privatisation of public enterprises were some of the areas for actions pointed out by the Commission. The Tenth Commission was the first Commission to refer to the presence and persistence of a large number of Centrally Sponsored Schemes. These have their advantages and disadvantages. The Commission also talked about the tax reforms at the Central and the State level. The Commission touched upon the distinction of plan and non plan expenditure. The Commission talked of the process of decentralisation after 73rd and 74th amendments to the constitution and advocated strengthening of these institutions. At the end, the Commission also reiterated the need for a Finance Commission division in the Ministry of Finance.

In their concluding observations, the Eleventh Finance Commission said that their Commission was established at a time, when the fiscal profile of the country was, perhaps, worse than ever before with almost key fiscal variable sinking into high disturbing magnitude and moving in a negative direction. All States had fallen into large revenue deficits as well as fiscal deficits and were showing no signs of improvement. The Commission made its recommendations against this background and hoped that their recommendations will be able to reverse the negative trends.

One important point raised by the Commission was regarding adopting 1971 population figures for devolution purpose. The Commission felt that it is better to avoid conditionality like this in the ToR and a decision on such matters should be left to the best judgments of the Finance Commission. The Commission also talked of synchronization of period of two Commissions, setting up of division, relative data base in the general observations.

The Twelfth Finance Commission in concluding observations summarised the recommendations made by them on the ToR. The Thirteenth Finance Commission did not have any chapter titled "concluding observations", but had a chapter "Looking Ahead: Towards a New Architecture for Federal Finance". In this chapter, the Commission talks of new areas, which the Commission has suggested for fiscal correction. Improving governance and incentivising change in governance, creation of council of finance ministers, a fiscal council, a local body ombudsman, are some of the noble steps suggested by the Finance Commission.

11. Implementation of Recommendations

Article 281 of the Constitution has prescribed that "The President shall cause every recommendation made by the Finance Commission under the provisions of this Constitution together with an explanatory memorandum as to the action taken thereon to be laid before each House of Parliament".

Thus, the Government mandatorily has to present the implementation report, which is known as the "Action Taken Report"(ATR). The Action Taken Reports presented the by Govt. of India since the First Finance Commission have been presented in the Annexure.

Before discussing the ATRs of various Finance Commissions, it will be worthwhile to discuss the common procedures followed by the Govt. of India in case of all ATRs. As is evident from the reading of ATRs, the recommendations, from the point of view of implementations, have been categorized into four groups:

(a) Recommendations to be implemented by an order of President.

(b) Recommendations to be implemented by law of Parliament.

(c) Recommendations to be implemented by the executive orders.

(d) Recommendations to be examined further.

Before the Constitutional amendment, the recommendation regarding income tax and grants-in-aid only were implemented through a Presidential order and Union Excise duty proceeds and proceeds of additional duty were implemented by law of Parliament as contained in earlier Article 272 of the Constitution. But, after the Constitutional amendment, recommendations regarding all taxes and grants in aid are now transferred through a Presidential order. These orders are open ended i.e. they continue to be effective till they are repealed by the next order.

The Recommendations regarding grants-in-aid for Calamity Relief, upgradation grants, State specific, special problem grants and debt relief grants are implemented by an executive order.

The ATR clearly mentions the above procedure and categorises the recommendations into three categories only after the Eightieth Constitutional Amendment. So far as the recommendations "to be acted upon in due course" are concerned, the results of considerations are not known publicly and it is doubtful whether the decisions are presented before the Parliament or not.

The status of recommendations as presented in ATRs is given below:

(i) The report of the First Finance Commission was presented before the Parliament on 13th February, 1953, but there is no mention about the acceptance or rejection of the recommendations.

(ii) As per the ATR of the Second Finance Commission, all the recommendations were accepted by the Govt. The ATR talked of legislation to be presented to the Parliament to implement recommendations regarding distribution of Union Excise duties, Estate Duty and tax on railway fares. It, further, said that the question of levy of additional duty of excise, in lieu of Sales Tax on Textiles, Tobacco and Sugar is still under discussion with the States and once the decision is taken these will be distributed as per the recommendations of the Commission. Regarding recommendations on loans, these will be implemented after consultation with the States. Regarding other recommendations, the Govt., generally, accepted them and will implement, as far as possible, in consultation with the States.

The Govt. presented a second ATR regarding loans to the State Governments. Though the first ATR referred to in consultation with the State Govt. but the second ATR talked of a discussion with Planning Commission before finalizing the action taken. The Govt. argued that the scheme of consolidation suggested by the Commission would affect the ways and means position of the Central Govt. and reduce the resources available at its disposal to assist the States. It did not find any justification for fixation of uniform rate of interest. After due consideration, the Govt. discussed each category of loan and modified the recommendations accordingly. The details are given in para 3 of the second ATR.

(iii) As there were two dissenting notes in the report of Third Finance Commission, the ATR has straightway accepted those recommendations which were unanimous. After discussing the dissenting notes and the view of the majority, the Govt. accepted the majority view regarding a special purpose grant be made to certain States for improvement of communication. The majority had also recommended that 75% of the revenue component of the States Plans be included in the scheme of devolution. In this case, the Govt. did not accept the majority view and gave detailed reasons for not accepting these recommendations. It was the first case of its kind, when the recommendations of a Commission were not accepted by the Govt.

(iv) The ATR of the Fourth Commission mentioned the acceptance of the recommendations, but with certain modifications. It has been observed that the Commission did not consider the increases in pay scales and DAs of the State Govt. employees of A.P, Mysore and U.P. But the Commission, while recommending grants, said that the effect of these liabilities might also be taken into account in fixing the grants under Article 275 and to be included in the order of President. Accordingly, the Govt. of India requested Prof. D.G. Karve, a member of Commission to undertake an assessment of these liabilities. The recommendations made by Prof. Karve were then accepted and additional amounts were given to the concerned States.

The Commission had also excluded from assessment of some requirements of States of Assam, M.P., and Mysore, because the proposals were not accepted. As these proposals, could not be finalised till the finalisation of the order of President, these could not be included in the order and the ATR observed that such liabilities would be taken into account during the computation of the resources of the plan and their needs of central assistance.

(v) The ATR of Fifth Finance Commission shows that all the major recommendations made have been accepted by the Govt. of India. Regarding the Commission's recommendation that it would not be desirable to maintain the existing arrangement in respect of additional excise duties, in lieu of State Sales Tax formerly levied unless the Govt., after discussing the matter, further, with the States can arrive at a general agreement for the continuance of the present arrangements with suitable modification. The matter was proposed to be put up before the National Development Council (NDC).

(vi) The recommendations of the Sixth Finance Commission were accepted, except the establishment of National Fund for financing the relief expenditure of the States. The GoI reported that instead the Commission made detailed suggestions in this regard and these were to be examined jointly in discussion with the Planning Commission.

(vii) The ATR of the Seventh Finance Commission shows that all the recommendations except the following two were accepted by the Govt. of India.

(a) The loss equal to the difference between the amount of excise revenue realised on sale of potable liquor and that assumed by the Commission may be compensated by the Centre to the full extent. The GoI adhered to its decision to compensate the States to the extent of one half of the loss in revenues from the State Excise.

(b) The Govt. of India was not convinced with the logic given by the Commission for treating Small savings loan as loan in perpetuity,

A note of dissent was appended to the report by

one of the members suggesting an alternative formula of devolution of central taxes and duties as also statutory grants in aid to the States. The Govt. of India went by the majority view by saying that in regard to devolution of resources, which involves a delicate issue of Centre-State financial relations.

(viii) The Eighth Commission submitted two reports, one interim in November 1983 and the final report on 30th April, 1984. As per the ToR, the recommendations contained in interim report were accepted by the Govt. of India. The GOI accepted the recommendations of Eighth Finance Commission. Three notes of dissent were appended to the report but the Govt. of India went by the majority views of the Commission. As the final report of the Commission was presented after the finalisation of the budget as well as Annual Plans of the States, hence, the implementation of the recommendation started after one year i.e. 1985-86.

The Sarkaria Commission deliberated upon this issue, because it was agitated by the States before the Commission. It was alleged that besides causing serious hardships to several States as their hopes for higher devolutions in that year were belied, this has adversely affected the prestige of the Finance Commission. The Sarkaria Commission asked the GoI to explain the position. As per the Sarkaria Commission (para 10.8.56), the Ministry of Finance gave three reasons to the Commission's query.

(i) If the Union Govt. had received the report in time, it would not have agreed to give to the States Central Assistance towards the annual plan of that order.

(ii) The recommendations "don't constitute an award". These are recommendations to the President. The Executive may or may not accept these recommendations, considering their feasibility and desirability of implementation on objective considerations.

(iii) Finding additional resources to implement the final recommendations would have required unpleasant measures like Additional Taxation or deficit financing.

The Sarkaria Commission examined reply given by GoI, in detail, and gave five facts to arrive at the conclusion:

(a) The delay in presentation was also in case of Fifth Commission, yet it was implemented from that very year;

(b) The release of high order of Central Assistance cannot be a justification for non-implementation of recommendations, because Central Assistance and devolutions are two different types of transfers.

(c) The corresponding loss to States due to non-implementation was much larger than the loss because of mid-year implementation of report.

(d) Assistance given on the basis of Interim Report could be adjusted against dues based on the final report.

(e) There existed an expectation of more funds becoming available to the States during the course of the year.

The Commission, then, observed that "non implementation of recommendations of Finance

Commission not only causes damage to its prestige but may give rise to serious frictions in Centre-State relations in future, while the recommendations are not binding on Union Govt. in a technical sense, the expectation is that, as far as possible, these would not be departed from without compelling reasons" (para 10.8.58).

In this context, the Commission suggested that the time schedule of the completion of work of the Finance Commission should be so drawn up that it can reasonably submit its final report 4 to 5 months before the beginning the period of operation. Such a step would also give the Union Govt. sufficient lead time to get the recommendations examined, place the explanatory memorandum before the parliament and make necessary budgetary provisions.

(ix) The ATR on the first report of Ninth Finance Commission shows that GoI had accepted all the recommendations except grants in aid for meeting the requirement of revenue content of State Plan with the proviso that the Planning Commission may take into consideration this recommendation, while finalising funding arrangements for Annual Plans for 1989-90. The Govt. of India amended the shares of some of the States because of some computational errors in the report.

The ATR on Second report mentioned that GoI had accepted the recommendations regarding relief expenditure and setting of Calamity Relief Fund in each State. The ATR said that the arrangement for the custody and operation of the fund will be separately worked out in consultation with C & AG and RBI.

So far as the plan deficit grant is concerned, the GoI had observed that these grants will be taken into account by the Planning Commission as a resource for financing the States plans. Excepting rescheduling/write off of certain loans, other recommendations on debt relief require in depth examination and will be considered in due course. Regarding a note a dissent by one of the members, the GoI has accepted the majority view.

(x) The ATR of Tenth Commissions mentioned the acceptance of all the recommendations by the GoI.

(xi) The Eleventh Finance Commission gave two reports—one interim report on 15th January, 2000 and the final report on 7th July, 2000. As per the ToR, the Govt. of India accepted all the recommendations. The Commission was given an additional ToR on 28th April, 2000 to draw a monitarable fiscal reforms programme aimed at reduction of revenue deficit of the States and to recommend the manner in which the grant to States to cover the assessed deficit in their non plan revenue account may be linked to progress in implementing the progamme". The commission submitted a supplementary report on 20th August, 2000. The Commission had suggested a detailed fiscal reform programme which was duly accepted by the GoI.

(xii) The GoI submitted the ATR on *Twelfth Commission* on 26th February, 2005. The Govt. of India accepted the recommendations regarding share in Central Taxes, non plan revenue deficit grant for education, health, maintenance of roads, bridges and buildings and forests, heritage conservation, specific needs, local bodies and financing of Calamity Relief Expenditure. In case of sharing of profit emanating from petroleum, the Commission accepted the recommendations that this should be within the overall ceiling of transfers recommended by the Finance Commission i.e. 38% of the gross revenues. GoI also accepted the debt relief recommended by the Commission.

The recommendation regarding Central Assistance to State Plans was accepted by GoI, in principle, to be implemented in phases in consultation in with RBI. But, it actually implemented in one go. This was related to the 70% loan component of Central Assistance wherein the Commission had recommended that the Govt. should stop giving loans to States and States should raise this component from the market.

The Govt. also accepted the recommendations regarding external assistance loans and accounting procedures. In case of accounting procedures, the Govt. Accounting Standard Board in the office of C & AG would be asked to draw a detailed road map and operational framework for its implementation. Though the GoI has accepted the ceiling on total transfers to States yet it had put a condition that the acceptance does not imply the establishment of a principle of mandatorily sharing of the fixed percentage of the center's revenue receipts with the States.

(xiii) The GoI presented the ATR on Thirteenth Finance Commission report on 25th February, 2010. The GoI accepted the recommendations on sharing of union taxes, grants-in-aid, Local Bodies, Disaster Relief and accepted the recommendations on GST, Fiscal Road Map and debt relief to States with certain provisos.

In case of GST, the recommendation was accepted, in principle, but implementation may await the outcome of discussion in empowered committee. Regarding Fiscal Road Map, the detailed proposals for amendment of the FRBM Act, as may be necessary, will be taken up separately. Regarding debt relief, the Govt. accepted the recommendations but in case of NSSF loans, Ministry of Finance will constitute a committee to work out detailed modalities for implementation of recommendations. With regard to completely avoiding central loans to States in future, action will be taken in consultation with the respective Ministries.

It is, thus, evident that the recommendations of the Finance Commissions are, normally, accepted by the Govt. of India though technically it is not bound to accept them, because these are "recommendations" and not mandatory. In some cases, these recommendations were modified also but the Govt. of India gave cogent reasons for not accepting or modifying the recommendations. It is another matter that the State Governments may or may not agree with the logic given but ultimately they have no choice but to accept them.

Where there is note of dissent with respect to any recommendation, the Govt. of India have, generally, gone by the majority view but in one case, the Govt. of India went with the view of the dissenting member and did not accept the majority view. This happened in the case of the Third Finance Commission.

One very piquant and unparallel situation developed in case of the Eleventh Commission, when the Southern States vehemently criticised the recommendations. The Chairman had to call a press conference to clarify the position and the Govt. of India, in order to avoid the conflict with those States, had to give an additional ToR to the Commission even after the Commission had given its main recommendations. The Commission found out a via media, wherein the protesting States were given some incentive grants by adjusting the grants of other States. Such types of situation should be avoided and once the recommendations have been given, the Commission should not and must not defend the recommendations in the public platform or in press conference.

12. Centre-State Fiscal Relations: Emerging Trends

The history of Centre-State relations is, roughly, one hundred and fifty years old, which started with the assumption of sovereignty by the crown in 1858. The subject was always at the centre of attention and several attempts were made till the formation of Indian Constitution, when these relations were formalised. The question of provincial autonomy was always, in focus, and in this, the financial autonomy occupied a prominent place. There was always a conflict of interest between the Centre and the Provinces. This conflict passed through different stages and different mechanisms, in the form of deliberations of committees, commissions etc., which were adopted to come to a consensus or, at best, to satisfy the Provinces. These encompassed the issues of decentralisation of powers, functions, sources of finances and expenditure responsibilities.

I. The Govt. of India Act 1919

The first formal step in this process was the passing of the Government of India Act, 1919 in the formalisation of relations and provided for a division of legislative and administrative functions between the Centre and Provinces. It decided to separate financial resources by dividing existing heads of revenues between them. The Joint select committee of Parliament drafted the devolution rules under GoI Act 1919. These devolution rules were promulgated in December 1920. Thus, the Act of 1919 and devolution rules thereunder gave considerable latitude to the Provinces. But, there was no separation of cash balances of the Centre and Provinces. There was a single "public account" on which both operated. The provision of the "ways and means" was the sole responsibility of Centre. The provinces had no control over audit and accounts, borrowings and allied matters. Thus though some autonomy was given to the Provinces, yet the Centre controlled most of the matters.

II. The Govt. of India Act 1935

As the arrangement on the basis of GOI Act 1919 was not working satisfactorily because of lack of rational and acceptable distribution, the whole question of the division of revenue and taxation powers between the Centre & Provinces was examined by the High Power Taxation Enquiry Committee appointed in 1924. Simultaneously, a Committee called the Reforms Enquiry Committee was also appointed under Sir Alexander Muddiman. This Committee was to enquire into the difficulty arising out of implementation of provisions of GoI Act 1919. It recommended separation of audit and accounts. The separation scheme was introduced in 1924.

The matter was also examined by the Simon Commission on Constitutional Reforms and Joint Committee of British Parliament deliberated upon the recommendations of Simon Commission. The recommendations of Joint Committee were embodied in the GOI Act 1935, which was the major step in formalising the Centre-Province relations. The most important issue, under consideration at all the stages, was the division of revenues between the Centre and the provinces. This question, further, engaged the attention of the Round Table Conference and the Parliamentary Committee. This matter was discussed by the Lord Layton Committee, a sub-committee under Lord Peel. In 1931, a white paper was issued embodying the Govt's proposals for Constitutional Reforms. The White Paper contained, inter alia, the financial proposals, too. These Committees discussed, in great detail, the determination of principles, which should regulate the distribution as between the inter se. Centre and the Provinces and among provinces. Ultimately, the Govt. of India Act, 1935 came into being, which, generally, embodied the Federal concept of division of functions and resources. Thus, the passing of the Govt. of India Act, 1935 was the major step in formalising the Centre-Provinces relations. But, looking to the provisions of the Act, it is evident that the Central control over provinces was, further, strengthened and provinces dependence on Centre for finances indirectly increased.

As a prelude to the introduction of the Act, Sir Otto Niemeyer was asked to make recommendations on the assignment of revenues and sharing of taxes. He was requested to review the debt liability of the provinces and suggest relief measures, if any. Sir Otto Niemeyer made wide ranging recommendations, including the criteria of determination of shares, which included population, origin. These recommendations were fully accepted and embodied in the Govt. of India (Distribution of Revenues) order 1936. Looking at the overall scheme embodied in the GoI Act 1935, it would be observed that, though centralization was hidden, yet the basic principles of federal finance alongwith financial powers and authorities to the provinces were followed.

The Govt. of India Act, 1935 was in operation, when

the Constituent Assembly started deliberations on the draft of the Constitution placed before it. So far as the financial arrangement to be incorporated was concerned, the task was entrusted to NR Sankar Expert Committee.

III. Indian Constitution

The draft of the Constitution, by and large, had followed the provisions of Govt. of India Act 1935 regarding revenue sharing and expenditure. The draft also did not disturb the concept of shared revenues and retained the provisions for both obligatory and permissive sharing of few taxes. The Sankar Committee recommended the constitution of independent Finance Commission to deal periodically with financial questions. This recommendation was incorporated in the draft of the Constitution. As in the GoI Act 1935, the Constitution draft did not prescribe the shares as well as the basis of distribution. The framers of Indian Constitution, as the debates of constituent Assembly show, relied heavily on the Govt. of India Act of 1935 for the new constitutional framework, though there was difference of opinion about the strong Centre and the decentralised provinces. In the final analysis, the Indian Constitution incorporated the features of centralisation, which according to some, were not even present in earlier British legislation. The formation of Central, State and Concurrent List, the sharing of taxes and grants-in-aid were the subjects which were taken up from GOI Act 1935. There are many articles in the Constitution, which are more centralising. Article 246, which deals with Central, State and Concurrent List, is one of them which shows heavy concentration of sources of revenue in the central list while larger responsibilities of expenditure on the State list. Another Article is 249, which empowers the Rajya Sabha to transfer legislative jurisdictions from the States to the Centre. Article 250,

353(A) and Article 354 are some of few examples of centralized tendencies of the Constitution.

Thus, the Constitution of India was, formally, introduced in January 1950. Because of the not timely Constitution of Finance Commission, the matter of distribution was referred to a committee headed by Sir Chintamani Deshmukh in December 1949 as an interim measure. He had a limited mandate and he calculated the shares of the provinces.

IV. Change in Political Scenario

The end of the single party rule at the Centre and the States and the emergence of the regional parties at the State level capturing powers also increased the friction in the Centre State relations, in general, and fiscal relations, in particular. Having different ideology and political agenda, these State Governments came in frequent conflict with the Centre and some times, the situation became so tense that a compromise formula was worked out. There were so many examples of such conflict in the recent past. Sometimes, there were no easy solutions to these conflicts.

There were quite a few grey areas in the Indian Constitution, which were sufficient enough to stir the conflict between the Centre and State. But the system worked smoothly till 1967 because of the one party rule at the Centre as well as at the State level. In almost all the States, the Indian National Congress was in power and conflict did not surface during this period. But the Centre-State fiscal relationship became important issue after the one party dominance over Indian States ended. Regional parties emerged and these were voted to power. The first in this process was the emergence of left party and its coming to power in West Bengal and Kerala. Then DMK and AIDMK in Tamil Nadu, Assam Gan Parishad in Assam,

Telugu Desam in Andhra Pradesh, Party led by Biju Patnaik in Orissa were more prominent. BJP also came into prominence and captured power at the Centre and also in some States. Bihar by JD(U) and Punjab by Akali Dal and Haryana by Devi Lal also followed suit. Today the political scenario has completely changed. A new concept of coalition politics has come into being both at the Centre as well as in the States. With this changed complexion, the areas of conflict have also enlarged. Thus, there are three types of conflicts, which are emerging today—one between the Centre and State as such, second between coalition partners of the Centre and the third between coalition partners at the State level. Because of this changed political scenario, the zone of conflict is getting enlarged with the passage of time.

V. Finance Commission

The non correspondence of sources of revenue and expenditure responsibilities between Centre and States was always a cause of friction in the Centre-State fiscal relations. This conflict was sought to be managed by the institution of Finance Commission under Article 280 of the Constitution. In fact, the formation of this Commission was first recommended by Sri. N.R. Sankar Committee. The Constitution clearly prescribed the tasks to be performed by the Finance Commission. After the 73rd and 74th Constitution amendment, two more tasks were also assigned to the Finance Commission. These related to the grants-in-aid to local bodies—both urban and rural.

Hitherto, thirteen finance commissions have been constituted and the efficacy of the institution has been tested over time and the Commission has been successfully able to perform the responsibilities entrusted to it in the form of ToR and considerations. But some irritants always crop up when a new Finance Commission is constituted and the ToR and considerations are notified. Apart from the basic ToR, the notification contains a long list of "considerations", which the Commission has had to take into account, while making its recommendations. These considerations are heavily loaded in favour the of Centre. All along, the States have been protesting about these in their memoranda also, but neverthless. These are, by and large, ignored by the Centre. The Commissions could do nothing about these protests, as it was bound by the ToRs. A few Commissions have observed that the Commission should not be bound by placing these considerations in the ToRs. These issues were also raised before the various forums like Sarkaria Commission and Punchi Commission. The observations and recommendations have been ignored and the list has been increasing in the notifications of successive Commissions.

As per the ToR, the Finance Commission makes the recommendations regarding vertical and horizontal transfers and grants-in-aid of different kinds. So far as the vertical and horizontal transfers are concerned, the Commissions decide their own principles and norms and come out with the shares of each State in the divisible pool. As the taxes are compulsorily shareable with the States, the States take the shares as their constitutional right. The Finance Commission try to correct the horizontal imbalance, which is normally, caused by the mismatch between the revenue and the expenditure responsibilities between the Centre and States. The imbalance can arise either on the revenue side due to differences between the States in quality or quantity of public services provided, differences in the unit cost – cost differences may be due to factors beyond the control of States or due to differences in fiscal management. While deciding on the share of each State, the Commissions take into account all these factors and build these factors into the formula of devolution.

Apart from vertical and horizontal distribution, the Commissions recommend grants-in-aid to States in need of assistance under Article 275(1) of the Constitution. Though, the grants are given to the States in need of assistance and the need is assessed on the basis of budgetary needs but now the Commissions have been recommending grants-in-aid for various purposes. Excepting non-plan deficit grant, other grants have conditions attached to them. Even the grants given for local bodies have a long list of conditions attached to them. The States have been objecting to the conditional grants. Their argument is that if the grants are decided on the basis of needs, then attaching conditions is limiting the fiscal autonomy and flexibility for States. It is, further, stated that giving tied grants to achieve objectives in areas that are the basic functional responsibility of the State and forcing the States to enact legislation to be able to get the grant, is in a way, reinforcing the centralising tendencies. Thus, this part of the recommendation of the Finance Commission always causes some friction in the Centre-State fiscal relations.

During the last sixty years, the role of the Finance Commission has changed so also the list of considerations. The traditional role of Finance Commission of recommending share in central taxes and grants-in-aid has narrowed down. In the earlier few commissions, the Finance Commission was asked to look into the requirements of five years plans also. The Third Finance Commission's majority recommendations on grants-in-aid for plan funding were not accepted by GoI; instead, it went with the dissent note of the member. A few Finance Commissions discussed the problem faced by them in their working because of the existence of the Planning Commission as well as non-synchronization of award period and five year plan period.

The matter was raised by the States before the Sarkaria Commission, which went with the status quo. The later Finance Commissions stopped recommending grants-in-aid for plan and confined only to non-plan grants. Gradually, few areas were added for consideration of non-plan grants like upgradation of standards of administration, outcome related and environment related grants. But, by and large, those related to non-plan side only.

But, it was in case of the Eleventh Finance Commission that the scope of Finance Commission was enlarged by making it recommend measures for restructuring public finances of the Centre and the States with the ToRs entering into realms of macro economic stability and equitable growth. This will be evident from the "consideration" added in the ToR of the Eleventh Finance Commission.

"The Commission shall review the State of finances of the union and the States and suggest ways and means by which the Governments, collectively and severally, may bring about a restructuring of the public finances restoring budgetary balance and maintain macro-economic stability and debt reduction along with equitable growth."

The scope of the recommendations of the Twelfth Finance Commission was, further, enlarged, when the objective of reduction of fiscal deficit was added to it. The Commission was asked to review the fiscal reform facility introduced by the Central Govt. on the basis of recommendations of the Eleventh Finance Commission and suggest measures for effective achievement of these objectives. In pursuance of this objective, the Twelfth Finance Commission recommended, among other things the enactment of Fiscal Responsibility and Budget Management legislation and made it a condition precedent to getting debt write off facility. Most of the States enacted the legislation and as a result, most of the States were out of the revenue deficit regime and were near to the target of fiscal deficit fixed in the FRL. It is another matter that because of economic slowdown and slump in central tax revenue, the States got a less share of taxes than budgeted and their own revenue receipts were also affected and there was, therefore, some slippage in the target of RD and GFD.

The Thirteenth Finance Commission moved a step further. The Commission was asked to review the operation of States Debt Consolidation and Relief facility (2005-2010) introduced by the Central Govt. on the basis of recommendations of the Twelfth Finance Commission and suggest measures for maintaining a stable and sustainable fiscal environment consistent with equitable growth. Further, it was also asked to suggest a road map for implementation of Goods and Service Tax (GST) which, if implemented, will be a major reform measure in the field of taxation and usher in a new relationship between the Centre and States. The Thirteenth Finance Commission recommended a road map for Goods and Services tax and also set apart about ₹ 50,000 crore for meeting the loss of revenue if any, faced by the States. But as the matter was under active consideration of the Empowered Committee of Finance Ministers and there was non consensus between the Centre and the States regarding tax structure and the powers of taxation and revision of rates, the Govt. of India, in its ATR has deferred the decision till a consensus is emerged.

The Thirteenth Commission recommended a fiscal correction path separately for the Centre and for the States and fixed different targets of fiscal correction for them and linked the release of grants to fulfillment of these conditions. Thus, the role as facilitator for fiscal reforms both at central as well as at State level was, further, strengthened.

The Commission also recommended certain grants in

aid to achievement of certain outcomes. In this way, the Commission, it is hoped, will enable the States to follow the outcome budgeting in selected areas, which the Central Govt. could not do. Thus, with the changing times and the need of the hour, the role of the Finance Commission has shifted from the traditional area to new areas and instead of adjucating the shares of taxes between the centre and the States and among States inter se, it has become a facilitator between the Centre and the States.

As is evident, these are relatively new tasks which have been assigned to the Finance Commission. The scope of recommendations has been enlarged to restructure the public finances to achieve equitable growth, debt reduction and macro-economic stability. Thus, the Finance Commission helped the States remarkably in the area of fiscal reforms.

A unique problem arises before the States because of the non-synchronization of the award period of Finance Commission and Five Year Plan period. This created problem for the Finance Commission also in making their assessment of revenues and expenditure requirements. The State also has to make two different forecasts for two different time periods, which creates problem of uniformity of approach etc. The Finance Commission as well as Commissions on Centre-State relations have made recommendations in this regard and a Constitutional amendment was also suggested but nothing substantial has been done on this account uptil.

VI. Emergence of Planning Commission and National Development Council

Though, the Constitution makers visualised only one channel of transfer of funds from the Centre to the State and the institution of Finance Commission was put in place with this objective in view, but immediately after the adoption of the Constitution, the Govt. of India established a parallel institution in the name of the Planning Commission by the resolution of the Cabinet with comprehensive terms of reference. These were:

(1) to make an assessment of the material, capital and human resources of the country, including technical personnel, and investigate the possibilities of augmenting such of these resources as are found to be deficient in relation to the nation's requirements;
(2) to formulate a plan for the most effective and balanced utilization of the country's resources;
(3) on a determination of priorities, to define the stages in which the plan should be carried out and propose the allocation of resources for the due completion of each stage;
(4) to indicate the factors which are tending tiwards a retarded economic development and determine the conditions which, in view of the current social and political situation, should be established for the successful execution of the plan;
(5) to determine the nature of the machinery which will be necessary for securing the successful implementation of each stage of the plan in all its aspects;
(6) to appraise, from time to time, the progress achieved in the execution of each stage of the plan and to recommend the adjustments of policy and measures that such appraisal might show to be necessary; and
(7) to make such interim or ancillary recommendations as might be appropriate on a consideration of the prevailing economic conditions, current policies,

> measures and development programmes, or on an examination of such specific problems as may be referred to it for advice by the Central or the State governments for facilitating the discharge of the duties assigned to it.

Unlike Finance Commission whose strength has been statutorily fixed and qualifications etc. prescribed, the resolution constituting the Planning Commission was silent on both the matters and the Govt. of India retained the freedom about these matters. In the initial stages, some problems arose regarding coordination between the Commission and the Ministries. This matter was decided by making Ministers as members of the Commission. As the then Prime Minister Nehru was behind the concept, he brushed aside the criticism, and a via-media was found out.

There is no constitutional sanction behind planning. The Commission has not been constituted by parliamentary legislation. This aspect was debated at many levels like States Reorganization Commission (1956), Parliament Estimates Committee etc. But, it has continued to be so. But, the areas of conflict have widened with the passage of time. It is not the problem of coordination between the Planning Commission and the Central ministries, but more so it was the point of conflict with the States. This conflict has arisen because the Planning Commission exhaustively deals with the subjects like education, medical and public health, agriculture and allied activities, social welfare etc. which are mainly State subjects. The States feel aggrieved that their autonomy is being extremely frustrated by the national plans in the shaping of which they have little or no hand.

The institution of Planning Commission had an impact on the constitutional responsibility of the Finance

Commission. The States are asked to submit the projections of revenues and expenditures on separate formats and parameters to decide the total resources for funding of the plan. The Planning Commission has, thus, assumed the responsibility for coordinating with the States with regard to all aspects of planning and development starting from selection of schemes, their location, social infrastructure facilities, infrastructure development plans. Thus, all the activities of the States on the plan side came under overall scrutiny and control of the Planning Commission. The Planning Commission also decides the sectoral priorities as well as earmarks the schemes for closer examination. In the overall scheme of financing, the contribution of Planning Commission in the form of Central Assistance was substantial in the earlier plan periods. But, after the Twelfth Finance Commission recommendations, the Govt. of India has stopped giving loan part of Central Assistance and has confined itself only to grant portion of Central Assistance. As a result of this policy, the contribution of Central Assistance has been reduced to the minimum yet the Planning Commission has maximum control on all activities of the States with regard to Five Year and Annual Plans. This excessive control by an executive authority has been resented by the States at various fora, but nothing concrete has been done so far in this direction. Even the Central Ministries also feel the pinch. In the changed scenario of liberalization, more prominent role of the private sector, shifting from centralized planning to outsourcing and PPP model of execution, there should be a serious thinking regarding changing role of the Planning Commission so that the Centre-State relations because of excessive control of Planning Commission, may not be affected adversely and a situation may not arise of the direct confrontation between the Centre and the States.

The institution of National Development Council was set up on August 6, 1952. The objective of setting up of NDC was to strengthen and mobilise efforts and resources of the nation in support of plan to promote common economic policies in all vital spheres and to ensure the balanced and rapid development of all parts of the country. The NDC was reconstituted on October 7, 1967. The functions of NDC are:

(1) To review the working of plan from time to time and to recommend such measures as are necessary for achieving the aims and targets articulated in the national plans.
(2) To review the social and economic policies affecting the development of the nation.
(3) To ensure maximum cooperation of people in the planning and improvement of administrative capacity.
(4) To suggest programmes and schemes for the development of less developed and backward classes and regions.
(5) To assess resources required for implementing plans and to suggest ways and means for raising national resources.
(6) To prescribe guidelines for the formulation of national plans.
(7) To consider national plans as formulated by Planning Commission and to approve of the same.

Consisting the Prime Minister, Chief Ministers of States and members of Planning Commission, the Council was created to satisfy the States' complaints that the States had no role to play in formulation of Five Year Plans. It was created as a forum, where the States could air their views and try to sort out differences. Though the function of the Council was to strengthen and normalise the efforts and resources of the nation in support of the plans, to promote common economic policies in all vital spheres and to ensure the balanced and rapid development of all parts of the country. While, the charter of the NDC is both comprehensive and impressive, but as the working of NDC over the years have shown, the occasional meeting of the NDC with long intervals and with predetermined approach and strategy have failed to reach a consensus on the approach to five year plans or mid-term appraisal. It seems to be a ritual to get the seal of approval on these two documents, though many of the States might not agree to the contents of the prepared documents. Thus, at the end of the days deliberations, the States remain dissatisfied except that the Chief Ministers in their written speeches air their views knowing fully well that these will not find place in the plan document and the Mid term Appraisal document.

VII. Policies of Govt. of India

Because of the dominant role of the Centre in the development process of the economy, many new initiatives have been taken in the past by the Govt. of India. With the introduction of new Central plan schemes and Centrally sponsored schemes, the expenditure incurred by Centre has gone up considerably. All these expenditures are discretionary transfers in the shape of central share, additional central assistance and special plan assistance. These discretionary transfers have distorted States priorities. Over the years, the inter-state imbalances have grown and have become matters of concern in the Centre-State relations. These imbalances are reflected in almost all areas specially in education, health and other social sector needs. Many committees at the national level have examined these issues and have made recommendations. Though the objective of removing regional imbalances is always a goal of each five year plan, yet these still persist and still a cause of conflict and grave concern.

In the recent past, a new tendency on the part of centre is seen, when a number of central legislations have been enacted on the State subjects, the compliance and enforcement cost of which are entirely borne by the States. The list of these legislations is quite long. To mention a few like Environment Protection Act, Wildlife Protection Act, Forest Conservation Act, the Biodiversity Conservation Act, the Tribal Conservation Act. The States have to comply with the provisions of the Acts but are not compensated for the cost of compliance and the revenue loss on account of compliance.

The latest addition to the list is the Right of children to Free and Compulsory Education (RTE) Act, 2009. The Food Security Act is in the process. This legislation along with RTE Act, will impose additional burden on the States in terms of compliance and inforcement. There will always be conflict with regard to cost sharing as was seen in case of RTE Act.

The periodic revision of pay scales and pension by the Govt. of India impacts heavily on the State finances. When the demand for sharing of burden is made by the States, the stock reply of Central Govt. is that the Govt. of India has not forced the States to revise pay scales and pensions accordingly. But as is the experience, it is very difficult for the States to resist the demand of employees and their unions and have to revise the pay scales and pension sooner or later adversely impacting the finances.

The proposed Goods and Services Tax (GST) is another area of conflict between the Centre and the States. There is no consensus between Centre and States on the proposed amendment of the Constitution, as the States feel that this impinges upon the autonomy of the States.

Another legislation imposed on the States through the Finance Commission is the Fiscal Responsibility and Budget Management Act (FRBMA), because the debt consolidation and relief facility recommended by the Twelfth Finance Commission and the State specific grants recommended by the Thirteenth Finance Commission have been made conditional to passing/ amending the FRBM Act and also achieving the targets of revenue surplus, fiscal deficit and debt stock in a specified time frame. Though the achievement of targets are all right, but fixing the same targets for all States indiscriminately is not at all reasonable, which adversely affects the less developed States in their development efforts.

The Govt. of India on the recommendations of the Twelfth Finance Commission, have stopped giving loan assistance for plan financing to the States. This policy has two implications for the States. The Central support for state plan funding has drastically gone down. Secondly, the budgetary support for central plan schemes including CSS has gone up considerably. The changing pattern of Central Assistance is, thus, a major cause of strain in Centre-State financial relations and this is increasing, because of the larger size of central plan assistance and ever increasing number of central plan and centrally sponsored schemes.

The Govt. of India, on the one hand, has stopped giving loan assistance to the States and, on the other, have started fixing the overall borrowing ceiling for each State every year. The States have a grudge against the Govt. of India that their share in total borrowings of the Centre and the States is going down. Thus, the States suffer on these two counts. This point was part of the joint memorandum of the States to the Thirteenth Finance Commission. But the

Commission was silent on this issue.

Over the years, the Govt. of India has been transferring Central Sector and Centrally Sponsored Scheme money directly to executing agencies bypassing the State budget. Setting up the execution of scheme and its proper utilisation is the responsibility of the States. This not only erodes the accountability, but also undermines the role of the States. In many cases, the Govt. of India insists that the State Govt should create a society under the Societies Registration Act and open a Bank Account, where the central money is directly credited. Though, delay in passing the money from State level to district and field level agencies is cited as a major reason for direct transfers, but it creates more problems for the States as well as the Centre. There is no proper accounting of these funds and no audit by C & AG. The Thirteenth Finance Commission has taken note of these tendencies and has clearly stated that all money transactions from the Govt. of India should pass through the State budget and must be part of regular audit by the C & AG. The system of bypassing the States is, thus, a major conflict area between the Centre and the States.

The economic reforms initiated by the Government of India in the wake of severe balance of payments crisis had for reaching repercussions on the States also. With the increasing role of private sector in economic infrastructure development, the roles of States have not only increased in social sector, but in creating an environment and setting conditions for attracting private sector investment. The States, which have poor infrastructure facilities, have lagged behind in attracting private investment. This has resulted in increasing disparities in economic growth in those districts which indirectly accentuates inter state imbalance and is, thus, a major cause of concern.

VIII. Periodic attempts for Conflict Resolution

As has been discussed earlier, too, the Govt. of India, in order to diffuse the tension periodically, constituted Commissions to review the existing arrangement of Centre-State relations. So far, two Administrative Reforms Commissions have been constituted, which have, among other things, looked into various aspects of the Centre-State relations and recommended certain measures. Two Commissions, one R.S. Sarkaria Commission (CSRC-I) on Centre-State relations and another M.M. Punchi Commission (CSRC-II) on the same aspect have also been constituted. These Commissions examined, in great details, all the issues concerning the Centre-State relations, including fiscal relations in the light of Constitutional provisions and recent development and have come out with constructive recommendations to ease the tensions between the Centre and the States. The Govt. of India, partly, acted upon these recommendations through the deliberations in the Inter-State council.

(1) Inter State Council

As the Indian Constitution was framed largely on the lines of the Govt. of India Act, 1935, the Constitution makers provided for the establishment of "Inter-State Council (ISC)", in confermity with the provisions embodied under Section 135 of the Govt. of India Act, 1935. The Act provided for the establishment of "Inter-provincial council" with the rationale that "if departments or institutions of coordination and research are to be maintained at the Centre in such matters as Agriculture, Forestry, Irrigation, Education and Public Health; and if such institutions are to be able to rely upon appropriations of public funds sufficient to enable them to carry on their work, the joint interest of provincial Govt. in them must be expressed in some regular and recognized machinery of inter-governmental consultations." The said council was envisaged to be advisory in character for facilitating inter provincial cooperation, but no such council had been set up till the time India became independent.

The Article 263 of the Constitution provides for the establishment of Inter-State council. This provision is on the lines of section 135 of GoI Act, 1935. The Article 263 provides as under:

"If at any time it appears to the President that the public interest would be served by the establishment of a Council charged with the duty of—

(a) inquiring into, and advising upon, disputes, which may have arisen between the States;
(b) investigating and discussing subjects in which some or all of the States, or the Union and one or more of the States, have a common interest; or
(c) making recommendations on any such subject and, in particular, recommendations for the better co-ordination of policy and action with respect to that subject.

In spite of the provision contained in the Constitution, this council had not been established even after 40 years of adoption of Constitution in 1950. The Sarakria Commission, besides the first Administrative Reforms Commission in its recommendation, reiterated the need for setting up of the Council. Even though a considerable period had since elapsed the Govt. of India took the decision only as late as in 1990 for setting up the Council. The presidential order was issued on 28th May 1990 constituting the Inter-State Council, consisting of the Prime Minister, The Chief Ministers of all States, the Chief Ministers of Union Territories, having a Legislative Assembly and administrators of Union Territories and six ministers of cabinet rank in the union council of ministers to be nominated by the Prime Minister.

The Presidential Order also defined the duties of the Council as:

(a) investigating and discussing such subjects, in which some or all of the States or the Union and one or more of the States, have a common interest as may be brought up before it;
(b) making recommendations on any such subject and; in particular; recommendations for the better coordination of policies and actions with respect to that subject; and
(c) deliberating upon such matters of general interest to the States as may be referred to by the chairman to the Council.

While formulating the guidelines for identifying and selecting issues, the Council prepared a negative list of issues, which may not be brought up before the Inter State Council. The negative list consists of the following issues:

(i) Any issue which can be resolved by discussion at the official level, or at the level of the Ministers—between the Central Government and the State Governments concerned.
(ii) Any issue which has to be considered or dealt with by the National Development Council, the National Integration Council, the Finance Commission, the Planning Commission or such other body or authority of a like nature as may be set up from time to time to deal with specific subjects relating to Centre-State relations.
(iii) Any issue which is currently under consideration

or discussion in either House of Parliament or which is subjudice.

(iv) Any issue relating to a matter which, under the Constitution, is left for the decision of a specified authority other than the Central Government such as the Election Commission or the Supreme Court etc.

(v) Any other issue the discussion of which may, in the opinion of the Chairman; createa discord between the States; or otherwise be against the public interest; or against the interests of the sovereignty or integrity of India, the security of the State, friendly relations with foreign State or Public Order.

(vi) Any issue which relates to the discharge of any duty or special responsibility of the Union under the provisions of the Constitution or any law of Parliament. Provided that if majority of the members of Inter-State Council propose the discussion of an issue or keeping in view the importance of a particular issue, it is considered desirable to do so, the Council may consider such an issue with the approval of the Chairman in terms of provisions of Clause 4(c) of the Presidential Order dated the 28th May, 1990.

"N.B.—The sub-clause (i-vi) mentioned above are only illustrative and not comprehensive."

The Inter State Council was established after roughly 40 years of the acceptance of the Constitution of India and it is not clear as to what prompted the Govt. of India to do so. The Council itself preparing a negative list, has restricted its role in coordination between the Union and the States and between States inter se. Further, the experience of working of the Council for the last ten years shows that it held only 6 meetings during this long period and most of the time was devoted to the discussion on the report of Sarkaria Commission. It is, thus, evident that the Inter-State Council, though an effective Constitutional mechanism of coordination between union and the States, and also among States, has played a limited role during its existence.

(2) Administrative Reforms Commission

Administrative Reforms Commission set up after the general election of 1967, under the first chairmanship Sri K. Hanumanthaiya was specifically assigned the task of reviewing existing arrangement of the Centre-State relations and making recommendations accordingly. The Commission after extensive review made its recommendations regarding fiscal matters in the Thirteenth Report.

The ARC came to the conclusion that "it is our firm view that the basic Constitutional fabric of ours is quite sound and must remain intact. The Constitution is flexible enough to ensure its successful working irrespective of which party may be in power. We are convinced that it is not in the amendment to the Constitution that the solutions of the problems of Centre State relations is to be sought, but in the working of the provisions of the Constitution by all concerned in the latter and spirit in which the founding fathers intended them to be worked. There is no other way of ensuring cordial and fruitful Centre-State relations" (p. 7, para 12).

For effective coordination between the Finance Commission and the Planning Commission, the ARC recommended that a member of Planning Commission may be appointed to the Finance Commission. The ARC, further, recommended that the Finance Commission should include two persons—one having experience of financial administration at the Centre and the other with such experience at State level. The practice of appointing a member of Planning Commission in charge of resource division was followed in case of few Commissions, but was abandoned at a later stage. It was again in the Thirteenth Finance Commission that a member of Planning Commission was also a member of the Finance Commission. In case of second recommendation, it was not strictly followed except that the member secretary or the Secretary of the Commission is, normally, appointed, who has the experience of working at both the levels.

Though, the Constitution had provided for the setting up of Inter State Council under Article 263 of the Constitution, but it was not set up. Hence, the ARC recommended for the setting up of the Inter State Council for settling the Inter-State or Centre-State differences.

The ARC recommended that powers should be delegated to the maximum extent to the States with regard to their work on projects in which the Centre is directly interested or which are carried out by them as agents to the Central Govt. (recommendation No.22).

The ARC also observed that the Centre's encroachment upon the State subjects has also increased in another form. The introduction of Centrally Sponsored Schemes (CSS) and flagship programmes is encroachment upon the State's autonomy. Without any consultation with the States, the Govt. of India floats those schemes and requires the States to contribute to funding on a matching basis. This, not only distorts States priorities, but in order to get such funds, the state has to make provision in the budget by cutting other expenditure. Further, these schemes are formulated on a uniform basis disregarding regional dissimilarity and needs. Sometimes, these schemes prove of little utility to the State. Thus, this irritant in the Centre-State relations started as far back as 1967 and as the present position shows, the number of schemes has gone up over the years.

This matter is being raised by the States, time and again, in all the forums, including National Development Council. Many a Committee went into this serious question and recommended reducing the number of schemes as well as transferring the schemes to the States alongwith the funds. **Though the recommendations were accepted by the NDC, yet because of lack of political will and bureaucratic opposition at the Centre, these decisions have not been implemented; instead, the number of CSS has been going up unaccompanied by or centrally disbursed, funds, all, very much to the annoyance and dismay of the State. Thus, the National Development Council has failed to resolve this recurring conflict of interest between the Center and States, which casts doubts about the efficiency and independence of this institution in conflict resolution.**

(3) R.S. Sarkaria Commission on Centre-State Relations

The Commission devoted a full chapter on Centre-State financial relations. The Commission invited suggestions from the States and on the basis of the historical background and States' memoranda, formulated their own issues, which encompassed all the subjects relating to fiscal relations. In section 4 of the report, the Commission also reviewed, in detail, the factual position on the ground. Then, the Commission discussed the issues under (a) enlargement of the States' resources (b) enlargement of divisible pool, pattern of devolution, role of Finance Commission and indebtedness etc. The Commission made detailed recommendations on all aspects of the financial relations. A few important ones are narrated here:

Though the Commission had recommended that the

surcharge of Income Tax should not be levied by the Union Govt., except for a specific purpose and for a strictly limited period only, yet this recommendation is followed more in breach than in compliance. With regard to the clash of role of Finance Commission and Planning Commission, the Sarkaria Commission was in favour of maintaining status quo, by saying that "The present division of responsibilities between the two bodies, which has come to be evolved with mutual understanding of their comparative advantage in dealing with various matters in their respective fields, may continue".

Though the Commission had suggested a State level Finance Commission for a different purpose, yet it came into being after the Seventy Third and the Seventy Fourth amendment of the Constitution but only for Local Bodies. The Commission also made specific recommendation for additional resource mobilisation not only at the Central level, but also at the State level. Levy of consignment tax, tax under Article 296; taxation of advertisement, broadcast by radio etc. to be added to Entry 92, list one and Article 269(1)(f), review of royalty rates on minerals, petroleum and natural gas after every two years.

The Commission also made its recommendations regarding calamity relief, small savings loan and flow of institutional finance to the States. One of the important recommendations of the Commission was the permissible sharing of proceeds of corporation tax by an appropriate amendment to the Constitution. The reason given was that this will enlarge the base of devolution, so that, in the revenues of the States, there would be greater stability and predictability in future. Being an elastic resource, the States would benefit from its growth. After a long gap, the Constitution was amended to include all taxes in divisible pool. But the basic theme of the recommendations was the continuing of the existing constitutional and other arrangements regarding the Centre-State financial relations.

(4) Second Administrative Reforms Commission

On 31st August, 2005, the second Administrative Reform Commission (ARC) was constituted under the chairmanship of Sri Veerappa Moily. Apart from other matters, the Commission was asked to exclude from its purviews the detailed examination of administration of Defence, Railways, External Affairs, Security and Intelligence as also subjects such as Centre-State relations etc. which are already being examined by other bodies.

But the Commission in Chapter 5 of the Report, favourably considered the flow of funds from the Union to States through the Centrally Sponsored Schemes. Though this subject was very important from States' point of view and a factor adversely affecting the relationship between the Centre and States because of the proliferation of CSS on State subject, yet the Commission confined its recommendations to the flow and accounting of funds. The ARC (II) talked of principles for implementing the system of flow of sanctions/approvals etc. Robust financial information should be created in a time bound manner. Thus, the basic issue of the proliferation of CSS on the State subject was neglected by the ARC (II).

(5) M.M. Punchi Commission on Centre State Relations

After a gap of about twenty eight years of the constitution of Sarkaria Commission, the Second Commission, to review the Centre-State relations, was constituted in 2007 under the chairmanship of Sri Justice M.M. Punchi, former Chief Justice of India. The ToRs of the Commission were very wide in the sense that the Commission was asked to examine and review the working of the existing arrangements between Union and the States as per the Constitution of India, the healthy precedents being followed and pronouncements of the Court in regard to powers, functions and responsibilities, inter alia, in the sphere of financial relations, economic and social planning and sharing of resources.

So far as financial relations aspect is concerned, the Commission was asked to take into consideration the following:

(i) the role, responsibility and jurisdiction of the Centre *vis-a-vis* the States in promoting the concept and practice of independent planning and budgeting at the district level;

(ii) the role, responsibility and jurisdiction of the Centre *vis-a-vis* the States in linking Central Assistance of various kinds with the performance of the States;

(iii) the role, responsibility and jurisdiction of the Centre in adopting approaches and policies based on positive discrimination in favour of backward States;

(iv) the impact of the recommendations made by the Eighth to the Twelfth Finance Commissions on the fiscal relations between the Centre and the States, especially the larger and growing dependence of the States on devolution of funds from the Centre; and

(v) the need and relevance of separate taxes on the production and on the sales of goods and services subsequent to the introduction of Value Added Tax (VAT) regime.

The Commission submitted a comprehensive report (Vol. III) on the Centre-State Financial Relations and Planning.

The Punchi Commission has made its recommendations after extensive discussion with the States and the Centre, as well as review of the development after the first Commission on Centre-State relations (Sarkaria Commission). This forum gave ample opportunity to the States to air their grievances as well as causes of conflict in the relations with the Centre. A few major recommendations, which may help in conflict resolution are narrated below:

(a) A comprehensive review of all transfers to States, with a view to minimising the component of discretionary transfers, particularly those channeled through CSS.
(b) All future central legislations involving States' involvement should provide for cost sharing.
(c) The proposed enactment for providing food security to the poor should clearly delineate the responsibilities of the Central and the State Governments in meeting additional costs of implementing the provisions of the Act.
(d) The ToR of future Finance Commissions should be formulated in such a way that the additional commitments of the States on account of pay revision are fully taken into account.
(e) The scope of raising more revenue from the taxes mentioned in Article 268 should be examined afresh.
(f) State specific targets of fiscal deficit should be fixed in the FRBM legislation of State.
(g) Direct transfers to implementing agencies should be stopped.
(h) "Considerations" specified in the ToR of Finance Commission should be even handed as between the Centre and the States.

(i) There should be a better coordination between the Finance Commission and the Planning Commission and there should be synchronization of the periods covered by the Finance Commission and the Five year plans.

The recommendations made by the Commission specially in the field of fiscal relations, if implemented, will go a long way in easing the tension between the Centre and States. The report of the Commission will be examined by the Inter-State Council; then only final decision will be taken.

IX. Joint Front

In order to bring consensus among the States regarding implementation of Value Added Tax (VAT), an Empowered Committee of State Finance Ministers was constituted under the chairmanship of Dr. Asim Das Gupta, the then Finance Minister of West Bengal. The empowered committee deliberated upon the various common issues regarding VAT and, as a result, there was smooth transition from the Sales/ Trade Tax to Value Added Tax. In between, the Empowered Committee also prepared a joint memorandum on behalf all States and presented it before the Thirteenth Finance Commission. This happened for the first time in the history of Central State relations. Now, this committee is deliberating upon the various issues relating to Goods and Service Tax (GST) and had presented a model draft to the GOI. The process of consultation is going on. In the meantime, the Thirteenth Finance Commission also recommended a draft of GST and set apart a sum of ₹ 50,000 crore as compensation amount for the States. The ATR says that the recommendations will be implemented only after a consensus is emerged and a dialogue is going on between the Govt. of India in the Ministry of Finance and the

Empowered Committee of Finance Ministers of the States.

A new trend is emerging in the sphere of Centre-State fiscal relations. Whenever a new scheme or Act is contemplated by the Govt. of India on the subject of State list, the States administered by same party or regional parties put together, form a sort of joint front to put forward their point of view. This was clearly visible in case of Right to Education Act and Right to Food Security Act etc.

Thus, in the changing political scenario and emergence, and then dominance of regional parties at the State level, new situations are cropping up which are creating conflicting situations in the Centre-State fiscal relations.

13. Report of Thirteenth Finance Commission: An Assessment

The report of the Commission was presented to the President on 30.12.2009. The Government of India, after examining the recommendations at length, placed the report of the Commission alongwith ATR before the two Houses of Parliament on 25.02.2010 and now, it has become a public document. It was just coincidence that the FC report was placed on the same day when the Economic Survey was presented in Parliament. Next day, the budget was presented. Hence, all attention was diverted to discussing the economic survey and the budget and the F.C. report did not get the attention, which it duly deserved.

After the presentation of the report, not much debate was generated. Barring a very few items in daily papers, a special issue of in "Economic and Political Weekly" and one write up in the Hindu and the Economic Times and some comments in the Front Line, nothing has appeared in the print media heitherto. Only three States, namely, Uttar Pradesh, Kerala and West Bengal sharply reacted to the recommendations. Whatever may be the reason behind the less coverage and debate on the recommendations, it is unfortunate in the sense that the Finance Commission being a Constitutional body, its recommendations have far reaching consequences on the Centre-State fiscal relations.

I
Issues before the Commission

Article 280 of the Constitution provides for the constitution of Finance Commission at five yearly intervals. The President of India, in that process, constituted the Thirteenth Finance Commission (henceforth referred to as FC-XIII) under the Chairmanship of Sri. Vijay L. Kelkar vide notification No. SO1937 (E) dated 13th November, 2007.

Subsequently, vide notification No. S.O. 780(E) dated 27th March, 2008, Dr. Sanjiv Misra, Secretary (Expenditure) was appointed as Member of the Finance Commission in place of Dr. Abusaleh Shariff of NCAER. The notification contained usual Terms of Reference (ToR) along with "Other Considerations". Though "Other Considerations" contain a long list with some altogether new ones yet some of the major issues confronting the Finance Commission have been discussed in this section.

Constitution of Commission

The Finance Commission (miscellaneous provisions) Act prescribes that other members should be selected from among persons who (a) are, or have been, or are qualified to be appointed as Judges of High Court, or (b) have special knowledge of finances and accounts of the Government or (c) have had wide experience in financial matters and in administration or (d) have special knowledge of economics. The Administrative Reform Commission (ARC) had recommended that a member of the Planning Commission should also be made a Member of the Finance Commission to have a proper coordination among two bodies. The member in charge of resources in the Planning Commission was appointed part time member of FC-XIII also. In this way, the old practice was restored. The member incidentally has the vast experience of working in State and Central Govt. But, no member was appointed, who was qualified to be appointed as Judge of High Court. Such a member has always been there in earlier Commissions. All the other members of the Commission were eminent economists in their own field and had good theoretical background of the subject.

The Constitution of thirteenth in number clearly shows that the system of Finance Commission has been functioning satisfactorily and the States are fairly satisfied with the recommendations. Though there has been some squeeze in the role of Finance Commission over the years, because of the emergence of Planning Commission, yet it has played a significant role in trying to balance the Central-State fiscal relations and also providing right direction to it.

Role of Finance Commission

Successive Finance Commissions have highlighted in their reports about the diminishing role of the Finance Commission in the matter of distribution of funds from the Centre to the States. The increasing role of Planning Commission and the Central Ministries and subjects related to these issues were matters of scrutiny by the Sarkaria Commission (CSRC-I) as well as by Punchi Commission (CSRC-II).

The Constitution makers had visualised a single source of transfer of funds from the Centre to the States. This had its own advantages. The emergence of Planning Commission as a parallel body deciding upon transfer of plan funds to the States has led to an overlap with the Finance Commission, which was, perhaps, not the intention of the Constitution makers, as laid down in the Constitution. Later on, there also appeared overlap of the award period of Finance Commission and the Five Year Plan Period. This mismatch created problems for the States in preparing the budgets and reflecting the plans in their budgets and to the Finance Commission in deciding the committed liabilities of completed plan schemes on the non-plan side.

Another major development, which is continuously impinging upon the transfer of resources to the States, is the proliferation of the Centrally Sponsored Schemes of various Central Ministries, specially dealing with the subjects in the State list. These schemes have varying shares of expenditure between the Centre and the States. The assistance is, normally, given in the form of grants. These schemes are approved by the Planning Commission, funded by the Central Ministries and executed by the State agencies and in some cases directly by the executing agencies. This assistance is over and above the assistance given by the Planning Commission for state plan funding. A new system has also been created outside the budget by creating new institutions and the funds are channeled through these agencies outside the State budget.

The assistance going to the States through Planning Commission and Central Ministries is quite substantial and is much more than the amount transferred through Finance Commission. Thus, many a time, the role of Finance Commission, which is a Constitutional body, is diluted in favour of an executive institution and also by the Central Ministries. In such an anamalous situation, it becomes difficult for the States to take a holistic view of the total assistance flowing from the Centre through these institutions because of the different timeframe, some grants fixed and certain and some uncertain conditionalities to be fulfilled and the institutional mechanism to be put in place etc.

Terms of Reference

The notification sets out the terms of reference as well as "other considerations" which the Commission was asked to look into while making its recommendations. The Government of India, before finalising ToRs of the Commission, solicitated the views of the State Governments. Apart from this communication, there was no discussion with the States in finalising "other considerations" because ToRs. are already set out in the Constitution. Though, the States have been pleading for it and CSRC I and II strongly recommending for the same.

The Presidential Order, constituting the Thirteenth Finance Commission, divided the ToR in two parts. Para 4 deals with the matters for which the Commission "shall" make recommendations. The points, on which the recommendation has to be made, are those which are prescribed in Article 280 of the Constitution.

Para 6 of the notification deals with the "Other Considerations", which the Commission "shall have regard to" while making recommendations. The list of "considerations" appeared, for the first time, in the Fifth Finance Commission's ToR and ever since the list of considerations has been expanding Commission after Commission.

Other Considerations

The issue of "other considerations" was hotly debated before the CSRC I. As has been mentioned in para 10.8.39 of the report, "the Government of India reported to the Commission that these considerations are, therefore, to be viewed as "an illustrative list of the factors considered germane to the task of the Finance Commissions" by the Government. The Sarkaria Commission clearly stated that "we are not convinced that any reference to the Finance Commission, unless constituting a term of reference vide Article 280(3) of the Constitution, can bind or delimit its approach. However, it will only be appropriate and befitting the statutory and high status of the Finance Commission that any consideration suggested to it, besides its terms of reference under Article 280(3), are put in a language, which does not give an impression of formally binding it to adhere to a given approach or methodology". It is felt by all the State Governments that, in practice, these other considerations have conditioned the approach and methodology of the Commission. Ideally, these considerations should be even handed as between the Centre and the States. But contrary to the expectations, "other considerations" as handed down to, and acted upon by the past few Commissions have been so framed as to tilt the balance in favour of the Centre and against the States.

Population Figures

So far as the adoption of population figure of 1971 is concerned, this was introduced through a resolution of Parliament, which was valid upto the year 2001. The State Government had been, continuously, pleading before the Government of India and successive Finance Commissions about the non existence of any mandate of Parliament about the extension of Resolution beyond 2001, but the pleas of the State Government in this regard have continuously been ignored without assigning any reasons. Without extending the validity period through Parliament resolution, again, the extension of it beyond 2001 cannot be said to be regular and proper.

Further, two developments have taken place after the expiry of this resolution. Apart from the validity of the concerned resolution, the census figures of 2001 have now come and secondly, in case of Uttar Pradesh, Madhya Pradesh and Bihar, new successor States have come into being from the year 2000. Thus, the population figures of 1971 have no relevance to these States now. Moreover, and the Central Government's stored, with respect to this has also all along been unternable in terms of the Constitutional provisions. In the light of ToR and other considerations handed down to FC-XIII, the Commission was not able to do anything in the matter.

Further after 1971, three censes have taken place (1981, 1991 and 2001) and new population figures have come up and there is a sea change in the situation at the ground level. It is relevant to point out here that the population of a place is one of the basic determinants for assessing the "needs" of the States. The basic minimum facilities like basic education, basic health, housing, sanitation, drinking water etc. reflect the need of the people. Article 275 of the Constitution talks about the States who are "in need" of grants-in-aid. Hence, while assessing the needs of the States, if the population figures of 1971 census were taken, then the true reflection of the needs of the States would not be there and in such a situation, the States will be deprived of a good quantum of grants-in-aid.

Tax: Grant Ratio

Another important area of concern for the States is the decline in the tax share in the total transfers to the States. Tenth Finance Commission award consisted of 91% of share in central taxes and 9% as grants-in-aid. In the EFC period, this ratio changed to 87% and 13% respectively. But in the Twelfth Finance Commission period, the tax share portion went down further to 81% with the grant portion rising to 19%. As per the Constitution, the share in Central Taxes is the legitimate right of the States and it comes to the States on a regular basis without any strings attached to it. However, the grants-in-aid recommended by the FC (excluding NPRD) have some conditionalities attached to the releases; hence, uncertainty regarding regular flow is always there. The Twelfth Finance Commission had more relied upon the conditional grants to States for social sectors, road maintenance, etc. Though there has been overall increase in the quantum of central transfers to the States, yet the compulsory sharing of tax revenue has been continuously, going down from one Finance Commission to another.

Review of Debt Position

Para 5 of the notification desires the Commission to review the state of Finances of the Union and the States, keeping in view, in particular, the operation of the States' DCRF 2005-2010 introduced by the Central Government on the basis of the recommendations of the Twelfth Finance Commission and suggest remedial measures for maintaining a stable and sustainable fiscal environment, consistent with equitable growth.

It is evident from the above that the usual clause relating to debt-relief has been changed and instead of debt relief, the Commission was asked to maintain a stable and sustainable fiscal environment consistent with equitable growth and thus, indirectly the question of debt was, thus, linked to fiscal consolidation.

Debt relief recommended by the earlier Finance Commissions is normally, restricted to loans advanced to States by GoI. The scope of debt relief has come down with the share of Central loans in outstanding debt coming down to about 12 per cent from over 60 per cent in the early nineties because of debt-swap scheme and termination of on lending facility to State for Plan proposes, after the recommendations of the Twelfth FC. This makes it all the more important to work out a special package for developing States to provide them with relief and resources for investment. If lower borrowing limits are fixed for these States to meet the fiscal deficit targets laid down under the FRBM legislations, then the States need to be compensated in terms of higher revenue transfers.

Though the mandate given to the FC-XIII is specific to the review of the debt relief recommended by the Twelfth Finance Commission, reference to maintaining stable fiscal environment consistent with equitable growth gave enough scope to the FC-XIII to recommend a special package of relief to debt stressed States.

New Dimensions

Many new dimensions have been added in the ToR of Thirteenth Finance Commission. One relates to quality of public expenditure to obtain better outputs and outcomes and second, to need to manage ecology, environment and climate change, consistent with sustainable development.

Gross Budgetary Support

As per para 6(ii) of the notification, the FC-XIII has been asked to estimate the Gross Budgetary Support (GBS) to the Central and State Plans as a demand on the resources of the Central Government. This consideration has far-reaching implications not only for the working of the Finance Commission but also for the entire gamut of the Centre-State fiscal relations. The Finance Commission is a constitutional body and as such cannot be bound by the estimates of GBS prepared by extra constitutional authority like the Planning Commission. It can only said that, as the GBS consists mostly for funding centrally sponsored schemes and special assistance, the consideration by FC-XIII of the GBS amounted to perpetuating the increasing role of Centrally sponsored schemes and increasing the discretionary element of assistance to the State Plans.

In addition, clause 9(ii) of the other considerations required the FC-XIII to consider "the demands on the resources of the Central Government, in particular, on account of the projected Gross Budgetary Support to the Central and the State Plan expenditure on civil administration, defence, internal and border security, debt-servicing and other committed expenditure and liabilities". This gave priority to providing for Central Government's committed expenditure, and implied that the FC-XIII would be transferring only the residual resources for the States to share. This is unconstitutional as it violates Article-280 of the Constitution, which mandates the entire pool as divisible between the Central Government and the States. It also gives priority to the committed expenditure of the Central Government over that of the States, even when the States may be burdened with high committed expenditure on interest, pension and salaries wholly on account of the deviated Central Policies which are violative of the Constitutional provisions.

Goods and Services Tax

The Thirteenth Finance Commission was also asked to examine the proposed implementation of Goods and Services Tax with effect from 1st April, 2010 including its impact on the country's foreign trade. Thus, the FC-XIII was given the task of preparing a model GST which can be an alternative model to the one being prepared the Empowered Committee of Finance Ministers. A consensus has to emerge between the Centre and the States before finalising the draft Act.

Fiscal Responsibility and Budget Management

On the recommendations of FC-XII, by and large, all the States enacted the FRBM Act. The performance during the period 2005-2007 shows that some of the States including Uttar Pradesh strictly followed the Act and fulfilled the targets of the Act well in advance of the target date.

Almost uniform targets for reduction of fiscal and revenue deficits were set by the FC-XII for all the States. It would not be incorrect to say here that the implementation of these forced targets resulted in cuts in developmental expenditure amongst the less developed States like Uttar Pradesh.

As is evident from the Central budgets, the Government of India seems not having followed the fiscal targets set for itself. The recent decisions of the Government of India regarding loan waiver, the increased oil, food and fertilizer "off budget" subsidy and now the Sixth Pay Commission burden have resulted in higher revenue and fiscal deficit and thus adversely affecting the FRBM targets. Further, the Government of India unilaterally extended the target date of reduction of fiscal deficit from 2008-09 to 2009-10 and also revised the target of GFD from 3.5% in 2008-09 to 4% of GSDP for 2009-10 for all the States while its GFD was more than 5% of GDP for 2009-10.

Grants-in-aid: Conditional or unconditional

The FC-XII had recommended grants-in-aid for education and health sector subject to the condition that the State Government will spend a certain minimum level on the non-plan expenditure side. This resulted in the increase in the non-plan revenue component of the budget and in a way adversely affected the revenue account balance.

Another contentious issue is that grants from the FC to the States based on the need of assistance be released automatically without any conditionalities from the Central government. It seems that the intentions of the Constitution makers are gradually being negated by the recent Finance Commissions by making their transfers more and more conditional. The increasing trend of conditionality of statutory transfers (Transfers through FC's) is evident from the way the grants were provided by the Twelfth Finance Commission.

The Finance Commissions have had to contend with two contradictory demands from the States. On the one hand are States that are better-off, show better tax effort and manage their finances better; they naturally want to maintain the tempo of development within their States and have the Finance Commissions' recommendations tailored to that end. On the other hand, mostly Hindi speaking States are weak in all these respects, and are in a state of constant dependence on grants and reliefs recommended by the Finance Commissions to make up their revenue gaps. The practice of passing on higher and higher amounts to the financially weaker States to help them catch up with the better-off States has been severely criticised as unfair and inequitable in that it punishes the better governed States, and provided, in effect; rewards for inefficiency and fiscal profligacy. To get round this dilemma, Finance Commissions have customarily taking the route of assigning relative weights, both for determining inter se sharing of taxes and for working out inter se allocation of grants.

It has been observed that changing macroeconomic policies of the Centre affect State finances adversely. The Central Government announces unilaterally "relief packages" for those who are hit by distress caused by

Economic slow down. Giving relief on the Central Taxes adversely affects the States share of the Central Taxes. At the request of Government of India, many of the States including U.P. reduced the petroleum prices affecting adversely their revenue receipts further.

II
Approach of the Commission

As per the FC-XIII, the overall approach of the commission "is to foster inclusive and green growth promoting fiscal federalism" (para 3.7). This has been taken as a "vision" underlying the Commission's recommendations. But the FC has observed that the recommendations, however, are subject to contours as specified in the Constitution.

I. Approach towards Fiscal Consolidation

As per the Commission, "inclusivity" is the corner stone of all the recommendations and is justified for long term economic efficiency reasons, so as to minimise the burden of fiscally induced migration on high income States. Because of this objective in mind the FC-XIII has substantially enhanced grants for local bodies (para 3.11).

The Commission has defined "Fiscal Consolidation" as measures to improve the quality and effectiveness of the process of public expenditure and resource mobilization (para 3.12), which involves ways to incentivise such consolidation. The Commission has, in the process, coined a new phase "expansionary fiscal consolidation", which according to FC-XIII means no compression of development expenditure. This type of consolidation will ensure that the Govt. gets the best value for money foregone as incentives to the growth of the industry in general, and the industry's investment backed by integrated efforts directed towards export promotion in particular.

The FC-XIII has mentioned its three challenges of different States viz very high degree of vertical imbalances, spatial inequality in fiscal capacity and needs. Thirdly recent decentralizations initiatives and the increasing pace of urbanization have increased the obligations of ULBs. There are other challenges also which have been narrated by the Commission which have to be kept in view not only in the short term but also in long term, as implications of these challenges are of varying degrees. (para 3.17, 3.18 and 3.19).

The approach to fiscal correction starts with the determination of the feasible target for debt-GSDP ratio, consolidated for the Centre and States put together and for States separately. This combined ratio has been fixed at 68% to be achieved by 2014-15 and 45% for the Central Government, keeping in mind the targets of elimination of revenue deficit and fixing ceiling of GFD. Another important point about this path of fiscal correction is that this will start with a time lag of one year. Year 2010-11, has been taken as an "adjustment year" and fiscal consolidation path to start from 2011-12. Further, important aspect of this process is the recognition of the fact that one size does not fit all unlike previous FCs which fixed the uniform target for each and every State (para 3.24).

Thus, fiscal consolidation has been linked to incentives like the FC-XII, which linked it to DCRF facility. The incentives are linked to higher tax collections on the one hand and change in the type of expenditure on the other. Thus, the Commission has given directions for expenditure reforms. This is an important element in the approach to fiscal road map for the future. The expenditure reforms include improved supply of public goods, which includes reduction of existing integrated and regressive subsidies and also improving the productivity of expenditure. Thus, the FC-XIII has assumed the role of facilitator in the sphere of fiscal reforms at the State level.

II. Approach towards Grants-in-aid

In the words of the Commission, "grants have been designed with a view to "incentivising" improvements in accountability of transparency in and innovation at the cutting edge of the public goods delivery process" (para 3.26). This is altogether a new way on focusing on outcome, instead of aiming at the utilization of grants without any reference to outcome, as has been the practice uptil now with the previous Commissions. Though this will result in effective and proper utilization of grants-in-aid, yet the States will have to gear their machinery to implement the targets in a time bound manner.

Keeping in mind environmental sustainability and environmental resources available to poor and vulnerable groups, the Commission has tried to incentivise fiscal policies that promote measures for energy conservation, renewable energy, soil conservation, aforestration and affordable access to safe drinking water. This is indeed altogether a new approach, which this Commission has adopted keeping in view the "Consideration" given to the Commission in para 6(viii) of the notification.

There is thus a fundamental change in the approach of the FC-XIII regarding principles as well as types of grants-in-aid. The grants have been designed in a "forward looking" manner and to areas beyond the FRBML. Secondly, grants have a conditionality element but in the words of FC-XIII, care has been taken that these conditions do not affect decision-making by the State Government and Local Bodies. "Mere utilization" of grant is not good enough, hence, this has been linked to some measurable output targets. Three objectives have been cited in this regard (i) to ensure additionality of resources i.e. the grant will not substitute, what the State Government was doing from its own resources, but will do some additional public good with this fund (ii) Grants will help improve transparency and accountability, thus enabling a feed back-route in improving public policy formulation and implementation and (iii) the conditions will help in better monitoring of expenditure. Thus, these are performance based grants and will require the States and ULBs to adopt and undertake green policy actions (para 3.52). All these incentives are built in the grants given for renewable energy, water and solid management and potable drinking water and public health, aiming at reduction of infant mortality rates as well as targeting the judicial reforms at the State and the district level.

Target oriented grants as designed by the FC-XIII are a welcome step, though most of the States had pleaded for unconditional grants. The basic reason put forward by the States that as these grants are given to those States, which are "in need of assistance", hence, the grants should be untied and the States should be given freedom to appply the funds, as per their needs. Secondly, the States have also pleaded that the conditional grants reduce the autonomy of the States. But FC-XIII had different argument to offer. FC-XIII has observed that the level of utilization of XII-FC grant even without conditions, specially in case of education, health and maintenance of buildings fell short of targets and many a State did not utilise the part of grants released; hence, they could not get the remaining part of the grant. In case of grant given for education and health sector on the non-plan side, the amount was mostly spent on salary and other items, which was, otherwise, being borne by the States from their own resources. The utilization level of FC-

XII grants as shown by FC-XIII clearly indicates that the level of utilization was not hundred percent. So the grant did not help in the objective of better quality education and health facilities. Thus, in the light of these observations steps initiated by FC-XIII will help in the direction of improved governance and effectiveness of public institutions.

It is further to be seen that non-plan revenue deficit (NPRD) grants component has drastically come down in quantum as well as in number, as has been observed by FC-XIII while assessing the revenues and expenditures of the States. At least, this is a welcome signal as most of the States will be in surplus after taking into account the share in central taxes and this revenue surplus will help States in reducing GFD to a desired level.

In case of grants relating to ULBs & PRIs, four issues have been taken up for consideration by FC-XIII viz. issues related to devolution, issues relating to preparation of accounts & audit, issues relating to functioning of SFCs and other issues. These grants have also been linked to performance and totally nine conditions have been cited by the Commission. Some of the conditions infringes on the legislative powers of the States, which may be objected to by the States. However, the States were given one year (2010-11) to prepare the ground for the release of grants from 2011-12 onwards.

III. Design of Fiscal Transfers

The design of fiscal transfer as recommended by FC-XIII centres around four principles (i) symmetry between the Centre and the States, meaning thereby, a normative discipline has been applied both for the Centre and the State, (ii) equal treatment, meaning thereby, no priority has been accorded to any level of govt. and equalization and not equity is the main concern (iii) there is predictability and certainty in resource flows and finally (iv) incentives have been built into devolution formula and in the release of grants.

In case of **vertical transfers**, the non correspondence between the sources of revenue between the Centre and the States, and their expenditure responsibilities as given in the Constitution has been cited as the main reason for the transfer from the Centre to the States. Other arguments given in para 3.36 of the report are (i) equalisation of the fiscal capacities of the States (ii) to achieve national standards in social programmes and to induce efficiency in internal economic union and finally, as instruments for insuring regions against shocks to their fiscal capacities (para 3.36). Like FC-XII, the FC-XIII has increased the divisible pool marginally.

The **horizontal distribution** centres around four issues (i) fiscal need (ii) fiscal capacity (iii) cost of providing similar levels of public goods and services (iv) efficiency in pubic management, fiscal effort and outcomes. The Commission has not attempted explicitly to assign specific criteria as measures of fiscal capacity or needs. The Commission has given weightage to efficiency and performance in its overall design of transfer. In order to arrive at the weightage, the FC-XIII has applied group specific averages to conform to the criteria adopted.

IV. Approach towards Assessment of Revenue and Expenditure

As per FC-XIII, it has adopted a "normative approach" in the assessment of revenues as well as expenditure of centre and States. However, the overall resource availability has been taken into account. One of the objectives, which the Commission has taken into consideration, is that there are no widespread variations in the transfers to the States from the shares recommended by the earlier Commissions. As per FC-XIII, there is a marked tendency towards stability in the relative share of the Centre in respect of aggregate transfers (para 3.30).

The Commission deals, at the length, with the questions relating to the food and fertilizer subsidies and the regressive incidence of these subsidies largely on account of leakages and highly imperfect targeting system. In the fiscal road map, these subsidies have been clearly targeted and the Commission has sought to discourage public spending on subsidies.

So far as the approach regarding assessment of revenues and expenditure of the Centre and States is concerned, the Commission has adopted the following approach:

1. Assumption for GSDP Growth Rate

(i) The constant growth rate has not been taken for the award period but a calibrated approach has been adopted. The nominal growth rate of 12.5% for 2010-11, 13% for 2011-12, 13.5% for 2012-13, 2013-14 and 2014-15 has been assumed by the FC-XIII.

(ii) As a first step, the Commission has normatively assessed the base year figures of 2009-10 and then projected on this base year figure for the award period (2010-15).

2. Norms for Central Receipt and Expenditure

Having said this, the Commission has adopted the BE figures of 2009-10 tax and non-tax revenue as base year figures, but in case of expenditures, some modifications have been done. On this basis, the following norms have been applied on central finances.

(a) A buoyancy of 1.33 has been taken for tax revenue, resulting in Tax GDP ratio as 11.35, 11.78, 12.24, 12.72 and 13.22 for the award period.

(b) Under non-tax revenue separate norms for each item have been followed:
   (i) Interest receipts to go down by 2%.
   (ii) Profits from PSUs/Banks to grow at the same rate as in the.
   (iii) Economic services to grow @18% per annum.
   (iv) NTR to grow from 2.01% in 2010-11 to 2.24% in 2014-15.

(c) For Non-Plan revenue Expenditure
- Interest payments would range between 35.21% and 39.99% during the award period taking average interest rate at 7.35%.
- Food subsidy to grow at 8.87% per annum.
- Contain the fertilizer subsidy, other subsidies to be reduced also.
- Pension to grow at 9% per annum.
- Expenditure on other general and economic services to grow at 5% per annum.
- Non-Plan grants and loans to PSUs to remain constant.
- In the aggregate, the NPRE as proportion of GDP to decrease from 10.06% in 2010-11 to 7.73% in 2014-15.

(d) Non debt capital receipts will increase equi-proportionately from 0.5% of GDP in 2010-11 to 1% of GDP in 2014-15.

(e) Total capital expenditure is projected at 3, 3.13, 3.75, 3.88 and 4.50% of GDP during each year of the award period.

3. Norms for States' Revenues and Expenditure

In case of the States also the FC-XIII has, normatively, fixed the GSDP for the base year 2009-10 and then normatively fixed the incremental growth rate.

The GSDP projections methodology has been described in para 7.9 to 7.15. In assuming the GSDP growth rate, the Commission has assumed that the ratio of aggregate GSDP to GDP is held constant at the level used for estimation of base year GSDP. The incremental growth has been distributed across the States, in such a way, that the ratio of year on year improvement for each State to the total improvement to be achieved during the award period is same for all the States.

(i) Own Tax Revenue

In case of Own Tax Revenue, the Commission has calculated the buoyancy over 2001-08 and with GSDP growth, derived the tax growth rate for 2008-09 and 2009-10 on the actuals of 2007-08. This figure has been compared with the BE of 2009-10 and higher of the two has been taken as base figure.

Two different projections have been suggested, one for the general category States and another for special category States. Further, the general category States have been divided, further, into three groups. The FC-XIII has calculated the mean tax-GSDP ratio and Standard Deviation. The mean is 8.6% and Standard Deviation is 1.7 in the base year. Depending on the respective tax: GSDP ratio, each State has been given an improvement path over five year period (para 7.25)

Where the Tax: GSDP ratio is more than one standard deviation below mean have been projected to reach one standard deviation below mean level by the end of projection period. The States with Tax: GSDP ratio less than one standard deviation below mean, which includes U.P. also have been projected to reach the mean level by the end of the projected period. For rest of the States, the Tax-GSDP ratio has been projected to remain at their base year level. In this way, the Tax: GSDP ratio to improve to 8.9% and standard deviation will reduce to 1.4%.

(ii) Non-Tax Revenue

In case of non-tax revenue, trend based growth has been taken except in cases, which do not follow general trend. Because of the accounting procedure differences across the States, receipts from power, transport and dairy have been excluded.

- Interest receipts have been calculated on the normative basis. The outstanding loans and advances at the end of 2009-10 have been projected as constant over the period and a 7% rate of interest has been taken and receipts taken accordingly.
- Dividents have been projected at the rate of 5% on the total amount of investment at the end of 2007-08 including those in power utilities.
- Election receipts have been taken at a five year interval, assuming a 5% growth for five years over the receipts of 2005-06.
- Receipts from other miscellaneous general services, a growth rate of 5% has been assumed.
- In case of lottery, major minerals and power, these have been taken based on the indicators given by GoI and respective States.
- Receipts on irrigation have been taken on cost recovery basis, current level of recovery is 23% of the NPRE on irrigation. A normative approach has been taken and 25% in 2010-11, 35% in 2011-12, 45% in 2012-13, 60% in 2013-14 and 75% in 2014-15 have taken in the receipts.

- In case of residual items under general, social and economic services, higher of the TGR of 2001-08 and BE 2009-10 has been taken. Rest to grow at 8%, 12% and 13% during the award period.

(iii) Non-Plan Revenue Expenditure

In case of Non-Plan Revenue Expenditure, the following norms have been applied to arrive at the base year figure and then for the award period (2010-2015).

- Expenditure on Power, Transport and dairy have been excluded like in case of receipts. Non subsidy has been taken in this section.
- Expenditure on Calamity Relief has been taken out as this is treated separately.
- Contra entries have been removed from the expenditure side.
- Some of the grants have been excluded from the expenditure side, as these have not been projected on the receipt side.
- In case of salary, the FC-XIII has followed the norm of FC-XII that the salary expenditure should not increase beyond 35% of revenue expenditure net of interest payment and pensions. To bring the salary expenditure to this level, the expenditure has to be reduced by 10% of the amount every year.
- Pension payment for the base year has been estimated at 21% over 2008-09 arrived at by applying TGR over actuals of 2007-08; pension payments over base year are expected to grown at 10%.
- Arrears have not been taken into account because of the difficulty in assessing the liabilities of the States..
- After assessing the debt stock, at 7.5% interest rate, the interest payment has been calculated for each State.

- The same procedure has been followed for election expenditure as was followed for election receipt.
- Assignment to ULBs/PRIs has been assumed as per the base year BE with 8% increase per year.
- Thirty percent of plan expenditure on 2011-12 has been assumed as committed liability for 2012-13 and 5% growth has been assumed for 2013-14 and 2014-15.
- ₹ 1175.00 crore for utilized and ₹ 588.00 crore for unutilized potential maintenance cost has been assumed in the base year and an annual growth of 5% has been assumed, which will ultimately reach to ₹ 1500.00 crore and ₹ 750.00 crore respectively.
- Similar procedure has been adopted for minor irrigation works.
- For Roads and Bridges, expenditure in 2007-08 has been projected to grow at TGR to arrive at 2009-10 and then 5% growth has been assumed.

Based on the above, the revenues and expenditure of each State have been assessed and predevolution non-plan deficit has been assumed. After assessing the revenues and expenditures of the States, the FC-XIII has suggested structural reforms at the State level, which include PSU, Power Sector, data base, new pension scheme, cash management, Accounts system.

III
Recommendations of the Commission

The FC-XIII has prepared a transfer scheme, which includes determination of divisible pool, inter se distribution and the principles determining the grants-in-aid, the conditionalties and shares of States in grants-in-aid and also a road map for fiscal correction. In the process, it has suggested amendment to FRL and broad based MTFP frame work for the Centre as well as the States.

I. Vertical Transfer

In order to determine the vertical transfer, the FC-XIII has taken into account the following facts:

(a) Vertical devolution should be informed by the revenue raising capacity of the Centre as well as the States and also the emerging pressures on their expenditure commitments.

(b) The shares of surcharges and cesses in gross tax revenue of the Centre has increased sharply from 9.51% in 2001-02 to 13.63% in 2009-10, resulting in considerable reduction in divisible pool as percentage of gross tax revenue receipts of centre.

(c) There has been significant increase in non-tax revenues of the Centre.

(d) The sharp increase in CSS outlays requires greater contribution from the States.

(e) Because of various Central Acts like RTE, and a new Natural Food Security Act coming into being, the expenditure commitments of the States will increase.

(f) The buoyancy of central taxes has been higher than the State taxes.

Keeping the above factors into account, the Commission has gone ahead with the determination of divisible pool.

A. Divisible Pool

The FC-XIII has recommended a higher share (32%) than the share (30.5%) as recommended by FC-XII. The

Commission has not earmarked any portion for additional excise duty, in lieu of Sales Tax on textiles, tobacco and sugar, and has also not recommended any reduction in the share of the States in the event of levy of VAT on Textiles, Tobacco and Sugar by the States.

B. Overall Ceiling

The FC-XIII has indicated 39.5% of the Centre's gross revenue receipts as a ceiling of all central transfers as percentage of gross revenue receipts against the ceiling of 38% recommended by FC-XII.

C. Horizontal/Vertical Transfer

After deciding the overall ceiling and the divisible pool for vertical transfer, the Commission has approached the issues relating to horizontal transfer. Like earlier FCs, the FC-XIII has also relied on the broadly accepted principles of equity and efficiency.

The Commission did not find feasible to adopt forward-looking indicators for tax devolution involving yearly updating of inter se shares and fixed percentage share has been determined by the Commission for the entire award period. While assuming the formula for vertical transfer, the FC-XIII kept in mind the stability in the relative shares of the States. Keeping all these factors in background, the Commission has, further, decided to have stability in the relative shares of the States. The Commission has said that the share will be constant "only if" their share in central taxes exceeds the buoyancy of combined tax revenue.

D. Formula for Inter se distribution

The Commission has retained the "Population and the Area Criteria" as well as the weightage assigned to them by the

FC-XII. Though the Commission has retained the "fiscal discipline" as the criteria yet has raised its weightage from 7.5% in FC-XII to 17.5%. A new criterion it "Fiscal Capacity Distance" has been introduced and highest weightage of 47.5% has been assigned to it. The formula as recommended by FC-XIII is given in Table 13.1 below.

TABLE 13.1
Formula for Inter se Transfers

Criteria	*Weightage (%ge)*
1. Population (1970)	25.0
2. Area	10.0
3. Fiscal Capacity Index	47.5
4. Fiscal Discipline	17.5

The Commission has not included the criteria of income distance and tax effort. The Commission has used separate averages for general category States and for special category States.

In deciding the shares of States, a three years' average per capita GSDP of each of the States for years 2004-05 to 2006-07 and average tax to GSDP ratio was obtained as a weighted mean separately for general and special category States. Group specific revenues averages are applied to the States. In this way, per capita fiscal capacity was observed.

Fiscal distance was obtained from Haryana, the second highest in per capita ranking. These per capita entitlements are multiplied by respective population figures of 1971. The criteria of fiscal discipline and tax effort have been combined and a weightage of 17.5% has been given to it.

Using the above formula, the shares of each of the States have been worked out. The Commission at the end (para 8.41) has emphasized that relative to FC-XII, there is an increase in the ratio of devolution to GSDP as projected by the Commission for each State and every State taken individually gains in terms of devolution relative to its GSDP.

E. Revised Road Map

The Commission has recommended a revised road map for the award period (2010-15). It has said that a target based FRBM framework needs to be maintained for the award period. The Commission has fixed different targets for the Centre as well as for different the States. The targets for the Central Government include:

(a) All items of consumption expenditure which need to be financed from current receipts.
(b) A feasible level of outstanding liabilities of the Centre at 45% of GDP by 2014-15.
(c) Revenue deficit to decline from 4.8% in 2009-10 to zero in 2013-14 and remain so thereafter.
(d) Guarantees ceiling is fixed at 5% of GDP for the stock of guarantees at the end of every year.
(e) A detailed Medium Term Fiscal Plan (MTFP) should be prepared with a three year forward estimates of revenues & expenditure.
(f) A detailed economic and functional classification of expenditure budget be prepared as part of MTFP.
(g) All the Central transfers to the States be set out in an independent statement.
(h) Compliance cost of major tax proposals in the MTFP from 2013-14 budget.
(i) Budget should accompany a statement of the Revenue Consequences of Capital (ROC) expenditure for the lifetime of the proposed project. This should be modified annually to take into account price changes in price inflation etc. and other charges.
(j) New policy initiatives that are known to involve

future expenditure commitments should be reflected in the MTFP. The MTFP should provide the projections for transfer to the State. This should be done from 2013-14.

(k) The MTFP should contain detailed information regarding PPP projects.

(l) Inventory of vacant lands and buildings to be prepared based on market value.

(m) Because of the reversal of the path of the economy on account of economic slow down, the FC-XIII felt the need to allow the fiscal system to adopt to exogenous stocks and/or changes in exogenous parameter values. Against these backgrounds, FC-XIII has recommended changes in the design of existing FRBM legislation.

(i) MTFP should make explicit the values of the parameters underlying expenditure and revenue projections and the band within which these parameters can vary while remaining consistent with FRBMA targets.

(ii) Act should specify the nature of shocks that require a relaxation of shocks.

(iii) Macro-Economic stabilization and counter recessionary actions are the primary responsibility of the Central Government. Assuming the responsibility of ARM the money to be distributed to the States as per FC formula.

(iv) In case of future Pay Commission, the FC-XIII has recommended that the recommendation of CPC should be made effective from future date.

(v) The Independent review and monitoring mechanism for FRBM Act should be put in place.

(vi) Finally, a full fledged fiscal Council should be

set up—which should act as an autonomous body reporting the MOF, which should report to Parliament.

The 13th Finance Commission has recomended the setting up of an *autonomous body* christened as "Fiscal Council". There is incongruity in the recommendation in the sense that an autonomous body should not be expected to report to the Ministry of Finance; the correct nomenclature of this new autonomous body may be considered as "Fiscal Correction and Budget Management Commission" and it should be allowed to report to the Parliament direct.

Road Map for State Finances

(n) Commission has suggested a separate roadmap for state finances with the following features.

(i) Debt: GSDP ratio at 25% by 2014-15.
(ii) Zero revenue deficit throughout but by 2011-12 must.
(iii) GFD of U.P. should be able to come to 3% of the GSDP by 2011-12 and maintained thereafter.
(iv) Amending the Act accordingly. It should be conditionality for release of all State specific grants and debt relief.
(v) Structure of MTFP should change on the lines recommended for GOI.
(vi) Independent / Review mechanism should be put in place.
(vii) States should attempt to incorporate statements on RCCE, PPP and related liabilities.
(viii) The Central Govt. should set net borrowing ceiling for the States based on the fiscal system path.

Road Map for PSU and Power Sector Reforms

The Commission has suggested a separate road map for power sector reforms so that its impact on overall State Finances is minimal. Similarly, it has proposed a time-bound action plan for liquidating the loss making PSUs and bringing on track other PSUs which are not loss making. But these corrective measures are, in no way, linked to any grant-in-aid. Thus, it depends on the States to follow or not the road map suggested for PSUs and Power Sector utilities.

Debt Relief

(o) Debt Relief has been recommended as below:

(i) DCRF of FC-XII will continue for those States, which could not avail of this facility. The relief will be confined to interest relief only.

(ii) NSSF Loans contracted till 2006-07 and outstanding at the end of 2009-10 be reset at a common interest rate of 9%. The facility is subject to enactment of FRBM legislation.

(iii) Loans given under CSS/CS outstanding on 2009-10 be written off subject to FRBM legislation.

ULB and PRI Grants

The Grants to the Urban Local Bodies and the PRIs will be allotted on the basis of following formula:

(p) After discussing various issues concerning ULBs and PRIs, the FC-XIII has made the following recommendations:

(i) For the first time, FC-XIII has recommended a certain percent of divisible pool. The volume of divisible pool for the previous year be used as a basis for computing the grant eligibility of local bodies for a particular year. Yearly breakup has been given in **Table 13.2**

(ii) The grants will have two components viz. basic component and performance based component.

(iii) All States will have access to basic component and the performance grant will be subject to conditions as per para 10.161.

(iv) Special area grants are also recommended subject to para 10.162.

(vi) Both the component have been divided into Urban and Rural shares.

(vii) FC-XIII has suggested the criteria and weightage for grants to Local Bodies, which is given in para 10.158. The State-wise break-up has been given in Annexure 10.15(a), 15(b), 15(c) and 15(d).

(viii) The FC-XIII has also suggested incentive framework for general performance grants.

(1) grants in 2 installments per year subject to submission of UC.

(2) For years 2011-12 to 2014-15 the State Govt. will be eligible to draw its share subject to compliance with 9 conditions stipulated in para 10.161

(a) put in place a supplement to budget furnishing details given in para 10.110, maintain accounts as specified in para 10.111 & 10.112; Urban Bodies to maintain accounts as per para 10.116.

(b) put in place an audit system;

TABLE 13.2
Recommended Grants for Local Bodies

(' Crore)

Item	*2009-10*	*2010-11*	*2011-12*	*2012-13*	*2013-14*	*2014-15*	*2010-15*
Percentage of the previous years' divisible pool to be given to all the states as grant under Article 275 of the Constitution–General Basic Grant and Total Special Areas Grant		1.50%	1.50%	1.50%	1.50%	1.50%	1.50%
General Performance Grant			0.50%	1.00%	1.00%	1.00%	0.78%
Aggregate Grant to Local Bodies		**1.50%**	**2.00%**	**2.50%**	**2.50%**	**2.50%**	**2.28%**
Projected Divisible Pool 2009-14 (Rs. Crore)	**545463**	**636183**	**746179**	**880156**	**1038188**	**1224595**	**3846169**
General Basic Grant and Total Special Area Grant		8182	9543	11193	13202	15573	57693
General Basic Grant		8022	9303	10873	12883	15253	56335
General Performance Grant		0	3182	7462	8802	10382	20826
General Basic Grant & General Performance Grant		**8022**	**12484**	**18335**	**21685**	**25636**	**86161**
Total Special Areas Grant		**160**	**239**	**319**	**319**	**319**	**1357**
Special Area Basic grant		160	160	160	160	160	798
Special Areas Performance Grant		0	80	160	160	160	559
Aggregate Grants to Local Bodies		**8182**	**12724**	**18654**	**22004**	**25955**	**87519**

TABLE 13.3
Weightage Allotted to Criterion for Grants to Local Bodies

Criterion	*Weightage Allotted (%)*	
	PRIs	*ULBs*
Population	50	50
Area	10	10
Distance from the highest per capita sectoral income	10	20
Index of devolution	15	15
SC/STs proportion in the total population	10	—
FC local body grants utilisation index	5	5
Total :	**100**	**100**

(c) Independent Local Body Ombudsman;
(d) System of electronically transferable of grants within 5 days of their receipt from GoI;
(e) the State must prescribe through Act the qualification of persons eligible for appointment as members of SFC;
(f) fully enabled to levy property taxes;
(g) put in place of a Property Tax Board;
(h) put in place standards for delivery of all essential services provided by local bodies; and
(i) all municipal corporations must put in place a five hazard response and mitigation plan.

(3) Incentive frame work for Special Area Programme grant consists of four conditions, which have been proposed to be fulfilled before those grants are drawn.

The Commission has also recommended that other developmental authorities must share a certain percentage of their income with Local Bodies. Further, the development plans should be brought into the District Planning Committee.

Editorial Comments

This suggestion if implemented, will result in weakning the State's powers to augment its own total revenue resources and, hence, it has to be reviewed by the NDC.

The Commission has also suggested other measures to strengthen the Local Bodies like payment of service charges and sharing of mining royalties etc.

Disaster Management

(q) With the introduction of Disaster Management Act 2005, the earlier scheme of Calamity Relief has undergone a fundamental change. The Commission has made the following recommendations:

  (i) CRF merged with SDRF and NCCF with NDRF.
  (ii) Performance incentive grants—only to three States.
  (iii) Contribution of the Centre and the States by 75 : 25.
  (iv) Balance as on 31.03.2010 transferred to respective funds.
  (v) Total size of SDRF to be ₹ 33581 crore and an additional grant of ₹ 525 crore for capacity building.
  (vi) Mitigation and construction activities to be kept out of scheme.
  (vi) List of disasters covered under the Act to

remain the same.

(vii) Prescribed norms to be adhered.

Grants, Incentives and Outcome

(r) The Commission has recommended various types of grants aggregating to ₹ 3,18,581 crore, which is 18.03% of the total transfer. Various types of grants have been recommended by the Commission are as follows:

(i) Non-Plan Revenue Deficit Grant (NPRD)—only eight States have been recommended for this grant.

(ii) Performance related grants only—there States have been given.

(iii) Grant for elementary education.

(iv) Grant for quality of public expenditure.

(v) For management of ecology and environment.

(vi) For maintenance of roads.

F.C. has stipulated the conditions for release of grants on attainment of certain bench mark targets.

Grants for elementary education has been given to eight States only viz. Assam, Bihar, Jharkhand, Madhya Pradesh, Orissa, Rajasthan, Uttar Pradesh and West Bengal. It is stipulated that the expenditure (plan + non-plan) under elementary education (major head 2202, sub-major head 01, exclusive of grants recommended therein should grow at least by 8% per annum.

The first of the environment related grants is in relation to density of area under forest cover for calibrating the incentive grant. Incentive is reward for the maintenance of present stock. The only conditionality is that States develop working plans for each of the zones within a period of three years. The grant will be based on detailed action plans.

The second grant is the forward looking incentive for generation of grid electricity from renewable energy. The reward will be given in the fiscal year 2014-15 when the capacity comes into production in four years.

The third grant under Environment is for the purpose of incentivising the States to establish an independent regulatory mechanism for the water sector and improved maintenance for irrigation network. The grant is subject to setting up of Independent Water Regulatory Authority by 2011-12. Further, it is conditional to achieving the recovery rates of irrigation as stipulated in para 12.58(ii).

Grants for improving outcomes are subject to the following conditions. Before setting the conditions, the FC-XIII had identified three issues (i) how to ensure that intended expenditure reaches the target group? (ii) how to ensure that expenditure contains the right mix of inputs? and (iii) how to ensure that the service provider has the required capacity? and is fully incentivised to provide the service at the desired standard.

For this purpose, the FC-XIII has identified three areas (i) putting in place an incentive framework to target public expenditure (ii) promote innovation to improve outcomes in public policy and district governance and (iii) improving transparency in Govt. accounts to better reflect and measure output and outcome.

Keeping the above in mind, the Commission has proposed UID (Unique Identification Data) grant to the States with conditions stipulated in para 12.71. After first year's grant, subsequent grants will be on reimbursement basis.

Second is incentive for reducing infant mortality. The result of sample registration system will form the essential basis. The grant will cover a period of 2012-15. This will give States a period of 2 years to make improvement. The method of determination of improvement is given in para 12.94.

Another is for improving justice delivery. For the first time, the FC-XIII has thought about the reforms in judiciary and has recommended a total grant of ₹ 5000 crore. This is related to courts working in shifts, establishing ADR centrs, Lok Adalats, Legal Aid, training of Judicial Officers, State Judicial Academies, training of public prosecutors and creation of posts of court managers, maintenance of heritage court buildings. The condition precedent to that is the State puts a State Litigation Policy before the end of fiscal year.

Grants for Police training and promoting innovations have been provided.

For improving transparency in Govt. Accounting & establishing a data base for Govt. employees and pensioners, grants have been given, but with a condition attached to it.

Finally, the FC-XIII has recommended State specific grants, keeping in view, the following issues in mind. Para 12.116 narrates the priority given by FC-XIII, while recommending State specific grants. On this basis, we find that priority should be accorded to State-specific grants to address the following issues:

(i) The specific needs of marginal areas and marginal groups within States.

(ii) Provision of infrastructure to alleviate some of the problems faced by the local population in blocks and tehsils along the international borders.

(iii) Protection of historical monuments, archaeological sites and heritage buildings, which are not with the Archaeological Survey of India (ASI).

(iv) Provision of safe drinking water, especially in regions afflicted with arsenic, salinity and fluoride related problems.

(v) Gaps in critical infrastructure for health, including

care for children.

(vi) Setting up and strengthening of skill building institutions to help provide employable skills.

A total of ₹ 27945 crore has been recommended for State specific issues and the State of U.P. has been given grants worth ₹ 1679 crore under the category, which includes grants for Border Roads, Varanasi City, Bundelkhand area, Police, Heritage Conservation and for upgradation of Civil Service Training facilities.

Model GST

The FC-XIII has suggested a model GST. In its ATR, the GoI has accepted these recommendations in principle. But, it has observed that in view of the on going discussions between the Centre and the States through the empowered committee of Finance Ministers, implementation of these recommendations regarding GST alongwith modalities may await the outcome of the discussions. Because of these reasons, this recommendation has not been discussed in this chapter.

IV
Implication of Recommendation

This section deals with the implications of approach and recommendations on the State Finances with particular reference to Uttar Pradesh.

I. Implications of Approach

Having discussed the general approach and the approach adopted by FC-XIII on different issues as well as the normative approach adopted for assessment of revenues and expenditures of the Centre as well as the States, it is now proposed, in this sub section, to discuss the implications of the general and normative approach with regard to revenues and expenditures of the State of U.P. and also on other issues for assessing the impact on State finances, the conventional approach adopted by the State for projecting the revenues and expenditure and the normative method adopted by FC-XIII has been discussed in detail. The comparative picture is presented in **Annexure 13.2** for revenues. **Annexure 13.3** presents the comparative position on the expenditure side.

But before this analysis is done, it is worth mentioning that the FC-X, FC-XI and FC-XII also adopted some norms for assessment of revenues and expenditures of the States. **Table 13.4** presents a comparative picture for FC-X, FC-XI and FC-XII award period.

The **Table** gives an interesting reading. The estimates of Finance Commission, State and finally the actuals do not correspond with each other. The variations between the Finance Commission's and State's forecasts can be explained, because different norms were adopted by them in forecasting. But the States forecast and the actuals also do not tally with each other and the variations are quite large, which cannot be explained without going into itemwise analyais.

There is another aspect to this situation, if we look to actuals for FC-X, FC-XI and FC-XII and adding the actual share in Central taxes, one still finds a gap between the revenues and the NPRE, making the State of U.P. eligible for Non-plan gap grant. Thus, the State of U.P. lost the sizable amount of grant during these years based on the forecast as well as actuals.

So far as the FC-XIII is concerned, a summary statement is presented in **Table 13.5.**

TABLE 13.4

Comparative position of the Forecasts made by FC and State of Uttar Pradesh

(₹ in crore)

Period	Revenue Receipt			Non-Plan Revenue Expenditure		
	Projected by State	*Reassessed by FC*	*Actual **	*Projected by State*	*Reassessed by*	*Actual **
FC-X (1995-2000)	36,663	42,986	45,421	1,13,019	74,512	97,046
FC-XI (2000-2005)	71,543	92,500	75,728	2,06,254	1,53,279	1,71,076
FC-XII (2005-2010)	1,29,099	1,48,887	1,67,980	2,31,595	2,06,115	2,75,631

* *The figures of 2009-10 are Revised Estimates*

TABLE 13.5
Comparative Position of assessment by FC-XIII and Uttar Pradesh

(' in Crore)

Item	*2010-11*	*2011-12*	*2012-13*	*2013-14*	*2014-15*	*2015-16*
State Own Revenue Receipt	43682 *(44903)*	50315 *(50295)*	58024 *(56552)*	66986 *(63700)*	77410 *(71734)*	296417 ***(287184)***
Non-Plan Revenue Expenditure	83680 *(59806)*	86717 *(64421)*	99266 *(76310)*	109397 *(82043)*	120685 *(88219)*	499745 ***(370799)***
Non-Plan Revenue Deficit (+)/ Surplus (-)	39998 *(14903)*	36402 *(14126)*	41242 *(19758)*	42411 *(18343)*	43275 *(16485)*	203328 ***(83616)***

Figures in parenthesis are assessed by FC-XIII.

Insofar as the assessment of revenue is concerned, the following trend emerges:

(1) There are variations in GSDP figures, hence the buoyancy and the Tax: GSDP ratio will change and, therefore, the OTR figures. All the five year estimates of the State are higher than the FC assessment. The State had taken a trend growth rate of individual taxes as the basis of forecast, the FC has calculated the tax estimates on the basis of tax-GSDP ratio.

(2) But the major variation has been in case of non-tax revenue. In this case, the FC-XIII has normatively fixed the receipts from interest, dividend and profit. The normative rates have no relationship with the past actuals. These have been normatively kept at a higher level, which are not likely to occur. Another major area of variation is in the irrigation sector. The receipt has been linked

to NPRE and has fixed recovery as 25% of NPRE in 2010-11, 35% in 2011-12, 45% in 2012-13 and 75% of NPRE in 2014-15. The irrigation rates have not been revised in the State since 1994 and the receipt is very low as per cent of NPRE. Thus, on all the three counts viz. interest, dividend and profit, and irrigation receipts are on a very high side and which are not likely to be achieved. The receipt on royalty, power, forestry have been excluded. The exclusion of royalty, power and forestry should not have been done in case of U.P., because the royalty is only on minor minerals as there are no major minerals. The forestry royalty should also not have been excluded. Because of these reasons, over a five year period, the State's forecasts are higher by ₹ 31205 crore.

(4) Similarly, different growth rates have been assumed by the FC-XIII for economic and social services.

But the variations in the expenditure are much more pronounced.

(i) In the salary and pension, the main reason for variation is that FC-XIII has excluded the arrear part, which falls in 2010-11. If arrear part is added, then the variation is marginal.

(ii) In case of general services, the variations are marginal excluding Interest and Pension.

(iii) But, there are sharp variations in case of Economic and Social services. Regarding these variations the report only says that, apart from specific items, the other NPRE under each service has been projected at the respective 2001-08 TGR or 7.5%, whichever is higher, to reach the base year level and then 8% growth has been taken. But, this does not fully explain the variation.

It can only be said that the normative approach is all right, but looking against the past actuals, it will be a difficult task to achieve these norms and fixed estimates of revenues and expenditure and in the final analysis, the same situations will emerge at the end of the award period as in case of FC-XI and FC-XII period.

II. Implication of Recommendation

(1) *Overall Ceiling on Transfer to States*

The ceiling of overall transfers from revenue account to the States has been set at 39.5% of gross revenue receipt of the centre against 38% recommended by FC-XIII. Thus, there is only 1.5% increase. The Commission has observed the increasing trend in the overall transfers on revenue account. It has been further observed that the transfers on revenue account had been above 39% of the revenue receipts of the Centre in the 2008-09(RE) and 2009-10(BE). But the actual story is different, as and when, the actuals are received, because it is a common experience that there are wide variations in the BE, RE and actuals. However, a true picture of total transfers from the Centre has been presented in **Table 13.6.**

Table 13.6 shows the Finance Commission transfers, Planning Commission transfers and ministries transfers as well as total transfers against gross revenue receipts of the GOI. The highest transfers came during the award period of FC-IX, when total transfers were 40.33% of centre's gross tax revenue. During the tenth and eleventh FC period, this percentage was around 35%. Though, the ceiling was 38% during FC-XII period, but in three years for which actuals were received, the percentage did not touch the desired limit of 38%. Though 2008-09(RE) and 2009-10(BE), the share is shown at 39.57% and 39.35%, it is likely to change,

TABLE 13.6
Total Transfers and FC Transfers to State.

(per cent)

Year	*Finance Commission Transfers*			*Other Transfers*		*Total*	
	Share in Central Taxes	*Grants*	*Total Transfers through*	*Grants through Planning FC (2+3)*	*Non-Plan Grants (Non-Commission*	*Total Transers (5+6) statutory)*	*Transfers (4+7)*
FC-VII	22.39	1.96	24.35	12.11	1.66	13.77	38.11
FC-VIII	20.25	2.52	22.77	13.56	1.54	15.10	37.87
FC-IX	21.37	3.42	24.79	14.48	1.06	15.54	40.33
FC-X	22.22	2.34	24.56	10.57	0.67	11.24	35.79
FC-XI	20.59	3.88	24.47	10.10	0.70	10.80	35.27
FC-XII	21.75	4.45	26.20	10.99	1.32	12.31	38.51
2005-06	21.71	5.69	27.41	9.66	1.03	10.69	38.08
2006-07	21.77	5.11	27.08	9.69	1.16	10.85	37.21
2007-08	21.88	3.80	25.68	10.32	1.22	11.53	37.21

when the actuals come.

(2) *Divisible Pool*

The FC-XIII has raised the divisible pool from 30.5% in FC-XII period to 32% for FC-XIII award period. In this context, the FC-XIII has considered the increase in divisible pool on account of increasing expenditure responsibilities of States as well as higher buoyancy of central taxes in comparison to State taxes. The Commission has also observed that there has been a long term stability in the relative shares of the centre and States in the combined revenue receipts and in the combined revenue expenditure. FC has tried to maintain the stability in relative shares, hence raised the divisible pool to 32%. The joint memorandum, submitted by the States through the august offices of Empowered Committee of State Finance Ministers, had requested that the divisible pool be raised to 50%, The reason behind this demand was the higher expenditure responsibility with less buoyant resources. Because of the more and more centrally sponsored schemes (CSS) on the States subjects, the States have to bear the burden, some times, to the extent 50% or more leaving less elbow room for their own priorities. But, this was not accepted and majority of the States were disappointed on this account.

(3) *Share in Central Taxes (SCT) and Grant Ratio*

The Finance Commission has changed the ratio of SCT and grant. Leaving aside the grant portion of GST, because this has yet to be accepted, the ratio comes to 91 : 9 as will be evident from **Table 13.7**.

As will be evident from the **Table 13.7** the SCT and grant ratio, by and large, has reached to a level of FC-X, where it was 91:9. But the FC-XII had raised the ratio of grant to 19 against 81 of SCT. Most of the States had urged

TABLE 13.7

SCT and Grant Component under Various Commissions

(*₹ in Crore*)

Item	*Xth FC*	*XIth FC*	*XIIth FC*	*XIIIth FC*
Share in Central Taxes 1448096.00	206345.00376318.01613112.02			
	(91.04%)	(86.53%)	(81.13%)	(91.4%)
	(92.72%)	***(95.31%)***	***(88.57%)***	***(84.8%)***
Total Grants in Aid	20300.30	58587.39	142639.60258581.00	
	(8.96%)	(13.47%)	(18.87%)	(8.6%)
	(7.28%)	***(4.69%)***	***(11.43%)***	***(15.2%)***
Total Transfer to All States 1706676.00	**226643.30434905.40755751.62**			

Figures in Bold & Italics shows UP's figures

Source : Finance Commission reports.

the FC-XIII that the share of SCT should be raised and grants reduced. The argument advanced was that there is always a predictability and stability in the transfer of SCT, whereas the grants being conditional, their timing and quantum cannot be predicted and hence, create difficulty in managing the cash flow throughout the year. Thus, the Commission partly accepted the plea of the States, by raising the share of SCT, but instead made the grants conditional.

But, in case of U.P., the impact of this ratio is discouraging. During FC-XI period, the ratio of share & grant was 95:5 in the total transfer to U.P. But, this went down to 89:11 during FC-XII period, it has further gone down to 85 : 15 in FC-XIII award period. Thus, there is complete reversal of the ratio for U.P. State's share of grants to total transfer to State has gone up from 5% in FC-XI to 15% in FC-XIII. The grants being highly conditional and result oriented, the normal flow will be difficult unless the State gears up its efficiency level.

(4) Horizontal Sharing Formula

The FC has suggested a formula for sharing of Central taxes which is given in **Table 13.8** along with the formula suggested by FC-XI, FC-XII and FC-XIII for the sake of comparison.

TABLE 13.8
Horizontal Sharing Formula

Item	*XIth FC*	*XIIth FC*	*XIIIth FC*	*Change from XIIth FC*
Population	10.0	25.0	25.0	0.0
Income Distance	62.5	50.0	—	(–) 50.0
Area	7.5	10.0	10.0	0.0
Tax Effort	5.0	7.5	—	(–) 7.5
Fiscal Capacity Distance	—	—	47.5	47.5
Fiscal Discipline	7.5	7.5	17.5	10.0
Index of Infrastructure	7.5	0.0	—	0.0
Total:	**100.0**	**100.0**	**100.0**	—

Source: Finance Commission Reports.

While, the Commission has retained the criteria of population, area and fiscal discipline, it has dropped the criteria of Income distance and tax effort and, instead, has added a new criterion of fiscal capacity distance. The weightage to income distance had come down from 62.5% in FC-XI to 50% in FC-XII and completely eliminated in FC-XIII. Further, FC-XIII retained the weightage given by FC-XII to population and area, but raised the weightage of **fiscal discipline** from 7.5% to 17.5%. The FC-XIII has thus given the highest weightage of 47.5% to fiscal capacity distance.

As per FC-XIII, the population is an important indicator of needs of a State, but it has taken 1971 population into account as per the ToR handed down to FC-XIII. Many of the States had taken strong exception to it because the Parliament resolution on this account had expired in 2001 and had not been extended. If the population represents the need of the State then the Commission is relying on the needs of the States as back as 30 years. The States had represented to GoI, when it was preparing the ToR, but the plea was not accepted.

The FC-XIII did not take into account the income distance criteria an index of general backwardness of the States though all the previous Commissions had taken this factor into account, while determining the shares of States. As per FC-XIII, distance criteria measured by per capita GSDP is a proxy for the distance between the States in tax capacity and when the proxy is so applied the procedure implicitly provided a single average tax to GSDP ratio to determine fiscal capacity of States. Instead, FC-XIII has recommended the use of separate averages for measuring tax capacity one for general category and another for special category States. The FC-XIII has advanced the argument that the overall GSDP does not accurately capture the fiscal distance between the two groups. Overall GSDP does not capture the taxable base. The overall GSDP varies across the States and the sectors are not uniform in their taxability. Hence, discarding the distance criteria, it has adopted a new criteria of fiscal capacity.

Further, the FC-XIII has done away with income distance criteria, which had 50% weightage and added the new fiscal capacity distance factor with weightage of 47.5%. Thus FC-XIII in a way, reduced the weightage of backwardness by 2.5%.

Thus, the FC-XIII gave more emphasis on taxable or fiscal capacity, rather than general disability as depicted by GSDP alone. A study has been done by following the distance method formula of FC-XII and the fiscal capacity distance formula of FC-XIII and the results are given in **Table 13.9.**

TABLE 13.9
Income Distance Method and Fiscal Capacity Distance Method—Share of States

State	*Income Distance*	*Fiscal Capacity Distance*	*Increase/ Decrease*
Andhra Pradesh	7.56	6.12	(–) 1.44
Bihar	12.87	16.29	(+) 3.42
Gujarat	3.10	0.87	(–) 2.23
Haryana	0.10	0.10	(–) 0.10
Karnataka	4.58	3.17	(–) 1.41
Kerala	2.71	1.14	(–) 1.57
Madhya Pradesh	7.47	8.43	(+) 0.96
Maharashtra	0.26	0.01	(–) 0.25
Orissa	5.05	5.39	(+) 0.34
Punjab	1.48	0.28	(–) 1.20
Rajasthan	5.85	6.19	(+) 0.34
Tamil Nadu	5.66	2.99	(–) 2.67
Uttar Pradesh	22.21	26.06	(+) 3.85
West Bengal	8.55	7.81	(–) 0.74

It is seen that only States like Orissa, Bihar, Madhya Pradesh, Rajasthan and Uttar Pradesh have gained by applying the Fiscal Capacity Distance Index as applied by FC-XIII. Major losers are Andhra Pradesh, Karnataka, Kerala, Punjab & Tamil Nadu.

So far as the fiscal discipline factor is concerned, it has been given a weightage of 17.5%. The tax effort weightage of 7.5%, fiscal discipline weight of 7.5% and 2.5% weightage taken out of income distance weightage has been added to fiscal discipline criteria and the weightage has thus been raised to 17.5%. Thus, the two criteria of fiscal capacity distance (47.5%) and fiscal discipline (17.5%) have together been given weightage of 65%.

The weightage has to be seen in the light of fiscal consolidation road map suggested by the FC-XIII. The amendments suggested by the FC-XIII in the FRBM legislation are all linked to the fiscal capacity factor and based on the different levels of capacity of the States and, hence, can be good for the States.

(5) Inter se Shares of Central Taxes

The share of each State in the net proceeds of all sharable Central taxes during 2010-15 have been specified in para 8.38 and 8.39 of the report. For the sake of comparison, the shares of general category States for XI, XII and XIII FC have been presented in **Table 13.10.** An overview of shares of the States from the FC-I to FC-XIII has been presented at **Annexure 13.6.**

TABLE 13.10
Inter-se share of non special category States

States	*XIth FC*	*XIIth FC*	*XIIIth FC*	*+/– over FC-XII*
Andhra Pradesh	7.701	7.356	6.937	(–) 0.419
Bihar	14.597	11.028 *	10.917	(–) 0.111
Gujarat	2.821	3.569	3.041	(–) 0.528
Haryana	0.944	1.075	1.048	(–) 0.027
Karnataka	4.930	4.459	4.328	(–) 0.131
Kerala	3.057	2.665	2.341	(–) 0.324
Madhya Pradesh	8.838	6.711 *	7.120	(+) 0.409
Maharashtra	4.632	4.997	5.199	(+) 0.202
Orissa	5.056	5.161	4.779	(–) 0.382
Punjab	1.147	1.299	1.389	(+) 0.090
Rajasthan	5.473	5.609	5.853	(+) 0.244
Tamil Nadu	5.385	5.305	4.969	(–) 0.336
Uttar Pradesh	19.140	19.264 *	19.677	(+) 0.413
West Bengal	8.116	7.057	7.264	(+) 0.207

* *Percentage share of successor State only*
Source: Finance Commission Report

In para 8.41, FC-XIII has tried to justify the respective shares of the States by saying that there is an increase in the ratio of devolution to GSDP (as projected by FC-XIII) for each State. Every State taken individual gains in terms of devolution relative to its GSDP (Table 8.4 of FC-XIII report) **(Table 13.11).**

TABLE 13.11
Devolution as a percent of GSDP

States	*FC-XIII*	*FC-XII*	*Difference FC-XIII-FC-XII)*
Andhra Pradesh	3.34	2.80	0.54
Bihar	19.44	13.57	5.87
Gujarat	1.48	1.44	0.04
Haryana	1.10	0.93	0.17
Karnataka	2.69	2.21	0.48
Kerala	2.13	1.94	0.19
Madhya Pradesh	8.61	5.61	3.01
Maharashtra	1.36	1.04	0.32
Orissa	6.73	5.69	1.04
Punjab	1.92	1.22	0.70
Rajasthan	5.52	3.88	1.64
Tamil Nadu	2.58	2.07	0.51
Uttar Pradesh	10.09	6.79	3.30
West Bengal	3.67	2.82	0.85

But when one looks to the relative shares of individual States in the divisible pool, i.e. the actual amount to be received by each State gets a different picture as shown in **Table 13.10.** Each State is concerned with the actual share which it gets in absolute numbers and percentage share in the kitty to be distributed. The ratio to GSDP does not matter because both the GSDP as well as the amount are assumed numbers but share as has come out of formula is fixed number.

It is evident from the **Table 13.10** that out of 14 States, the share of 8 States have gone down and only 6 States namely Madhya Pradesh, Maharashtra, Punjab, Rajasthan, Uttar Pradesh and West Bengal have gained in comparison to FC-XII shares. Out of these eight States, Andhra Pradesh,

Gujarat, Haryana, Karnataka and Tamil Nadu come under the category of Developed States and Bihar and Orissa come under the underdeveloped category. The major decline is in case of Andhra Pradesh, Gujarat, Kerala, Orissa and Tamil Nadu. But comparing the shares as recommended by three Commissions viz. XI, XII and XIII, the following trends emerge:

(a) There are four States, namely Andhra Pradesh, Karnataka, Kerala and Tamil Nadu, whose individual share has gone down continuously from XI Commission.

(b) Gujarat, Haryana, Orissa show an increase in share from 11th to 12th FC, but a decline in the FC-XIII.

(c) Uttar Pradesh is the only State whose share has consistently increased from 19.14% in XI to 19.264% in XII and to 19.677% in FC-XIII.

Thus, there is continuous fall in the share of richer States. The under developed States have a mixed bag except Uttar Pradesh, which has a rising share after every Commission. Bihar has a continuous declining share. Orissa share went slightly up in FC-XII period, but came down in FC-XIII. Madhya Pradesh's share after falling in FC-XII, increased in FC-XIII but still it was lower than FC-XI share. All these trends go to raise the question as to whether the Commission has succeeded in following the principles of equity and efficiency or not ? Further, the stability and consistency factor in the allotment has also not been there as has been claimed by the FC-XIII.

(6) Inter se Share of Grants

Before discussing the inter se share of grants, it is worthwhile to look into the quantum of grants distributed by the F.C. Though in absolute terms, the grants have gone up from ₹ 20300 crore in FC-X to ₹ 258581 crore in FC-XIII, but it does not show any trend when looked as percent of total FC transfers. In FC-X it was about 9%, which went upto 13.5% in FC-XI. The share jumped up to about 19% in FC-XII and went down to a low of 8% in FC-XIII.

As has been discussed in the earlier sections, the grants-in-aid have been recommended by FC-XIII under various heads taking different factors into account. The FC-XII had tried to correct the imbalance created in the shares of States because of their distribution formula by adjusting the grants. But as the FC-XIII has recommended grants under different considerations. Hence, it cannot be said that the FC-XIII has applied some correction factor as was applied by FC-XII. The Inter se grant share as recommended by FC-XIII is presented in **Table 13.12.**

TABLE 13.12
Inter State Share of Grants

(Percent)

States	*XIth FC*	*XIIth FC*	*XIIIth FC*	*Change*
Andhra Pradesh	3.47	3.66	5.23	(+) 1.57
Bihar	3.06	5.59	5.65	(+) 0.06
Gujarat	2.36	2.60	3.75	(+) 1.15
Haryana	1.12	1.01	1.65	(+) 0.64
Karnataka	1.94	2.84	4.49	(+) 1.65
Kerala	1.39	2.28	2.46	(+) 0.18
Madhya Pradesh	2.97	3.60	5.15	(+) 1.55
Maharashtra	3.34	3.88	6.31	(+) 2.43
Orissa	2.95	3.70	3.74	(+) 0.04
Punjab	1.90	3.44	2.14	(–) 1.30
Rajasthan	5.11	3.26	5.01	(+) 1.75
Tamil Nadu	2.28	2.90	4.40	(+) 1.50
Uttar Pradesh	6.06	10.70	10.34	(–) 0.36
West Bengal	7.99	5.31	4.89	(–) 0.42

Source: Finance Commission Report

It is evident from **Table 13.12** that except Punjab, Uttar Pradesh and West Bengal, all the States have gained in percentage share from FC-XII. Andhra Pradesh, Gujarat,

Karnataka, Madhya Pradesh, Maharashtra, Rajasthan and Tamil Nadu have gained more. It seems that these States have been compensated to some extent for the loss of share in Central taxes.

In order to assess the impact of overall transfer on respective shares of the States, the combined shares of States in total transfers have been presented in **Table XIII.13.**

TABLE 13.13
Overall Transfer from Finance Commission

State	*FC-XII*	*FC-XIII*	*Change*
Andhra Pradesh	6.660	6.688	(+) 0.028
Bihar	10.010	10.133	(+) 0.123
Gujarat	3.390	3.152	(–) 0.238
Haryana	1.060	1.141	(+) 0.081
Karnataka	4.160	4.358	(+) 0.198
Kerala	2.590	2.363	(–) 0.227
Madhya Pradesh	6.130	6.832	(+) 0.702
Maharashtra	4.790	5.374	(+) 0.584
Orissa	4.890	4.627	(–) 0.263
Punjab	1.700	1.505	(–) 0.195
Rajasthan	5.170	5.733	(+) 0.563
Tamil Nadu	4.860	4.889	(+) 0.029
Uttar Pradesh	17.660	18.289	(+) 0.629
West Bengal	6.730	6.914	(+) 0.184

The table shows that though the overall shares of 10 States have increased and the shares of 4 States, namely, Gujarat, Kerala, Orissa and Punjab have gone down from FC-XII shares, but the increase or decrease is very marginal except in case of Madhya Pradesh, Maharashtra, Rajasthan and Uttar Pradesh.

It emerges that the recommendations of FC-XIII have not made any substantial change in the shares of different States. Thus in overall terms also, the FC-XIII has not been able to achieve the twin objectives of progressivity and equity.

(7) Conditional Grants to States

As the Commission has explained, because of some of the "considerations" in the ToRs being different from earlier Commissions "considerations", the Commission has ventured into new grounds and given grants, which were not considered earlier. The new areas include performance incentive grant, environment grant, improving outcome grants all of the 6 new areas selected under this head. Though conditions have been attached to each grants, but they have termed them as "Incentives". As per the Commission, "future performance" has been taken into account, not the "past trend". Further, mere utilization certificate will not be the sufficient condition for release of grants, but will be one of the conditions. But the main consideration will be the outcome targets and their achievement. These incentives have been built up into the pattern of transfers and also into the recommendations for the road map to pursue them.

Though conditional grants were recommended by earlier FCs, but those were different from those recommended by FC-XIII. Linking the grants to outcome is a welcome step and must be appreciated. There is difference of opinion on this point, while the joint memorandum submitted by the Empowered Committee on behalf of States advocated about the conditional grants but many of the Political parties in their interaction with FC-XIII on its State visits, had insisted on conditional and specific purpose grants so that the funds are not misappropriated or not utilised at all. The FC-XIII has stuck to the FC-XII recommendations of grants being conditional, though it calls them incentives. The FC-XIII has given one year time (2010-11) to prepare the ground and galvanise the administrative machinery for the utilisation of grants. The Commission describes year 2010-11 as the "Adjustment Year". The States will have no reason to complain as one year is a sufficient time to take off.

Except performance incentive grant, which has been given for past performance, others have been given on achieving the set targets. It can only be said that conditions attached are not such, which cannot be achieved. But the States will have to raise their performance level, gear the machinery and have close monitoring at all level and then only, they will be eligible for release of grants in subsequent years. As per observation made by FC-XIII, the States with difficulty could utilise the grants in aid other than Calamity Relief and Local Body Grants.

In case of State specific grants, the State's enactment/ amendment of their FRLs incorporating the specified targets has been made a condition precedent to release of grants and the debt relief.

To judge the performance on outcome targets, the data requirements may create problems. This issue of outcome data has also been discussed by FC-XIII, because, normally, the data is received after a time lag. In this connection the FC-XIII has formulated the incentive targets with the following specific outcomes:

(i) For elementary education the expenditure (Plan + Non-Plan) under elementary education (major head 2202, sub major head 01) exclusive of grants recommended, should grow by at least 8%.

(ii) In case of forest grant, the preparation of working plans and its implementation has been made the condition precedent.

(iii) In case of renewable energy, the incentive to be based on States achievement in renewable energy capacity addition in MW from April 2010 to 31st

March 2014.

(iv) So far as the grants-in-aid for water sector management in concerned, the Commission has set four conditions:

1. Establishment of Water Regulatory Authority by 2011-12.
2. States are required to achieve the irrigation rates as assessed by FC-XIII.
3. Minimum expenditure on maintenance of canal system.
4. If Water Regulatory Authority fixes its own rates, then these will replace FC-XIII rates.

(v) Grant for improving outcome, separate outcome targets have been fixed as below:

(1) Better targeting of subsidies through UIDA. For this following conditions have been given:

(a) First installment will be released on July 1, 2010. All subsequent installments will be released on reimbursement basis.

(b) The UIDA (Unique Identification Authority) will certify the numbers of persons of beneficiaries of NREGS, RSBS, PDS, old age pension and other welfare schemes, which have been registered in the State and on the basis of that number grant of ₹ 100 per UIDA issued will be given.

(2) Incentive for reducing Infant Mortality.

(1) Within HDI, IMR has been taken and the results of the survey under the Sample Registration scheme conducted by RGI.

(1) Formula has two components one is to reward

positive movement in the value of the parameter and the second is to provide a premium if such change is made above the medium value of the parameter for all the States.

(3) Justice Delivery: State should put up a State litigation policy.

(vi) Promoting innovations

(i) District Innovation Fund (DIF)

(vii) Police Training

(a) The first installment will be released in 2011-12 after the State Govt. finalises the detailed guidelines for implementation of scheme and notifies the authority at the district level.

(b) The second installment will be released after the State Govt. submits the utilization of first installment.

(viii) Improving transparency in Govt. Accounts

(i) Improving statistical infrastructure at State H.Q.

(ii) Setting up a data base for Govt. Employees & Pensioners.

(iii) 75% of the grant will be utilised for strengthening statistical infrastructure at district level.

(iv) a maximum of 25% can be used for improving statistical infrastructure at State H.Q.

(a) The grant will be drawn in five annual installments. First installment when expenditure plan is submitted and rest after utilization of grant.

(b) It will be built in common foundation

across the States as suggested by FC-XIII ₹ 10 crore for each general category state and ₹ 5 crore for special category State has been recommended by the FC-XIII.

(c) ₹ 2.50 crore during 2010-11 without any precondition and the balance will be released after the State certificate that it has created a database and this has been functionally integrated with the treasury on a transactional basis.

Thus, there is no consistency in vogue in the fixation of outcome targets and are achievable.

(8) State Specific Grants

FC-XIII has also recommended State specific grants. U.P. has been granted ₹ 1679.00 crore for 6 items viz Varanasi Development (₹ 125.00 crore), Boarder Roads (₹ 250.00 Crore) Bundhelkhand (₹ 500.00 crore), Police (₹ 330.00 crore), Agriculture Mandis (₹ 354.00 crore), Heritage roads (₹ 100.00 crore) and development of Civil Services Training Institute (₹ 18.00 crore).

Thus, FC-XIII has recommended new types of grants with specific outcome targets. The Commission has given one year period (2010-11) to put in place the required infrastructure to achieve the targets in the next four years. It is to be seen whether the conditions specified by the FC-XIII will be fulfilled by the States. Thus, all depends on the willingness and commitment of the respective departments to fulfill the conditions in order to be able to get the recommended grants in aid.

(9) Local Body Grants

FC-XIII has, for the first time, recommended conditions for

release of grants-in-aid to local bodies. These grants have been classified in two categories, basic grant and general performance grant. Basic grant will be given in 2010-11 and the general performance grant from 2011-12. From year 2011-12 onwards, a State meets the conditionalities specified in para 10.160 and para 10.161 it will be eligible to receive both the basic grants and the general performance grant. These conditions, in short, are:

(i) A supplement to budget document for both ULBs and PRIs.
(ii) Put in place an audit system.
(iii) Put in place independent local body Ombudsman.
(iv) A system to transfer electronically the grant to ULBs/PRIs within 5 days.
(v) Prescribe through an Act the qualifications of members of SFC.
(vi) ULBs should be fully enabled to levy property tax.
(vii) Put in place a State level Property Tax Board.
(viii) Put in place standards of delivery of all essential services provided by local bodies.
(ix) All municipal corporations must put in place a fire hazard response and mitigation plan.

The Govt. will have to give documentary proof of the compliance with the conditionalities. After the release of basic grant in 2010-11, the Govt. will have to fulfill these conditions in one year framework. The creation of the office of ombudsman is one of the most important conditions. A bill will have to be passed within one year. The FC-XIII has reduced the period of transfer of funds to local bodies within 5 days instead of 15 days in FC-XII period. This system must be put in place otherwise the State Govt. will have to pay penal interest beyond a period of 5 days.

Thus, incentivising grants with the outcome will be both incentive to do better and achieve the targets and also a deterrent in terms of loss of grant if the outcome targets are not achieved. This is the better way of proper, effective and target oriented use of grants.

(10) Fiscal Road Map for States

FC-XIII has recommended a target based fiscal framework separately for Centre and States. For this the enactment/ amendment of FRBM Act is the condition precedent. FRBM Act has also been made a condition for availing the State specific grants and debt relief. The FRBM and MTFP framework has been designed keeping in view the experience of economic slow down, effect on resources and the stimulus package of GOI. The FC-XIII has designed the road map with the specific steps to combat the likely future shocks etc.

Target based framework will contain the following:

1. Debt to GDP ratio—25% by 2014-15—GoI to assume the responsibility for all borrowings due to unanticipated shock in the international economics and/or
2. Long term target of zero RD, but by 2011-12 RD must be zero and continue onwards.
3. U.P. in spite of Revenue Surplus had FD at 3.9%. It should also come to 3% by 2011-12 and maintained thereafter.
4. Amend the FRL to incorporate the above targets.
5. Standard reforms recommended for the Centre must be replicated at State level.

   (i) Structure of MTFP to be changed—Economic and Functional classification of budget to be part of MTFP—the process to commence from

2011-12.

(ii) All Central transfers to States to be set out in independent statement.

(iii) Compliance cost of major tax proposal—this should be done from 2013-14.

(iv) All capital expenditure proposals included in the budget are accompanied by a statement of the Revenue consequences of capital expenditure (RCCE) for the life time of proposed project. RCCE statement should be made annually & modified to take into account price and other charges. This should begin to be provided from 2013-14.

(v) New Policy initiatives that are know to involve future expenditure commitments should be reflected in MTFP. This should be done from year 2013-14 budgets.

(vi) Limits to Govt. guarantees should be fixed. In case of GoI 5% of GDP for the stock of outstanding guarantees at the end of every year.

(vii) Contingent liabilities on account of PPP projects (Explicit or implicit) should also be reflected in FRBM Act.

(viii) A detailed statement quantifying the obligation of public sector in PPP arrangement should be included in MTFP.

(ix) Inventory of vacant land and buildings valued at market price should also form part of MTFP from 2013-14 onwards.

(x) MTFP should make explicit the values of the parameters underlying expenditure and revenue projections and the lands within the parameters can vary, while remaining consistent with FRBM targets (9.61)

(xi) FRBMA should specify the nature of shocks that would require to relaxation of targets (9.62).

(xii) GoI should assume the entire responsibility of ARM instead of raising borrowing ceiling of States.

(xiii) Recommendations of Pay Commission to be implemented from the date of acceptance.

(xiv) Central Govt. should fix net borrowings ceiling for each State.

(xv) Independent monitoring and review apparatus to be put in place. This should be included in the FRL.

(xvi) Loans against CSS/CS outstanding at the end of 2009-10 to be written off, subject to the same condition for interest relief on NSSF.

State of U.P. had enacted the FRL much before the recommendations of FC-XII with specific targets of reduction of revenue deficit, fiscal deficit and debt as percent of GSDP. The Act had also provided for the preparation of MTFP and its presentation alongwith the budget. The Act also provides for half yearly and yearly review by the Finance Minister and its presentation before the legislature.

Recently, the State Government amended the section 5(4) of the Act, where in the fiscal deficit: GSDP target was prescribed. Now, the State Government has proposed to replace the section 5(4) with the new section, which gives powers to the State Government to fix the targets, as it deems fit. Thus, at the moment, the Act does not have any target for GFD : GSDP.

Now, with the recommendation of FC-XIII being accepted by the GoI and linking it with the release of State specific grants and debt relief, the State Govt. will have to amend the existing FRBM Act in order to qualify for the grants-in-aid. Not only the three targets of RD, GFD, GSDP and debt: GSDP targets, the FC-XIII has recommended major changes in the MTFP and has also added many new statements alongwith MTFP and also put in place an independent monitoring and review mechanism.

The proposed new FRL shows that the time frame of fiscal targets have been changed, keeping in view the impact of economic slowdown on receipt and expenditure by the States. At least one year (2010-11) has been given for adjustments. The MTFP, as suggested by FC-XIII, will contain more information reflecting the level of decision making by the States with regard to revenue raising and expenditure priorities as well as future expenditure commitments. An independent review and monitoring apparatus has also been put in place, which will judge the compliance of FRL.

After the recommendations of FC-XII, most of the States had passed the FRBM Act with some common provisions as recommended by the FC-XII and linking it with DCRF. This worked well from 2005-06 to 2008-09 and many of the States had achieved the RD reduction target much before the target date and had reduced the GFD target to a considerable extent. As a result, the States got the benefit of DCRF. U.P. also got the facility for four years and could not get in the last year because, of the high GFD : GSDP ratio. But, because of the global economic slow down, the situation started deteriorating by the end of 2008-09 and its full impact was felt in 2009-10. The revenues of Centre as well as States were affected adversely, the expenditure level was maintained and in some cases raised also, in order to give stimulus to the economy. Further, the Centres Pay Commission Recommendations were willy nilly followed by many a State and as a result of revision of pay, allowances and pensions from the retrospective effect, the expenditure liabilities of both Centre and States increased sharply.

In the light of this, the GoI relaxed the GFD:GSDP targets for States. First, the target was raised from 3% to 3.5% and then to 4% to be achieved by 2009-10. The Centre did not revise its own FRBM targets but only of the States. The centre's targets went haywire and rose to around 7% in 2009-10(BE). The GOI, simultaneously, raised the borrowing ceilings of the States, in order to compensate them for the loss of tax revenue from Centre as well as their own revenue. In case of U.P., the share in central taxes in 2008-09 was reduced from ₹ 34,706.10 crore (BE) to actuals of ₹ 30,905.72 crore, which resulted in loss of ₹ 3800 crore of SCT and the share for 2009-10 was pegged at less than the RE of 2008-09, which is only ₹ 31,711 crore i.e. an increase of 2.6% over actuals of 2008-09. As a result of loss in Central share and its own revenue and to keep up the tempo of developmental expenditure, the GFD of the State rose sharply and as a result lost 2 years (2008-10) debt relief.

The FC-XIII has taken note of these developments and has, in turn, suggested measures in the event of likely shocks. It has devoted ten paras (9.55 to 9.64) to these issues. As per FC-XIII, the important lesson drawn from the events between 2005-2010 is the need to allow the fiscal system to adapt the exogenous shocks and/or changes in exogenous parameters. The FC-XIII has suggested three changes in the design of existing fiscal responsibility legislation to address this challenge.

First, the MTFP to make explicit the values of the parameters underlying expenditure and revenue projections and the band within which, these parameters can vary while remaining consistent with FRBMA targets, should such circumstances arise.

Second, the FRBMA to specify the nature of shocks that would require a relaxation of targets. These shocks would affect some target more than others. Thus, shocks requiring a boost to aggregate demand or sharp increases in oil prices would require temporary relaxation of revenue deficit targets. Shocks addressed through expanding public investment would impact the debt to GSDP ratio and, therefore, the fiscal deficit targets.

Thirdly, macro economic stabilisation and counter necessary actions are the primary responsibility of Central Govt. Hence, rather than raising the borrowing ceiling for the States, the GOI should assume the entire responsibility of ARM and pass on the resources to the States. Such a policy would also maintain the integrity and improve the expenditure predictability of State budgets as well as the medium term fiscal plan.

Apart from these, many policy decisions of the Centre also affect the expenditure requirement of the States. The Pay Commission recommendation is an important example of this. The FC-XIII has recommended that the recommendations should be accepted from the date on which the recommendations are accepted by the Govt. The logic behind this, in the view of FC-XIII, is that when the transfers recommended are without any retrospective effect, then the same should be possible for Pay Commissions recommendations also. But, this decision is, normally, not based on strict financial principles..

But, the other three steps, suggested by FC-XIII, are in the right direction and will give some flexibility to the States and will not result in unnecessary penalisation for the reasons beyond the control of States, as was done in case of DCRF recommended by FC-XII and linked to fixed targets of RD and GFD uniformly throughout the States..

Debt Relief

The FC-XIII has recommended three types of debt relief. One to those State, which had not availed the DCRF, as recommended by FC-XII. For them, the facility has been extended, subject to enactment of FRBM Act. This facility will be limited to consolidation and interest rate reduction only. Second, loans to States from NSSF contracted till 2006-07 and outstanding at the end of 2009-10 to be reset at 9% rate of interest, subject to conditions prescribed in para 9.106. Third, loans from GoI to States and administered by ministries/ departments, other then MOF, outstanding as at the end of 2009-10, to be written off, subject to conditions given in para 9.114.

The FC-XIII also recommended a window for borrowings from Central Govt. to be available for the fiscally weak States that are unable to raise loans from market, which was closed by FC-XII for all States.

So far as the case of U.P. is concerned, it got the debt waiver for four years under DCRF, but was found ineligible for the last year (2009-10), as it could not fulfil the target of GFD as percentage of GSDP. Most of the general category States availed of this facility and got benefit not only in interest payment and principal write off also.

So far as the loans against NSSF are concerned, this was the only loan which was left by the FC-XII under DCRF. This loan has, now, been covered and the total interest relief is ₹ 13,516.62 crore for twenty eight States. U.P. will get the benefit of ₹ 1,414.85 crore in five year period, subject to the condition of FRL.

The central loans administered by Ministries, other than MOF, are only ₹ 4,506 crore for all the States and U.P.'s share of outstanding loans is only ₹ 442 crore. These loans will be written off, subject to the condition of passing of FRL.

Finally, the FC-XIII has recommended that the debt write off recommended is accounted in such a manner that it does not artificially affect the revenue or fiscal deficit of the States.

Thus, within Commissions FC-XII and FC-XIII all the loans, given by MoF as well as by various Ministries, have been covered for debt and interest relief and all these measures have helped the States in the matter of not only repayment of principal amount, but in the interest payment also. This will give some space to the States to relocate expenditure priorities.

Disaster Relief

The ToR of FC-XIII was different from the ToR of FC-XII because during this period, a new Act "Disaster Management Act, 2005" (An Act 53 of 2005) was passed. The Act has a new scheme in place and the word "calamity" has been replaced with the word "Disaster". The definition has also been made wider, which includes "While previous Finance Commissions have taken such a view, the DM Act provides a far wider, definition of disaster as 'a catastrophe, mishap, calamity or grave occurrence in any area, arising from natural or man-made causes, or by accident or negligence, which results in substantial loss of life or human suffering or damage to, and destruction of property, or damage to, or degradation of environment, and is of such a nature or magnitude as to be beyond the coping capacity of the community of the affected area"

Further, two funds have been created at the national level viz. National Disaster Response Fund and National Disaster Mitigation Fund. Similar funds at the State level and district level have also been envisaged.

The Act envisages the formation of National Disaster Management Authority (NDMA) at the appex level. For its assistance, National Executive Committee (NEC) has been put in place. Similarly, State Disaster Management Authority and SEC have also been provided in the Act. At the district level, a District Disaster Management Authority under District Magistrate has also been provided.

(i) Total size of SDRF has been worked out at ₹ 33581 crore, U.P.'s share comes to ₹ 2129.51 crore.
(ii) Additional grant of ₹ 525 crore has been provided.
(iii) Creation of District DRF has been left to the discretion of the States.
(iv) FC-XIII has kept mitigation and reconstruction activities out of the scheme.
(v) Though "Disaster" has been defined under the Act, but FC-XIII has kept the current list of disasters but has included man made disasters of high intensity.
(vi) The FC-XIII has prescribed the accounting norms (para 11.94).

The Disaster Management Act, 2005 is a much improved version and has a better management approach to deal with the calamity, whether natural or man made. A three tier system of management, funding and monitoring will not only result in avoiding but also managing the calamity in a quick response time.

Road Map for PSU Reforms

The FC-XIII also talks of a road map for PSU reforms, specially for loss making PSUs, which has been presented in the earlier section. The road map is all right and attempts must be made in this direction so as to (a) lessen the burden on State exchequer and (b) run the rest with efficiency and on their own without any budgetary support. The experience at the State level shows that this subject was always at the forefront with every Govt., many working groups recommended the direction also. The Govt. made several attempts to sell the loss making PSUs, but could sell only one big PSU i.e. Cement Corporation. But, the Govt. could not make any headway in case of sugar, textile, tourism, transport sectors to name a few. The employees' agitation lengthy auction process, cautious approach of bureaucrats and legal battle were some of the main bottlenecks. But, sooner or later all these will have to be done because a stage has already come, when the State Govt. burdened with its own huge committed liability will not be able to give budgetary support to them in the form of loans, share capital and Govt. guarantees, which has, in many cases, resulted in contingent liability to the State. Hence, the recommendation by the Commission is timely. Linking this recommendation to MTFP, which will be part of FRL, will strengthen the State Governments hands to move ahead.

Reforms in the Accounting Procedure

The Commission has also suggested some steps in the direction of reforms in the accounting process. The clear depictions of "contra entries" and "transfer to and from funds" are two main examples. In case of U.P., there are many contra entry cases, which though affect the budgetary figures, but do not affect the cash flow position of the State. Similarly, the example of "Sinking Fund" is a case in point with regard to "Transfer to and from Fund". The State transfers a huge amount from its expenditure budget to the Public Account and, thus, it affects the budgetary figure of revenue expenditure, but there is no return entry and no debit entry in the Sinking Fund. On the one hand, the Sinking Fund gets inflated, so also the revenue expenditure. This is a welcome step and if followed will give the real picture of State finances, as presented in the annual budget. Though, no contra entries are separately shown, but the budget of 2010-2011 has tried to correct entries with regard to the Sinking Fund, so that the balance in the Sinking Fund is correctly reflected. As the statement of contra entries has been made a precondition of MTFP, this will also be implemented. The annual budget will, thus, show true and correct picture of receipt and expenditure without any notional entries.

The Commission has discouraged the tendency of transferring money to PLA at the end of year, to avoid its lapse. It has also recommended that the tendency to divert public expenditure from the budget to "nominated funds", which are operated outside the authority of the legislature should be discouraged. The money is transferred to PLA through the treasury, hence technically, the money is shown as spent during the year. But actual expenditure takes place in the future year. In the next year, because the money is available with the Department in PLA, they spend this money first and then take up expenditure against budgeted amount. It is always less and gives a wrong picture of actual budgeted expenditure. Hence, it is a welcome thing, which will result in curbing this tendency and bringing the entire expenditure under legislature scrutiny and will also depict the actual expenditure during the year. So far as the PLA is concerned, the State Govt. has recently issued instructions not to transfer any amount in PLA at the end of the year 2009-10. It is hoped that this will be strictly adhered to and no money will be transferred to PLA. But giving money to agencies outside the purview of budget is many a time at the direction of GoI, where GoI insists on formation of a society and then only transfers money directly to the society. Hence, the State willy nilly succumbs to centre's pressure. Hence, this process of correction should start from the Centre.

The presumption of separate statements in the budget with regard to subsidies, maintenance expenditure, salary, pension etc. are steps in the right direction and will make the budget more transparent and easy to understand. In U.P., many of the disclosure statements, as prescribed by FC-XII and FC-XIII, are being published alongwith the budget document. As regards different types of funds in Public Account, the Govt. has closed as many as 16 Funds maintained in the Public Account in the budget of 2010-11, as these were inoperative since long. The amount shown in these head have been transferred to the Consolidated Fund under general miscellaneous services..

Power Sector

One of the most worrying part is the power sector. Because of the importance of energy as a pre-condition of economic development it is always in the forefront of any discussion on reforms. Many attempts were made in the power sector to improve its workings. But finally, the process of reform started in January 2000 with the unbundling, corporatisation and then privatisation. During these years, many committees, task forces were constituted, World Bank studies were done, recommendations made, new energy policies formulated and Electricity Acts amended. But, in spite of all that, the picture which emerges, is not very encouraging. This is also evident from the review made by the FC-XIII. The situation is alarming, because it is very adversely affecting the State budget. In case of U.P., after the unbundling of the UPSEB into three corporations, the State has pumped directly and indirectly more than ₹ 50,000 crore in the power sector since 14.01.2000. Many of the liabilities like pension, GPF, arrears of central utilities were taken over and loans given by the State Govt. and interest thereon worth ₹ 19,000 crore were written off in order to give a clean balance sheet to the three corporations created at that time. But after ten years, we are at the same situation, which was these prior to reforms. There are huge cash losses, huge Govt. guarantees and share capital have been given. In many cases the liabilities of guaranteed loans have been taken over by State Govt. Huge subsidy has also been given. But, the sector is, any how, managing its affairs with working capital and short term loans and is in a "debt trap" situation. The sector is lagging in three basic parameters, PLF, AT&D losses and collection efficiency. There are many reasons some of which are beyond the control of the utility like revision of tariff, which is not done at regular intervals and is not adequate and some are within its control likely PLF, AT & D losses and collection efficiency. The Commission has suggested some of the measures and if sincerely followed may result in some improvement.

V
Concluding Observations

The issues, recommendations and their implications, specially for the State of U.P., have been discussed, in detail, and some comparison has also been made with the recommendations of FC-XII. All these discussions lead us to believe that the FC-XIII has followed the path traversed by FC-XII, but in many cases, it has deviated and ventured into new areas because of the "other considerations" listed in the TOR.

The FC-XIII has increased the divisible pool and in it, the share portion and thereby reduced the grant component. Further, the shares as percent of total transfers through FC have gone down from FC-XII. Even the grants have not been able to make good the reduction in shares. Thus, the recommendation on this account does not fulfil the twin objective of equity and progressivity.

If compared with the conditionalties, the FC-XIII has tried to convince that these are incentives and not conditions. Conditions in many cases are more stringent and somewhere may interfere with the Constitutional obligations of the States. The case, in point, is the target fixed for reduction of Revenue Deficit and fiscal deficit by 2011-12. The GOI had relaxed the GFD/GSDP target and fixed it at 4% for 2009-10, but now, it has asked the States to reduce it to 3% by 2011-12. Thus it has withdrawn the facility given to States in the face of economic slowdown and the States will have to face the hard budget constraint, specially on the capital side.

Further, even though the State may be in a revenue surplus regime, a restriction has been imposed on States not to increase its capital expenditure to bring GFD to 3% of GSDP by 2011-12. To put a restriction on capital expenditure just to bring the GFD:GSDP ratio to 3% is not desirable, because this expenditure is done, normally, for infrastructure creation in the State. But the State will have to willy nilly accept this imposed discipline in order to get the huge grants in aid.

Reducing revenue deficit to zero and maintaining it at that level in future, will naturally mean that revenue expenditure in social sectors would be cut because of the less space available to States as most of the revenue expenditure is consumed by the committed expenditure. Further, there are many Centrally Sponsored Schemes of GOI, which are on the revenue side and where the State share is, gradually, increasing. How can the State fulfill this condition, while maintaining revenue surplus. Other revenue expenditure cannot be slashed. It mostly consists of salary, interest, pension payments and assignment to local bodies. In this way, the States are forced to reduce not only their revenue expenditure, but the capital expenditure also. The FC-XIII has clearly stated that any State that has a revenue surplus along with a higher fiscal deficit should compress its capital expenditure or alternatively increase its surplus on revenue account. Thus, it means that the States not only just cut in capital expenditure, but also squeeze the revenue expenditures to reduce fiscal deficit.

Another stringent condition imposed on the States is to bring the Debt Stock/GDP ratio to 25% by 2014-15. Its a very tall order to comply in a short span of five years. This is the target fixed for all States put together.

The amendment of FRBM Act on the lines suggested by FC-XIII, though will enforce the fiscal discipline, but with the force of law. But attaching this condition for release of grants will, further, result in harder constraints. On the whole, it can be concluded that from the very start, the GOI built, a bias against the States as "Other considerations" narrated in the TOR, were heavily loaded against the States. As a result, the same bias is reflected in the recommendations made by FC-XIII also.

ANNEXURES

Annexure 1.1

Extract from Govt. of India 1935

PART VII[1]

FINANCE, PROPERTY, CONTRACTS AND SUITS

CHAPTER I: FINANCE

Distribution of Revenues between the Federation and the Federal Units

Meaning of "Revenues of Federation" and "Revenues of Province".

136. Subject to the following provisions of this chapter with respect to the assignment of the whole or part of the net proceeds of certain taxes and duties to Provinces and Federal States, [1a][and subject to the provisions of this Act with respect to the Federal Railway Authority], the expression "revenues of the Federation" includes all revenues and public moneys raised or received by the Federation and the expression "revenues of the Province" includes all revenues and public moneys raised or received by a Province.

Certain succession duties, stamp duties, terminal taxes and taxes on fares and freights.

137. Duties in respect of succession to property other than agricultural land,[2] estate duty in respect of property other than agricultural land, such stamp duties as are mentioned in the Federal Legislative List, terminal taxes on goods or passengers carried by railway, or air, and taxes on railway fares and freights, shall be levied and collected by the [Federation][1b], but the net proceeds in any financial year of

any such duty or tax, except in so far as those proceeds represent proceeds attributable to Chief Commissioners' provinces, shall not form part of the revenues of the [Federation][1b], but shall be assigned to the Provinces and to the [Federated][1c] States, if any, within which that duty or tax is leviable in that year, and shall be distributed among the Provinces and those States in accordance with such principles of distribution as may be formulated by Act of the [Federal][1b] Legislature:

Provided that the [Federal][1b] Legislature may at any time increase any said duties or taxes by a surcharge for [Federal]1b purposes and the whole proceeds of any such surcharge shall form part of the revenues of the [Federation][1b].

Taxes on Income.

138. (1) Taxes on income other than agricultural income shall be levied and collected by the Federation, but a prescribed percentage of the net proceeds in any financial year of any such tax, except in so far as those proceeds represent proceeds attributable to Chief Commissioners' Provinces or to taxes payable in respect of [Federal][1b] emoluments, shall not form part of the revenues of the [Federation][1b], but shall be assigned to the Provinces and to the [Federated][1c] States, if any, within which that tax is leviable in that year, and shall be distributed among the Provinces and those States in such manner as may be prescribed[3]:

Provided that—

(a) the percentage originally prescribed under this sub-section shall not be increased by any [subsequent Order in Council][3a] .

(b) The [Federal][1b] Legislature may at any time increase the said taxes by a surcharge for [Federal][1b] purposes and the whole proceeds of any such surcharge shall form part of the revenues of the [Federation][1b]

[4][For the purposes of this sub-section, in each financial year [1a][one per cent, or] such [1a][other] percentage as may be prescribed, of so much of the net proceeds of taxes on income as does not represent the net proceeds of taxes on income as does not represent the net proceeds of taxes payable in respect of [Federal][1b] emoluments shall be deemed to represent proceeds attributable to the Chief Commissioners' Provinces].

(2) Notwithstanding anything in the preceding sub-section, the [Federation][1b] may retain out of the moneys assigned by that sub-section to Province and States—

(a) in each year of a prescribed period such sum as may be prescribed [or 4, if it is so prescribed, the whole of those moneys]; and

(b) in each year of a further prescribed period a sum less than that retained in the preceding year by an amount, being the same amount in each year, so calculated that the sum to be retained in the last year of the period will be equal to the amount of each such annual reduction:

Provided that —

(i) neither of the periods originally prescribed shall be reduced by any subsequent Order in Council ;

(ii) the Governor-General in this discretion may in any year of the second prescribed period direct that the sum to be retained in the preceding year, and that the second prescribed period shall be correspondingly extended, but he shall not give any such direction except after consultation with such representatives of [Federal][1b], Provincial and State interest as he may think desirable, not shall be give any such direction unless he is satisfied that the maintenance of the financial stability of the [Federal]1b Government requires him so to do.

(3) Where an act of the [Federal][1b] Legislature imposes a surcharge for [Federal][1b] purposes under this section, the Act shall provide for the payment of each [Federated][1c] State in which taxes on income are not leviable by such basis as may be prescribed with a view to securing that the contribution shall be the equivalent, as near as may be, of the net proceeds which it is estimated would result from the surcharge if it is were leviable in that State, and the State shall become liable to pay that contribution accordingly.

(4) In this section —
"taxes on income" does not include a corporation tax;
"prescribed" means prescribed by [His Majesty in Council][4a]; and of the revenues of the [Federation][1b] or of the Federal Railway Authority in respect of which income-tax is chargeable.

[4b][139. (1) Corporation tax shall not be levied by the Federation in any Federated State until ten years have elapsed from the establishment of the Federation.

Corporation tax

(2) Any Federal law providing for the levying of corporation tax shall contain provisions enabling the Ruler of any Federated State in which the tax could otherwise be leviable to elect that the tax shall not be levied in the State, but that in lieu thereof there shall be paid by the State to the revenues of the Federation a contribution as near as may be equivalent to the net proceeds which it is estimated would result from the tax if it were levied in the State.

(3) Where the Ruler of a State so elects as aforesaid, the

officers of the Federation shall not call for any information or returns from any corporation in the State, but it shall be the duty of the Ruler thereof to cause to be supplied to the Auditor-General of India such information as the Auditor-General may reasonably require to enable the amount of any such contribution to be determined.

If the Ruler of a State is dissatisfied with the determination as to the amount of the contribution payable by his State in any financial year, he may appeal to the Federal Court, and if he establishes to the satisfaction of that Court that the amount determined is excessive, the Court shall reduce the amount accordingly and no appeal shall lie from the decision of the Court on the appeal.

Salt duties, excise duties and export duties.

140. (1) Duties on salt, Federal duties of excise and export duties shall be levied and collected by the Federation, but, if an Act of the Federal Legislature so provides, these shall be paid out of the revenues of the Federation to the Provinces and to the Federated States, if any, to which the act imposing the duty extends, sums equivalent to the whole or any part of the net proceeds of that duty, and those sums shall be distributed among the Provinces and those States in accordance with such principles of distribution as may be formulated by the Act.

(2) Notwithstanding anything in the preceding sub-section, [one half, or such great proportion as His Majesty in Council may determine][5], of the net proceeds in each year of any export duty on jute products shall not form part of the revenues of the Federation, but shall be assigned to the Provinces or Federated States in which jute is grown in proportion to the respective amounts of jute grown therein.

141. (1) No Bill or amendment which imposes or varies any tax or duty in which Provinces are interested or which varies the meaning of the expression "agricultural income" as defined for the purposes of the enactments relating to Indian income-tax, or which affects the principles on which under any of the foregoing provisions if this chapter moneys are or may be distributable to Provinces or States, or which imposes any such Federal surcharge as is mentioned in the foregoing provisions of this chapter, shall be introduced or moved in either Chamber of the Federal Legislature except with the previous sanction of the Governor-General in this discretion.

Prior sanction of Governor-General required to Bill affecting taxation in which Provinces are interested.

(2) The Governor General shall not give his sanction to the introduction of any Bill or the moving if any amendment imposing in any year any such Federal surcharge as aforesaid unless he is satisfied that all practicable economies and all practicable measures for otherwise increasing the proceeds of Federal taxation or the portion thereof retainable by the Federation would not result in the balancing of Federal receipts and expenditure on revenue account in that year.

(3) In this section the expression "tax or duty in which Provinces are interested" means—

(a) a tax or duty the whole or part of the net proceeds whereof are assigned to any Province; or

(b) a tax or duty by reference to the net proceeds whereof sums are for the time being payable out of the revenues of the Federation to any Provinces.

142. Such sums as may be prescribed by [His Majesty in Council][6] shall be charged on the revenues of the Federation in each year as grants-in-aid of the revenues of such Provinces as His Majesty may determine to be in need of assistance, and different sums may be prescribed for different Provinces:

Grants from Federation to certain Provinces.

Provided that, except in the case of the North-West Frontier Province, no grant fixed under this section shall be increased by a subsequent Order, unless an address has been presented to the Governor-General by both Chambers of the Federal Legislature for submission to [His Majesty][6a] praying that the increase may be made.

7[**142-A.** (1) Notwithstanding anything in section one hundred of this Act, no Provincial law relating to taxes for the benefit of a Province or of a municipality, district board, local board or other local authority therein in respect of professions, trades, callings or employments shall be invalid on the ground that it relates to a tax on income.

Taxes on professios, trades, callings and employments.

(2) The total amount payable in respect of any one person to the Province or to any one municipality, district board, local board, or other local authority in the Province by way of taxes on professions, trades, callings and employments shall not, after the thirty-first day of March nineteen hundred and thirty-nine, exceed fifty rupees per annum:

Provided that, if in the financial year ending with that date there was in force in the case of any Province or any such municipality, board or authority a tax in professions, trades callings or employments the rate, or the maximum rate, of which exceeded fifty rupees per annum, the preceding provisions of this sub-section shall, unless for the time being provision to the contrary is made by a law of the Federal Legislature, have effect in relation to that Province, municipality, board or authority as if for the reference to fifty rupees per annum these were substituted a reference to that rate or maximum rate, of such lower rate, if any (being a rate greater than fifty rupees per annum), as many for the time being be fixed by a law of the Federal Legislature; and any law of the Federal Legislature made for any of the purposes of this proviso may be made either generally or in relation to any specified Provinces, municipalities, boards or authorities.

(3) The fact that the Provincial Legislature has power to make laws as aforesaid with respect to taxes on professions, trades, callings and employments, the generality of the entry in the Federal Legislative List relating to taxes on income].

Savings

143. (1) Nothing in the foregoing provisions of this chapter affects any duties or taxes levied in any Federated State otherwise than by virtue of an Act of the Federal Legislature applying in the State.[7a]

[7][(1A) Nothing in the foregoing provisions of this chapter authorises the levy of any duty or tax by the Dominion in any Acceding State unless provision in that behalf is made in the Instrument of Accession of that State.]

(2) Any taxes, duties, cesses or fees which, immediately before the commencement of Part III of this Act, were being lawfully levied by any Provincial Government, municipality or other local authority or body for the purposes of the Province, municipality, district or other local area under a law in force on the first day of January, nineteen hundred thirty-five[8], may notwithstanding that those taxes, duties, cesses or fees are mentioned in the Federal Legislative List,

continue to be levied and to be applied to the same purposes until provision to the contrary is made by the Federal Legislature.

144. (1) In the foregoing provision of this chapter "net proceeds" means in relation to any tax or duty the proceeds thereof reduced by the cost of collection and for the purposes of those provisions the net proceeds of any tax or duty, or of any part of any tax or duty, in or attributable to any area shall be ascertained and certified by the Auditor-General of India, whose certificates shall be final.

Calculation of "net proceeds", etc.

(2) Subject as aforesaid, and to any other express provision of this chapter, an Act of the Federal Legislature may, in any case where under this Part of this Act to proceeds to any duty or tax are, or may be, assigned to any Province or State, or a contribution is, or may be, made to the revenues of the Federation by any State, provide for the manner in which the proceeds of any duty or tax and the amount of any contribution are to be calculated, for the times in each year and the manner at and in which any payments are to be made, for the making of adjustments between one financial year and another, and for any other incidental or ancillary matters.

The Crown and the States

[8a]**145.** There shall be paid to His Majesty by the Federation in each year the sums stated by His Majesty's Representative for the exercise of the functions of the Crown in its relation with Indian States to be required, whether on revenue account or otherwise, for the discharge of those functions, including the making of any payments in respect of any customary

Expenses of the Crown in connection with Indian States.

allowances to members of the family or servants of any former Ruler of any territories in India.

Payments from or by Indian States.

[8a]**146.** All cash contributions and payments in respect of loans and other payments due from or by any Indian State which, if this Act had not been passed, would have formed part of the revenues of India, shall be received by His Majesty, and shall if His Majesty has so directed, be placed at the disposal of the Federation, but nothing in this Act shall derogate from the right of His Majesty, if he thinks fit so to do, to remit at any time the whole oar any part or any such contributions or payments.

Remission of States' contributions.

[8a]**147.** (1) Subject to the provisions of sub-section (3) of this section His Majesty may, in signifying his acceptance of the Instrument of Accession of a State, agree to remit over a period not exceeding twenty years from the date of the accession of the State to the Federation any cash contributions payable by that State.

(2) Subject as aforesaid, where any territories have been voluntarily ceded to the crown by a Federated State before the passing of this Act—

(a) in return for specific military guarantees, or

(b) in return for the discharge of the State from obligations to provide military assistance, there shall, if His Majesty, in signifying his acceptance of the Instrument of Accession of that State, so directs be paid to that State, but in the first mentioned case, on condition that the said guarantees are waived, such sums as in the opinion of His Majesty ought to be paid in respect of any such cession as aforesaid.

(3) Notwithstanding anything in this section—

(a) every such agreement or direction as aforesaid shall be such as to secure that no such remission or payment shall be made by virtue of the agreement or direction until the Provinces have begun to receive moneys under the section of this chapter relating to taxes on income, and, in the case of a remission, that the remission shall be complete before the expiration of twenty years from the date of the accession to the Federation of the State in question, or before the end of the second prescribed period referred to in sub-section (2) of the said section whichever first occurs; and

(b) no contribution shall be remitted by virtue of any such agreement save in so far as it exceeds the value of any privilege of immunity enjoyed by the State; and

(c) in fixing the amount of any payments in respect of ceded territories, account shall be taken of the value of any such privilege or immunity.

(4) This section shall apply in the case of any cash contributions the liability for which has before the passing of this Act been discharged by payment of a capital sum or sums, and accordingly His Majesty may agree that the capital sum or sums so paid shall be repaid either by instalments or otherwise, and such repayments shall be deemed to be remissions for the purposes of this section.

(5) In this chapter "cash contributions" means—

(a) periodical contributions in acknowledgement of the suzerainty of His Majesty, including contributions payable in connection with any arrangement for the aid and protection of a State by His Majesty, and contributions in commutation of any obligation of a State to provide military assistance to His Majesty, or in respect of the maintenance by His Majesty of a special force for service in connection with a State, or in respect of the maintenance of local military forces or police or in respect of the expenses of an agent ;

(b) periodical contributions fixed on the creation or restoration of a State, or on a re-grant or increase of territory, including annual payments for grants of land on perpetual tenure or for equalization of the value of exchanged territory;

(c) periodical contributions formerly payable to another State but now payable to His Majesty by right of conquest, assignment or lapse.

(6) In this chapter "privilege or immunity" means any such right, privilege, advantage or immunity of a financial character as is hereinafter mentioned, that is to say—

(a) rights, privileges or advantages in respect of, or connected with, the levying of sea customs or the production and sale of untaxed salt ;

(b) sums receivable in respect of the abandonment or surrender of the right to levy internal customs duties, or to produce or manufacture salt, or to tax salt or other commodities or goods in transit, or sums receivable in lieu of grants of free salt ;

(c) the annual value to the Ruler of any privilege or territory granted in respect of the abandonment or surrender of any such right as is mentioned in the last preceding paragraph ;

(d) privileges in respect of free service stamps or the

free carriage of State mails on government business ;

(e) the privilege of entry free from customs duties of goods imported by sea and transported in bond to the State in question; and

(f) the right to issue currency notes, not being a right, privilege, advantage or immunity surrendered upon the accession of the State, or one which in the opinion of His Majesty, for any other reason ought not to be taken into account for the purposes of this chapter.

(7) An Instrument of Accession of a State shall not be deemed to be suitable for acceptance by His Majesty, unless it contains such particulars as appear to His Majesty to be necessary to enable due effect to be given to the provisions of this and the next but one succeeding sections, and in particular provisions for determining from time to time the value to be attributed for the purposes of those provisions to any privilege or immunity the value of which is fluctuating or uncertain.

Certain payments to Federated States, etc. to be charged on Federal revenues.

[8a]**148.** Any payments made under the last preceding section and any payments heretofore made to any State by the Governor-General in Council or by any Local Government under any agreements made with that State before the passing of this Act, shall be charged on the revenues of the Federation or on the revenues of the corresponding Province under this Act, as the case may be.

149. Where under the foregoing provisions of this chapter there is made in any year by the Federation to a Federated State any payment or distribution of, or calculated by

Value of privileges and immunities to be set off against share of taxes, etc., assigned to Federated States.

reference to, the net proceeds of any duty or tax, the value in and for that year of any privilege or immunity enjoyed by that State in respect of any former or existing source of revenue from a similar duty or tax or from goods of the same kind, being a privilege or immunity which has not been otherwise taken into account shall, if and in so far as the Act of the Federal Legislature under which the payment or distribution is made so provides, be set off against the payment or distribution.

Miscellaneous Financial Provisions

Expenditure defrayable out of Indian Revenues.

150. (1) No burden shall be imposed on the revenues of the Federation or the Provinces except for the purposes of [India][8b] or some part of [India][8b].

(2) Subject as aforesaid, the Federation or a Province may make grants for any purpose, notwithstanding that the purpose is not one with respect to which the Federal or the Provincial Legislature, as the case may be, may make laws.

Provisions as to the custody of public moneys.

151. (1) Rules may be made by the Governor General and by the Governor of a Province for the purpose of securing that all moneys received on account of the revenues of the Federation or of the Province, as the case may be, shall, with such exceptions, if any as may be specified in the rules, be paid into the public account of the Federation or of the Province, and the rules so made may prescribe, or authorise some person to prescribe, the procedure to be followed in respect of the payment of moneys into the said account, the withdrawal with or ancillary to the matters aforesaid.

[8c][(2) In the exercise of the powers under this section the Governor General or a Governor shall exercise his individual judgment].

Exercise by Governor-General of certain powers with respect to Reserve Bank.

[8c]152. (1) The functions of the Governor General with respect in the following matters shall be exercised by him in this discretion, that is to say—

(a) the appointment and removal from office of the Governor and Deputy Governors of the Reserve Bank of India, the approval of their terms of office ;

(b) the appointment of an officiating Governor or Deputy Governor of the bank ;

(c) the supersession of the Central Board of the bank and any action consequent therein ; and

(d) the liquidation of the Bank.

(2) In nominating directors of the Reserve Bank of India and in removing from office any director nominated by him, the Governor-General shall exercise his individual judgement.

Previous sanction of Governor-General to legislation with respect to Reserve Bank, currency and coinage.

153. No Bill or amendment which affects the coinage or currency of the Federation or the constitution or functions of the Reserve Bank of India shall be introduced into or moved in [8c][either chamber] of the Federal Legislature without the previous sanction of the Governor General in his discretion.

Exemption of certain public property from taxation.

154. Property vested in His Majesty for purposes of the government of the Federation shall, save in so fare as any Federal law may otherwise provide, be exempt from all taxes imposed by, or by any authority within, a Province or Federated State:

Provided until any Federal law otherwise provides, any property so vested which was immediately before the commencement of Part III of this Act, liable, or treated a liable, to any such tax, shall, so long as that tax continues, continue to be liable, or to be treated as liable, thereto.

Exemption from taxes on electricity.

[9][**154-A.** Save in so far as any Federal law may otherwise provide, no Provincial law or law of a Federated State shall impose, or authorise the imposition of, a tax on the consumption or sale of electricity (whether produced by a Government or other persons) which is—

(a) consumed by the Federal Government, or sold to the Federal Government for consumption by that Government ; or

(b) consumed in the construction, maintenance or operation of Federal Railway by [8c][the Federal Railway Authority or] a railway company operating that railway, or sold to [8c][that authority or] any such railway company for consumption in the construction, maintenance or operation of a Federal Railway;

and any such law imposing, authorising the imposition of a tax on the sale of electricity shall secure that the price of electricity sold to the Federal Government for consumption by the Government, or to the Federal Railway Authority or any such railway company as aforesaid for consumption in the construction, maintenance or operation of a Federal Railway, shall be less by the amount of a tax than the price charged to other consumers of a substantial quantity of electricity.]

155. (1) Subject as hereinafter provided, the Government of a Province and the Ruler of a Federated State shall not be

Exemption of Provincial Governments and Rulers of Federated States in respect of Federal taxation.

liable to Federal taxation in respect of lands or buildings situated in [8c][British] India or income accruing, arising or received in British India;

Provided that—

(a) where a trade or business of any kind is carried on by or on behalf of the Government of a Province in any part of British India outside that Province or by a Ruler in any part of British India, nothing in this sub-section shall exempt that Government or Ruler from any Federal taxation in respect of that trade or business, or any operations connected therewith, or any income arising in connection therewith, or any property occupied for the purposes, thereof ;

(b) nothing in this sub-section shall exempt a Ruler from any Federal taxation in respect of any lands, buildings or income being his personal property or personal income.

(2) Nothing in this Act affects any exemption from taxation enjoyed as of right at the passing of this Act by the Ruler of an Indian State in respect of any Indian Government securities issued before that date.

Adjustment in respect of certain expenses and pensions.

156. Where under the provisions of this Act the expenses of any court or commission, or the pension payable to or in respect of a person who has served under the Crown in India, are charged on the revenues of the Federation or the revenues of a Province, then if—

(a) in the case of a charge on the revenues of the Federation the court or commission serves any of the separate needs of a Province, or the person has served wholly or in part in connection with the affairs of a Province ; or

(b) in the case of charge on the revenues of a Province, the court or commission serves any of the separate needs of the Federation or another Province, or the person who has served wholly or in part in connection with the affairs of the Federation or another Province, these shall be charged on an paid out of the revenues of the Province or, as the case may be, the revenues of the Federation or of the other Province, such contribution in respect of the expenses or pension as may agreed, or as may in default of agreement be determined by an arbitrator to be appointed by the Chief Justice of India.

Duty of Federation and Provinces to supply Secretary of State with Funds.

[10]157. (1) The Federation and every Province shall secure that there are from time to time in the hands of the Secretary of State sufficient moneys to enable him to make such payments as he may have to make in respect of liability which falls to be met out of the revenues of the Federation or of the Province as the case may be.

(2) Without prejudice to their obligations under the preceding sub-section, the Federation and every Province shall secure that there are from time to time in the hands of the Secretary of State and the High Commissioner sufficient moneys to enable payment to be made of all pensions payable out of the revenues of the Federation or the Province, as the case may be, in the United Kingdom or through officers accounting to the Secretary of State or to the High Commissioner.

Provisions as to relation of Burma monetary system with India.

[10]158. (1) His Majesty to Council may make such provision[10] as may appear to him to be necessary or proper for defining and regulating the relations between the monetary

systems of India and Burma and for purposes connected with or ancillary to those purposes, and in particular, but without prejudice to the generality of this section, such provision as may appear to His Majesty to be necessary or proper for the purpose of giving effect to any arrangement with respect to the said matters made before the commencement of Part III of this Act with the approval of the Secretary of State by the Governor of Burma in Council with the Governor General in Council or any other persons.

(2) Any sums required by an order under this section to be paid by the Federation shall be charged on the revenues of the Federation[11].

Relief in respect of tax on income taxable both in India and Burma.

[10]159. His Majesty in Council may make provision for the grant of relief from any Federal tax on income taxed or taxable in Burma.[11]

Provisions as to customs duties on India-Burma trade.

[10]160. With a view to preventing undue disturbance of trade between India and Burma in the period immediately following the separation of India and Burma and with a view to safeguarding the economic interests of Burma during this period, His Majesty may by Order in Council[12] give such directions as he thinks fit for those purposes with respect to the duties which are, while the Order is in force, to be levied on goods imported into or exported from India or Burma and with respect to ancillary aid related matters.

Notes

1 This part came into effect on 01.04.1937—See the Government of India (Commencement and Transitory Provisions) Order, 1936, para 3.

1a Omitted by the India, (Provisional Constitution) Order, 1947.

2 Inserted by India (Estate Duty) Act, 1945 (8 & 9 Geo., 6, Ch. 7) S.1.

1b Substituted, by *ibid*, by the word "Dominion".
1c Substituted, by *ibid*, by the word "Acceeding".
3 See the Government of India (Distribution of Revenues) Order, 1936 [3.7.1936].
3a Substituted by *ibid*, by the words "Order of the Governor General"
4 Inserted by the India and Burma (Miscellaneous Amendments) Act, 1940 (3 & 4 Geo 6,Ch.5), S.1.
4a Substituted by *ibid*., by the words "Order of the Governor General."
4b Omitted by *ibid*.
5 Substituted, by *ibid*, by the words "such proportion as the Governor General may be order determine".
6 Substituted, by *ibid*, by the words 'Order of the Governor-General'.
6a Substituted, by *ibid*, by the words 'the Governor-General'.
7 *Inserted* by the India and Burma (Miscellaneous Amendment) Act, 1940 (3 & 4 Geo 6, Ch. 5), S.2.
7a Sub-sec (1A) was inserted, by the India (Provisional Constitution) Order, 1947, as follows—
8 To be *construed* as reference to the 1-4-1937 for a period of two years thereafter under the India and Burma (Transitory Provisions) Order, 1937. para 3.
8a Omitted by the India (Provisional Constitution) Order, 1947.
8b Substituted, by ibid, by the word "Dominion".
8c Omitted, by *ibid*.
9 *Inserted* by the India and Burma (Miscellaneous Amendments) Act, 1940 (3 & 4 Geo. 6, Ch. 5, S. 3.
10 Omitted by the India (Provisional Constitution) Order, 1947.
11 See the India and Burma (Burma Monetary Arrangements) Order, 1937 [18-3-1937].
12 See the India and Burma (Trade Regulation) Order, 1937 [18-3-1937].

CHAPTER II: BORROWING AND AUDIT

Borrowing

Cessation of borrowing by Secretary of State in Council.

[1]**161.** Upon the commencement of Part III of this Act all powers vested in the Secretary of State in Council of borrowing on the security of the revenues of India shall cease and determine, but nothing in this section affects the provisions of Part XIII of this Act with respect to borrowing in sterling by the Secretary of State.

162. [1][Subject to the provisions of Part XIII of this Act with respect of the Federation extends to borrowing in sterling], the executive authority of the Federation extends to borrowing upon the security of the revenues of the Federation within such limits, if any, as may from time to time be fixed by Act of the Federal Legislature and to the giving of guarantees within such limits, if any, as may be so fixed.

Borrowing by Federal Government.

163. (1) Subject to the provisions of this section the executive authority of a Province extends to borrowing upon the security of the revenues of the Province within such limits, if any, as may from time to time be fixed by the Act of the Provincial Legislature and to the giving of guarantees within such limits, if any, as may be so fixed.

Borrowing by Provincial Governments.

(2) The Federation may, subject to such conditions, if any, as it may think fit to impose, make loans to, or, so long as any limits fixed under the last preceding section are not exceeded, give guarantees in respect of loans raised by, any Province and any sums required for the purpose of making loans to a Province shall be charged on the revenues of the Federation.

(3) A Province may not without the consent of the Federation borrow outside India, nor without the like consent raise any loan if there is still outstanding any part of loan made to the Province by the Federation or by the Governor General in Council, or in respect of which a guarantee has been given by the Federation or by the Governor General in Council.

A consent under this sub-section may be granted subject to such conditions, if any, as the Federation may think fit to impose.

(4) A consent required by the last preceding sub-section

shall not be unreasonably withheld, not shall the Federation refuse, if sufficient cause is shown, to make a loan to, or to give a guarantee in respect of a loan raised by, a Province, or seek to impose in respect of any of the matters aforesaid any condition which is unreasonable, and, if any dispute arises whether a refusal of consent, or a refusal to make a loan or to give a guarantee, or any condition insisted upon, is or is not justifiable, the matter shall be referred to [2][the Governor General and the decision of the Governor General in his discretion shall be final].

Loans by Federal Government to Federated States.

164. The Federation may, subject to such conditions, if any, as it may think fit to impose, make loans to, or so long as any limits fixed under the last but one preceding section are not exceeded, give guarantees in respect of loans raised by, any Federated State.

Application of Colonial Stock Acts to stock issued by Federation.

[1][165. (1) The Colonial Stock Acts, 1877 to 1900, shall, notwithstanding anything to the contrary in those Acts, apply in relation to sterling stock issued after the establishment of the Federation and forming part of the public debt of the Federation as they apply in relation to stock forming part of the public debt of any British Possession mentioned in those Acts, so however that nothing in section twenty of the Colonial Stock Act, 1877, shall be construed as compelling a person, desirous of bringing proceedings to proceed in the manner therein specified and that, until Parliament otherwise determines, any conditions prescribed by the Treasury under section two of the Colonial Stock Act, 1900 shall be deemed to have been complied with respect to all such stock so issued by the Federation.

(2) The expression "colonial stock" in section eleven of the Trusts (Scotland) Act 1921 shall include any stock in

relation to which the said Acts apply by virtue of this section.

(3) In paragraph (d) of sub-section (1) of section one of the Trustee act, 1925, the words "or any other securities the interest in sterling whereon is payable out of, and charged on, the revenues of India" shall be repealed:

Provided that, notwithstanding anything in this Act, any securities which by virtue of the said words were immediately before the commencement of Part III of this Act securities in which a trustee might invest trust funds shall continue to be securities in which a trustee may invest such funds .]

Audit and Accounts

Auditor-General of India.

166. (1) There shall be an Auditor-General of India who shall be appointed by [3][His Majesty] and shall only be removed from office in like manner and on the like grounds as a judge of the Federal Court.

(2) The conditions of service of the Auditor-General shall be such as may be prescribed by [4][His Majesty in Council] and he shall not be eligible for further office under the Crown in India after he has ceased to hold his office:

Provided that neither the salary of an Auditor-General nor his rights in respect of leave of absence, pension or age of retirement shall be varied to his disadvantage after his appointment.

(3) The Auditor-General shall perform such duties and exercise such powers in relation to the accounts of the Federation and of the Provinces as may be prescribed by, or by rules made under, an order of [3][His Majesty in Council], or by any subsequent Act of the [5][Federal] Legislature varying or extending such an Order:

(4) The salary, allowances and pension payable to or in respect of an Auditor-General shall be charged on the

revenues of the [5][Federation], and the salaries, allowances and pensions payable to or in respect of members of his staff shall be paid out of those revenues.

167. (1) If a Provincial Legislature [5a][after the expiration of two years from the commencement of Part III of this Act] charging the salary of an Auditor-General for that Province on the revenues of the Province, an Auditor-General of the Province may be appointed by [6][His majesty] to perform the same duties and to exercise the same powers in relation to the audit of the accounts of the Province as would be performed and exercised by the Auditor-General of India, if any Auditor-General of the Province had not been appointed:

Provisional Auditor-General

Provided that no appointment of an Auditor-General in a Province shall be made until the expiration of at least three years from the date of the Act of the Provincial Legislature by which provision is made for an Auditor-General of that Province.

(2) The provisions of the last preceding section shall apply in relation to the Auditor-General of a Province and his staff as they apply in relation to the Auditor-General of India and his staff, subject to the following modifications that is to say—

(a) a person who is, or has been, Auditor-General of a Province shall be eligible for appointment as Auditor-General of India ;

(b) In [7][Sub-section (3)] of the said section, for the reference to the Federal Legislature there shall be substituted a reference to the Provincial Legislature, and for the reference to the Governor-General there shall be substituted a reference to the Governor; and

(c) in sub-section (4) of the said section for the reference to the revenue of the Federation there shall be substituted a reference to revenues of the Province:

provided that nothing in this section shall derogate from the power of the Auditor-General of India to give such directions in respect to the accounts of Provinces as are mentioned in the next succeeding section.

168. The accounts of the Federation shall be kept in such form as the Auditor-General of India may, with the approval of the Governor-General, prescribe and, in so far as the Auditor-General of India may, with the like approval, give any directions with regard to the methods or principles in accordance with which any accounts or Provinces ought to be kept, it shall be the duty of every Provincial Government to cause accounts to be kept accordingly.

Power of Auditor-General of India to give directions to accounts.

169. The reports of the Auditor-General of India relating to the accounts of the Federation shall be submitted to the Governor-General, who shall cause them to be laid before the Federal Legislature, and the reports of the Auditor-General of India or of the Auditor-General of the Province, as the case may be, relating to the accounts of a Province shall be submitted to the Governor of the Province, who shall vause them to be laid before the Provincial Legislature.

Audit Reports

[5a][**170.** (1) There shall be an auditor of India Home Accounts who shall be appointed by the Governor-General in his discretion and shall only be removed from office in like manner and on the like grounds as a judge of the Federal Court.

Auditor of Indian Home Accounts

(2) The conditions of service of the Auditor of Indian Home Accounts shall be such as may be prescribed by the Governor-General in his discretion:

Provided that neither the salary of an Auditor of Indian Home Accounts nor his rights in respect of leave of absence, pension or age of retirement shall be varied to his disadvantage after his appointment.

(3) The Auditor of Indian Home Accounts shall perform such duties and exercise such powers in relation to transactions in the United Kingdom affecting the revenues of the Federation, of the Federal Railway Authority, or of any Province, as may be prescribed by, or by rules made under, an Order of His Majesty in Council, or by any Act of the Federal Legislature varying or extending such an Order:

Provided that no Bill or amendment for the purpose aforesaid shall be introduced or moved without the prior sanction of the Governor-General in his discretion:

(4) The reports of the Auditor of Indian Home Accounts relating to such transactions as aforesaid shall be submitted to the Auditor-General of India, or, in the case of transactions affecting the revenues of a Province which has an Auditor-General, to the Auditor-General of the Province, and shall be included by any such Auditor-General in the reports which under this part of this Act he is required to submit to the Governor-General or, as the case may be, to the Governor.

(5) The Auditor of Indian Home Accounts shall be subject to the general superintendence of the Auditor-General of India.

(6) The salary, allowances and pension payable to or in respect of the Auditor of Indian Home Accounts shall be charged on the revenues of the Federation, and the salaries, allowances and pensions payable to or in respect of members of his staff shall be paid out of those revenues.

(7) His Majesty in Council may require the Auditor of Indian Home Accounts to perform in relation to Burma all or any of the functions which he performs in relation to India, and may fix the payments to be made in respect of his services from the revenues of Burma to the revenues of the Federation, any may make such incidental and consequential provision

as may appear to him to be proper.

[6a]**171.** The accounts relating to the discharge of the functions of the Crown in its relations with Indian States shall be audited by the Auditor-General of India, or, in so far as those accounts concern transactions in the United Kingdom, by the Auditor of Indian Home Accounts acting on his behalf and under his general superintendence, and the Auditor-General of India shall make to the Secretary of State annual reports on the accounts so audited by him or on his behalf.

Audit of accounts relating to the discharge of the functions of the Crown in relation to Indian States.

Notes

1. Omitted by the India (Provisional Constitution) Order, 1947.
2. Substituted, by *ibid.*, by the words "an arbitrator appointed by the Chief Justice of India, whose decision shall be final".
3. Substituted, by *ibid.*, by the word "Governor General".
4. Substituted, by *ibid.*, by the words "Order of the Governor General".
5. Substituted by *ibid.*, by the words "Dominion".

5a. Omitted by *ibid.*

6. Substituted, by *ibid.*, by the word "Governor".
7. Substituted, by *ibid.*, by the words "sub-sections (2) and (3).

Articles of Constitution Relevant to Finance Commission

Article 268. Duties levied by the Union but collected and appropriated by the States

(1) Such stamp duties and such duties of excise on medicinal and toilet preparations as are mentioned in the Union List shall be levied by the Government of India but shall be collected—

(a) in the case where such duties are leviable within any [1][Union territory], by the Government of India, and

(b) in other cases, by the States within which such duties are respectively leviable.

(2) The proceeds in any financial year of any such duty leviable within any State shall not form part of the Consolidated Fund of India, but shall be assigned to that State.

Article 269. Taxes levied and collected by the Union but assigned to States—

[2][(1) Taxes on the sales or purchase of goods and taxes on the consignment of goods shall be levied and collected by the Government of India but shall be assigned and shall be deemed to have been assigned to the States on or after the 1st day of April, 1996 in the matter provided in clause (2).

Explanation—For the purposes of this clause—

(a)the expression 'taxes on the sale or purchase of goods'

shall mean taxes on sale or purchase of goods other than newspapers, where such sale or purchase takes place in the course of inter-State trade or commerce;

(b) the expression 'taxes on the consignment of goods' shall mean taxes on the consignment of goods (whether the consignment is to the person making it or to any other person), where such consignment takes place in the course of inter-State trade or commerce.

(2) The net proceeds in any financial year of any such tax, except in so far as those proceeds represent proceeds attributable to Union territories, shall not form part of the Consolidated Fund of India, but shall be assigned to the States within which that tax is leviable in that year, and shall be distributed among those States in accordance with such principles of distribution as may be formulated by Parliament by law.]

[3][(3) Parliament may by law formulate principles for determining when a [4][sale or purchase of, or consignment of, goods] takes place in the course of inter-State or commerce.]

[5]**[Article 270.** Taxes levied and distributed between the Union and the States—

(1) All taxes and duties referred to in the Union List, except the duties and taxes referred to in articles 268 and 269, respectively, surcharge on taxes 1and duties referred to in article 271 and any cess levied for specific purposes under any law made by Parliament shall be levied and collected by the Government of India and shall be distributed between the Union and the States in the manner provided in clause (2).

(2) Such percentage, as may be prescribed, of the net proceeds of any such tax or duty in any financial year shall not form part of the Consolidated Fund of India, but shall be assigned to the States within which that tax or duty is leviable in that year, and shall be distributed among those States in such manner and from such time as may be prescribed in the manner provided in clause (3).

(3) In this article, 'prescribed' means—

(a) until a Finance Commission has been constituted, prescribed by the President by order, and

(b) after a Finance Commission has been constituted, prescribed by the President by order after considering the recommendations of the Finance Commission'.]

Article 271. Surcharge on certain duties and taxes for purposes of the Union—

Notwithstanding anything in Arts. 269 and 270, Parliament may at any time increase any of the duties or taxes referred to in those articles by a surcharge for purposes of the Union and the whole proceeds of any such surcharge shall form part of the Consolidated Fund of India.

[6]**Article 272.** Taxes which are levied and collected by the Union and may be distributed between the Union and the States.—[Repealed by the Constitution (Eightieth Amendment) Act, 2000, sec. 4 (w.e.f. 9-6-2000).]

Article 274. Prior recommendation of President required to Bills affecting taxation in which States are interested—

(1) No Bill or amendment which imposes or varies any tax or duty in which States are interested, or which varies the meaning of expression 'agricultural income' as defined for the purposes of the enactment relating to Indian Income tax, or which affects the principles

on which under any of the foregoing provisions of this Chapter moneys are or may be distributable to the States, or which imposes any such surcharge for the purposes of the Union as is mentioned in the foregoing provisions of this Chapter; shall be introduced or moved in either House of Parliament except on the recommendations of the President.

(2) In this article the expression 'tax or duty in which States are interested' means—

(a) a tax or duty the whole or part of the net proceeds whereof are assigned to any State;

or

(b) a tax or duty by reference to the net proceeds whereof sums are for the time being payable out of the Consolidated Fund of India to any State.

Article 275. Grants from the Union to certain States—

(1) Such sums as Parliament may be law provide shall be charged on the Consolidated Fund of India in each year as grants-in-aid of the revenues of such States as Parliament may determine to be in need of assistance and different sums may be fixed for different States:

Provided that there shall be paid out of the Consolidated Fund of India as grants-in-aid of the revenues of a State such capital and recurring sums as may be necessary to enable that State to meet the costs of such schemes of development as may be undertaken by the State with the approval of the Government of India for the purpose of promoting the welfare of the Scheduled Tribes in that State or raising the level of administration of the Scheduled Areas therein to that of the administration of the rest of the areas of that State:

Provided further that there shall be paid out of the Consolidated Fund of India as grants-in-aid of the revenues of the State of Assam sums, capital and recurring, equivalent to—

(a) the average excess of expenditure over the revenues during the two years immediately preceding the commencement of this Constitution in respect of the administration of the tribal areas specified in [7][Part I] of the table appended to paragraph 20 of the Sixth Schedule; and

(b) the costs of such schemes of development as may be undertaken by that State with the approval of the Government of India for the purpose of raising the level of the administration of the said areas to that of the administration of the rest of the areas of that State.

[8][(1A) On and from the formation of the autonomous State under article 244A—

(i) any sums payable under clause (a) of the second proviso to clause (1) shall, if the autonomous State comprises of all the tribal areas referred to therein, be paid to the autonomous State, and, if the autonomous State comprises only some of those tribal areas, be apportioned between the State of Assam and the autonomous State as the President may, by order, specify;

(ii) there shall be paid out of the Consolidated Fund of India as grants-in-aid of the revenues of the autonomous State sums, capital and recurring, equivalent to the costs of such schemes of development as may be undertaken by the autonomous State with the approval of the

Government of India for the purpose of raising the level of administration of that State to that of the administration of the rest of the State of Assam.]

(2) Until provision is made by Parliament under clause (1), the powers conferred on Parliament under that clause shall be exercisable by the President by order and any order made by the President under this clause shall have effect subject to any provision so made by Parliament:

Provided that after a Finance Commission has been constituted no order shall be made under this clause by the President except after considering the recommendations of the Finance Commission.

Article 279. Calculation of 'net proceeds', etc.—

(1) In the foregoing provisions of this Chapter, 'net proceeds' means in relation to any tax or duty the proceeds thereof reduced by the cost of collection, and for the purposes of those provisions the net proceeds of any tax or duty, or of any part of any tax or duty, in or attributable to any area shall be ascertained and certified by the Comptroller and Auditor-General of India, whose certificate shall be final.

Article 280. Finance Commission—

(1) The President shall, within two years from the commencement of this Constitution and thereafter at the expiration of every fifth year or at such earlier time as the President considers necessary, by order constitute a Finance Commission which shall consist of a Chairman and four other members to be appointed by the President.

(2) Parliament may by law determine the qualifications which shall be requisite for appointment as members of the Commission and the manner in which they shall be selected.

(3) It shall be the duty of the Commission to make recommendations to the President as to—

(a) the distribution between the Union and the States of the net proceeds of taxes which are to be, or may be, divided between them under this Chapter and the allocation between the States of the respective shares of such proceeds;

(b) the principles which should govern the grants-in-aid of the revenues of the States out of the Consolidated Fund of India;

[9][(bb) the measures needed to augment the Consolidated Fund of a State to supplement the resources of the Panchayats in the State on the basis of the recommendations made by the Finance Commission of the State;]

[10][(c) the measures needed to augment the Consolidated Fund of a State to supplement the resources of the Municipalities in the State on the basis of the recommendations made by the Finance Commission of the State;]

[11][(d)] any other matter referred to the Commission by the President in the interests of sound finance.

(4) The Commission shall determine their procedure and shall have such powers in the performance of their functions as Parliament may by law confer on them.

Article 281. Recommendations of the Finance Commission—

The President shall cause every recommendation made by the Finance Commission under the provisions of this Constitution together with an explanatory memorandum as to the action taken thereon to be laid before each House of Parliament.

Article 282. Expenditure defrayable by the Union or a State out of its reserves—

The Union or a State may make any grants for any public purpose, notwithstanding that the purpose is not one with respect to which Parliament or the Legislature of the State, as the case may be, may make laws.

Articles Relevant to Panchayats

[12](Part IX) The Panchayats

In this part, unless the context otherwise requires—

(a) 'district' means a district in a State ;
(b) 'Gram Sabha' means a body consisting of persons registered in the electoral rolls relating to a village comprised within the area of Panchayat at the village level;
(c) 'intermediate level' means a level between the village and district levels specified by the Governor of a State by public notification to be the intermediate level for the purposes of this Part;
(d) 'Panchayat' means an institution (by whatever name called) of self-government constituted under article 243B, for the rural areas;
(e) 'Panchayat area' means the territorial area of a Panchayat;
(f) 'population' means the population as ascertained at the last preceding census of which the relevant figures

have been published;

(g) 'village' means a village specified by the Governor by public notification to be a village for the purposes of this Part and includes a group of villages so specified.

243A. Gram Sabha—

A Gram Sabha may exercise such powers and perform such functions at the village level as the Legislature of a State may by law, provide.

243B. Constitution of Panchayats—

(1) There shall be constituted in every State, Panchayats at the village, intermediate and district levels in accordance with the provisions of this Part.

(2) Notwithstanding anything in clause (l), Panchayats at the intermediate level may not be constituted in a State having a population not exceeding twenty lakhs.

243C. Composition of Panchayats—

(1) Subject to the provisions of this Part, the Legislature of a State may, by law, make provisions with respect to the composition of Panchayats:

Provided that the ratio between the population of the territorial area of a Panchayat at any level and the number of seats in such Panchayat to be filled by election shall, so far as practicable, be the same throughout the State.

(2) All the seats in a Panchayat shall be filled by persons chosen by direct election from territorial constituencies in the Panchayat area and, for this purpose, each Panchayat area shall be divided into territorial constituencies in such manner that the ratio between the population of each constituency and the number of seats allotted to it shall, so far as practicable, be

the same throughout the Panchayat area.

(3) The Legislature of a State may, by law, provide for the representation—

(a) of the Chairpersons of the Panchayats at the village level, in the Panchayats at the intermediate level or, in the case of a State not having Panchayats at the intermediate level, in the Panchayats at the district level;

(b) of the Chairpersons of the Panchayats at the intermediate level, in the Panchayats at the district level;

(c) of the members of the House of the People and the members of the Legislative Assembly of the State representing constituencies which comprise wholly or partly a Panchayat area at a level other than the village level, in such Panchayat;

(d) of the members of the Council of States and the members of the Legislative Council of the State, where they are registered as electors within—

(i) a Panchayat area at the intermediate level, in Panchayat at the intermediate level;

(ii) a Panchayat area at the district level, in Panchayat at the district level.

(4) The Chairperson of a Panchayat and other members of a Panchayat whether or not chosen by direct election from territorial constituencies in the Panchayat area shall have the right to vote in the meetings of the Panchayats.

(5) The Chairperson of—

(a) Panchayat at the village level shall be elected in such manner as the Legislature of a State may, by law, provide ; and

(b) a Panchayat at the intermediate level or district level, shall be elected by, and from amongst, the elected members thereof.

243D. Reservation of seats—

(1) Seats shall be reserved for—

(a) the Scheduled Castes ; and

(b) the Scheduled Tribes, in every Panchayat and the number of seats so reserved shall bear, as nearly as may be, the same proportion to the total number of seats to be filled by direct election in that Panchayat as the population of the Scheduled Castes in that Panchayat area or of the Scheduled Tribes in that Panchayat area bears to the total population of that area and such seats may be allotted by rotation to different constituencies in a Panchayat.

(2) Not less than one-third of the total number of seats reserved under clause (1) shall be reserved for women belonging to the Scheduled Castes or, as the case may be, the Scheduled Tribes.

(3) Not less than one-third (including the number of seats reserved for women belonging to the Scheduled Castes and the Scheduled Tribes) of the total number of seats to be filled by direct election in every Panchayat shall be reserved for women and such seats may be allotted by, rotation to different constituencies in a Panchayat.

(4) The offices of the Chairpersons in the Panchayats at the village or any other level shall be reserved for the Scheduled Castes, the Scheduled Tribes and women in such manner as the Legislature of a State may, by law, provide:

Provided that the number of offices of

Chairpersons reserved for the Scheduled Castes and the Scheduled Tribes in the Panchayats at each level in any State shall bear, as nearly as may be, the same proportion to the total number of such offices in the Panchayats at each level as the population of the Scheduled Castes in the State or of the Scheduled Tribes in the State bears to the total population of the State:

Provided further that not less than one third of the total number of offices of Chairpersons in the Panchayats at each level shall be reserved for women:

Provided also that the number of offices reserved under this clause shall be allotted by rotation to different Panchayats at each level.

(5) The reservation of seats under clauses (1) and (2) and the reservation of offices of Chairpersons (other than the reservation for women) under clause (4) shall cease to have effect on the expiration of the period specified in article 334.

(6) Nothing in this Part shall prevent the Legislature of a State from making any provision for reservation of seats in any Panchayat or offices of Chairpersons in the Panchayats at any level in favour of backward class of citizens.

243E. Duration of Panchayats etc.—

(1) Every Panchayat, unless sooner dissolved under any law for the time being in force, shall continue for five years from the date appointed for its first meeting and no longer.

(2) No amendment of any law for the time being in force shall have the effect of causing dissolution of a Panchayat at any level, which is functioning immediately before such amendment, till the

expiration of its duration specified in clause (1).

(3) An election to constitute a Panchayat shall be completed—

(a) before the expiry of its duration specified in clause (1);

(b) before the expiration of a period of six months from the date of its dissolution:

Provided that where the remainder of the period for which the dissolved Panchayat would have continued is less than six months, it shall not be necessary to hold any election under this clause for constituting the Panchayat for such period.

(4) A Panchayat constituted upon the dissolution of a Panchayat before the expiration of its duration shall continue only for the remainder of the period for which the dissolved Panchayat would have continued under clause (1) had it not been so dissolved.

243F. Disqualification for membership—

(1) A person shall be disqualified for being chosen as, and for being, a member of a Panchayat—

(a) if he is so disqualified by or under any law for the time being in force for the purposes of elections to the Legislature of the State concerned: Provided that no person shall be disqualified on the ground that he is less than twenty five years of age, if he has attained the age of twenty one years;

(b) if he is so disqualified by or under any law made by the Legislature of the State.

(2) If any question arises as to whether a member of a Panchayat has become subject to any of the

disqualifications mentioned in clause (1), the question shall be referred for the decision of such authority and in such manner as the Legislature of a State may, by law, provide.

243G. Powers, authority and responsibilities of Panchayat—

Subject to the provisions of this Constitution the Legislature of a State may, by law, endow the Panchayats with such powers and authority and may be necessary to enable them to function as institutions of self-government and such law may contain provisions for the devolution of powers and responsibilities upon Panchayats, at the appropriate level, subject to such conditions as may be specified therein, with respect to—

(a) the preparation of plans for economic development and social justice;

(b) the implementation of schemes for economic development and social justice as may be entrusted to them including those in relation to the matters listed in the Eleventh Schedule.

243H. Powers to impose taxes by, and Funds of, the Panchayats—

The Legislature of a State may, by law—

(a) authorise a Panchayat to levy, collect and appropriate such taxes, duties, tolls and fees in accordance with such procedure and subject to such limits;

(b) assign to a Panchayat such taxes, duties, tolls and fees levied and collected by the State Government for such purposes and subject to such conditions and limits;

(c) provide for making such grants-in-aid to the Panchayats from the Consolidated Fund of the State; and

(d) provide for constitution of such Funds for crediting all moneys received, respectively, by or on behalf of the Panchayats and also for the withdrawal of such moneys there from, as may be specified in the law.

243I. Constitution of Finance Commission to review financial position—

(1) The Governor of a State shall, as soon as may be within one year from the commencement of the Constitution (Seventy-third Amendment) Act, 1992, and thereafter at the expiration of every fifth year, constitute a Finance Commission to review the financial position of the Panchayats and to make recommendations to the Governor as to—

(a) the principles which should govern—

(i) the distribution between the State and the Panchayats of the net proceeds of the taxes, duties, tolls and fees leviable by the State, which may be divided between them under this Part and the allocation between the Panchayats at all levels of their respective shares of such proceeds;

(ii) the determination of the taxes, duties, tolls and fees which may be assigned to, or appropriated by, the Panchayats;

(iii) the grants-in-aid to the Panchayats from the Consolidated Fund of the State;

(b) the measures needed to improve the financial position of the Panchayats;

(c) any other matter referred to the Finance Commission by the Governor in the interests of sound finance of the Panchayats.

(2) The Legislature of a State may, by law, provide for

the composition of the Commission, the qualifications which shall be requisite for appointment as members thereof and the manner in which they shall be selected.

(3) The Commission shall determine their procedure and shall have such powers in the performance of their functions as the Legislature of the State may, by law, confer on them.

(4) The Governor shall cause every recommendation made by the Commission under this article together with an explanatory memorandum as to the action taken thereon to be laid before the Legislature of the State.

243J. Audit of accounts of Panchayats—

The Legislature of a State may, by law, make provisions with respect to the maintenance of accounts by the Panchayats and the auditing of such accounts.

243K. Elections to the Panchayats—

(1) The superintendence, direction and control of the preparation of electoral rolls for, and the conduct of, all elections to the Panchayats shall be vested in a State Election Commission consisting of a State Election Commissioner to be appointed by the Governor.

(2) Subject to the provisions of any law made by the Legislature of a State the conditions of service and tenure of office of the State Election Commissioner shall be, such as the Governor may by rule determine: Provided that the State Election Commissioner shall not be removed from his office except in like manner and on the like ground as a Judge of a High Court and the conditions of service of the State Election Commissioner shall not be varied to his disadvantage

after his appointment.

(3) The Governor of a State shall, when so requested by the State Election Commission, make available to the State Election Commission such staff as may be necessary for the discharge of the functions conferred on the State Election Commission by clause (l).

(4) Subject to the provisions of this Constitution, the Legislature of a State may, by law, make provision with respect to all matters relating to, or in connection with, elections to the Panchayats.

243L. Application to Union territories—

The provisions of this Part shall apply to the Union territories and shall, in their application to a Union territory, have effect as if the references to the Governor of a State were references to the Administrator of the Union territory appointed under 239 and references to the Legislature or the Legislative Assembly of a State were references, in relation to a Union territory having a Legislative Assembly, to that Legislative Assembly:

Provided that the President may, by public notification, direct that the provisions of this Part shall apply to any Union territory or part thereof subject to such exceptions and modifications as he may specify in the notification.

243M. Part not to apply to certain areas—

(1) Nothing in this Part shall apply to the Scheduled Areas referred to in clause (l), and the tribal areas referred to in clause (2), of article 244.

(2) Nothing in this Part shall apply to—

(a) the States of Nagaland, Meghalaya and Mizoram;

(b) the Hill areas in the State of Manipur for which District Councils exist under any law for the time being in force.

(3) Nothing in this Part—

(a) relating to Panchayats at the district level shall apply to the Hill areas of the District of Darjeeling in the State of West Bengal for which Darjeeling Gorkha Hill Council exists under any law for the time being in force;

(b) shall be construed to affect the functions and powers of the Darjeeling Gorkha Hill Council constituted under such law.

[13]**(3A)** Nothing in article 243, relating to reservation of seats for the Scheduled Castes, shall apply to the State of Arunachal Pradesh.

(4) Notwithstanding Constitution—

(a) the Legislature of a State referred to in sub-clause (a) of clause (2) may, by law, extend this Part to that State, except the areas, if any, referred to in clause (1), if the Legislative Assembly of that State passes a resolution to that effect by a majority of the total membership of that House and by a majority of not less than two-thirds of the members of that House present and voting

(b) Parliament may, by law, extend the provisions of this Part to the Scheduled Areas and the tribal areas referred to in clause (1) subject to such exceptions and modifications as may be specified in such law, and no such law shall be deemed to be an amendment of this Constitution for the purposes of article 368.

243N. Continuance of existing laws and Panchayats—

Notwithstanding anything in this Part, any provision of any law relating to Panchayats in force in a State immediately before commencement of the Constitution (Seventy-third Amendment) Act, 1992, which is inconsistent with the provisions of this part, shall continue to be in force until amended or repealed by a competent Legislature or other competent authority or until the expiration of one year from such commencement whichever is earlier:

Provided that all the Panchayats existing immediately before such commencement shall continue till the expiration of their duration, unless sooner dissolved by a resolution passed to that effect by the Legislative Assembly of that State or, in the case of a State having a Legislative Council, by each house of the Legislature of that State.

243 O. Bar to interference by courts in electoral matters—

(a) the validity of any law relating to the delimitation of constituencies or the allotment of seats to such constituencies made or purporting to be made under article 243K, shall not be called in question in any court;

(b) no election to any Panchayat shall be called in question except by an election petition presented to such authority and in such manner as is provided for by or under any Law made by the Legislature of a State.

Articles Relevant to Municipalities

[14][Part IXA] The Muncipalities

243P. Definitions—

(a) 'Committee' means a Committee constituted under article 243S;

(b) 'district' means a district in a State;

(c) 'Metropolitan area' means an area having a population of ten lakhs or more, comprised in one or more districts and consisting of two or more Municipalities or Panchayats or other contiguous areas, specified by the Governor by public notification to be Metropolitan area for the purposes of this Part;

(d) 'Municipal area' means the territorial area of a Municipality as is notified by the Governor;

(e) 'Municipality' means an institution of self government constituted under article 243Q;

(f) to 'Panchayat' means a Panchayat constituted under article 243B;

(g) 'population' means the population as ascertained at the last preceding census of which the relevant figures have been published.

243Q. Constitution of Muncipalities—

(1) There shall be constituted in every State—

(a) a Nagar Panchayat (by whatever name called) for a transitional area, that is to say, an area in transition from a rural area to an urban area.

(b) a Municipal Council for a smaller urban area; and

(c) a Municipal Corporation for a larger urban area, in accordance with the provisions of this Part:

Provided that a Municipality under this clause may not be constituted in such urban area or part thereof as the Governor may, having regard to the size of the area and the municipal services being provided or proposed to be provided by an industrial establishment in that area and such other factors as he may deem fit, by public notification, specify to be an industrial township.

(2) In this article, 'a transitional area', 'a smaller urban area' or 'a larger urban area' means such area as the Governor may, having regard to the population of the area, the density of the population therein, the revenue generated for local administration, the percentage of employment in non-agricultural activities, the economic importance or such other

factors as he may deem fit, specify by public notification for the purposes of this Part.

243R. Composition of Municipalities—

(1) Save as provided in clause (2), all the seats in a Municipality shall be filled by persons chosen by direct election from the territorial constituencies in the Municipal area and for this purpose each Municipal area shall be divided into territorial constituencies to be known as wards.

(2) The Legislature of a State may, by law, provide—

(a) for the representation in a Municipality of—

(i) persons having special knowledge or experience in Municipal administration;

(ii) the members of the House of the People and the members of the Legislative Assembly of the State representing constituencies which comprise wholly or partly the Municipal area;

(iii) the members of the Council of States and the members of the Legislative Council of the State registered as electors within the Municipal area;

(iv) the Chairpersons of the Committees constituted under clause (5) of article 243S:

Provided that the persons referred to in paragraph (i) shall not have the right to vote in the meetings of the Municipality;

(b) the manner of election of the Chairperson of a Municipality.

243S. Constitution and composition of Wards Committees, etc.—

(1) There shall be constituted Wards Committees,

consisting of one or more Wards, within the territorial area of a Municipality having a population of three lakhs or more.

(2) The Legislature of a State may, by law, make provision with respect to—

(a) the composition and the territorial area of a Wards Committee;

(b) the manner in which the seats in a Wards Committee shall be filled.

(3) A member of a Municipality representing a ward within the territorial area of the Wards Committee shall be a member of that Committee.

(4) Where a Wards Committee consists of—

(a) one ward, the member representing that ward in the Municipality; or

(b) two or more wards, one of the members representing such wards in the Municipality elected by the members of the Wards Committee, shall be the Chairperson of that Committee.

(5) Nothing in this article shall be deemed to prevent the Legislature of a State from making any provision for the Constitution of Committees in addition to the Wards Committees.

243T. Reservation of seats—

(1) Seats shall be reserved for the Scheduled Castes and the Scheduled Tribes in every Municipality and the number of seats so reserved shall bear, as nearly as may be, the same proportion to the total number of seats to be filled by direct election in that Municipality as the population of the Scheduled Castes in the Municipal area or of the Scheduled Tribes in the Municipal area bears to the total population of that

area and such seats may be allotted by rotation to different constituencies in a Municipality.

(2) Not less than one-third of the total number of seats reserved under clause (1) shall be reserved for women belonging to the Scheduled Castes or, as the case may be, the Scheduled Tribes.

(3) Not less than one-third (including the number of seats reserved for women belonging to the Scheduled Castes and the Scheduled Tribes) of the total number of seats to be filled by direct election in every Municipality shall be reserved for women and such seats may be allotted by rotation to different constituencies in a Municipality.

(4) The offices of Chairpersons in the Municipalities shall be reserved for the Scheduled Castes, the Scheduled Tribes and women in such manner as the Legislature of a State may, by law, provide.

(5) The reservation of seats under clauses (1) and (2) and the reservation of offices of Chairpersons (other than the reservation for women) under clause (4) shall cease to have effect on the expiration of the period specified in article 334.

(6) Nothing in this Part shall prevent the Legislature of a State from making any provision for reservation of seats in any Municipality or offices of Chairpersons in the Municipalities in favour of backward class of citizens.

243U. Duration of Municipalities, etc.—

(1) Every Municipality, unless sooner dissolved under any law for the time being in force, shall continue for five years from the date appointed for its first meeting and no longer:

Provided that a Municipality shall be given a

reasonable opportunity of being heard before its dissolution.

(2) No amendment of any law for the time being in force shall have the effect of causing dissolution of a Municipality at any level, which is functioning immediately before such amendment, till the expiration of its duration specified in clause (1).

(3) An election to constitute a Municipality shall be completed,—

(a) before the expiry of its duration specified in clause (1);

(b) before the expiration of a period of six months from the date of its dissolution:

Provided that where the remainder of the period for which the dissolved Municipality would have continued is less than six months, it shall not be necessary to hold any election under this clause for constituting the Municipality for such period.

(4) A Municipality constituted upon the dissolution of a Municipality before the expiration of its duration shall continue only for the remainder of the period for which the dissolved Municipality would have continued under clause (1) had it not been so dissolved.

243V. Disqualifications for membership—

(1) A person shall be disqualified for being chosen as, and for being a member of a Municipality—

(a) if he is so disqualified by or under any law for the time being in force for the purposes of elections to the Legislature of the State concerned:

Provided that no person shall be disqualified on the ground that he is less than twenty-five years of age, if he has attained the age, of twenty-one years;

(b) if he is so disqualified by or under any law made by the Legislature of the State.

(2) If any question arises as to whether a member of a Municipality has become subject to any of the disqualifications mentioned in clause (1), the question shall be referred for the decision of such authority and in such manner as the Legislature of a State may, by law, provide.

243W. Powers, authority and responsibilities of Municipalities, etc.—

Subject to the provisions of this Constitution, the Legislature of a State may, by law, endow—

(a) the Municipalities with such powers and authority as may be necessary to enable them to function as institutions of self-government and such law may contain provisions for the devolution of powers and responsibilities upon Municipalities, subject to such conditions as may be specified therein, with respect to—

(i) the preparation of plans for economic development and social justice;

(ii) the performance of functions and the implementation of schemes as may be entrusted to them including those in relation to the matters listed in the Twelfth Schedule;

(b) the Committees with such powers and authority as may be necessary to enable them to carry out the responsibilities conferred upon them including those in relation to the matters listed in the Twelfth Schedule.

243X. Power to impose taxes by, and Funds, of, the Municipalities.

The Legislature of a State may, by law—

(a) authorise a Municipality to levy, collect and appropriate such taxes, duties, tolls and fees in accordance with such procedure and subject to such limits;

(b) assign to a Municipality such taxes, duties, tolls and fees levied and collected by the State Government for such purposes and subject to such conditions and limits;

(c) provide for making, such grants-in-aid to the Municipalities from the Consolidated Fund of the State; and

(d) provide for constitution of such Funds for crediting all moneys received, respectively, by or on behalf of the Municipalities and also for the withdrawal of such moneys there from, as may be specified in the law.

243Y. Finance Commission—

(1) The Finance Commission constituted under article 243I shall also review the financial position of the Municipalities and make recommendations to the Governor as to—

(a) the principles which should govern—

(i) the distribution between the State and the Municipalities of the net proceeds of the taxes, duties, tolls and fees leviable by the State, which may be divided between them under this Part and the allocation between the Municipalities at all levels of their respective shares of such proceeds;

(ii) the determination of the taxes, duties, tolls

and fees which may be assigned to, or appropriated by, the Municipalities;

(iii) the grants-in-aid to the Municipalities from the Consolidated Fund of the State;

(b) the measures needed to improve the financial position of the Municipalities;

(c) any other matter referred to the Finance Commission by the Governor in the interests of sound finance of the Municipalities.

(2) The Governor shall cause every recommendation made by the Commission under this article together with an explanatory memorandum as to the action taken thereon to be laid before the Legislature of the State.

243Z. Audit of accounts of Municipalities—

The Legislature of a State may, by law, make provisions with respect to the maintenance of accounts by the Municipalities and the auditing of such accounts.

243ZA. Elections to the Municipalities—

(1) The superintendence, direction and control of the preparation of electoral rolls for, and the conduct of, all elections to the Municipalities shall be vested in the State Election Commission referred to in article 243K.

(2) Subject to provisions of this Constitution, the Legislature of a State may, by law, make provision with respect to all matters relating to, or in connection with, elections to the Municipalities.

243ZB. Application to Union territories—

The provisions of this Part shall apply to the Union territories and shall, in their application to a Union territory, have effect, as if the references to the Governor of a State were references to the Administrator of the Union territory appointed under article 239 and references to the Legislature or the Legislative Assembly of a State were references in relation to a Union territory having a Legislative Assembly, to that Legislative Assembly:

Provided that the President may, by public notification, direct that the provisions of this Part shall apply to any Union territory or part thereof subject to such exceptions and modifications as he may specify in the notification.

243ZC. Part not to apply to certain areas—

(1) Nothing in this Part shall apply to the Scheduled Areas referred to in Clause (l), and the tribal areas referred to in clause (2), of article 244.

(2) Nothing in this part shall be construed to affect the functions and powers of the Darjeeling Gorkha Hill Council constituted under any law for the time being in force for the hill areas of the district of Darjeeling in the State of West Bengal.

(3) Notwithstanding anything in this Constitution, Parliament may, by law, extend the provisions of this Part to the Scheduled Areas and the Tribal Areas referred to in clause (l) subject to such exceptions and modifications as may be specified in such law, and no such law shall be deemed to be an amendment of this Constitution for the purposes of article 368.

243ZD. Committee for district planning.—[15]

(1) There shall be constituted in every State at the district level a District Planning Committee to consolidate the plans prepared by the Panchayats and the Municipalities in the district and to prepare a draft development plan for the district as a whole.

(2) The Legislature of a State may, by law, make provision with respect to—

(a) the composition of the District Planning Committees;

(b) the manner in which the seats in such Committees shall be filled—

Provided that not less than four fifths of the total number of members of such Committee shall be elected by, and from amongst, the elected members of the Panchayat at the district level and of the Municipalities in the district in proportion to the ratio between the population of the rural areas and of the urban areas in the district;

(c) the functions relating to district planning which may be assigned to such Committees;

(d) the manner in which the Chairpersons of such Committees be chosen.

(3) Every District Planning Committee shall, in preparing the draft development plan,

(a) have regard to—

(i) matters of common interest between the Panchayats and the Municipalities including spatial planning, sharing of water and other physical and natural resources, the integrated development of infrastructure and environmental conservation;

(ii) the extent and type of available resources whether financial or otherwise;

(b) consult such institutions and organizations as the Governor may, by order, specify.

(4) The Chairperson of every District Planning Committee shall forward development plan, as recommended by such Committee, to the Government of the State.

243ZE. Committee for Metropolitan planning.—[16]

(1) There shall be constituted in every Metropolitan area a Metropolitan Planning Committee to prepare a draft development plan for the Metropolitan area as a whole.

(2) The Legislature of a State may, by law, make with respect to—

(a) the composition of the Metropolitan Planning Committees;

(b) the manner in which the seats in such Committees shall be filled:

Provided that not less than two thirds of the members of such Committee shall be elected by, and from amongst, the elected members of the Municipalities and Chairpersons of the Panchayats in the Metropolitan area in proportion to the ratio between the population of the Municipalities and of the Panchayats in that area;

(c) the representation, in such Committees of the Government of India and the Government of the State and of such organisations and institutions as may be deemed necessary for carrying out the functions assigned to such Committees;

(d) the functions relating to planning and coordination for the Metropolitan area which may be assigned to such Committees;

(e) the manner in which the Chairpersons of such Committees shall be chosen.

(3) Every Metropolitan Planning Committee shall, in preparing the draft development plan,—

(a) have regard to—

(i) the plans prepared by the Municipalities and the Panchayats in the Metropolitan area;

(ii) matters of common interest between the Municipalities and the Panchayats, including co-ordinated spatial planning of the area, sharing of water and other physical and natural resources, the integrated development of infrastructure and environmental conservation;

(iii) the overall objectives and priorities set by the Government of India and the Government of the State;

(iv) the extent and nature of investments likely to be made in the Metropolitan area by agencies of the Government of India and of the Government of the State and other available resources whether financial or otherwise;

(b) consult such institutions and organisations as the Governor may, by order, specify.

(4) The Chairperson of every Metropolitan Planning Committee shall forward the development plan, as recommended by such Committee, to the Government of the State.

243ZF. Continuance of existing laws and Municipalities.

Notwithstanding anything in this Part, any provision of any law relating to Municipalities in force in a State immediately before the commencement of the Constitution

(Seventy-fourth Amendment) Act, 1992, which is inconsistent with the provisions of this Part, shall continue to be in force until amended or repealed by a competent Legislature or other competent authority or until the expiration of one year from such commencement, whichever is earlier:

Provided that all the Municipalities existing immediately before such commencement shall continue till the expiration of their duration, unless sooner dissolved by a resolution passed to that effect by the Legislative Assembly of that State or, in the case of a State having a Legislative Council, by each House of the Legislature of that State.

243ZG. Bar to interference by courts in electoral matters—

Notwithstanding anything in this Constitution—

(a) the validity of any law relating to the delimitation of constituencies or the allotment of seats to such constituencies, made or purporting to be made under article 243ZF shall not be called in question in any court;

(b) no election to any Municipality shall be called in question except by an election petition presented to such authority and in such manner as is provided for by or under any law made by the Legislature of a State.

Source: Constitution of India

Notes

1. *Subs.* by the Constitution (Seventh Amendment) Act, 1956 Sec. 29 and Sch., for 'State specified in Part C of the First Schedule.'
2. *Subs.* by the Constitution (Eightieth Amendment) Act, 2000, Sec. 2. Prior to amendment clauses (1) and (2) read as follows:
   '(1) Taxes on the sale or purchase of goods on the consignment of

goods shall be levied and collected by the Government of India but shall be assigned and shall be deemed to have been assigned to the States on or after the 1st day of April, 1996 in the manner provided in clause (2).

Explanation. —For the purposes of this clause—

(a) the expression "taxes on the sale or purchase of goods" shall mean taxes on sale or purchase of goods other than newspaper, where such sale or purchase takes place in the course of inter-State trade or commerce;

(b) the expression "taxes on the consignment of goods" shall mean taxes on the consignment of goods (whether the consignment is to the person making it or to any other person), where such consignment takes place in the course of inter-State trade or commerce.

(2) The net proceeds in any financial year of any such tax, except in so far as those proceeds represent proceeds attributable to Union territories, shall not form part of the Consolidated Fund of India, but shall be assigned to the states within which that tax is leviable in that year, and shall be distributed among those States in accordance with such principles of distribution as may be formulated by Parliament by law.'

3 *Ins.* by the Constitution (Sixth Amendment) Act, 1956, Sec. 3.

4 *Subs.* by the Constitution (Forty-sixth Amendment) Act, 1982, Sec. 2 for 'sale or purchase of goods'(w.e.f. 2-2-1983).

5. *Subs.* by the Constitution (Eightieth Amendment) Act, 2000, Sec. 3, and deemed to have been substituted w.e.f. 1-4-1996. Prior to substitution Art. 270 read as follows:

'Article 270

(1) taxes on income other than agricultural income shall be levied and collected by the Government of India and distributed between the Union and the States in the manner provided in clause (2).

(2) Such percentage, as may be prescribed, of the net proceeds in any financial year of any such tax, except in so far as those proceeds represent proceeds attributable to Union territories or to taxes payable in respect of Union emoluments, shall not form part of the Consolidated Fund of India, but shall be assigned to the States within which that tax is leviable in that year, and shall be distributed among those States in such manner and from such time as may be prescribed.

(3) For the purposes of clause (2). in each financial year such percentage as may prescribed of so much of the net proceeds of taxes on 3 income as does not represent the net proceeds of taxes payable in respect of Union emoluments shall be deemed to represent proceeds attributable to Union territories.

(4) In this article:
(a) "taxes on income" does not include a corporation tax;
(b) "prescribed" means:
(i) until a Finance Commission has been constituted, prescribed by the President by order, and
(ii) after a Finance Commission has been constituted, prescribed by the President by order after considering the recommendations of the Finance Commission;
(c) "Union emoluments" includes all emoluments and pensions payable out of the Consolidated Fund of India in respect of which income tax is chargeable.

6. Omitted by the Constitution (Eightieth Amendment) Act 2000 Prior to omission Art 272 read as follows:
'272. Taxes which are levied and collected by the union and may be distributed between the Union and the States.—Union duties of excise other than such duties of excise on medicinal and toilet preparations as are mentioned in the Union list shall be levied and collected by the Government of India, but, if Parliament by law so provides, these shall be paid out of the Consolidated Fund of India to the States to which the law imposing the duty extends sums equivalent to the whole or any part of the net proceeds of that duty, and those sums shall be distributed among those states in accordance with such principles of distribution as may be formulated by such law.'
7. *Subs.* by the North eastern areas (Reorganisation) Act, 1971 (81 of 1971), Sec 71 for 'Part A' (w.e.f. 21.1.1972).
8. Ins. by the Constitution (Twenty-second Amendment) Act, 1969, Sec. 3
9. *Ins.* by the Constitution (Seventy-third Amendment) Act, 1992, Sec. 3 (w.e.f. 24.4.1993).
10. Ins. by the Constitution (Seventy-Fourth Amendment) Act, 1992, sec. 3 (w.e.f. 1.6.1993)
11. Sub-clause (c) relettered as sub-clause (d) by the Constitution (Seventy-fourth Amendment) Act, 1992, sec. 3 (w.e.f. 1.6.1993).
12. PART IX—The territories in Part D of the First Schedule and other territories not specified in that Schedule was rep. by the Constitution (Seventh Amendment) Act, 1956, sec. 29 and Sch. and *ins.* by the Constitution (Seventy-third Amendment) Act, 1992. sec. 2 (w.e.f. 1.6.1993).
13. *ins.* by the Constitution (Eighty-third Amendment) Act, 2000, sec. 2 (w.e.f. 8.9.2000).
14. *ins.* by the Constitution (Seventy-fourth Amendment Act, 1992, sec. 2 (w.e.f. 1.6.1993).
15. The provisions of article 243ZD shall not apply to the National

Capital Territory of Delhi vide S.O. 1125(E) dated 12th November, 2001.

16. The provisions of article 243ZE shall not apply to the National Capital Territory of Delhi vide S.O. 1125(E) dated 12th November, 2001.

** ATR upto FC-XI based on FC-XII document "Fifty years of Fiscal Federalism—Finance Commission of India April, 2003 ARTs of FC-XII and FC-XIII based on GOI Notification.*

Source: Constitution of India

Annexure III.2

The Finance Commission (Miscellaneous Provisions) Act, 1951

An Act

to determine the qualifications requisite for appointment as members of the Finance Commission and the manner in which they shall be selected, and to prescribe their powers.

Be it enacted by Parliament as follows—

(1) Short title—

This Act may be called the Finance Commission (Miscellaneous Provisions) Act, 1951 (Act XXXIII of 1951).

(2) Definition—

In this Act, 'the Commission' means the Finance Commission constituted by the President pursuant to clause (1) of article 280 of the Constitution.

(3) Qualifications for appointment as, and the manner of selection of members of, the Commission—

The Chairman of the Commission shall be selected from among persons who have had experience in public affairs, and the four other members shall be selected from among persons who—

(a) are, or have been, or are qualified to be appointed as Judges of a High Court; or

(b) have special knowledge of the Finances and accounts of the Government; or

(c) have had wide experience in financial matters and in administration ; or

(d) have special knowledge of economics.

(4) Personal interest to disqualify members—

Before appointing a person to be member of the Commission, the President shall satisfy himself that the person will have no such financial or other interest as is likely to affect prejudicially his functions as a member of the Commission; and the President shall also satisfy himself from time to time with respect to every member of the Commission that he has no such interest and any person who is, or whom the President proposes to appoint to be a member of the Commission shall, whenever required by the President so to do, furnish to him such information as the President considers necessary for the performance by him of his duties under this section.

(5) Disqualifications for being a member of the Commission—

A person shall be disqualified for being appointed as, or for being a member of the Commission

(a) if he is of unsound mind;
(b) if he is an undischarged insolvent;
(c) if he has been convicted of an offence involving moral turpitude; and
(d) if he has such financial or other interest as is likely to affect prejudicially his functions as a member of the Commission.

(6) Terms of office of members and eligibility for re-appointment—

Every member of the Commission shall hold office for such period as may be provided for in the order of the President appointing him, but shall be eligible for re-appointment:

Provided that he may, by letter addressed to the President, resign his office.

(7) Conditions of service and salaries and allowances of members whole time or part time service to the Commission as the President may in each case specify and there shall be paid to the members of the Commission such fees or salaries and such allowances as the Central Government may, by rules made in this behalf, determine.

(8) Procedure and Powers of the Commission—

(1) The Commission shall determine their procedure and in the performance of their functions shall have all the powers of a civil court under the Code of Civil Procedure, 1908 (Act V of 1908) while trying a suit in respect of the following matters, namely—

(a) summoning and enforcing the attendance of witnesses;

(b) requiring the production of any document; and

(c) requisitioning any public record from any court or office.

(2) The Commission shall have power to require any person to furnish information on such points or matters as in the opinion of the Commission may be useful for, or relevant to, any matter under the consideration of the Commission and any person so required shall, notwithstanding anything contained in sub-section (2) of section 54 of the Indian Income-tax Act, 1922, or in any other law for the time being in force be deemed to be legally bound to furnish such information within the meaning of section 176 of the Indian

Penal Code.

The Commission shall be deemed to be a civil court for the purposes of sections 480 and 482 of the Code of Criminal Procedure, 1898 (Act V of 1898).

Explanation—

For the purposes of enforcing the attendance of witnesses, the local limits of the Commission's jurisdiction shall be the limits of the territory of India.

Annexure III.3

Finance Commissions Constituted so far

Finance Commission	*Year Constituted*	*Year Report Submitted*	*Period of Award (1st April to 31st March*	*Name of Chairman*
1	2	3	4	5
First	November, 1951	December, 1952	1952-1957	Sri K.C. Neogi
Second	June, 1956 .	December, 1957	1957-1962	Sri. K. Santhanam
Third	December, 1960	December, 1961	1962-1966	Sri. A.K. Chanda
Fourth	May, 1964	August, 1965	1966-1969	Dr. P.V. Rajamannar
Fifth	February, 1968	July, 1969	1969-1974	Sri. Mahabir Tyagi
Sixth	June, 1972	October, 1972	1974-1979	Sri. K. Brahmanand Reddi
Seventh	June, 1977	October, 1978	1979-1984	Sri. J.M. Shelat
Eighth	June, 1982	April, 1984	1984-1989	Sri. Y.S. Chawan
Ninth	June, 1987	July, 1988 (1st Report)		
		December, 1989	1989-1990	
		(2nd Report)	1990-1995	Sri N.K.P. Shalve
Tenth	June, 1992	November, 1993	1995-2000	Sri K.C. Pant
Eleventh	July, 1998		2000-2005	Prof. A.M. Khusro
Twelfth	November, 2002	December, 2004	2005-2010	Dr. C. Rangarajan
Thirteenth	November, 2007	December, 2009	2010-2015	Dr. Vijay L. Kelkar

Annexure III.4

Finance Commission Award Period and Plan Period

FC Award Period		Plan Period	
First Finance Commission	1952-57	1st Plan	1951-56
Second Finance Commission	1957-62	2nd Plan	1956-61
Third Finance Commission	1962-66	3rd Plan	1961-66
Fourth Finance Commission	1966-69	3 Annual Plan	1966-69
Fifth Finance Commission	1969-74	4th Plan	1969-74
Sixth Finance Commission	1974-79	5th Plan	1974-78
			1978-79
			1979-80
Seventh Finance Commission	1979-84	6th Plan	1981-85
Eighth Finance Commission	1984-89	7th Plan	1985-90
Ninth Finance Commission (1st Report)	1989-90	2 Annual Plans	1990-91 1991-92
Ninth Finance Commission (2nd Report)	1990-95	8th Plan	1992-97
Tenth Finance Commission	1995-00	9th Plan	1997-02
Eleventh Finance Commission	2000-05	10th Plan	2002-07
Twelfth Finance Commission	2005-10	11th Plan	2007-12
Thirteenth Finance Commission	2010-15	11th Plan	2007-12
		12th Plan	2012-17

Annexure III.5

Terms of Reference of Finance Commissions

First Finance Commission

Composition

Chairman	**Shri K.C. Neogy**
Members	**Shri V.P. Menon (Resigned 18th Feb., 1952)** **Shri V.L. Mehta (in place of Shri V.P. Menon)** **Shri Justice R. Kaushalendra Rao** **Shri B.K. Madan** **Shri M.V. Rangachari, Member Secretary**

Terms of Reference

The Commission constituted by an Order dated 22nd November, 1951 listed the functions of the Commission under Article 280 of the Constitution as follows:

(a) the distribution between the Union and the States of the net proceeds of taxes which are to be, or may be divided, between them under the provisions of Chapter I of Part XII of the Constitution and the allocation between the States of the respective shares of such proceeds;

(b) the principles which should govern the grants-in-aid of the revenues of the States out of the Consolidated Fund of India;

(c) the continuance or modification of the terms of any agreement entered into by the Government of India with the Government of any State specified in Part B of the First Schedule under Clause (l) of Article 278 or under Article 306; and

(d) any other matter referred to the Commission by the President in the interests of sound finance.

Former Clause (c) has since been deleted and Clause (d) has now been renumbered as Clause (c).

(2) On 6th April, 1952, the Commission was formally requested to make recommendations to the President in regard to—

(a) the sums to be prescribed by him as grants-in-aid of the revenues of the States of Assam, Bihar, Orissa and West Bengal in lieu of assignment of any shares of the net proceeds in each year of the export duty on jute and jute products to these States in accordance with the provisions of Article 273 of the Constitution; and

(b) the States in need of assistance and the sums payable to such States as grants-in-aid of their revenues under the substantive portion of Clause (1) of Article 275 of the Constitution.

Second Finance Commission

Composition

Chairman	**Shri K. Santhanam**
Members	**Shri Ujjal Singh** **Shri L.S. Misra (Retired Chief Justice, Hyderabad)** **Shri M.V. Rangachari** **Dr. B.N. Ganguli** **Shri H.B. Bhar, Secretary**

Terms of Reference

Para 4 of the Presidential Order dated 1st June, 1956 stated as follows—

(4) The Commission shall, in addition to making recommendations as to the matters specified in sub-clauses (a) to (c) of clause (3) of article 280, make recommendations as to the following matters, namely:

(a) the sums which may be prescribed under article 273 as grants-in-aid of the revenues of the States of Assam, Bihar, Orissa and West Bengal in lieu of assignment of any share of the net proceeds in each year of export duty on jute and jute products to those States;

(b) the States which are in need of assistance by way of grants-in-aid of the revenues of those States under article 275, and the sums to be paid to those States, having regard, among other considerations, to

(i) the requirements of the Second Five Year Plan, and

(ii) the efforts made by those States to raise additional revenue from the sources available to them;

(c) the principles which should govern the distribution under article 269 of the net proceeds in any financial year of estate duty in respect of property other than agricultural land, levied by the Government of India in the States within which such duty is leviable; and

(d) the modifications, if any, in the rates of interest and the terms of repayment of the loans made to the various States by the Government of India between the 15th day of August, 1947 and the 31st day of March, 1956.

The following two matters were added to the terms of reference on 22.05.1957.

(e) the principles which should govern the distribution among the States of the net proceeds of the additional duty of excise on mill made textiles, sugar and tobacco (including manufactured tobacco) and the amounts which should be assured to the States as the income now derived by them from the levy on these commodities and the States Sales Tax which is to be replaced by the additional duty of excise.

(f) the principles which should govern the distribution, under article 269 of the Constitution of the net proceeds in any financial year of the tax on railway fares proposed to be levied by the Railway Passenger Fares Bill, 1957, introduced in the Lok Sabha on 15th May, 1957.

Third Finance Commission

Composition

Chairman	**Shri Ashok Kumar Chanda**
Members	**Shri P. Govinda Menon**
	Shri Dwijendra Nath Roy (Retired High Court Judge)
	Prof. M.V. Mathur
	Shri G.R. Kamat, Member Secretary

Terms of Reference

Para 4 of the Presidential Order dated 2nd December, 1960 issued by the Department of Economic Affairs as modified by that Department's letters Nos. 4(14)B/60 dated 28.02.1961 and 13(4)-B/61 dated 21.04.1961 stated as follows—

(4) In addition to the matters on which under the provisions of sub-clauses (a) and (b) of the clause 3 of article 280 of the Constitution, the Commission is required to make recommendations, the Commission

should also make recommendations in regard to—

(a) the States which are in need of assistance by way of grants-in-aid of their revenues under article 275, and the sums to be paid to those States other than the sums specified in the provisos to clause (1) of that article, having regard, among other considerations, to—

(i) the requirements of the Third Five Year Plan; and

(ii) the efforts to be made by those States to raise additional revenues from the sources available to them;

(b) the changes, if any, to be made in the principles governing the distribution amongst the States under article 269, of the net proceeds in any financial year of estate duty in respect of property other than agricultural land;

(c) the manner in which the sums of Rs. 12.5 crores, which the Railway have agreed to pay to the General Revenues every year consequent on the decision taken to merge the tax on Railway Fares with the passenger fares and repeal the Railway Passenger Fares Act, 1957, should be distributed amongst the States;

(d) the changes, if any, to be made in the principles governing the distribution of the net proceeds in any financial year of the additional excise duties levied on each of the following commodities, namely—

(i) cotton fabrics.

(ii) rayon or artificial silk fabrics.

(iii) silk fabrics.

(iv) woolen fabrics.

(v) sugar, and

(vi) tobacco, including manufactured tobacco, in replacement of the sales taxes formerly levied by the State Governments:

Fourth Finance Commission

Composition

Chairman	**Dr. P.V. Rajamannar**
Members	**Shri Mohan Lal Gautam** **Shri D.G. Karve** **Prof. Bhabatosh Datta** **Shri P.C. Mathew, Member Secretary**

Terms of Reference

Para 4 of the Presidential Order dated 5th May, 1964 stated as follows—

(4) In addition to the matters on which, under the provisions of sub-clauses (a) and (b) of clause (3) of the article 280 of the Constitution, the Commission is required to make recommendations, the Commission should also make recommendations in regard to—

(a) the States which are in need of assistance by way of grants-in-aid of their revenues under article 275, and the sums to be paid to those States other than the sums specified in the provisos to clause (1) of that article, having regard, among other consideration to—

(i) the revenues resources of those States for the five years ending with the 25 financial year 1970-71 on the basis of the levels of taxation likely to be reached in financial year 1965-66;

(ii) the requirements of those States to meet the committed expenditure on maintenance and upkeep of plan schemes completed during the Third Plan;

(iii) further expenditure likely to devolve upon those States for the servicing of their debt;

(iv) creation of a fund out of the excess, if any, over a limit to be specified by the Commission of the net proceeds of estate duty on property other than agricultural land accruing to a State in any financial year, for the repayment of the State's debt to the Central Government; and

(v) the scope for economy consistent with efficiency, which may be effected by the States in their administrative expenditure;

(b) the changes, if any, to be made in the principles governing the distribution amongst the States under article 269 of the net proceeds in any financial year of estate duty in respect of property other than agricultural land;

(c) the changes, if any, to be made in the principles governing the distribution amongst the States of the grant to be made available to the States in lieu of taxes on railway fares;

(d) the changes, if any, to be made in the principles governing the distribution of the net proceeds in any financial year of the additional excise duties levied on each of the following commodities, namely—

(i) cotton fabrics.

(ii) silk fabrics.
(iii) rayon and artificial silk fabrics.
(iv) woolen fabrics.
(v) sugar, and
(vi) tobacco (including manufactured tobacco) in replacement in the States' sales taxes formerly levied by the State Governments.

(e) the effect of the combined incidence of a State's sales tax and Union duties of excise on the production, consumption or export of commodities or products, the duties on which are shareable with the States, and the adjustments, if any, to be made in the State's share of Union excise duties if there is any increase in the States sales tax on such commodities or products over a limit to be specified by the Commission.

Fifth Finance Commission

Composition

Chairman	**Shri Mahavir Tyagi**
Members	**Shri P.C. Bhattacharrya (Died on 13th Feb. 1969)** **Shri G. Swaminathan (From 21st Feb. 1969, in place of Shri P.C. Bhattacharrya)** **Shri M. Seshachalapthy (Retired Judge)** **Dr. D.T. Kakdawala** **Shri V.L. Gidwani, Member Secretary**

Terms of Reference

Paras 4 and 5 of the Presidential Order dated 29th February, 1968 containing the terms of reference of the Fifth

Finance Commission are reproduced below—

(4) The Commission shall make recommendations as to the following matters—

(a) the distribution between the Union and States of the net proceeds of taxes which are to be, or may be, divided between them under Chapter I of part XII of the Constitution and the allocation between the States of the respective shares of such proceeds;

(b) the principles which should govern the grants-in-aid of the revenues of the States out of the Consolidated Fund of India and the sums to be paid to the States which are in need of assistance by way of grants-in-aid of their revenues under Article 275 for purposes other than those specified in the provisos to clause (1) of that Article and other than the requirements of the Five Year Plan, having regard, among other considerations, to—

(i) the revenues resources of those States for the five years ending with the financial year 1973-74 on the basis of the levels of taxation likely to be reached at the end of the financial year 1968-69;

(ii) the requirements on revenue account of those States to meet the expenditure on administration, interest charges in respect of their debt, maintenance and upkeep of plan schemes completed by the end of 1968-69, transfer of funds to local bodies and aided institutions and other committed expenditure;

(iii) the scope for better fiscal management as

also for economy consistent with efficiency which may be effected by the States in their administrative, maintenance, developmental and other expenditure;

(c) the changes, if any, to be made in the principles governing the distribution amongst the States of the grant to be made available to the States in lieu of the repealed tax on railway passenger fares;

(d) the changes, if any, to be made in the principles governing the distribution amongst the States under Article 269 of the net proceeds in any financial year of estate duty in respect of property other than agricultural land;

(e) the desirability or otherwise of maintaining the existing arrangements under the Additional Duties of Excise (Goods of Special Importance) Act, 1957 in regard to the levy of additional duties of excise on sugar, textiles and tobacco in lieu of the States' sales taxes thereon, with or without any modifications, and the scope for extending such arrangements to other items or commodities;

(f) irrespective of the recommendation made under item (e) above, the change, if any to be made in the principles governing the distribution of the net proceeds in any financial year of the additional excise duties leviable under the 1957 Act aforesaid on each of the following commodities, namely—

(i) Cotton fabrics.

(ii) Silk fabrics

(iii) Woolen fabrics.

(iv) Rayon or artificial silk fabrics.

(v) Sugar, and
(vi) Tobacco including manufactured tobacco, in replacement of the States' sales taxes formerly levied by the State Governments.

Provided that the share accruing to each State shall not be less than the revenue realized from the levy of the sales tax for the financial year 1956-57 in that State;

(g) the principles which should govern the distribution of the net proceeds of such additional items or commodities as may be recommended under item (e) above for levy of additional excise duties in lieu of the States' sales taxes thereon;
(h) the scope for raising revenue from the taxes and duties mentioned in article 269 of the Constitution but not levied at present;
(i) the scope for raising additional revenue by the various State Governments from the sources of revenue available to them; and
(j) the problem of unauthorised over-drafts of certain States with the Reserve Bank and the procedure to be observed for avoiding such over-drafts.

(5) The Commission in making its recommendations on the various matters aforesaid shall have regard to the resources of the Central Government and the demands thereon on account of the expenditure on civil administration, defence and border security, debt servicing and other committed expenditures or liabilities.

(6) The Commission shall make an interim Report by the 30th September, 1968 covering as many of the matters mentioned in para 4 above as possible and in particular, in respect of the financial year 1969-70; and

make the final Report by the 31st July, 1969 on each of the said matters and covering a period of five years commencing from the 1st day of April, 1969, indicating in its Reports the basis on which it has arrived at its findings and making available the relevant documents.

The supplementary reference dated 1.5.1969 made to the Commission is reproduced below—

Whereas since the commencement of the Constitution, Advance Tax collections made under the Income Tax Act have been taken into account in determining the net proceeds of taxes on income for purposes of article 270(2) of the Constitution only on completion of regular assessment;

And whereas successive Finance Commissions have recommended the distribution between the Union and the States of the net proceeds of taxes on income under article 280(3) (a) of the Constitution on the said basis;

And whereas the Comptroller and Auditor General of India has also certified the net proceeds of taxes on income under article 279(1) of the Constitution in each of the financial years until and including 1966-67 on the said basis;

And whereas it is now considered that the Advance Tax collections made in a financial year should be taken into account in determining the net proceeds of taxes on income in that year and not be left over for such determination in subsequent years on completion of regular assessment as hitherto;

Now, therefore, in pursuance of sub-clause (a) and (c) of clause (3) of article 280 of the Constitution of India the President is pleased to refer to following further matters to the Finance Commission, constituted by S.O. No. 812 dated the 29th February, 1968, namely —

(a) The distribution of the Advance Tax already collected and not included in the net proceeds of taxes on income in the financial years until and including 1966-67 as certified by the Comptroller and Auditor General of India;

(b) The changes, if any, in the distribution between the Union and the State of the net proceeds of taxes on income as prescribed in the Constitution (Distribution of Revenue) Order, 1965, in so far as the taxes on income collected in the financial years 1967-68 and 1968-69 are concerned, in the event of the net proceeds thereof being certified by the Comptroller and Auditor General of India after taking into account the Advance Tax collected in the respective years; and

(c) The distribution of the net proceeds of taxes on income in each of the financial years 1969-70 to 1973-74 as determined on the revised basis.

(2) The Commission shall take into account the effect of the recommendations made by them on the matters specified in paragraph 1 above in making their recommendations under S.O. 812 aforesaid, as to the distribution between the Union and the States of the net proceeds of taxes which are to be, or may be, divided between them and the allocation between the States of the respective share of such proceeds under sub-clause (a) of clause (3) of Article 280 of the Constitution and also as to the determinations of the sums to be paid as grants-in-aid of the revenues of the States in need of assistance under clause (1) of Art

Sixth Finance Commission

Composition

Chairman **Shri K. Brahmananda Reddi**

Members **Shri Justice S.S. Abal Masud**
Dr. B.S. Minhas
Dr. I.S. Gulati
Shri G. Ramachandran, Member Secretary

Terms of Reference

Paragraphs 4-7 of the Presidential Order dated 28th June, 1972, containing the Terms of Reference of the Sixth Finance Commission are reproduced below—

(4) The Commission shall make recommendations as to the following matters—

(a) the distribution between the Union and the States of the net proceeds of taxes which are to be, or may be, divided between them under Chapter I of Part XII of the Constitution and the allocation between the States of the respective shares of such proceeds;

(b) the principles which should govern the grants-in-aid of the revenues of States out of the Consolidated Fund of India and the sums to be paid to the States which are in need of assistance by way of grants-in-aid 29 of their revenues under Article 275 of Constitution for purposes other than those specified in the provisos to clause (1) of that article having regard, among other considerations, to—

(i) the existing practice in regard to determination and distribution of Central assistance for financing State Plans;

(ii) the revenue resources of those States for the five years ending with the financial year 1978-79 on the basis of the levels of taxation likely to be reached at the end of the financial year 1973-74;

(iii) the requirements on revenue account of those States to meet the expenditure on administration taking also into account such provision for emoluments of Government employees, teachers and local body employees as obtaining on a specified date as the Commission deem it proper in the light of the States' capacity and needs, interest charges in respect of their debt, transfer of funds to local bodies and aided institutions and other committed expenditure;

(iv) adequate maintenance and upkeep of the capital assets and maintenance of Plan schemes completed by the end of 1973-74, the norms, if any, on the basis of which specified amounts are allowed for the maintenance of different categories of capital assets being indicated by the Commission;

(v) the requirements of States which are backward in standards of general administration for upgrading the administration with a view to bringing it to the levels obtaining in the more advanced States over a period of ten years; and

(vi) the scope for better fiscal management and

economy consistent with efficiency which may be effected by the States in their administrative, maintenance, developmental and other expenditure;

(c) the changes, if any to be made in the principles governing the distribution amongst the States of the grant to be made available to the States in lieu of tax under the repealed Railway Passenger Fares Tax Act, 1957;

(d) the changes, if any, to be made in the principles governing the distribution amongst the States under Article 269 of the Constitution of the net proceeds of any financial year of estate duty in respect of property other than agricultural land;

(e) the changes, if any, to be made in the principles governing the distribution of the net proceeds in any financial year of the additional excise duties leviable under the Additional Duties of Excise (Goods of Special Importance) Act, 1957, on each of the following commodities, namely -

(i) cotton fabrics.

(ii) woolen fabrics.

(iii) rayon or artificial silk fabrics.

(iv) sugar ; and

(v) tobacco including manufactured tobacco, in replacement of the States' sales taxes formerly levied by the State Governments;

Provided that the share accruing to each State shall not be less than the revenue realised from the levy of sales tax for the financial year 1956-57 in that State; and

(f) The principles governing the distribution among the States of the grant to be made available to the States on account of wealth tax on agricultural property.

(5) The Commission may make an assessment of the non-plan capital gap of the States on a uniform and comparable basis for the five years ending with 1978-79. In the light of such an assessment, the Commission may undertake a general review of the States' debt position with particular reference to the Central loans advanced to them and likely to be outstanding as at the end of 1973-74 and suggest changes in the existing terms of repayment having regard inter-alia to the overall non-plan gap of the States, their relative position and the purposes for which the loans have been utilised, and the requirements of the Centre.

(6) The Commission may review the policy and arrangements in regard to the financing of relief expenditure by the States affected by natural calamities and examine inter-alia the feasibility of establishing a National Fund to which the Central and State Governments may contribute a percentage of their revenue receipts.

(7) The Commission in making its recommendations on the various matters aforesaid shall have regard to the resources of the Central Government and the demands thereon on account of the expenditure on civil administration, defence and border security, debt servicing and other committed expenditure or liabilities.

Seventh Finance Commission

Composition

Chairman	**Shri J.M. Shelat**
Members	**Dr. Raj Krishna**

Dr. C.H. Hanumantha Rao
Shri H.N. Ray
Shri V.B. Eswaran, Member Secretary

Terms of Reference

Paras 4 to 9 of the Presidential Order dated the 22nd June, 1977 containing the terms of reference of the Seventh Finance Commission are reproduced below —

(4) The Commission shall make recommendations as to the following matters —

(a) the distribution between the Union and the States of the net proceeds of taxes which are to be, or may be, divided between them under Chapter I of Part XII of the Constitution and the allocation between the States of the respective shares of such proceeds;

(b) the principles which should govern the grants-in-aid of the revenues of the States out of the Consolidated Fund of India and 31 the sums to be paid to the States which are in need of assistance by way of grants-in-aid of their revenues under Article 275 of the Constitution for purposes other than those specified in the provisos to clause (l) of that Article.

(5) In making its recommendations, the Commission shall have regard, among other considerations, to—

(i) the resources of the Central Government and the demands thereon on account of the expenditure on civil administration, defence and border security, debt servicing and other committed expenditure or liabilities;

(ii) the existing practice in regard to determination and distribution of Central assistance for financing State Plans;

(iii) the revenue resources of those States for the five years ending with the financial year 1983-84 on the basis of the levels of taxation likely to be reached at the end of the financial year 1978-79 and the targets set for additional resource mobilisation for the Plan;

(iv) the requirements on revenues account of those States to meet the expenditure on administration and other non-plan commitments or liabilities, keeping however in view national policies and priorities. In assessing such requirements, the Commission shall take into account—

(a) such provision for emoluments of Government employees, teachers and local body employees as obtaining on a specified date as the Commission deem it proper and with reference to appropriate objective criteria rather than in terms of actual increases that may have been given effect to; and

(b) commitments in regard to interest charges on their debt, transfer of funds to local bodies and aided institutions.

(v) adequate maintenance and upkeep of capital assets and maintenance of plan schemes completed by the end of 1978-79, the norms, if any, on the basis of which specified amounts are allowed for the maintenance of different categories of capital assets and the manner in which such maintenance expenditure could be monitored being indicated by the Commission;

(vi) the requirements of States which are backward in general administration for upgradation of standards in non-developmental sectors and services with a view to bringing them to the levels obtaining in the more advanced States over the period covered by the Report of the Commission; the manner in which such expenditure could be monitored, being also indicated by the Commission;

(vii) the scope for better fiscal management and economy in expenditure consistent with efficiency; and

(viii) the need for ensuring reasonable returns on investments in irrigation and power projects, transport undertakings, industrial and commercial enterprises and the like.

(6) The Commission may suggest changes, if any, to be made in the principles governing the distribution among the States of—

(a) the net proceeds in any financial year of estate duty in respect of property other than agricultural land;

(b) the net proceeds in any financial year of the additional excise duties leviable under the Additional Duties of Excise (Goods of Special Importance) Act, 1957, in replacement of the sales tax levied formerly by the State Governments on each of the following commodities, namely—

(i) Cotton fabrics.

(ii) Woollen fabrics.
(iii) Rayon or artificial silk fabrics.
(iv) Sugar, and
(v) Tobacco including manufactured tobacco.

Provided that the share accruing to each State shall not be less than the revenue realised from the levy of sales tax for the financial year 1956-57 in that State;

(c) the grant to be made available to the States in lieu of the tax under the repealed Railway Passenger Fares Tax Act, 1957; and
(d) the grant to be made available to the States on account of Wealth Tax on agricultural property.

(7) In making its recommendations on the various matters aforesaid, the Commission shall adopt the population figures of 1971 in all cases where population is regarded as a factor for determination of devolution of taxes and duties and grants-in-aid.
(8) The Commission may make an assessment of the non-plan capital gap of the States on a uniform and comparable basis for the five years ending with 1983-84. In the light of such an assessment, the Commission may undertake a general review of the States' debt position with particular reference to the Central Loans advanced to them and likely to be outstanding as at the end of 1978-79 and suggest appropriate measures to deal with the non-plan capital gap, having regard inter-alia to the overall non-plan gap of the States, their relative position and the purposes for which the loans have been utilised, and the requirements of the Centre.
(9) The Commission may review the policy and arrangements in regard to the financing of relief expenditure by the States affected by natural

calamities and suggest such modifications as it considers appropriate, in the existing arrangements, having regard, among other considerations, to the need for avoidance of wasteful expenditure.

Eighth Finance Commission

Composition

Chairman	**Shri Y.B. Chavan**
Members	**Shri Justice Sabyasachi Mukherjee (Resigned on 28th April, 1983)** **Shri Justice T.P.S. Chawala (From 3rd June, 1983 in place of Shri Justice Sabyasachi Mukherjee)** **Dr. C.H. Hanumantha Rao** **Shri G.C. Baveja** **Shri A.R. Shirali** **Shri N.V. Krishnan, Secretary**

Terms of Reference

Paras 4 to 10 of the Presidential Order dated the 20th June, 1982 containing the terms of reference of the Eighth Finance Commission are reproduced below—

(4) The Commission shall make recommendations as to the following matters -

(a) The distribution between the Union and the States of the net proceeds of taxes which are to be, or may be, divided between them under Chapter I of Part XII of the Constitution and allocation between the States of the respective shares 33 of such proceeds;

(b) The principles which should govern the grants-in-aid of the revenues of the States out of the Consolidated Fund of India and the sums to be paid to the States which are in need of assistance by way of grants-in-aid of their revenues under article 275 of the Constitution for purposes other than those specified in the provisos to clause (1) of that article.

(5) In making its recommendations, the Commission shall have regard, among other considerations, to—

(i) the resources of the Central Government and the demands thereon on account of expenditure on civil administration, defence and border security, debt servicing and other committed expenditure or liabilities;

(ii) the existing practice in regard to determination and distribution of Central Assistance for financing State Plans;

(iii) the revenue resources of those States for the five years ending with the financial year 1988-89 on the basis of the levels of taxation likely to be reached at the end of the financial year 1983-84 and the targets set for additional resource mobilisation for the Plan;

(iv) the requirements on revenue account of those States to meet the expenditure on administration and other non-Plan commitments or liabilities, keeping however in view national policies and priorities. In assessing such requirements, the Commission shall take into account—

(a) such provision for emoluments and terminal benefits of Government employees, teachers and employees of local bodies as obtaining on a specified date as the Commission deems it proper and with reference to appropriate objective criteria rather than in terms of actual increases that may have been given effect to; and

(b) commitments in regard to interest charges on their debt, transfer of funds to local bodies and aided institutions;

(v) adequate maintenance and upkeep of capital assets and maintenance of plan schemes completed by the end of 1983-84, the norms, if any, on the basis of which specified amounts are allowed for the maintenance of different categories of capital assets and the manner in which such maintenance expenditure could be monitored, being indicated by the Commission;

(vi) the requirements of States for upgradation of standards in non-developmental sectors and services particularly of States which are backward in general administration with a view to bringing them to the levels obtaining or likely to obtain in the more advanced States, the manner in which such expenditure could be monitored, being also indicated by the Commission;

(vii) the scope for better fiscal management and economy in expenditure consistent by the Commission; and

(viii) the need for ensuring reasonable returns on investments in irrigation and power projects, transport undertakings, industrial and commercial enterprises and the like.

(6) The Commission may suggest changes, if any, to be

made in the principles governing the distribution among the States of—

(a) the net proceeds in any financial year of estate duty in respect of property other than agricultural land;

(b) the net proceeds in any financial year of the additional excise duties leviable under the Additional Duties of Excise (Goods of Special Importance) Act, 1957, in replacement of the sales tax levied formerly by the State Governments on each of the following commodities; namely—

(i) cotton fabrics.

(ii) woollen fabrics.

(iii) rayon or artificial silk fabrics.

(iv) sugar, and

(v) tobacco including manufactured tobacco.

Provided that the share accruing to each State shall not be less than the revenue realised from the levy of sales tax for the financial year 1956-57 in that State.

(c) the grant to be made available to the States in lieu of the tax under the repealed Railway Passenger Fares Tax Act, 1957; and

(d) the grant to be made available to the States on account of wealth tax on agricultural property.

(7) In making its recommendations on the various matters aforesaid, the Commission shall adopt the population figures of 1971 in all cases where population is regarded as a factor for determination of devolution of taxes and duties and grants-in-aid.

(8) The Commission may examine the scope for raising revenue from the taxes and duties mentioned in article 269 of the Constitution but not levied at present and the scope for enhancing revenue from the duties

mentioned in Article 268.

(9) The Commission may make an assessment of the non-plan capital gap of the States on a uniform and comparable basis for the five years ending with 1988-89. In the light of such an assessment, the Commission may undertake a general review of the States' debt position with particular reference to the Central loans advanced to them and likely to be outstanding as at the end of 1983-84 and suggest appropriate measures to deal with the non-Plan capital gap, having regard inter-alia to the overall non-Plan gap of the States, their relative position and the purposes for which the loans have been utilised and the requirements of the Centre.

(10) The Commission may review the policy and arrangements in regard to the financing of relief expenditure by the States affected by natural calamities and suggest such modifications as it considers appropriate, in the existing arrangements, having regard, among other considerations, to the need for avoidance of wasteful expenditure.

Ninth Finance Commission

Composition

Chairman	**Shri N.K.P. Salve**
Members	**Shri Justice Abdus Sattar Qureshi** **Shri Raja J. Chelliah** **Shri Lal Thanhawla** **(Resigned on 24th January, 1989)** **Shri S Venkitaramanan (From 3rd May, 1989, in place of Shri Lal Thanhawla Subsequently resigned)** **Shri R. Keishing (From 25th Nov., 1989 in place of Shri S. Venkitaramanan)**

Shri Mahesh Prasad (Member Secretary Resigned)
Shri K.V.R. Nair (Member Secretary from 13th July, 1989 in place of Shri Mahesh Prasad)

Terms of Reference

Paras 3-10 of the Presidential Order dated 17th June, 1987 containing the terms of reference of the Ninth Finance Commission are reproduced—

(3) The Commission shall make recommendations 35 as to the following matters—

(a) the distribution between the Union and the States of the net proceeds of taxes which are to be, or may be, divided between them under Chapter I of Part XII of the Constitution and the allocation between the States of the respective shares of such proceeds;

(b) the principles which should govern the grants-in-aid of the revenues of the States out of the Consolidated Fund of India and the sums to be paid to the States which are in need of assistance by way of grants-in-aid of their revenues under article 275 of the Constitution for purposes other than those specified in the provisos to clause (1) of that article.

(4) In making its recommendations, the Commission shall—

(i) adopt a normative approach in assessing the receipts and expenditures on the revenue account of the States and the Centre and, in doing so, keep in view the special problems of each State, if any, and the special requirements of the Centre such as defence, security, debt servicing and other committed expenditure or liabilities;

(ii) have due regard to the need for providing adequate incentives for better resource mobilisation and financial discipline as well as closer linking of expenditure and revenue raising decisions;

(iii) take into account the need for speed, efficiency and effectiveness of Government functioning and of delivery systems for Government programme; and

(iv) keep in view the objective of not only balancing the receipts and expenditure on revenue account of both the States and the Centre, but also generating surpluses for capital investment.

(5) The Commission may suggest changes, if any, to be made in the principles governing the distribution among the States of—

(a) the net proceeds in any financial year of the additional duties of excise leviable under the Additional Duties of Excise (Goods of Special Importance) Act, 1957 (58 of 1957); and

(b) the grants to be made available to the States in lieu of the tax under the repealed Railway Passenger Fares Tax Act, 1957 (25 of 1957).

(6) In making its recommendations on the various matters aforesaid, the Commission shall adopt the population figures of 1971 in all cases where population is regarded as a factor for determination of devolution of taxes and duties and grants-in-aid.

(7) The Commission may examine the feasibility of the

merger of additional duties of excise in lieu of sales tax with basic duties of excise and evolve a suitable formula for allocating a part of the duties of excise in respect of the goods described in column (3) of the First Schedule to the Additional Duties of Excise (Goods of Special Importance) Act, 1957 (58 of 1957) for distribution among the States, in lieu of sales tax.

(8) The Commission may make an assessment of the debt position of the States as on the 31st day of March, 1989 and suggest such corrective measures as deemed necessary keeping in view the financial requirements of the Centre. The corrective measures will be with particular reference to investments made in infrastructure projects and shall have linkage with improvements in financial and managerial efficiency.

(9) The Commission may review the policy and arrangements in regard to the financing of relief expenditure by the States affected by natural calamities and suggest such modifications as it considers appropriate, in the existing arrangements, having regard, among other considerations, to the need for avoidance of wasteful expenditure. The Commission may examine, inter-alia, the feasibility of establishing a national insurance fund to which the State Governments may contribute a percentage of their revenue receipts.

(10) On the matters aforesaid, the Commission shall make two reports, the first report covering a period of one year commencing on the 1st day of April, 1989, by the 30th June, 1988, and the second report covering a period of five years commencing on the 1st day of April, 1990, by the 30th June, 1989.

(By subsequent notifications dated the 30th June, 1988 and 13th June, 1989 respectively the Commission was to make their first report by 31st July, 1988 and second report by 31st December, 1989)

Tenth Finance Commission

Composition

Chairman	**Shri K.C. Pant**
Members	**Dr. Debi Prosad Pal, MP** **Shri B.P.R. Vithal** **Dr. C. Rangarajan** **(Resigned 21st December, 1992)** **Shri Manu R. Shroff (From 14th October, 1993 in place of Dr. C. Rangarajan)** **Shri M.C. Gupta (Member Secretary (Relinquished charge on 31st January, 1994)** **Shri Arun Sinha, Member Secretary (From 1st March, 1994 in place of Shri. M.C. Gupta)**

Terms of Reference

Paras 3-9 of the Presidential Order dated 15th June, 1992 containing the terms of reference of the Tenth Finance Commission are reproduced below—

(3) The Commission shall make recommendations relating to the following matters—

(a) the distribution between the Union and the States of the net proceeds of taxes 37 which are to be, or may be, divided between them under Chapter I of Part XII of the Constitution and the allocation between the States of the respective shares of such proceeds;

(b) the principles which should govern the grants-in-aid of the revenues of the States out of the

Consolidated Fund of India and the sums to be paid to the States which are in need of assistance by way of grants-in-aid of their revenues under article 275 of the Constitution for purposes other than those specified in the provisos to clause (1) of that article.

(4) In making its recommendations, the Commission shall have regard, among other considerations, to—

(i) the objective of not only balancing the receipts and expenditure on revenue account of both the States and the Central Government, but also generating surplus for capital investment and reducing fiscal deficit;

(ii) the resources of the Central Government and the demands thereon, in particular, on account of expenditure on civil administration, defence and border security, debt servicing and other committed expenditure or liabilities;

(iii) the maintenance and upkeep of capital assets and maintenance expenditure on plan schemes to be completed by 31st March, 1995 and the norms on the basis of which specified amounts are recommended for the maintenance of the capital assets and the manner of monitoring such expenditure;

(iv) the requirements of States for modernisation of administration, e.g. computerisation of land records and providing faster channels of communication upto and above district level, and for upgrading the standards in non-developmental sectors and services, and the manner in which such expenditure can be monitored;

(v) the revenue resources of the States for the five years commencing on 1st April, 1995, on the basis of the levels of taxation likely to be reached in 1993-94, targets set for additional resource mobilisation for the plan and the potential for raising additional taxes;

(vi) the requirements of the States for meeting the non-Plan revenue expenditure also keeping in view the potential for raising additional taxes;

(viii) the need for ensuring reasonable returns on investment by the States in irrigation projects, power projects, state transport undertakings, departmental commercial undertakings, public sector enterprises, etc; and

(ix) the scope for better fiscal management consistent with efficiency and economy in expenditure.

(5) The Commission may suggest changes, if any, to be made in the principles governing the distribution of—

(a) the net proceeds in any financial year of the additional excise duties leviable under the Additional Duties of Excise (Goods of Special Importance) Act, 1957, in replacement of the sales tax levied formerly by the State Governments; and

(b) the grants to be made available to the States in

lieu of the tax under the repealed Railway Passenger Fares Act, 1957.

(6) In making its recommendations on the various matters aforesaid, the Commission shall adopt the population figures of 1971 in all cases where population is regarded as a factor for determination of devolution of taxes and duties and grants-in-aid.

(7) The Commission may review the present scheme of Calamity Relief Fund and may make appropriate recommendations thereon.

(8) The Commission may make an assessment of the debt position of the State as on 31st March, 1994, and suggest such corrective measures as are deemed necessary also keeping in view the financial requirements of the Centre.

Eleventh Finance Commission

Composition

Chairman	**Prof. A.M. Khusro**
Members	**Shri N.C. Jain** **Shri J.C. Jetly IAS (Retd.)** **Dr. Amaresh Bagchi** **Shri T.N. Srivastava, Member Secretary**

Terms of Reference

Paras 3-12 of the Presidential Order dated 3rd July, 1998 containing the terms of reference of the Eleventh Finance Commission are reproduced below—

(3) The Commission shall make recommendations as to the following matters—

(a) the distribution between the Union and the States

of the net proceeds of taxes which are to be, or may be, divided between them under Chapter I of Part XII of the Constitution and the allocation between the States of the respective shares of such proceeds;

(b) the principles which should govern the grants-in-aid of the revenues of the States out of the Consolidated Fund of India and the sums to be paid to the States which are in need of assistance by way of grants-in-aid of their revenues under article 275 of the Constitution for purposes other than those specified in the provisos to clause (1) of that article;

(c) the measures needed to augment the Consolidated Fund of a State to supplement the resources of the Panchayats in the State on the basis of the recommendations made by the Finance Commission of the State;

(d) the measure needed to augment the Consolidated Fund of a State to supplement the resources of the Municipalities in the State on the basis of the recommendations made by the Finance Commission of the State.

(4) The Commission shall review the state of the finances of the Union and the States and suggest ways and means by which the governments, collectively and severally, may bring about a restructuring of the public finances so as to restore budgetary balance and maintain macro-economic stability.

(5) In making its recommendations, the Commission shall have regard, among other considerations, to—

(i) the resources of the Central Government and the demands thereon, in particular, on account of expenditure on civil administration, defence and border security, debt servicing and other committed expenditure or liability;

(ii) revenue resources of the States for the five years commencing on 1st April, 2000, on the basis of levels of taxation possible to be reached in 1998-99, targets set for additional resources mobilisation for the Plan and the potential for raising additional taxes;

(iii) the requirement of the States for meeting the Plan and non-Plan revenue expenditure; keeping in view the need for generating surplus for capital investment and reducing fiscal deficit;

(iv) the maintenance and upkeep of capital assets and maintenance expenditure of plan schemes to be completed by 31st March, 2000 and the norms on the basis of which specified amounts are recommended for the maintenance of the capital assets and the manner of monitoring such expenditure;

(v) the requirements of States for upgradation of standards in non-developmental and social sectors and services particularly of States which are backward in general administration with a view to modernise and rationalise the administrative set up in the interest of speed, efficiency and sound fiscal management.

(vi) the need for ensuring reasonable returns on investment by the States in irrigation projects, power projects, State Transport Undertaking, departmental commercial undertakings, public sector enterprises etc.;

(vii) such provisions for emoluments and terminal benefits of Government employees including teachers and other employees of aided institutions as obtaining on a specified date as the Commission deems it proper and with reference to appropriate objective criteria rather than in terms of actual increases that may have been given effect to;

(viii) the scope for better fiscal management consistent with efficiency and economy in expenditure including the incentives that need to be provided for better realisations of tax and non tax revenue.

(6) In the case of local bodies—

(a) the Commission shall take into account the recommendations of the State Finance Commissions; and

(b) where the State Finance Commissions have not been constituted as yet, or have not submitted their report giving recommendations, the Commission will make its own assessment about the manner and extent of augmentation of Consolidated Fund of the State to supplement the resources of the Panchayats and Municipalities in the State. While making such assessment, the Commission—

(i) shall take into account the provisions required to be made for the emoluments and terminal benefits of the employees of local bodies including those of teachers;

(ii) shall take into account the existing powers of the Panchayats and Municipalities to raise financial resources including those by way of raising additional taxes by the Panchayats and Municipalities; and

(iii) the powers, authority and responsibility transferred to Panchayats and Municipalities under Article 243 G and 243 W of the Constitution read with Schedules Eleven and Twelve.

(7) The Commission may suggest changes, if any, to be made in the principles governing the distribution amongst the States of—

(a) the net proceeds in any financial year of the additional duties of the excise leviable under the Additional Duties of Excise (Goods of Special Importance) Act, 1957 (58 of 1957) in lieu of the sales tax levied formerly by the State Governments; and

(b) the grants to be made available to the States in lieu of the tax under the repealed Railway Passenger Fares Tax Act, 1957 (25 of 1957).

(8) In making its recommendations on the various matters aforesaid, the Commission shall adopt the population figures of 1971 in all cases where population is regarded as a factor for determination of devolution of taxes and duties and grants-in-aid.

(9) The Commission may make an assessment of the debt position of the States as on 31st day of March, 1999 and suggest such corrective measures as are deemed necessary, keeping in view the long term

sustainability for both the Centre and the States.

(10) The Commission may review the present scheme of Calamity Relief Fund and may make appropriate recommendations thereon.

Additional Term of Reference for The Eleventh Finance Commission

In pursuance of the provisions of article 280 of the Constitution read with sections 6 and 8 of the Finance Commission (Miscellaneous Provisions) Act, 1951 (33 of 1951), the President hereby directs that in the Order dated the 3rd July, 1998 published in the Notification of the Government of India in the Ministry of Finance (Department of Economic Affairs) No. S.O. 557(E), dated the 3rd July, 1998, in paragraph 4, the following shall be added at the end, namely—

'In particular, the Constitution shall draw a monitorable fiscal reforms programme aimed at reduction of revenue deficit of the State and recommended the manner in which the grants to States to cover the assessed deficit in their Non-Plan Revenue account may be linked to progress in implementing the programme'.

Twelfth Finance Commission

Composition

Chairman **Dr. C. Rangarajan**

Members **Shri Som Pal**
Shri T.R. Prasad IAS (Retd.)
Prof. D.K. Srivastava
Shri G.C. Srivastava IAS, Member Secretary

Terms of Reference

Paras 3-12 of the Presidential Order dated 1st November,

2002 containing the terms of reference of the Twelfth Finance Commission are reproduced below—

(4) The Commission shall make recommendations as to the following matters —

(i) the distribution between the Union and the States of the net proceeds of taxes which are to be, or may be, divided between them under Chapter I Part XII of the Constitution and the allocation between the States of the respective shares of such proceeds;

(ii) the principles which should govern the grants-in-aid of the revenues of the States out of the Consolidated Fund of India and the sums to be paid to the States which are in need of assistance by way of grants-in-aid of their revenues under article 275 of the Constitution for purposes other than those specified in the provisions to clause (1) of that article; and

(iii) the measures needed to augment the Consolidated Fund of a State to supplement the resources of the Panchayats and Municipalities in the State on the basis of the recommendations made by the Finance Commission of the State.

(5) The Commission shall review the state of the finances of the Union and the States and suggest a plan by which the governments, collectively and severally, may bring about a restructuring of the public finances restoring budgetary balance, achieving macro-economic stability and debt reduction along with equitable growth.

(6) In making its recommendations, the Commission shall have regard, among other considerations, to: —

(i) the resources, of the Central Government for five years commencing on 1st April 2005, on the basis of levels of taxation and non-tax revenues likely to be reached at the end of 2003-04;

(ii) the demands on the resources of the Central Government, in particular, on account of expenditure on civil administration, defence, internal and border security, debt-servicing and other committed expenditure and liabilities;

(iii) the resources of the State Governments, for the five years commencing on 1st April 2005, on the basis of levels of taxation and non-tax revenues likely to be reached at the end of 2003-04;

(iv) the objective of not only balancing the receipts and expenditure on revenue account of all the States and the Centre, but also generating surpluses for capital investment and reducing fiscal deficit;

(v) taxation efforts of the Central Government and each State Government as against targets, if any, and the potential for additional resource mobilization in order to improve the tax-Gross Domestic Product (GDP) and tax-Gross State Domestic Product (GSDP) ratio, as the case may be;

(vi) the expenditure on the non-salary component of maintenance and upkeep of capital assets and the non-wage related maintenance expenditure on plan schemes to be completed by the 31st March 2005 and the norms on the basis of which specific amounts are recommended for the maintenance of the capital assets and the manner of monitoring such expenditure;

(vii) the need for ensuring the commercial viability of irrigation projects, power projects, departmental undertakings, public sector enterprises etc. in the States through various means including adjustment of user charges and relinquishing of non-priority enterprises through privatisation or disinvestment.

(7) In making its recommendations on various matters, the Commission will take the base of population figures as of 1971, in all such cases where population is a factor for determination of devolution of taxes and duties and grants-in-aid.

(8) The Commission shall review the Fiscal Reform Facility introduced by the Central Government on the basis of the recommendations of the Eleventh Finance Commission, and suggest measures for effective achievement of its objectives.

(9) The Commission may, after making an assessment of the debt position of the States as on the 31st March 2004, suggest such corrective measures, as are deemed necessary, consistent with macro-economic stability and debt sustainability. Such measures recommended will give weightage to the performance of the States in the fields of human development and investment climate.

(10) The Commission may review the present arrangements as regards financing of Disaster Management with reference to the National Calamity Contingency Fund and the Calamity Relief Fund and make appropriate recommendations thereon.

(11) The Commission shall indicate the basis on which it has arrived at its findings and make available the State-wise estimates of receipts and expenditure.

Thirteenth Finance Commission

Composition

Chairman	**Dr. Vijay L. Kelkar**
Members	**Shri B.K. Chaturvedi**
	Dr. Indira Rajaraman
	Dr. Abusaleh Shariff
	Prof. Atul Sarma
	Shri Sumit Bose, Member Secretary

Terms of Reference

Paras 3-9 of the Presidential Order dated 31st October, 2009 containing the terms of reference of the Thirteenth Finance Commission are reproduced below —

(4) The Commission shall make recommendations as to the following matters, namely —

(i) the distribution between the Union and the States of the net proceeds of taxes which are to be, or may be divided between them under Chapter I Part XII of the Constitution and the allocation between the States of the respective shares of such proceeds ;

(ii) the principles which should govern the grants-in-aid of the revenues of the States out of the Consolidated Fund of India and the sums to be paid to the States which are in need of assistance by way of grants-in-aid of their revenues under article 275 of the Constitution for purposes other than those specified in the provisos to clause (1) of that article ; and

(iii) the measures needed to augment the Consolidated Fund of a State to supplement the resources of the Panchayats and Municipalities in the State on the basis of the recommendations made by the Finance Commission of the State.

(5) The Commission shall review the state of the finances of the Union and the States, keeping in view, in particular, the operation of the State's Debt Consolidation and Relief Facility 2005-2010 introduced by the Central Government on the basis of the recommendations of the Twelfth Finance Commission, and suggest measures for maintaining a stable and sustainable fiscal environment consistent with equitable growth.

6. In making its recommendations, the Commission shall have regard, among other considerations, to—

(i) the resources of the Central Government, for five years commencing on 1st April 2010, on the basis of levels of taxation and non-tax revenues likely to be reached at the end of 2008-06 ;

(ii) the demands on the resources of the Central Government, in particular, on account of the projected Gross Budgetary Support to the Central and State Plan, expenditure on civil administration, defence, internal and border security, debt-servicing and other committed expenditure and liabilities ;

(iii) the resources of the State Governments, for the five years commencing on 1st April 2010, on the basis of levels of taxation and non-tax revenues likely to be reached at the end of 2008-09 ;

(iv) the objectives of not only balancing the receipts and expenditure on revenue account of all the States and the Union, but also generating surpluses for capital investment ;

(v) the taxation efforts of the Central Government and each State Government and the potential for additional resource mobilisation to improve the tax Gross Domestic Product ratio in the case of the Union and tax-Gross State Domestic Product ratio in the case of the States;

(vi) the impact of the proposed implementation of Goods and Services Tax with effect from 1st April, 2010 including its impact on the country's foreign trade ;

(vii) the need to improve the quality of public expenditure to obtain better outputs and outcomes ;

(viii) the need to manage ecology, environment and climate change consistent with sustainable development ;

(ix) the expenditure on the non-salary component of maintenance and upkeep of capital assets and the non-wage related maintenance expenditure on plan schemes to be completed by 31st March, 2010 and the norms on the basis of which specific amounts are recommended for the maintenance of the capital assets and the manner of monitoring such expenditure ;

(x) the need for ensuring the commercial viability of irrigation projects, power projects, departmental undertakings and public sector enterprises through various means, including levy of user charges and adoption of measures to promote efficiency.

7. In taking its recommendations on various matters, the Commission shall take the base of population figures as of 1971, in all such cases where population is a factor for determination of devolution of taxes and duties and grants-in-aid.

8. The Commission may review the present

arrangements as regards financing of Disaster Management with reference to the National Calamity Contingency Fund and the Calamity Relief Fund and the funds envisaged in the Disaster Management Act, 2005 (53 of 2005), and make appropriate recommendations thereon.

9. The Commission shall indicate the basis on which it has arrived at its findings and make available the estimates of receipts and expenditure of the Union and each of the States.

Additional Terms of Reference for the Thirteenth Finance Commission

The Union cabinet today gave its approval for insertion of the following Additional Terms of Reference in the Term of Reference of the Thirteenth Finance Commission:

"Having regard to the need to bring the liabilities of the Central Government on account of oil, food and fertilizer bonds into fiscal accounting, and the impact of various other obligations of the Central Government on the deficit targets, the Commission may review the road map for fiscal adjustment and suggest a suitably revised roadmap with a view to maintaining the gains of fiscal consolidation through 2010 to 2015",

Source: 50 year of Fiscal Federalism.

List of Considerations referred in the TOR of Finance Commissions

First

(a) the sums to be prescribed by him as grants-in-aid of the revenues of the States of Assam, Bihar, Orissa and West Bengal in lieu of assignment of any shares of the net proceeds in each year of the export duty on jute and jute products to these States in accordance with the provisions of Article 273 of the Constitution;

(b) the States in need of assistance and the sums payable to such States as grants-in-aid of their revenues under the substantive portion of Clause (1) of Article 275 of the Constitution.

Second

(b) the States which are in need of assistance by way of grants-in-aid of the revenues of those States under article 275, and the sums to be paid to those States, having regard, among other considerations, to—

- (i) the requirements of the Second Five Year Plan, and
- (ii) the efforts made by those States to raise additional revenue from the sources available to them;

Third

(a) the States which are in need of assistance by way of grants-in-aid of their revenues under article 275, and the sums to be paid to those States other than the sums specified in the provisos to clause (1) of that article, having regard, among other considerations, to:

(i) the requirements of the Third Five Year Plan; and

(ii) the efforts to be made by those States to raise additional revenues from the sources available to them;

Fourth

(a) the States which are in need of assistance by way of grants-in-aid of their revenue under article 275, and the sums to be paid to those States other than the sums specified in the provisos to clause (1) of that article, having regard, among other consideration to:

(i) the revenues resources of those States for the five years ending with the financial year 1970-71 on the basis of the levels of taxation likely to be reached in financial year 1965-66;

(ii) the requirements of those States to meet the committed expenditure on maintenance and upkeep of plan schemes completed during the Third Plan;

(iii) and further expenditure likely to devolve upon those States for the servicing of their debt;

(iv) creation of a fund out of the excess, if any, over a limit to be specified by the Commission of the net proceeds of estate duty on property other than agricultural land accruing to a State in any financial year, for the repayment of the State's debt to the Central Government; and

(v) the scope for economy consistent with efficiency, which may be effected by the States in their administrative expenditure;

Fifth

(b) the principles which should govern the grants-in-aid of the revenues of the States out of the Consolidated Fund of India and the sums to be paid to the States which are in need of assistance by way of grants-in-aid of their revenues under Article 275 for purposes other than those specified in the provisos to clause (1) of that Article and other than the requirements of the Five Year Plan, having regard, among other considerations, to:

(i) the revenues resources of those States for the five years ending with the financial year 1973-74 on the basis of the levels of taxation likely to be reached at the end of the financial year 1968-69;

(ii) the requirements on revenue account of those States to meet the expenditure on administration, interest charges in respect of their debt, maintenance and upkeep of plan schemes completed by the end of 1968-69, transfer of funds to local bodies and aided institutions and other committed expenditure;

(iii) the scope for better fiscal management as also for economy consistent with efficiency which may be effected by the States in their administrative, maintenance, developmental and other expenditure;

Sixth

(b) the principles which should govern the grants-in-aid of the revenues of States out of the Consolidated Fund of India and the sums to be paid to the States which are in need of assistance by way of grants-in-aid of their revenues under Article 275 of Constitution for purposes other than those specified in the provisos to clause (1) of that article having regard, among other considerations, to:

(i) the existing practice in regard to determination and distribution of Central assistance for financing State Plans;

(ii) the revenue resources of those States for the five years ending with the financial year 1978-79 on the basis of the levels of taxation likely to be reached at the end of the financial year 1973-74;

(iii) the requirements on revenue account of those States to meet the expenditure on administration taking also into account such provision for emoluments of Government employees, teachers and local body employees as obtaining on a specified date as the Commission deem it proper in the light of the States' capacity and needs, interest charges in respect of their debt, transfer of funds to local bodies and aided institutions and other committed expenditure;

(iv) adequate maintenance and upkeep of the capital assets and maintenance of Plan schemes completed by the end of 1973-74, the norms, if any, on the basis of which specified amounts are allowed for the maintenance of different categories of capital assets being indicated by the Commission;

(v) the requirements of States which are backward in standards of general administration for upgrading the administration with a view to bringing it to the levels obtaining in the more advanced States over a period of ten years; and

(vi) the scope for better fiscal management and economy consistent with efficiency which may be effected by the States in their administrative, maintenance, developmental and other expenditure.

Seventh

(i) The resources of the Central Government and the demands thereon on account of the expenditure on civil administration, defence and border security, debt servicing and other committed expenditure or liabilities;

(ii) the existing practice in regard to determination and distribution of Central assistance for financing State Plans;

(iii) the revenue resources of those States for the five years ending with the financial year 1983-84 on the basis of the levels of taxation likely to be reached at the end of the financial year 1978-79 and the targets set for additional resource mobilisation for the Plan;

(iv) the requirements on revenues account of those States to meet the expenditure on administration and other non-plan commitments or liabilities, keeping however in view national policies and priorities. In assessing such requirements, the Commission shall take into account:

(a) such provision for emoluments of Government employees, teachers and local body employees as obtaining on a specified date as the Commission deem it proper and with reference to appropriate objective criteria rather than in terms of actual increases that may have been given effect to; and

(b) commitments in regard to interest charges on their debt, transfer of funds to local bodies and aided institutions;

(v) adequate maintenance and upkeep of capital assets

and maintenance of plan schemes completed by the end of 1978-79, the norms, if any, on the basis of which specified amounts are allowed for the maintenance of different categories of capital assets and the manner in which such maintenance expenditure could be monitored being indicated by the Commission;

(vi) the requirements of States which are backward in general administration for upgradation of standards in non-developmental sectors and services with a view to bringing them to the levels obtaining in the more advanced States over the period covered by the Report of the Commission; the manner in which such expenditure could be monitored, being also indicated by the Commission;

(vii) the scope for better fiscal management and economy in expenditure consistent with efficiency; and

(viii) the need for ensuring reasonable returns on investments in irrigation and power projects, transport undertakings, industrial and commercial enterprises and the like.

Eighth

(i) the resources of the Central Government and the demands thereon on account of expenditure on civil administration, defence and border security, debt servicing and other committed expenditure or liabilities;

(ii) The existing practice in regard to determination and distribution of Central Assistance for financing State Plans;

(iii) The revenue resources of those States for the five years ending with the financial year 1988-89 on the basis of the levels of taxation likely to be reached at the end of the financial year 1983-84 and the targets set for additional resource mobilisation for the Plan;

(iv) The requirements on revenue account of those States to meet the expenditure on administration and other non-Plan commitments or liabilities, keeping however in view national policies and priorities. In assessing such requirements, the Commission shall take into account:

   (a) such provision for emoluments and terminal benefits of Government employees, teachers and employees of local bodies as obtaining on a specified date as the Commission deems it proper and with reference to appropriate objective criteria rather than in terms of actual increases that may have been given effect to; and

   (b) commitments in regard to interest charges on their debt, transfer of funds to local bodies and aided institutions;

(v) adequate maintenance and upkeep of capital assets and maintenance of plan schemes completed by the end of 1983-84, the norms, if any, on the basis of which specified amounts are allowed for the maintenance of different categories of capital assets and the manner in which such maintenance expenditure could be monitored, being indicated by the Commission;

(vi) the requirements of States for upgradation of standards in non-developmental sectors and services particularly of States which are backward in general administration with a view to bringing them to the levels obtaining or likely to obtain in the more advanced States, the manner in which such expenditure could be monitored, being also indicated by the Commission;

(vii) The scope for better fiscal management and economy in expenditure consistent by the Commission; and

(viii) The need for ensuring reasonable returns on investments in irrigation and power projects, transport undertakings, industrial and commercial enterprises and the like.

Ninth

(i) adopt a normative approach in assessing the receipts and expenditures on the revenue account of the States and the Centre and, in doing so, keep in view the special problems of each State, if any, and the special requirements of the Centre such as defence, security, debt servicing and other committed expenditure or liabilities;

(ii) have due regard to the need for providing adequate incentives for better resource mobilisation and financial discipline as well as closer linking of expenditure and revenue raising decisions;

(iii) take into account the need for speed, efficiency and effectiveness of Government functioning and of delivery systems for Government programme; and

(iv) keep in view the objective of not only balancing the receipts and expenditure on revenue account of both the States and the Centre, but also generating surpluses for capital investment.

Tenth

(i) the objective of not only balancing the receipts and expenditure on revenue account of both the States and the Central Government, but also generating surplus for capital investment and reducing fiscal deficit;

(ii) the resources of the Central Government and the demands thereon, in particular, on account of expenditure on civil administration, defence and border security, debt servicing and other committed expenditure or liabilities;

(iii) the maintenance and upkeep of capital assets and maintenance expenditure on plan schemes to be completed by 31st March, 1995 and the norms on the basis of which specified amounts are recommended for the maintenance of the capital assets and the manner of monitoring such expenditure;

(iv) the requirements of States for modernisation of administration, e.g. computerisation of land records and providing faster channels of communication upto and above district level, and for upgrading the standards in non-developmental sectors and services, and the manner in which such expenditure can be monitored;

(v) the revenue resources of the States for the five years commencing on 1st April, 1995, on the basis of the levels of taxation likely to be reached in 1993-94, targets set for additional resource mobilisation for the plan and the potential for raising additional taxes;

(vi) the requirements of the States for meeting the non-Plan revenue expenditure also keeping in view the potential for raising additional taxes;

(vii) the tax efforts made by the States;

(viii) the need for ensuring reasonable returns on investment by the States in irrigation projects, power projects, state transport undertakings, departmental commercial undertakings, public sector enterprises, etc; and

(ix) the scope for better fiscal management consistent with efficiency and economy in expenditure.

Eleventh

(i) the resources of the Central Government and the demands thereon, in particular, on account of expenditure on civil administration, defence and border security, debt servicing and other committed expenditure or liability;

(ii) revenue resources of the States for the five years commencing on 1st April, 2000, on the basis of levels of taxation possible to be reached in 1998-99, targets set for additional resources mobilisation for the Plan and the potential for raising additional taxes;

(iii) the requirement of the States for meeting the Plan and non-Plan revenue expenditure, keeping in view the need for generating surplus for capital investment and reducing fiscal deficit;

(iv) the maintenance and upkeep of capital assets and maintenance expenditure of plan schemes to be completed by 31st March, 2000 and the norms on the basis of which specified amounts are recommended for the maintenance of the capital assets and the manner of monitoring such expenditure;

(v) the requirements of States for upgradation of standards in non-developmental and social sectors and services particularly of States which are backward in general administration with a view to modernise and rationalise the administrative set up in the interest of speed, efficiency and sound fiscal management;

(vi) the need for ensuring reasonable returns on investment by the States in irrigation projects, power projects, State Transport Undertaking, departmental commercial undertakings, public sector enterprises, etc.;

(vii) such provisions for emoluments and terminal benefits of Government employees including teachers and other employees of aided institutions as obtaining on a specified date as the Commission deems it proper and with reference to appropriate objective criteria rather than in terms of actual increases that may have been given effect to;

(viii) the scope for better fiscal management consistent with efficiency and economy in expenditure including the incentives that need to be provided for better realisations of tax and non-tax revenue.

Twelfth

(i) the resources, of the Central Government for five years commencing on 1st April 2005, on the basis of levels of taxation and non-tax revenues likely to be reached at the end of 2003-04;

(ii) the demands on the resources of the Central Government, in particular, on account of expenditure on civil administration, defence, internal and border security, debt-servicing and other committed expenditure and liabilities;

(iii) the resources of the State Governments, for the five years commencing on 1st April 2005, on the basis of levels of taxation and non-tax revenues likely to be reached at the end of 2003-04;

(iv) the objective of not only balancing the receipts and expenditure on revenue account of all the States and the Centre, but also generating surpluses for capital investment and reducing fiscal deficit;

(v) taxation efforts of the Central Government and each State Government as against targets, if any, and the potential for additional resources mobilization in order to improve the tax-Gross Domestic Product

(GDP) and tax-Gross State Domestic Product (GSDP) ratio, as the case may be;

(vi) the expenditure on the non-salary component of maintenance and upkeep of capital assets and the non-wage related maintenance expenditure on plan schemes to be completed by the 31st March 2005 and the norms on the basis of which specific amounts are recommended for the maintenance of the capital assets and the manner of monitoring such expenditure;

(vii) the need for ensuring the commercial viability of irrigation projects, power projects, departmental undertakings, public sector enterprises etc. in the States through various means including adjustment of user charges and relinquishing of non-priority enterprises through privatisation or disinvestment.

Thirteenth

(i) the resources of the Central Government, for five years commencing on 1st April 2010, on the basis of levels of taxation and non-tax revenues likely to be reached at the end of 2008-09;

(ii) the demands on the resources of the Central Government, in particular, on account of the projected Gross Budgetary Support to the Central and State Plan, expenditure on civil administration, defence, internal and border security, debt-servicing and other committed expenditure and liabilities;

(iii) the resources of the State Governments, for the five years commencing on 1st April 2010, on the basis of levels of taxation and non-tax revenues likely to be reached at the end of 2008-09;

(iv) the objective of not only balancing the receipts and expenditure on revenue account of all the States and the Union, but also generating surpluses for capital investment;

(v) the taxation efforts of the Central Government and each State Government and the potential for additional resource mobilisation to improve the tax-Gross Domestic Product ratio in the case of the Union and tax-Gross State Domestic Product ratio in the case of the States;

(vi) the impact of the proposed implementation of Goods and Services Tax with effect from 1st April, 2010, including its impact on the country's foreign trade;

(vii) the need to improve the quality of public expenditure to obtain better outputs and outcomes;

(viii) the need to manage ecology, environment and climate change consistent with sustainable development;

(ix) the expenditure on the non-salary component of maintenance and upkeep of capital assets and the non-wage related maintenance expenditure on plan schemes to be completed by 31st March, 2010 and the norms on the basis of which specific amounts are recommended for the maintenance of the capital assets and the manner of monitoring such expenditure;

(x) the need for ensuring the commercial viability of irrigation projects, power projects, departmental undertakings and public sector enterprises through various means, including levy of user charges and adoption of measures to promote efficiency.

Annexure III.7

Notes/Notes of Dissent

First Commission
- Note by Justice R. Kaushabendra Rao

Second Commission
- None

Third Commission
- Note of Dissent by Member Secretary G.R. Kamat

Fourth Commission
- Minutes by Sri Mohan Lal Gautam, Bhabatosh Datta, Justice P.V. Rajamannan

Fifth Commission
- Minutes by Sri. G. Swaminathan

Sixth Commission
- None

Seventh Commission
- Minutes—Sri H.N. Ray, Jointly by Raj Krishna and Sri H.N. Ray
- Minute of Dissent by Prof Raj Krishna

Eighth Commission
- Minutes of Dissent by Justice T.P.S. Chawla and G.C. Baveja
- Minute of Dissent by Y.B. Chavan and G.C. Baveja

Ninth Commission

- Three notes
  - One note of dissent by Justice A.S. Quareshi
  - A note by Majority
  - A note by majority minus Member Secretary

Tenth Commission

- None

Eleventh Commission

- A note by N.C. Jain
- A note of observation by Dr. Amresh Bagchi

Twelfth Commission

- None

Thirteenth Commission

- None

Annexure V.1

Shares of Central Taxes—Vertical Distribution

Commissions	*State's Share in Net Proceeds of*		
	Income Tax	*Union Excise Duty*	
1	2	3	
First	55%	40%	3 commodities
Second	60%	25%	8 commodities
Third	66.66%	20%	35 commodities
Fourth	75%	20%	all commodities
Fifth	75%	20%	all commodities
Sixth	80%	20%	all commodities
Seventh	85%	40%	all commodities
Eighth	85%	45%	all commodities
Ninth	85%	45%	all commodtiies
Tenth	77.5%	47.5%	all commodities

Source: Reports of Various Finance Commissions.

Annexure V.2

Table of Forecasts and Actuals of Eleventh & Twelfth Finance Commission

Statement of Revenue Receipt and Non-Plan Revenue Expenditure Forecast, as assessed by XIth Finance Commission and Actuals during 2000-01 to 2004-05

(U.P. Only)

(₹in lakh)

Year	*Revenue Receipts*			*Non-Plan Revenue Expenditure*		
	Forecast	*Assessed by FC-XI*	*Actuals*	*Forecast*	*Assessed by FC-XI*	*Actuals*
1	2	3	4	5	6	7
2000-01	1161180	1275556	1292465	2992561	2448483	2734660
2001-02	1279332	1520210	1210539	3500489	2696201	2821523
2002-03	1417368	1802307	1468039	4129410	3076250	2936369
2003-04	1558795	2128677	1588330	4707062	3378359	4694511
2004-05	1720046	2523249	1841290	5295927	3728624	3951226

Statement of Revenue Receipt and Non-Plan Revenue Expenditure Forecast, as assessed by XIIth Finance Commission and Actuals during 2005-06 to 2009-10

(U.P. Only)

(₹in lakh)

Year	*Revenue Receipts*			*Non-Plan Revenue Expenditure*		
	Forecast	*Assessed by FC-XII*	*Actuals*	*Forecast*	*Assessed by FC-XII*	*Actuals*
1	2	3	4	5	6	7
2005-06	2010898	2204653	2178823	4080112	3449483	4017233
2006-07	2261932	2539588	2953061	4285509	3714059	4600042
2007-08	2545321	2922330	3077533	4515816	4156150	5347929
2008-09	2865234	3360236	3542553	4733391	4467495	5867755
2009-10	3226582	3861858	5046037 (RE)	4981739	4824275	7730190 (RE)

Annexure V.3

Formula for Distribution of Income Tax

Commission	Population	Collection	Per capita Income	Income Distance	Poverty Ratio	Index of Back-wardnes	Area adjusted	Tax effort
1	2	3	4	5	6	7	8	9
I	80	20	---	---	---	---	---	---
II	90	10						
III	80	20						
IV	80	20						
V	90	10 *						
VI	90	10 *						
VII	90	10 *	22.5	45.0	---	---	---	---
VIII	22.5	10 *						
IX(i)	22.5	10 *	11.25	45.0	11.25	---	---	---
IX(ii)	22.5	10	11.25	45.0	---	11.25	---	---
X	20	---	---	60.0	---	5 +	5	10

* Assessment + Index of Infrastructure.

Source: Reports of Various Finance Commission.

Annexure V.4

Formula for Distribution of Excise Duty

Commission	*Population*	*Index of Backwardness*	*Per capita Income*	*Income Distance*	*Income Adjusted to Total Population*	*Poverty Ratio*	*Revenue Equalisation*	*Area*	*Tax effort*
1	2	3	4	5		6	7	8	9
I	100	---	---	---	---	---	---	---	---
II	90	---	---	---	---	---	---	---	---
III									
IV	80	20							
V	80	6.66	---	13.34	---	---	---	---	---
VI	75	---	---	25	---	---	---	---	---
VII	25	---	---	---	25	25	25	---	---
VIII	25	---	---	25	50	---	---	---	---
IX(i)	25	---	---	50	12.5	12.5	---	---	---
IX(ii)	25	12.5	---	33.5	12.5	---	---	---	---
X	20	5	---	60	---	---	---	5	10

Source: Reports of Various Finance Commission.

Formula Used for Sharing of Additional Excise Duty

Commission	*Guaranteed Amount (₹ in Crore)*	*Principles of Distribution*
1	2	3
Second	32.50	Percentage share on the basis of consumption with population as corrective. Weights not indicated.
Third	32.54	Percentage shares on the basis of %ge increase in Sales Tax collections since 1957-58 and population.
Fourth	32.54	Actual Sales Tax collections for 1961-64
Fifth	32.54	50% Sales Tax Collection 50% Population
Sixth	No guaranteed Amount	70% Population 20% Per Capita SDP 10% Production
Seventh	No guaranteed Amount	Sugar—average of dispatches to each State during 1974-77 Tobacco—SDP X Population
Eighth	No guaranteed Amount	50% Per capita SDP 50% Population
Ninth	No guaranteed Amount	50% Per capita SDP 50% Population
Tenth	No guaranteed Amount	50% Population 40% Per capita SDP 10% Sales Tax Collections

Source: Reports of Various Finance Commission.

Annexure V.6

Formula for Distribution of Divisible Pool

Indicator	*XI-FC*	*XII-FC*	*XIII-FC*
1	2	3	4
Population	10.0	25.0	25.0
Income Distance	62.5	50.00	---
Area	7.5	10.0	10.0
Tax effort	5.0	7.5	---
Fiscal Capacity Distance	---	---	47.5
Fiscal Discipline	7.5	7.5	17.5
Index of Infrastructure	7.5	---	---

Source: Reports of Various Finance Commission.

Indicators Used by Different Finance Commissions for Inter-se Allocation of Share in Central Taxes

S.No.	*Indicator*	*I*	*II*	*III*	*IV*	*V*	*VI*	*VII*	*VIII*	*IX*	*X*	*XI*	*XII*	*XIII*
1.	Population	√	√	√	√	√	√	√	√	√	√	√	√	√
2.	Collection	√	√	√	√	√	√	√	√	√	---	---	---	---
3.	Eco. & Social Backwardness	---	√	√	√	√	---	---	---	---	---	---	---	---
4.	Inverse of Per Capita income	---	---	---	---	---	---	---	√	---	---	---	---	---
5.	Distance of Per Capita income	---	---	---	---	---	---	---	√	√	√	√	√	---
6.	Generation of Electricity	---	---	---	---	---	---	---	---	---	---	---	---	---
7.	Poverty Ratio	---	---	---	---	---	---	---	---	√	---	---	---	---
8.	Composit Index of Backwardness	---	---	---	---	---	---	---	---	√	---	---	---	---
9.	Adjusted area	---	---	---	---	---	---	---	---	---	√	√	√	√
10.	Tax effort	---	---	---	---	---	---	---	---	---	---	---	---	---
11.	Poverty ratio	---	---	---	---	---	---	---	---	---	---	---	---	---
12.	Deficit Proportion	---	---	---	---	---	---	---	---	---	√	---	---	---
13.	Index of Backwardness	---	---	---	---	---	---	---	---	√	---	---	---	---
14.	Tax efforts	---	---	---	---	---	---	---	---	---	√	√	√	---
15.	Index of infrastructure	---	---	---	---	---	---	---	---	---	√	√	---	---
16.	Fiscal discipline	---	---	---	---	---	---	---	---	---	---	√	√	√
17.	Fiscal capacity index	---	---	---	---	---	---	---	---	---	---	---	---	√

Source: Report of various Finance Commissions

Annexure V.8

Share in Central Taxes and Duties of States from First Finance Commission to Thirteenth Finance Commission

(*₹ in Crore*)

State	*Share in Central Taxes & Duties*						
	FC-I	*FC-II*	*FC-III*	*FC-IV*	*FC-V*	*FC-VI*	*FC-VII*
1	2	3	4	5	6	7	8
1. Andhra Pradesh	32.18	70.05	84.12	99.96	347.78	570.08	1502.89
	8.9%	***8.2%***	***7.9%***	***7.6%***	***7.6%***	***8.0%***	***7.8%***
2. Assam	9.07	22.86	34.57	38.32	109.91	185.09	496.94
	2.5%	***2.7%***	***3.2%***	***2.9%***	***2.4%***	***2.6%***	***2.6%***
3. Bihar	39.35	74.16	99.63	120.61	508.73	738.44	2149.85
	10.9%	***8.7%***	***9.3%***	***9.1%***	***11.0%***	***10.4%***	***11.2%***
4. Chhatisgarh	---	---	---	---	---	---	---
	---	---	---	---	---	---	---
5. Gujarat	---	35.79	64.18	73.77	230.82	368.64	963.87
	---	***4.2%***	***6.0%***	***5.6%***	***5.0%***	***5.2%***	***5.0%***
6. Haryana	---	---	---	20.77	75.27	120.66	308.57
	---	---	---	***1.6%***	***1.6%***	***1.7%***	***1.6%***
7. Himachal Pradesh	---	---	---	---	22.54	43.10	110.26

	---	---	---	---	*0.5%*	*0.6%*	*0.6%*
8. Jammu & Kashmir	---	9.57	13.75	19.95	41.66	58.79	159.05
	---	*1.1%*	*1.3%*	*1.5%*	*0.9%*	*0.8%*	*0.8%*
9. Karnataka	3.53	43.46	54.23	68.10	229.29	383.64	1005.00
	1.0%	*5.1%*	*5.1%*	*5.1%*	*5.0%*	*5.4%*	*5.2%*
10. Kerala	1.29	29.16	43.45	51.21	183.13	271.04	766.16
	0.4%	*3.4%*	*4.1%*	*3.9%*	*4.0%*	*3.8%*	*4.0%*
11. Madhya Pradesh	27.53	56.54	74.81	89.67	343.10	543.57	1533.88
	7.6%	*6.6%*	*7.0%*	*6.8%*	*7.5%*	*7.7%*	*8.0%*
12. Maharashtra	62.86	109.85	119.52	157.19	486.82	711.53	1714.06
	17.4%	*12.9%*	*11.2%*	*11.9%*	*10.6%*	*10.0%*	*8.9%*
13. Manipur	---	---	---	---	3.43	13.48	37.76
	---	---	---	---	*0.1%*	*0.2%*	*0.2%*
14. Meghalaya	---	---	---	---	7.60	12.85	36.68
	---	---	---	---	*0.2%*	*0.2%*	*0.2%*
15. Nagaland	---	---	0.68	13.92	3.66	6.83	17.91
	---	---	0.1%	1.1%	0.1%	0.1%	0.1%
16. Orissa	14.22	30.05	48.20	52.67	182.70	272.59	815.27
	3.9%	**3.5%**	**4.5%**	**4.0%**	**4.0%**	**3.8%**	**4.2%**
17. Punjab	16.15	40.67	58.99	38.77	113.17	168.97	419.53
	4.5%	*4.8%*	*5.5%*	*2.9%*	*2.5%*	*2.4%*	*2.2%*
18. Rajasthan	13.93	35.52	49.21	58.69	213.56	333.39	883.52
	3.9%	**4.2%**	**4.6%**	**4.4%**	**4.6%**	**4.7%**	**4.6%**
19. Sikkim	---	---	---	---	---	---	0.48
	---	---	---	---	---	---	0.0%

1	2	3	4	5	6	7	8
20. Tamil Nadu	38.17	72.88	79.75	104.58	347.96	538.57	1476.39
	10.6%	***8.6%***	***7.5%***	***7.9%***	***7.6%***	***7.6%***	***7.7%***
21. Tripura	---	---	---	---	5.10	19.69	59.66
	---	---	---	---	***0.1%***	***0.3%***	***0.3%***
22. Uttar Pradesh	63.11	141.69	147.95	196.68	772.47	1150.22	3202.72
	17.5%	***16.6%***	***13.9%***	***14.9%***	***16.8%***	***16.2%***	***16.7%***
23. Uttaranchal	---	---	---	---	---	---	---
	---	---	---	---	---	---	---
24. West Bengal	40.22	79.52	93.72	118.33	376.30	588.07	1572.60
	11.1%	***9.3%***	***8.8%***	***8.9%***	***8.2%***	***8.3%***	***8.2%***
25. Goa	---	---	---	---	---	---	---
	---	---	---	---	---	---	---
26. Arunachal	---	---	---	---	---	---	---
	---	---	---	---	---	---	---
27. Jharkhand	---	---	---	---	---	---	---
	---	---	---	---	---	---	---
28. Mizoram	---	---	---	---	---	---	---
	---	---	---	---	---	---	---
Total:	361.61	851.77	1066.76	1323.19	4605.00	7099.24	19233.05
	100.0%	***100.0%***	***100.0%***	***100.0%***	***100.0%***	***100.0%***	***100.0%***

State	Share in Central Taxes & Duties						
	FC-VIII	FC-IX(i)	FC-IX(ii)	FC-X	FC-XI	FC-XII	FC-XIII
1	9	10	11	12	13	14	15
1. Andhra Pradesh	2754.78	848.70	6575.47	16325.94	28980.25	45138.68	100616.00
	7.7%	7.2%	7.5%	7.9%	7.7%	7.4%	6.9%
2. Assam	1251.67	404.28	2969.57	7064.14	12362.05	19850.69	52620.60
	3.5%	3.4%	3.4%	3.4%	3.3%	3.2%	3.6%
3. Bihar	4005.82	1372.99	9670.53	23302.45	54934.90	67671.04	158341.20
	11.2%	11.6%	11.0%	11.3%	14.6%	11.0%	10.9%
4. Chhatisgarh	---	---	---	---	---	16285.76	35825.20
	---	---	---	---	---	2.7%	2.5%
5. Gujarat	1417.18	422.13	3394.68	8014.95	10615.93	21900.47	44107.10
	4.0%	3.6%	3.9%	3.9%	2.8%	3.6%	3.0%
6. Haryana	427.97	137.05	1131.06	2554.96	3552.44	6596.46	15199.50
	1.2%	1.2%	1.3%	1.2%	0.9%	1.1%	1.0%
7. Himachal Pradesh	530.69	140.46	1269.43	3743.81	2570.25	3203.22	11327.30
	1.5%	1.2%	1.4%	1.8%	0.7%	0.5%	0.8%
8. Jammu & Kashmir	738.21	236.44	2217.32	5904.70	4854.50	7441.71	20182.70
	2.1%	2.0%	2.5%	2.9%	1.3%	1.2%	1.4%
9. Karnataka	1712.97	560.31	3962.02	10034.64	18552.48	27361.88	62774.90
	4.8%	4.8%	4.5%	4.9%	4.9%	4.5%	4.3%
10. Kerala	1258.94	404.41	2919.10	7217.00	11504.04	16353.21	33954.30
	3.5%	3.4%	3.3%	3.5%	3.1%	2.7%	2.3%

1	9	10	11	12	13	14	15
11. Madhya Pradesh	2788.11	909.56	6534.48	15275.50	33258.98	41180.59	103268.90
	7.8%	7.7%	7.4%	7.4%	8.8%	6.7%	7.1%
12. Maharashtra	2617.30	860.47	6036.36	12859.84	17431.05	30663.19	75406.90
	7.3%	7.3%	6.9%	6.2%	4.6%	5.0%	5.2%
13. Manipur	299.18	75.27	710.07	1689.63	1377.32	2221.44	6541.20
	0.8%	0.6%	0.8%	0.8%	0.4%	0.4%	0.5%
14. Meghalaya	242.88	59.67	558.21	1534.58	1287.01	2276.61	5918.50
	0.7%	0.5%	0.6%	0.7%	0.3%	0.4%	0.4%
15. Nagaland	325.47	73.38	781.88	2197.38	827.90	1613.67	4552.90
	0.9%	0.6%	0.9%	1.1%	0.2%	0.3%	0.3%
16. Orissa	1561.60	509.55	4263.81	8783.41	19026.64	31669.47	69316.10
	4.4%	4.3%	4.9%	4.3%	5.1%	5.2%	4.8%
17. Punjab	611.15	184.22	1515.22	3160.41	4316.37	7971.00	20146.40
	1.7%	1.6%	1.7%	1.5%	1.1%	1.3%	1.4%
18. Rajasthan	1538.18	574.68	4613.83	10255.26	20595.88	34418.56	84892.20
	4.3%	4.9%	5.3%	5.0%	5.5%	5.6%	5.9%
19. Sikkim	63.52	14.06	156.25	562.07	692.43	1392.94	3466.80
	0.2%	0.1%	0.2%	0.3%	0.2%	0.2%	0.2%
20. Tamil Nadu	2443.07	839.36	6008.16	12622.54	20264.72	32552.74	72070.40
	6.8%	7.1%	6.8%	6.1%	5.4%	5.3%	5.0%
21. Tripura	357.67	97.59	956.66	2325.81	1832.67	2626.09	7411.50
	1.0%	0.8%	1.1%	1.1%	0.5%	0.4%	0.5%

22. Uttar Pradesh	5915.60	2046.75	13876.54	33526.67	72015.41	118209.45	285397.10
	16.6%	17.4%	15.8%	16.2%	19.1%	19.3%	19.7%
23. Uttaranchal	---	---	---	---	2486.15	5762.22	16245.10
	---	---	---	---	0.7%	0.9%	1.1%
24. West Bengal	2820.62	851.90	6260.75	14104.85	30540.09	43303.91	105358.60
	7.9%	7.2%	7.1%	6.8%	8.1%	7.1%	7.3%
25. Goa	---	24.59	338.54	524.06	775.22	1589.14	3857.80
	---	0.2%	0.4%	0.3%	0.2%	0.3%	0.3%
26. Arunachal	---	65.30	524.59	1360.03	918.22	1767.34	4755.60
	---	0.6%	0.6%	0.7%	0.2%	0.3%	0.3%
27. Jharkhand	---	---	---	---	---	20624.02	40640.30
	---	---	---	---	---	3.4%	2.8%
28. Mizoram	---	72.52	637.47	1398.37	745.11	1466.52	3901.30
	---	0.6%	0.7%	0.7%	0.2%	0.2%	0.3%
Total:	35682.58	11785.64	87882.00	206343.00	376318.01	613112.02	1448096.40
	100.0%	100.0%	100.0%	100.0%	100.0%	100.0%	100.0%

Source: Reports of Various Finance Commission.

Annexure VI.1

Share of States in Total Transfers

(₹ *in Crore*)

State	*Ist Finance Commission (1952-57)*				*IInd Finance Commission (1957-62)*			
	Share of Taxes	*Grants*	*Total Transfers*	*%ge to Total Transfers*	*Share of Taxes*	*Grants*	*Total Transfers*	*%ge to Total Transfers*
1	2	3	4	5	6	7	8	9
1. Andhra Pradesh	32.18	1.20	33.38	8.11%	70.05	20.00	90.05	8.58%
2. Assam	9.07	8.75	17.82	4.33%	22.86	22.50	45.36	4.32%
3. Bihar	39.35	6.23	45.58	11.07%	74.16	21.16	95.32	9.09%
4. Gujarat	---	---	---	---	35.79	---	35.79	---
5. Haryana	---	---	---	---	---	---	---	---
6. Himachal Pradesh	---	---	---	---	---	---	---	---
7. Jammu & Kashmir	---	---	---	---	9.57	15.00	24.57	---
8. Karnataka	3.53	2.00	5.53	1.34%	43.46	30.00	73.46	7.00%
9. Kerala	1.29	2.25	3.54	0.86%	29.16	8.75	37.91	3.61%
10. Madhya Pradesh	27.53	2.04	29.57	7.18%	56.54	15.00	71.54	6.82%
11. Maharashtra	62.86	2.00	64.86	15.76%	109.85	---	109.85	10.47%
12. Manipur	---	---	---	---	---	---	---	---

13. Meghalaya	---	---	---	---	---	---	---	---
14. Nagaland	---	---	---	---	---	---	---	---
15. Orissa	14.22	5.47	19.69	4.78%	30.05	17.20	47.25	4.50%
16. Punjab	16.15	7.37	23.52	5.71%	40.67	11.25	51.92	4.95%
17. Rajasthan	13.93	1.19	15.12	3.67%	35.52	12.50	48.02	4.58%
18. Sikkim	---	---	---	---	---	---	---	---
19. Tamil Nadu	38.17		38.17	9.27%	72.88	---	72.88	6.95%
20. Tripura	---	---	---	---	---	---	---	---
21. Uttar Pradesh	63.11	---	63.11	15.33%	141.69	---	141.69	13.51%
22. West Bengal	40.22	11.50	51.72	12.57%	79.52	23.84	103.36	9.85%
23. Goa	---	---	---	---	---	---	---	---
24. Arunachal	---	---	---	---	---	---	---	---
25. Mizoram	---	---	---	---	---	---	---	---
Total:	361.61	50.00	411.61	100.00%	851.77	197.20	1048.97	100.00%

(₹ in Crore)

State	IIIrd Finance Commission (1962-66)				IVth Finance Commission (1966-69)			
	Share of Taxes	Grants	Total Transfers	%ge to Total Transfers	Share of Taxes	Grants	Total Transfers	%ge to Total Transfers
1		2	3	4	5	6	7	8 9
1. Andhra Pradesh	84.12	38.00	122.12	9.32%	99.96	40.53	140.49	8.05%
2. Assam	34.57	24.00	58.57	4.47%	38.32	49.56	87.88	5.04%
3. Bihar	99.63	3.00	102.63	7.83%	120.61	---	120.61	6.91%
4. Gujarat	64.18	21.00	85.18	6.50%	73.77	---	73.77	4.23%
5. Haryana	---	---	---	---	20.77	---	20.77	1.19%
6. Himachal Pradesh	---	---	---	---	---	---	---	---
7. Jammu & Kashmir	13.75	8.00	21.75	1.66%	19.95	19.71	39.66	---
8. Karnataka	54.23	27.00	81.23	6.20%	68.10	62.46	130.56	7.48%
9. Kerala	43.45	25.00	68.45	5.22%	51.21	62.46	113.67	6.51%
10. Madhya Pradesh	74.81	12.00	86.81	6.62%	89.67	8.10	97.77	5.60%
11. Maharashtra	119.52	---	119.52	9.12%	157.19	---	157.19	9.01%
12. Manipur	---	---	---	---	---	---	---	---
13. Meghalaya	---	---	---	---	---	---	---	---
14. Nagaland	0.68	---	0.68	0.05%	13.92	21.21	35.13	2.01%
15. Orissa	48.20	53.00	101.20	7.72%	52.67	87.54	140.21	8.03%
16. Punjab	58.99	---	58.99	4.50%	38.77	---	38.77	2.22%
17. Rajasthan	49.21	21.00	70.21	5.36%	58.69	20.19	78.88	4.52%

18. Sikkim	---	---	---	---	---	---	---	---
19. Tamil Nadu	79.75	12.00	91.75	7.00%	104.58	20.52	125.10	7.17%
20. Tripura	---	---	---	---	---	---	---	---
21. Uttar Pradesh	147.95	---	147.95	11.29%	196.68	29.55	226.23	12.96%
22. West Bengal	93.72	---	93.72	7.15%	118.33	---	118.33	6.78%
23. Goa	---	---	---	---	---	---	---	---
24. Arunachal	---	---	---	---	---	---	---	---
25. Mizoram	---	---	---	---	---	---	---	---
Total:	1066.76	244.00	1310.76	100.00%	1323.19	421.83	1745.02	100.00%

(₹ in Crore)

State	Vth Finance Commission (1962-66)				VIth Finance Commission (1966-69)			
	Share of Taxes	Grants	Total Transfers	%ge to Total Transfers	Share of Taxes	Grants	Total Transfers	%ge to Total Transfers
1	2	3	4	5	6	7	8	9
1. Andhra Pradesh	347.78	65.01	412.79	7.77%	570.08	205.93	776.01	8.08%
2. Assam	109.91	84.18	194.09	3.65%	185.09	254.53	439.62	4.58%
3. Bihar	508.73	---	508.73	9.57%	738.44	106.28	844.72	8.79%
4. Gujarat	230.82	---	230.82	4.34%	368.64	---	368.64	3.84%
5. Haryana	75.27	---	75.27	1.42%	120.66	---	120.66	1.26%
6. Himachal Pradesh	22.54	27.68	50.22	0.94%	43.10	160.96	204.06	2.12%
7. Jammu & Kashmir	41.66	73.68	115.34	2.17%	58.79	173.49	232.28	2.42%
8. Karnataka	229.29	17.99	247.28	4.65%	383.64	---	383.64	3.99%
9. Kerala	183.13	49.65	232.78	4.38%	271.04	208.93	479.97	5.00%
10. Madhya Pradesh	343.10	---	343.10	6.45%	543.57	---	543.57	5.66%
11. Maharashtra	486.82	---	486.82	9.16%	711.53	---	711.53	7.40%
12. Manipur	3.43	23.37	26.80	0.50%	13.48	114.53	128.01	1.33%
13. Meghalaya	7.60	11.24	18.84	0.35%	12.85	74.67	87.52	0.91%
14. Nagaland	3.66	77.95	81.61	1.54%	6.83	128.84	135.67	1.41%
15. Orissa	182.70	104.67	287.37	5.41%	272.59	304.73	577.32	6.01%
16. Punjab	113.17	---	113.17	2.13%	168.97	---	168.97	1.76%
17. Rajasthan	213.56	51.49	265.05	4.99%	333.39	230.53	563.92	5.87%

18. Sikkim	---	---	---	---	---	---	---	---
19. Tamil Nadu	347.96	22.82	370.78	6.97%	538.57	---	538.57	5.60%
20. Tripura	5.10	28.64	33.74	0.63%	19.69	112.50	132.19	1.38%
21. Uttar Pradesh	772.47	---	772.47	14.53%	1150.22	198.83	1349.05	14.04%
22. West Bengal	376.30	72.62	448.92	8.44%	588.07	234.86	822.93	8.56%
23. Goa	---	---	---	---	---	---	---	---
24. Arunachal	---	---	---	---	---	---	---	---
25. Mizoram	---	---	---	---	---	---	---	---
Total:	4605.00	710.99	5315.99	100.00%	7099.24	2509.61	9608.85	100.00%

(₹ in Crore)

State	VIIth Finance Commission (1979-84)					
	Share of Taxes	Grants Article 275			Total Transfers	%ge to Total Transfers
1	2	3	4	5	6	7
1. Andhra Pradesh	1502.89	---	19.60	19.60	1522.49	7.30%
2. Assam	496.94	---	21.71	21.71	518.65	2.49%
3. Bihar	2149.85	---	63.02	63.02	2212.87	10.62%
4. Gujarat	963.87	---	---	---	963.87	4.62%
5. Haryana	308.57	---	---	---	308.57	1.48%
6. Himachal Pradesh	110.26	207.07	7.74	214.81	325.07	1.56%
7. Jammu & Kashmir	159.05	199.56	18.28	217.84	376.89	1.81%
8. Karnataka	1005.00	---	---	---	1005.00	4.82%
9. Kerala	766.16	---	4.18	4.18	770.34	3.70%
10. Madhya Pradesh	1533.88	---	63.58	63.58	1597.46	7.66%
11. Maharashtra	1714.06	---	---	---	1714.06	8.22%
12. Manipur	37.76	146.32	9.95	156.27	194.03	0.93%
13. Meghalaya	36.68	92.61	4.86	97.47	134.15	0.64%
14. Nagaland	17.91	218.35	4.33	222.68	240.59	1.15%
15. Orissa	815.27	136.92	32.26	169.18	984.45	4.72%
16. Punjab	419.53	---	---	---	419.53	2.01%
17. Rajasthan	883.52	---	19.29	19.29	902.81	4.33%
18. Sikkim	0.48	35.72	0.65	36.37	36.85	0.18%

19. Tamil Nadu	1476.39	---	27.21	27.21	1503.60	7.21%
20. Tripura	59.66	136.57	3.61	140.18	199.84	0.96%
21. Uttar Pradesh	3202.72	---	112.02	112.02	3314.74	15.90%
22. West Bengal	1572.60	---	24.51	24.51	1597.11	7.66%
23. Goa	---	---	---	---	---	---
24. Arunachal	---	---	---	---	---	---
25. Mizoram	---	---	---	---	---	---
Total:	19233.05	1173.12	436.80	1609.92	20842.97	100.00%

(₹in Crore)

State	VIIIth Finance Commission (1984-89)						
	Share of Taxes	Grants Article 275			Total	Total Transfers	%ge to Total Transfers
		Revenue Gap	Upgrad-ation	Margin money			
1	2	3	4		5	6	7
1. Andhra Pradesh	2754.78	---	80.49	61.25	141.74	2896.52	7.34%
2. Assam	1251.67	274.33	63.35	18.13	355.81	1607.48	4.07%
3. Bihar	4005.82	---	130.27	84.38	214.65	4220.47	10.70%
4. Gujarat	1417.18	---	---	71.87	71.87	1489.05	3.77%
5. Haryana	427.97	---	---	11.25	11.25	439.22	1.11%
6. Himachal Pradesh	530.69	223.04	16.26	4.38	243.68	774.37	1.96%
7. Jammu & Kashmir	738.21	329.18	48.55	3.75	381.48	1119.69	2.84%
8. Karnataka	1712.97	---	---	15.00	15.00	1727.97	4.38%
9. Kerala	1258.94	---	16.81	12.50	29.31	1288.25	3.27%
10. Madhya Pradesh	2788.11	---	157.69	11.88	169.57	2957.68	7.50%
11. Maharashtra	2617.30	---	---	18.12	18.12	2635.42	6.68%
12. Manipur	299.18	146.95	22.30	0.62	169.87	469.05	1.19%
13. Meghalaya	242.88	119.15	19.20	0.63	138.98	381.86	0.97%
14. Nagaland	325.47	190.52	10.81	0.62	201.95	527.42	1.34%
15. Orissa	1561.60	207.60	74.84	65.62	348.06	1909.66	4.84%
16. Punjab	611.15	---	20.00	15.00	35.00	646.15	1.64%

1	2	3	4		5	6	7
17. Rajasthan	1538.18	42.63	53.48	41.88	137.99	1676.17	4.25%
18. Sikkim	63.52	36.16	4.14	0.63	40.93	104.45	0.26%
19. Tamil Nadu	2443.07	---	---	21.87	21.87	2464.94	6.25%
20. Tripura	357.67	187.05	14.59	1.87	203.51	561.18	1.42%
21. Uttar Pradesh	5915.60	---	108.18	81.25	189.43	6105.03	15.47%
22. West Bengal	2820.62	443.61	126.37	59.38	629.36	3449.98	8.74%
23. Goa	---	---	---	---	---	---	---
24. Arunachal	---	---	---	---	---	---	---
25. Mizoram	---	---	---	---	---	---	---
Total:	35682.58	2200.22	967.33	601.88	3769.43	39452.01	100.00%

(₹in Crore)

State	IXth Finance Commission (1989-90)							
	Share of Taxes	Grants Article 275				Total	Total Transfers	%ge to Total Transfers
		Deficit Grant	Upgradation	Margin Money	Special Problems			
1	2	3	4	5	6	7	8	9
1. Andhra Pradesh	848.70	---	10.75	21.62	20.44	52.81	901.51	6.60%
2. Assam	404.28	140.05	11.97	6.50	---	158.52	562.80	4.12%
3. Bihar	1372.99	---	24.01	16.87	41.07	81.95	1454.94	10.65%
4. Gujarat	422.13	---	---	14.37	---	14.37	436.50	3.19%
5. Haryana	137.05	---	---	2.88	24.88	27.76	164.81	1.21%
6. Himachal Pradesh	140.46	98.72	3.43	1.63	10.20	113.98	254.44	1.86%
7. Jammu & Kashmir	236.44	191.89	11.35	1.38	33.98	238.60	475.04	3.48%
8. Karnataka	560.31	---	---	3.00	12.64	15.64	575.95	4.22%
9. Kerala	404.41	---	2.11	4.50	---	6.61	411.02	3.01%
10. Madhya Pradesh	909.56	---	19.61	3.00	22.17	44.78	954.34	6.99%
11. Maharashtra	860.47	---	---	6.50	50.00	56.50	916.97	6.71%
12. Manipur	75.27	66.79	5.78	0.25	0.80	73.62	148.89	1.09%
13. Meghalaya	59.67	47.61	4.21	0.25	---	52.07	111.74	0.82%
14. Nagaland	73.38	79.78	3.37	0.13	14.50	97.78	171.16	1.25%
15. Orissa	509.55	57.14	18.22	23.12	10.58	109.06	618.61	4.53%
16. Punjab	184.22	---	---	5.38	89.01	94.39	278.61	2.04%

1	2	3	4	5	6	7	8	9
17. Rajasthan	574.68	38.82	6.06	8.37	23.37	76.62	651.30	4.77%
18. Sikkim	14.06	13.86	0.50	0.25	2.70	17.31	31.37	0.23%
19. Tamil Nadu	839.36	---	---	7.75	25.00	32.75	872.11	6.38%
20. Tripura	97.59	81.61	2.74	0.75	0.32	85.42	183.01	1.34%
21. Uttar Pradesh	2046.75	---	18.44	28.62	69.61	116.67	2163.42	15.83%
22. West Bengal	851.90	---	21.47	11.87	70.00	103.34	955.24	6.99%
23. Goa	24.59	16.68	2.55	0.13	3.00	22.36	46.95	0.34%
24. Arunachal	65.30	70.44	2.55	0.13	12.78	85.90	151.20	1.11%
25. Mizoram	72.52	80.67	2.55	0.25	14.50	97.97	170.49	1.25%
Total:	11785.64	984.06	171.67	169.50	551.55	1876.78	13662.42	100.00%

(₹ in Crore)

State	IXth Finance Commission (1990-95)							
	Share of Taxes	Grants Article 275					Total Transfers	%ge to Total Transfers
		Non-Plan Deficit	Plan Deficit	Total Plan & Non-Plan	Total Tax Plan & Non-Plan	Towards Relief Exp.		
1	2	3	4	5	6	7	9	10
1. Andhra Pradesh	6575.47	---	341.25	341.25	6916.72	322.50	7239.22	6.83%
2. Arunachal Pradesh	524.59	302.79	---	302.79	827.38	7.50	834.88	0.79%
3. Assam	2969.57	560.32	313.91	874.23	3843.80	112.50	3956.30	3.73%
4. Bihar	9670.53	---	1374.27	1374.27	11044.80	131.25	11176.05	10.54%
5. Goa	338.54	166.58	---	166.58	505.12	3.75	508.87	0.48%
6. Gujarat	3394.68	---	---	0.00	3394.68	318.75	3713.43	3.50%
7. Haryana	1131.06	---	---	0.00	1131.06	63.75	1194.81	1.13%
8. Himachal Pradesh	1269.43	523.09	---	523.09	1792.52	67.50	1860.02	1.75%
9. Jammu & Kashmir	2217.32	1083.12	13.30	1096.42	3313.74	45.00	3358.74	3.17%
10. Karnataka	3962.02	---	---	0.00	3962.02	101.25	4063.27	3.83%
11. Kerala	2919.10	---	412.54	412.54	3331.64	116.25	3447.89	3.25%
12. Madhya Pradesh	6534.48	---	1047.81	1047.81	7582.29	261.00	7843.29	7.40%
13. Maharashtra	6036.36	---	---	0.00	6036.36	165.00	6201.36	5.85%
14. Manipur	710.07	371.65	---	371.65	1081.72	3.75	1085.47	1.02%
15. Meghalaya	558.21	256.18	---	256.18	814.39	7.50	821.89	0.78%

1	2	3	4	5	6	7	9	10
16. Mizoram	637.47	379.79	---	379.79	1017.26	3.75	1021.01	0.96%
17. Nagaland	781.88	458.67	---	458.67	1240.55	3.75	1244.30	1.17%
18. Orissa	4263.81	528.48	554.50	1082.98	5346.79	176.25	5523.04	5.21%
19. Punjab	1515.22	---	53.91	53.91	1569.13	105.00	1674.13	1.58%
20. Rajasthan	4613.83	486.39	960.40	1446.79	6060.62	465.00	6525.62	6.15%
21. Sikkim	156.25	84.68	---	84.68	240.93	11.25	252.18	0.24%
22. Tamil Nadu	6008.16	---	43.79	43.79	6051.95	146.25	6198.20	5.85%
23. Tripura	956.66	466.01	---	466.01	1422.67	11.25	1433.92	1.35%
24. Uttar Pradesh	13876.54	348.60	2886.50	3235.10	17111.64	337.50	17449.14	16.46%
25. West Bengal	6260.75	---	998.65	998.65	7259.40	150.00	7409.40	6.99%
Total:	87882.00	6016.35	9000.83	15017.18	102899.18	3137.25	106036.43	100.00%

(₹ in Crore)

State	Xth Finance Commission (1984-89)								
	Share of Taxes	Grants Article 275						Total Transfers	%ge to Total Transfers
		Non-Plan Deficit	Upgradation	Special Problem	Local Bodies	Relief Exp.	Total Grants		
1	2	3	4	5	6		7	9	10
1. Andhra Pradesh	16325.94	686.45	88.88	65.00	424.95	490.33	1755.61	18081.55	7.98%
2. Arunachal Pradesh	1360.03	307.60	18.31	50.00	4.63	27.79	408.33	1768.36	0.78%
3. Assam	7064.14	712.03	146.86	60.00	147.56	197.46	1263.91	8328.05	3.67%
4. Bihar	23302.45	333.06	183.13	57.50	574.28	205.14	1353.11	24655.56	10.88%
5. Goa	524.06	77.26	3.79	7.00	5.91	4.23	98.19	622.25	0.27%
6. Gujarat	8014.95	0.00	0.00	50.00	259.47	551.17	860.64	8875.59	3.92%
7. Haryana	2554.96	0.00	0.00	40.00	99.22	98.93	238.15	2793.11	1.23%
8. Himachal Pradesh	3743.81	772.18	30.03	75.00	34.23	106.41	1017.85	4761.66	2.10%
9. Jammu & Kashmir	5904.70	1184.13	58.77	47.00	49.68	77.80	1417.38	7322.08	3.23%
10. Karnataka	10034.64	0.00	0.00	29.00	291.96	165.23	486.19	10520.83	4.64%
11. Kerala	7217.00	0.00	29.83	52.00	204.24	218.74	504.81	7721.81	3.41%
12. Madhya Pradesh	15275.50	0.00	146.37	60.00	410.43	201.67	818.47	16093.97	7.10%
13. Maharashtra	12859.84	0.00	0.00	100.00	479.96	269.28	849.24	13709.08	6.05%
14. Manipur	1689.63	350.92	24.74	50.00	11.54	9.79	446.99	2136.62	0.94%
15. Meghalaya	1534.58	316.42	11.72	5.00	10.12	11.01	354.27	1888.85	0.83%
16. Mizoram	1398.37	331.19	7.13	57.00	3.32	5.00	403.64	1802.01	0.80%

1	2	3	4	5	6		7	9	10
17. Nagaland	2197.38	529.78	23.96	30.00	5.21	6.71	595.66	2793.04	1.23%
18. Orissa	8783.41	371.74	86.79	51.00	220.10	193.51	923.14	9706.55	4.28%
19. Punjab	3160.41	0.00	81.31	0.00	133.95	213.80	429.06	3589.47	1.58%
20. Rajasthan	10255.26	33.45	79.87	70.00	255.40	706.89	1145.61	11400.87	5.03%
21. Sikkim	562.07	105.69	4.56	5.50	2.48	18.59	136.82	698.89	0.31%
22. Tamil Nadu	12622.54	0.00	40.84	60.00	402.86	234.33	738.03	13360.57	5.89%
23. Tripura	2325.81	488.78	13.90	12.00	14.97	17.75	547.40	2873.21	1.27%
24. Uttar Pradesh	33526.67	982.00	167.54	108.00	880.70	494.00	2632.24	36158.91	15.95%
25. West Bengal	14104.85	0.00	114.17	105.00	453.77	202.63	875.57	14980.42	6.61%
Total:	206343.00	7582.68	1362.50	1246.00	5380.94	4728.19	20300.31	226643.31	100.00%

STATEWISE TOTAL TRANSFER UNDER XI FINANCE COMMISSION
(2000 - 2005)

(Rs. Lakh)

Sl. No.	States	Share of Taxes	Grants under Article 275						Total Transfers (Col 2+ Col. 8)	%ge of Total Transfer
			Non-Plan Revenue Deficit	Upgradation & Special Probl-ems	Panchayats	Municipalties	Relief Expenditure	Total Grants (Col. 3 to Col 7)		
0	1	2	3	4	5	6	7	8	9	10
1	Andhra Pradesh	2898025	0	28523	76024	16466	82080	203093	3101118	7.13
2	Arunachal Pradesh	91822	122802	9059	2784	68	4983	139696	231518	0.53
3	Assam	1236205	11068	13254	23345	2154	42060	91881	1328086	3.05
4	Bihar *	5493490	0	40160	78504	9390	51246	179300	5672790	13.04
5	Goa	77522	0	2728	927	464	515	4634	82156	0.19
6	Gujarat	1061593	0	23485	34804	13252	66888	138429	1200022	2.76
7	Haryana	355244	0	13265	14709	3664	33695	65333	420577	0.97
8	Himachal Pradesh	257025	454926	9116	6567	389	18020	489018	746043	1.72
9	Jammu & Kashmir	485450	1121119	12782	7441	1566	14464	1157372	1642822	3.78
10	Karnataka	1855248	0	31153	39412	12482	30903	113950	1969198	4.53
11	Kerala	1150404	0	12914	32963	7525	27866	81268	1231672	2.83
12	Madhya Pradesh #	3325898	0	49452	71547	15601	37340	173940	3499838	8.05
13	Maharashtra	1743105	0	33197	65673	31625	65149	195644	1938749	4.46
14	Manipur	137732	174494	5859	1877	440	1189	183859	321591	0.74

0	1	2	3	4	5	6	7	8	9	10
15	Meghalaya	128701	157238	5739	2561	270	1632	167440	296141	0.68
16	Mizoram	74511	167630	8984	786	384	1232	179016	253527	0.58
17	Nagaland	82790	353624	6284	1287	179	812	362186	444976	1.02
18	Orissa	1902664	67360	21505	34559	3996	45366	172786	2075450	4.77
19	Punjab	431637	28421	11001	15464	5473	50857	111216	542853	1.25
20	Rajasthan	2059588	124468	29985	49095	9942	85785	299275	2358863	5.42
21	Sikkim	69243	84058	6678	529	21	2863	94149	163392	0.38
22	Tamil Nadu	2026472	0	25186	46612	19337	42536	133671	2160143	4.97
23	Tripura	183267	241416	6018	2846	402	2155	252837	436104	1.00
24	Uttar Pradesh	7201541	100900	53726	116713	22789	60620	354748	7556289	17.37
25	Uttranchal	248615	1774	13265	15200	2374	13413	46026	294641	0.68
26	West Bengal	3054009	324609	23945	57773	19749	41900	467976	3521985	8.10
	Total:	37631801	3535907	497263	800000	200000	825569	5858739	43490540	100.00

*Includes Bihar & Jarkhand.

#Includes Madhya Pradesh & Chhatisgarh.

STATEWISE TOTAL TRANSFER UNDER XII FINANCE COMMISSION

(₹ in crore)

Sl. No.	States	Share in Central Taxes & Duties (2005-10)	Grants-in-aid: Non-Plan Revenue Deficit (2005-10)	Health Sector (2005-10)	Education (2005-10)	Maintenance of Roads & Bridges (2006-10)	Maintenance of Buildings (2006-10)	Maintenance of Forests (2005-10)	Heritage Conservation (2006-10)	State Specific Needs (2006-10)	Local Bodies (2005-10)	Calamity Relief (2005-10)	Total Grants (Col. 3 to Col. 12)	Total Transfers (Col 2+ Col. 13)	%ge of Total Transfer
0	1	2	3	4	5	6	7	8	9	10	11	12	13	14	15
1	Andhra Pradesh	45138.68				980.12	242.53	65.00	40.00	500.00	1961.00	1425.93	5214.58	50353.26	6.663
2	Arunachal Pradesh	1767.34	1357.88			44.36	57.42	100.00	5.00	10.00	71.00	112.56	1758.22	3525.56	0.466
3	Assam	19850.69	305.67	966.02	1107.37	330.12	230.64	40.00	20.00	130.00	581.00	767.89	4478.71	24329.40	3.219
4	Bihar	67671.04		1819.69	2683.76	309.36	359.61	5.00	40.00	400.00	1766.00	592.37	7975.79	75646.83	10.009
5	Chhattisgarh	16285.76				262.40	183.09	85.00	10.00	300.00	703.00	444.45	1987.94	18273.70	2.418
6	Goa	1589.14				39.48	24.18	3.00	20.00	10.00	30.00	8.73	135.39	1724.53	0.228
7	Gujarat	21900.47				895.20	203.61	20.00	25.00	200.00	1345.00	1019.47	3708.28	25608.75	3.389
8	Haryana	6596.46				182.72	151.80	2.00	15.00	100.00	479.00	515.46	1445.98	8042.44	1.064
9	Himachal Pradesh	3203.22	10202.38			261.64	147.60	20.00	10.00	50.00	155.00	400.52	11247.14	14450.36	1.912
10	Jammu & Kashmir	7441.71	12353.46			117.68	164.54	30.00	10.00	100.00	319.00	343.89	13438.57	20880.28	2.763
11	Jharkhand	20624.02		360.98	651.73	409.04	159.61	30.00	10.00	330.00	580.00	501.46	3032.82	23656.84	3.130
12	Karnataka	27361.88				1458.12	205.12	55.00	50.00	600.00	1211.00	475.16	4054.40	31416.28	4.157
13	Kerala	16353.21	470.37			642.32	103.50	25.00	25.00	500.00	1134.00	354.32	3254.51	19607.72	2.594
14	Madhya Pradesh	41180.59		181.64	459.56	586.88	443.02	115.00	20.00	300.00	2024.00	1011.27	5141.37	46321.96	6.129
15	Maharashtra	30663.19				1189.68	223.61	70.00	50.00	300.00	2774.00	923.77	5531.06	36194.25	4.789

0	1	2	3	4	5	6	7	8	9	10	11	12	13	14	15
16	Manipur	2221.44	4391.98			76.96	37.71	30.00	5.00	30.00	55.00	22.11	4648.76	6870.20	0.909
17	Meghalaya	2276.61	1796.86			86.40	35.02	30.00	5.00	35.00	58.00	44.88	2091.16	4367.77	0.578
18	Mizoram	1466.52	2977.79			42.12	23.29	25.00	5.00	65.00	30.00	26.19	3194.39	4660.91	0.617
19	Nagaland	1613.67	5536.50			120.88	46.17	25.00	5.00	45.00	46.00	15.19	5839.74	7453.41	0.986
20	Orissa	31669.47	488.04	196.37	323.30	1475.08	389.14	75.00	50.00	170.00	907.00	1199.37	5273.30	36942.77	4.888
21	Punjab	7971.00	3132.67			420.96	151.80	2.00	10.00	96.00	495.00	605.16	4913.59	12884.59	1.705
22	Rajasthan	34418.56			100.00	633.32	213.09	25.00	50.00	450.00	1450.00	1722.50	4643.91	39062.47	5.169
23	Sikkim	1392.94	188.67			18.64	32.15	8.00	5.00	100.00	14.00	69.74	436.20	1829.14	0.242
24	Tamil Nadu	32552.74				1214.40	242.53	30.00	40.00	300.00	1442.00	866.46	4135.39	36688.13	4.855
25	Tripura	2626.09	5494.20			61.48	50.11	15.00	5.00	49.00	65.00	51.12	5790.91	8417.00	1.114
26	Uttar Pradesh	118209.45		2312.38	4454.07	2403.16	600.28	20.00	50.00	800.00	3445.00	1177.11	15262.00	133471.45	17.661
27	Uttranchal	5762.22	5114.68	50.00		324.56	97.60	35.00	5.00	240.00	196.00	369.28	6432.12	12194.34	1.614
28	West Bengal	43303.91	3044.72		391.86	412.92	181.23	15.00	40.00	890.00	1664.00	933.64	7573.37	50877.28	6.732
	Total:	613112.02	56855.87	5887.08	10171.65	15000.00	5000.00	1000.00	625.00	7100.00	25000.00	16000.00	142639.60	755751.62	100.00

Source: Reports of Various Finance Commission.

Statewise Total Transfer under XIII Finance Commission (2010-15)

(₹ in Crore)

Sl. No.	States	Share in Central Taxes & Duties NPRD	Post Devo-lution	Perfor-mance Incentive	Local Bodies	Disaster Relief (including capacity building)	Elemen-tary Educat-ion	Grants-in-aid Improving Outcomes: Impro-ment in Justice Delivery	Incentive for issu-ing UIDs	District Innovat-ion Fund	Improve-ment of statistical System at State & Dist. Level
0	1	2	3	4	5	6	7	8	9	10	11
1	Andhra Pradesh	100616.00	0.00	0.00	7195.10	2138.70	942.00	270.70	126.10	23.00	23.00
2	Arunachal Pradesh	4755.60	2516.20	0.00	305.70	187.70	24.00	77.60	2.00	16.00	16.00
3	Assam	52620.60	0.00	300.00	1892.80	1336.80	238.00	121.10	55.80	27.00	27.00
4	Bihar	158341.20	0.00	0.00	5682.10	1411.20	4018.00	385.00	369.20	38.00	38.00
5	Chhattisgarh	35825.20	0.00	0.00	2267.20	647.10	857.00	125.10	91.00	18.00	18.00
6	Goa	3857.80	0.00	0.00	172.00	17.30	11.00	15.00	2.00	2.00	2.00
7	Gujarat	44107.10	0.00	0.00	3757.60	2110.90	483.00	299.80	90.70	26.00	26.00
8	Haryana	15199.50	0.00	0.00	1521.30	824.40	229.00	124.20	32.10	21.00	21.00
9	Himachal Pradesh	11327.30	7888.80	0.00	641.50	670.30	113.00	64.80	6.40	12.00	12.00
10	Jammu & Kashmir	20182.70	15936.30	0.00	1122.60	877.60	449.00	104.50	5.90	22.00	22.00
11	Jharkhand	40640.30	0.00	0.00	2239.80	1100.20	1528.00	177.50	116.40	24.00	24.00
12	Karnataka	62774.90	0.00	0.00	6496.70	687.10	667.00	269.80	138.90	29.00	29.00
13	Kerala	33954.30	0.00	0.00	2676.10	563.20	140.00	140.10	49.60	14.00	14.00
14	Madhya Pradesh	103268.90	0.00	0.00	5833.50	1652.70	2216.00	407.40	249.70	50.00	50.00
15	Maharashtra	75406.90	0.00	0.00	8743.60	1859.60	744.00	542.70	317.40	35.00	35.00

16	Manipur	6541.20	6056.60	0.00	315.90	40.90	15.00	11.60	4.00	9.00	9.00
17	Meghalaya	5918.50	2810.90	0.00	432.40	77.90	52.00	4.20	4.50	7.00	7.00
18	Mizoram	3901.30	3991.40	0.00	310.70	47.50	5.00	13.00	1.20	8.00	8.00
19	Nagaland	4552.90	8146.10	0.00	415.70	29.70	7.00	6.20	4.00	11.00	11.00
20	Orissa	69316.10	0.00	0.00	3270.90	1647.80	1016.00	193.60	178.50	30.00	30.00
21	Punjab	20146.40	0.00	0.00	1753.80	948.80	224.00	120.80	21.60	20.00	20.00
22	Rajasthan	84892.20	0.00	0.00	5163.80	2519.30	1766.00	268.50	134.90	33.00	33.00
23	Sikkim	3466.80	0.00	200.00	187.20	118.10	5.00	21.80	1.10	4.00	4.00
24	Tamil Nadu	72070.40	0.00	0.00	5455.90	1241.40	700.00	252.40	145.60	31.00	31.00
25	Tripura	7411.50	4453.30	0.00	369.80	101.00	23.00	24.00	6.40	4.00	4.00
26	Uttar Pradesh	285397.10	0.00	0.00	12740.50	1622.10	5040.00	645.80	590.00	70.00	70.00
27	Uttarakhand	16245.10	0.00	1000.00	781.30	605.10	197.00	102.20	36.00	13.00	13.00
28	West Bengal	105358.60	0.00	0.00	5773.10	1288.30	2359.00	210.90	208.40	19.00	19.00
	Total:	1448096.40	51799.60	1500.00	87518.60	26372.70	24068.00	5000.30	2989.40	616.00	616.00

Source: Reports of Various Finance Commission.

(*Contd...*)

(Contd...)

Statewise Total Transfer under XIII Finance Commission (2010-15)

(₹ in Crore)

Sl. No.	States	Employee and Pension Data base	Env. Related Grants: Forests	Env. Related Grants: Water Sector Management	Maintenance of Roads and Bridges	State Specific	Total Grants (Col. 3 to Col. 16)	Total Transfers (Col 2+ Col. 13)	%ge of Total Transfer
0	1	12	13	14	15	16	17	18	19
1	Andhra Pradesh	10.00	268.60	284.00	981.00	1270.00	13532.20	114148.20	6.688
2	Arunachal Pradesh	5.00	727.80	8.00	162.00	300.00	4348.00	9103.60	0.533
3	Assam	5.00	184.60	88.00	336.00	600.00	5212.10	57832.70	3.389
4	Bihar	10.00	38.40	304.00	464.00	1845.00	14602.90	172944.10	10.133
5	Chhattisgarh	10.00	411.10	88.00	362.00	1281.00	6175.50	42000.70	2.461
6	Goa	10.00	36.90	8.00	40.00	200.00	516.20	4374.00	0.256
7	Gujarat	10.00	81.90	236.00	1261.00	1300.00	9682.90	53790.00	3.152
8	Haryana	10.00	8.80	212.00	267.00	1000.00	4270.80	19470.30	1.141
9	Himachal Pradesh	5.00	100.60	64.00	436.00	350.00	10364.40	21691.70	1.271
10	Jammu & Kashmir	5.00	133.00	88.00	140.00	1350.00	20255.90	40438.60	2.369
11	Jharkhand	10.00	151.40	108.00	334.00	1425.00	7238.30	47878.60	2.805
12	Karnataka	10.00	221.00	128.00	1625.00	1300.00	11601.50	74376.40	4.358
13	Kerala	10.00	135.50	176.00	953.00	1500.00	6371.50	40325.80	2.363
14	Madhya Pradesh	10.00	490.30	148.00	986.00	1231.00	13324.60	116593.50	6.832
15	Maharashtra	10.00	309.60	368.00	2103.00	1235.00	16302.90	91709.80	5.374
16	Manipur	5.00	150.30	8.00	100.00	301.00	7026.30	13567.50	0.795

17	Meghalaya	5.00	168.10	4.00	101.00	250.00	3924.00	9842.50	0.577
18	Mizoram	5.00	171.20	4.00	89.00	250.00	4904.00	8805.30	0.516
19	Nagaland	5.00	138.60	8.00	159.00	250.00	9191.30	13744.20	0.805
20	Orissa	10.00	331.00	184.00	1022.00	1745.00	9658.80	78974.90	4.627
21	Punjab	10.00	9.20	320.00	612.00	1480.00	5540.20	25686.60	1.505
22	Rajasthan	10.00	88.30	224.00	1509.00	1200.00	12949.80	97842.00	5.733
23	Sikkim	5.00	40.60	4.00	68.00	400.00	1058.80	4525.60	0.265
24	Tamil Nadu	10.00	142.50	192.00	1865.00	1300.00	11366.80	83437.20	4.889
25	Tripura	5.00	95.50	8.00	122.00	500.00	5716.00	13127.50	0.769
26	Uttar Pradesh	10.00	80.50	1364.00	2831.00	1679.00	26742.90	312140.00	18.289
27	Uttarakhand	5.00	205.40	76.00	329.00	700.00	4063.00	20308.10	1.190
28	West Bengal	10.00	79.00	296.00	673.00	1703.00	12638.70	117997.30	6.914
	Total	225.00	4999.70	5000.00	19930.00	27945.00	258580.00	1706676.70	1000.00

Source: Reports of Various Finance Commission.

Transfers by Various Finance Commissions

(₹Crore)

	State	FC-I	FC-II	FC-III	FC-IV	FC-V	FC-VI	FC-VI I	FC-VIII	FC-IX(i)	FC-IX(ii)	FC-X	FC-XI	FC-XI I	FC-XIII
	1	2	3	4	5	6	7	8	9	9	9	9	9	9	9
1.	Andhra	32.18	70.05	84.12	99.96	347.78	570.08	1502.89	2754.78	848. 70	6575.47	16325.94	28980.25	45138.68	100616.00
	Prades	8.9%	8.2%	7.3%	7.6%	7.6%	8.0%	7.8%	7.7%	7.2%	7.5%	7.9%	7.7%	7.4%	6.9%
2.	Assam	9.07	22. 86	34.57	38.32	109.91	185.09	496.94	1251.67	404.28	2969.57	7064.14	12362. 05	19850.69	52620.60
		2.5%	2.7%	3.2%	2.9%	2.4%	2.6%	2.6%	3.5%	3.4%	3.4%	3.4%	3.3%	3.2%	3.6%
3.	Bihar	39.35	74.16	99.63	120.61	508. 73	738.44	2149.85	4005.82	1372.99	9670.53	23302.45	54934. 90	67671. 04	158341. 20
		10.9%	8.7%	9.3%	9.1%	77.0%	10.4%	77.2%	77.2%	77.6%	77.0%	77.3%	74.6%	77.0%	70.9%
4.	Chhatisgarh	—	—	—	—	—	—	—	—	—	—	—	—	16285.76	35825. 20
		—	—	—	—	—	—	—	—	—	—	—	—	2.7%	2.5%
5.	Gujarat	—	35.79	64.18	73.77	230.82	368.64	963.87	1417.18	422.13	3394.68	8014.95	10615.93	21900.47	44107.10
		—	4.2%	6.0%	5.6%	5.0%	5.2%	5.0%	4.0%	3.6%	3.9%	3.9%	2.8%	3.6%	3.0%
6.	Haryana	—	—	—	20.77	75.27	120.66	308. 57	427.97	137. 05	1131 .06	2554.96	3552.44	6596.46	15199. 50
		—	—	—	7.6%	7.6%	7.7%	7.6%	7.2%	7.2%	7.3%	7.2%	0.9%	7.7%	7.0%
7.	Himachal	—	—	—	—	22.54	43.10	110.26	530.69	140.46	1269.43	3743.81	2570.25	3203.22	1 1327. 30
	Pradesh	—	—	—	—	0.5%	0.6%	0.6%	7.5%	7.2%	7.4%	7.8%	0.7%	0.5%	0.8%
8.	Jammu &	—	9.57	13.75	19.95	41.66	58.79	159. 0S	738.21	236.44	2217.32	5904.70	4854. S0	7441.71	20182.70
	Kashmir	—	1.1%	1.3%	7.5%	0.9%	0.8%	0.8%	2.7%	2.0%	2.5%	2.9%	7.3%	7.2%	7.4%
9.	Karnataka	3.53	43.46	54.23	68.10	229.29	383.64	1005.00	1712.97	560.31	3962. 02	10034.64	18552.48	27361.88	62774. 90
		1.0%	5.7%	5.1%	5.7%	5.0%	5.4%	5.2%	4.8%	4.8%	4.5%	4.9%	4.9%	4.5%	4.3%
10.	Kerala	1.29	29.16	43.45	51 .21	183.13	271.04	766.16	1258.94	404.41	2919. 10	7217. 00	1 1504.04	16353.21	33954. 30
		0.4%	3.4%	4.1%	3.9%	4.0%	3.8%	4.0%	3.5%	3.4%	3.3%	3.5%	3.7%	2.7%	2.3%
11.	Madhya	27.53	56.54	74.81	89.67	343.10	543.57	1533.88	2788.11	909.56	6534.48	15275.50	33258.98	41 180.59	103268.90
	Pradesh	7.6%	6.6%	7.0%	6.8%	7.5%	7.7%	8.0%	7.8%	7.7%	7.4%	7.4%	8.8%	6.7%	7.7%
12.	Maharashtra	62.86	109.85	119.52	157.19	486.82	71 1.53	1714.06	2617. 30	860.47	6036.36	12859.84	17431.05	30663.19	75406.90
		17.4%	12.9%	11.2%	77.9%	70.6%	70.0%	8.9%	7.3%	7.3%	6.9%	6.2%	4.6%	5.0%	5.2%
1 3.	Manipur	—	—	—	—	3.43	13.48	37.76	299.18	75.27	710.07	1689.63	1377.32	2221.44	6541.20
		—	—	—	0.7%	0.2%	0.2%	0.8%	0.6%	0.8%	0.8%	0.4%	0.4%	0.5%	
14.	Meghalaya	—	—	—	—	7.60	12.85	36.68	242.88	59.67	558.21	1534.58	1287. 01	2276.61	5918. S0

	—	—	—	—	0.2%	0.2%	*0.2%*	0.7%	0.5%	0.6%	0.7%	0.3%	0.4%	0.4%
15. Naqaland	—	—	0.68	13.92	3.66	6.83	17.91	325.47	73.38	781.88	2197.38	827. 90	1613.67	4552. 90
	—	—	*0.1%*	7.7%	*0.1%*	0.7%	0.7%	0.9%	0.6%	0.9%	7.7%	0.2%	0.3%	0.3%
16. Orissa	14.22	30.05	48. 20	52.67	182. 70	272.59	815.27	1561.60	509.55	4263.81	8783.41	19026.64	31669.47	69316. 10
	3.9%	3.5%	4.5%	4.0%	*4.0%*	3.8%	4.2%	4.4%	4.3%	4.9%	4.3%	5.7%	5.2%	4.8%
17. Punjab	16.15	40.67	58.99	38.77	1 13.17	168.97	419.53	61 1.15	184.22	1515.22	3160.41	4316.37	7971.00	20146.40
	4.5%	4.8%	5.5%	2.9%	2.5%	2.4%	2.2%	7.7%	7.6%	7.7%	7.5%	7.7%	7.3%	7.4%
18. Rajasthan	13.93	35.52	49.21	58.69	213.56	333.39	883.52	1538.18	574.68	4613.83	10255.26	20595.88	34418.56	84892. 20
	3.9%	4.2%	4.6%	4.4%	4.6%	*4.7%*	4.6%	4.3%	4.9%	5.3%	5.0%	5.5%	5.6%	5.9%
19. Sikkim	—	—	—	—	—	—	0.48	63.52	14. 06	156.25	562.07	692.43	1 392.94	3466. S0
	—	—	—	—	—	—	0.0%	0.2%	0.7%	0.2%	0.3%	0.2%	0.2%	0.2%
20. Tamil Nadu	38.17	72.88	79.75	104.58	347.96	538.57	1476.39	2443. 07	839.36	6008.16	12622.54	20264.72	32552.74	72070.40
	10.6%	8.6%	7.5%	7.9%	7.6%	7.6%	7.7%	6.8%	7.7%	*6,8 s0*	6.7%	5.4%	5.3%	5.0%
21. Tripura	—	—	—	—	5. 10	19.69	59.66	357.67	97.59	956.66	2325.81	1832.67	2626. 09	741 1.50
	—	—	—	—	0.7%	0.3%	0.3%	7.0%	0.8%	7.7%	7.7%	0.5%	0.4%	0.5%
22. Uttar Pradesh	63.1 1	141.69	147.95	196.68	772.47	1150.22	3202.72	5915. 60	2046.75	13876.54	33526.67	72015.41	1 18209.45	285397. 10
	17.5%	76.6%	73.9%	74.9%	76.8%	76.2%	76.7%	76.6%	77.4%	75.8%	76.2%	79.7%	79.3%	79.7%
23. Uttaranchal	—	—	—	—	—	—	—	—	—	—	—	2486.15	5762.22	16245. 10
	—	—	—	—	—	—	—	—	—	—	—	0.7%	0.9%	7.7%
24. West Bengal	40.22	79.52	93.72	1 18.33	376. 30	588. 07	1572.60	2820.62	851 .90	6260.75	14104.85	30540.09	43303.91	105358.60
	11.1%	9.3%	8.8%	8.9%	8.2%	8.3%	8.2%	7.9%	7.2%	7.7%	*6.8*%*	8.7%	7.7%	7.3%
25. Goa	—	—	—	—	—	—	—	—	24.59	338.54	524. 06	775.22	1589.14	3857. S0
	—	—	—	—	—	—	—	—	0.2%	0.4%	0.3%	0.2%	0.3%	0.3%
26. Arunachal	—	—	—	—	—	—	—	—	65. 30	524.59	1360.03	918.22	1767.34	4755. 60
	—	—	—	—	—	—	—	—	0.6%	0.6%	0.7%	0.2%	0.3%	0.3%
27. Jharkhand	—	—	—	—	—	—	—	—	—	—	—	—	20624.02	40640.30
	—	—	—	—	—	—	—	—	—	—	—	—	3.4%	2.8%
28. Mizoram	—	—	—	—	—	—	—	—	72.52	637.47	1398.37	745.1 1	1466.52	3901.30
	—	—	—	—	—	—	—	—	0.6%	0.7%	0.7%	0.2%	0.2%	0.3%
Total :	361.61	851.77	1066.76	1323.19	4605.00	7099.24	19233. 0S	35682.58	11785.64	87882. 00	206343. 00	376318.01	613112. 02	1448096.40
	100.0%	*100.0%*	700.0%	*100.0%*	*100.0%*	700.0%	*100.0%*	*100.0%*	*100.0%*	*100.0%*	7 00.0%	*100.0%*	*100.0%*	700.0%

Percent Share of Backward States in Total Transfers

(%)

Item	*Bihar*	*Jharkhand*	*M.P.*	*Chattisgarh*	*Orissa*	*Rajasthan*	*U.P.*
FC-I	11.07	---	7.19	---	4.78	3.67	15.33
FC-II	9.09	---	6.82	---	4.50	4.58	13.51
FC-III	7.83	---	6.62	---	7.72	5.35	11.29
FC-IV	6.91	---	5.60	---	8.04	4.52	12.96
FC-V	9.57	---	6.45	---	5.47	4.99	14.53
FC-VI	8.79	---	5.66	---	6.01	5.87	14.05
FC-VII	10.62	---	7.67	---	4.72	4.33	15.90
FC-VIII	10.72	---	7.50	---	4.82	4.25	15.47
FC-IX (i)	10.65	---	6.98	---	4.53	4.77	15.83
FC-IX(ii)	10.54	---	7.40	---	5.21	6.15	16.46
FC-X	10.88	---	7.10	---	4.28	5.03	15.95
FC-XI	13.04	---	8.05	---	4.77	5.42	17.37
FC-XII	10.00	3.13	6.13	2.42	4.89	5.17	17.66
FC-XIII	10.13	2.80	6.83	2.46	4.63	5.73	18.29

Source: Reports of Various Finance Commission.

Percent Share of Developed States in Total Transfers

(%)

Item	AP	Goa	Gujarat	Haryana	Karnataka	Kerala	Maharashtra	Punjab	Tamil Nadu	West Bengal
FC-I	8.11	---	---	---	1.34	0.86	15.76	5.72	9.27	12.57
FC-II	8.59	---	3.41	---	7.00	3.61	10.47	4.95	6.95	9.85
FC-III	9.32	---	6.50	---	6.20	5.22	9.12	4.50	7.00	7.15
FC-IV	8.05	---	4.23	1.19	7.48	6.52	9.01	2.22	7.17	6.78
FC-V	7.77	---	4.34	1.42	4.65	4.38	9.16	2.13	6.97	8.44
FC-VI	8.08	---	3.83	1.26	3.99	5.00	7.40	1.76	5.60	8.56
FC-VII	7.31	---	4.63	1.48	4.82	3.70	8.22	2.01	7.21	7.66
FC-VIII	7.34	---	3.77	1.11	4.38	3.27	6.88	1.64	6.25	8.74
FC-IX (i)	6.60	0.34	3.19	1.21	4.22	3.01	6.71	2.04	6.38	6.99
FC-IX(ii)	6.82	0.48	3.50	1.13	3.83	3.25	5.85	1.58	5.85	6.99
FC-X	7.98	0.28	3.92	1.23	4.64	3.41	6.05	1.58	5.90	6.61
FC-XI	7.13	0.19	2.76	0.97	4.53	2.83	4.46	1.25	4.97	8.10
FC-XII	6.66	0.29	3.39	1.06	4.16	2.59	4.79	1.70	4.85	6.72
FC-XIII	6.69	0.26	3.15	1.14	4.36	2.63	5.37	1.50	4.89	6.91

Action Taken on the Recommendations*

First Finance Commission

Report dated 31st December, 1952

The report of the Commission was laid on the table of Parliament on 13th February, 1953.

Second Finance Commission

Report dated 30th September, 1957

The recommendations of the Commission have been summarised in Section XVIII of their Report which is being laid on the table of Parliament. They have been accepted by Government.

The Commission's recommendations fall into three categories, those to be implemented by an Order of the President, those to be implemented by law of Parliament and those to be implemented by executive orders. The recommendations under Article 270, 273 and 275(1) of the Constitution fall in the first category and the necessary orders will be submitted to the President for approval. The recommendations relating to the distribution of certain Union duties of excise between the Union and the States, the distribution among the States under Article 269(2) of the Constitution of Estate Duty on property other than agricultural land and the tax on railway fares and the levy and distribution of additional duties of excise in replacement

* *ATR upto FC-XI based on FC-XII document "Fifty Years of Fiscal Federalism— Finance Commission of India April, 2003 ARTs of FC-XII and FC-XIII based on GOI Notification.*

of sales taxes on certain commodities fall in the second category. Legislation will be promoted, if possible in the current session of Parliament, to implement them. The question of the levy of additional duties of excise in replacement of sales taxes is still under discussion with the State Governments and if those duties are levied, they will be distributed as recommended by the Commission. The recommendation regarding loans has to be implemented by executive orders and necessary action will be taken in consultation with the State Governments.

The Commission have also made certain recommendations in paragraphs 164, 182, 191 to 197 and 202 of their Report. These recommendations are also generally acceptable to Government and will be implemented, as far as possible, in consultation with the State Governments and other authorities where necessary.

Sd/-

(H.M. Patel)

Principle Secretary to the Government of India

New Delhi
13th November, 1957

Recommendation Relating to Loan to State Governments

The recommendation of the Second Finance Commission together with an Explanatory Memorandum as to the action taken thereon was laid before the Lok Sabha on the 14th November, 1957 and the Rajya Sabha on the 18th November, 1957. The Memorandum stated inter-alia that the recommendations of the Commission had been accepted by Government and that so far as the recommendation regarding the loans made to State Governments was concerned, which had to be implemented by executive action, necessary action will be taken in consultation with the State Governments.

2. The Government of India, in consultation with the Planning Commission, have now examined the question. They consider that the scheme of consolidation suggested by the Commission, which would have the effect of postponing the repayment of loans normally due for the next 15 years, would affect the ways and means position of the Central Government and reduce the resources available for them to assist State Governments during the period by way of loans either for plan projects or projects outside the plan. They also consider that there is not sufficient justification for the fixation of a uniform rate of interest as suggested by the Commission for all loans irrespective of the purposes for which the loans had been taken and that the rates of interest should have some relevance to the purpose of the loan.

3. After a careful consideration of the matter, they have come to the following conclusions:

(a) Loans for rehabilitation of displaced persons and interest-free loans: The recommendation of the Commission should be accepted. In other words the terms of repayment of all interests free loans shall remain unaltered and in respect of loans for rehabilitation of displaced persons w.e.f. 1st April, 1957, the States should pay to' the Union the amounts of the principle and interests, they collect on account of these loans, including the arrears, if any.

(b) Loans for industrial and commercial enterprises and for industrial housing: The rate of interest applicable to each of the loans in this category should remain unaltered.

(c) Loans for electricity undertaking and for extension of Power facilities: The rate of interest should be refixed at 4% p.a. for all such loans.

(d) Loans against collection of Small Savings: The

existing rate of interest viz., 4 per cent per annum should continue.

(e) Loans for multi-purpose River Valley Projects: The loans for each project should be broken up into two parts, one for power and the other for irrigation and other purposes. The loans allocated for power should bear interest at 4 per cent and the balance of the loans at 3 per cent per annum. Where such an allocation is not possible, an ad-hoc rate should be settled for the composite loans in consultation with the State Government concerned and the Planning Commission.

(f) Other Loans: All other loans, i.e., those not falling in any of the categories (a) to (e) above, should have the rate of interest refixed at 3 per cent, except that where the rate now applicable is less than 3 per cent, the lower rate shall continue to apply.

(g) The Government of India also propose that this pattern of interest should also apply to outstandings of loans sanctioned during 1956-57 and 1957-58 and the revised arrangements should take effect in the case of all the loans, other than loans for rehabilitation, from 1st April, 1958.

(h) In regard to the scheme of consolidation suggested by the Commission, the Government of India consider, that this should be left for discussion with individual State Governments. For the present, therefore, they do not propose to vary the existing terms in regard to repayment except to the extent mentioned in sub. para (a) above.

(i) The Government of India expect that the effect of their proposal will be to reduce, on the whole, the interest burden on the States on account of the loans taken between the 15th August, 1947 and the 31st March, 1958 by about ₹ 4 crores a year.

4. The Government's conclusions have been communicated to the State Governments.

Sd/-
(M.V. Rangachari)
Special Secretary

New Delhi.
12th March, 1958.

Third Finance Commission

Report dated 14th December, 1961

The Report of the Third Finance Commission is being laid on the Table of Parliament. The recommendations of the Commission are summarised in Section VIII of the Report. All the unanimous recommendations of the Commission have been accepted.

The report is not unanimous and there are two recommendations on which there is a minute of dissent from one Member. These are:

(a) that a special purpose grant be made to certain States for improvement of communications; and
(b) that 75 per cent of the revenue component of the State Plans be included in the scheme of devolution recommended by the Commission.

The majority recommendation regarding the special purpose grant for improvement of communications has been accepted, but Government do not consider it either necessary or desirable to accept the other recommendation. The scheme for financing the Plans of States as set out in the Third Five Year Plan provides reasonable assurance to State Governments that, given the necessary effort to mobilise resources and subject to an assessment of the overall financial and economic situation, the necessary Central assistance will be available to State Governments through annual plans. There will be no real advantage in the States receiving assistance for their Plans partly by way of statutory grants-in-aid as recommended by the Commission and partly on the basis of annual reviews made by the Planning Commission at the time of the framing of the annual plans. It is desirable to take an integrated view of the entire financial picture of each State, both on revenue and capital accounts, in relation to the State Plan as a whole. The total amount of Central assistance which the States may expect to receive for their Plans is not likely to be affected either way by the decision taken on this recommendations of the Finance Commission. On the other hand, there are considerable advantages in continuing to work on the basis of annual Plans and yearly assessments of the financial resources of the Centre and the States, so that adjustments, if necessary, can be made from year to year. In view of its large size and the wide range of activities embodied in the Third Plan, annual plans and reviews are an essential means of improving performance in all sectors, ensuring the fullest effort to raise resources, maintaining a satisfactory balance between different types of projects, particularly those which are of high priority and in one way or another inter-dependent. These purposes will be better served through suitable changes, where appropriate, in the existing procedures, rather than by converting any portion of Central assistance for State Plans into statutory grants, which must by their very nature lack flexibility. At the same time, to enable State Governments to make any day-to-day adjustments that may become necessary within the framework of their annual plans, procedure relating to the administration of Central assistance towards Plan expenditure have been already simplified and it is proposed to make them more flexible after consultation with the States.

The Commission's recommendations fall into three categories, those to be implemented by an Order of the President, those to be implemented by law by Parliament and those to be implemented by executive orders. The recommendations under Articles 270(1) of the Constitution fall in the first category and the necessary Order will be submitted to the President for approval. The recommendations relating to the distribution of Union Duties of Excise, including Additional Duties and Estate Duty on property other than agricultural land fall in the second category. Necessary legislation is being promoted in the current session of Parliament to implement them. The recommendation regarding the distribution of the ad-hoc grant to the States in lieu of their share of tax on Railway fares will be implemented by executive orders.

The Commission has also made certain general observations in Chapter Vll of its Report. These do not require any immediate decision and will be considered in due course in consultation with the State Governments, where necessary.

Sd/-

(L. K. Jha)

Secretary to the Government of India

New Delhi.

12th March, 1962.

Fourth Finance Commission

Report dated 12th August, 1965

The Report of the Fourth Finance Commission is being laid on the Table of Parliament. The main recommendations of the Commission are summarised in Chapter 12 of the Report and these have been accepted subject to the modification indicated in paragraph 2 below.

The Commission has excluded from its assessment of

revenue expenditure certain increase in pay scales and dearness allowance increases relating to State Government employees and employees of Local Bodies and School teachers effected by the State Governments of Andhra Pradesh, Mysore and Uttar Pradesh through orders issued in July, in 1965, and listed in Part 2 of Annexure-1 of the Report. This was because either there was not sufficient time after receipt of these orders to re-assess the estimates already adopted or the proposals were not accompanied by basic particulars and other necessary data. The Commission's recommendation was that the effect of these liabilities might also be taken into account in fixing the Article 275 Grants to be included in the Order of the President. Accordingly, Government requested Prof. D.G. Karve, a Member of the Commission, to undertake an assessment of these liabilities applying thereto the same criteria as were applied to similar liabilities by the Commission. Prof. Karve has recommended additional grant of ₹ 6.29 crores to Andhra Pradesh and of ₹ 2.58 crores to Mysore and a grant of ₹ 9.85 crores to Uttar Pradesh, during each of the years from 1st April, 1966 to 31st March, 1971. The grant in the case of Uttar Pradesh has been recommended after taking into account the surplus of ₹ 17.02 crores otherwise available to the State for the five year period ending 31st March, 1971. These recommendations have been accepted.

The Commission had also excluded from its assessment of revenue expenditure provisions for special requirements of hill districts in Assam, improvement and strengthening of Police Organisation in Madhya Pradesh and grants to Panchayats in Mysore, as final orders on these proposals had not been issued. The Commission has recommended that if these proposals mature into commitments before the President issues Orders under Article 275 of the Constitution and the Union is approached by the State Governments, those requirements might also be taken into account by the President in determining the amounts to be granted under Article 275.

It would not be practicable to keep the Order under Article 275 pending or even open for an amendment later until these liabilities mature into commitments. Such liabilities would, therefore, be taken into account during the computation of the resources for the Plan of the respective States and their needs for purposes of Central assistance.

The Commission's recommendations fall into three categories; those to be implemented by an Order of the President, those to be implemented by law by Parliament and those to be implemented by executive orders. The recommendations under Articles 270 and 275 (1) of the Constitution fall in the first category and the necessary Order will be submitted to the President for approval. The recommendations relating to the distribution of Union duties of excise including additional duties and estate duty on property other than agricultural land fall in the second category. Necessary legislation will be promoted to implement them. The recommendations regarding the distribution of ad-hoc grants to States in lieu of their share of tax on Railway fares will be implemented by executive orders.

The Commission has made certain general observations in Chapter 11 of its Report. The Chairman of the Commission and one of the Members have also appended minutes in which some general issues have been raised. These do not require any immediate decision and will be considered in due course in consultation with the State Governments where necessary.

Sd/-
(G. Venkateshwara Ayyar)
Secretary to the Government of India

New Delhi.
Dated 10th September, 1965.

Fifth Finance Commission
Report dated 31st July, 1969

The Final Report of the Fifth Finance Commission is being laid on the Table of the House. A summary of the main recommendations in the Report relating to devolution of taxes and duties and grants-in-aid is summarised in Chapter 9 of the Report.

The Recommendations relating to the sharing of income tax, Union excise duties and additional duties of excise in lieu of States sales tax and payment of grants-in-aid of the revenues of certain States under Article 275(1) of the Constitution have been accepted. It will be recalled that recommendations in respect of estate duty and grants in lieu of the repealed tax on Railway fares made in the Commission's Interim Report submitted in October, 1968 have already been accepted. Necessary adjustments in the devolution of taxes and duties and grants-in-aid to States for the current year (1969- 70) consequent on the acceptance of the Commission's recommendations in the Final Report will be made. The Commission's recommendation that it would not be desirable to maintain the existing arrangements in respect of additional excise duties in lieu of State sales tax formerly levied thereon unless Government after discussing the matter further with the State Governments can arrive at a general agreement for the continuance of the present arrangements with suitable modification has been noted. The matter is proposed to be placed before the National Development Council.

The Commission's recommendations regarding devolution will result as pointed out in the Commission's Report in large revenue surpluses for certain States. The question of their utilisation is proposed to be discussed in consultation with the Planning Commission and the concerned States.

The Commission has expressed the view that there is hardly any scope in the present circumstances for levying any of the taxes and duties mentioned in Article 269 of the Constitution which are not levied at present, except in the case of tax on advertisement in newspapers where it sees some scope for raising revenue. The Commission has recommended that the question of the levy of this tax, its rate structure, exemptions etc. should be examined by Government. This question will be examined as recommended.

The Commission has made a number of comments in regard to the effort at resource mobilisation in various States and has also made several suggestions in respect of scope for raising revenue by the States. These also will be examined in consultation with the State Governments.

Sd/-

(I.G. Patel)

Special Secretary to the Government of India

New Delhi.
26th August, 1969.

Sixth Finance Commission

Report dated 28th October, 1973

The Report of the Sixth Finance Commission is being laid on the Table of the House. A summary of the main recommendations in the Report relating to devolution of taxes and duties and grants-in-aid and changes in the terms of repayment of Central loans outstanding against the States is summarised in Chapter XVIII of its report.

The recommendations of the Commission relating to sharing of income tax, union excise duties (including auxiliary duties in the three years 1976-77 to 1978-79), additional excise duties in lieu of States' sales tax, and Estate Duty, and to the payment of grants in lieu of the repealed tax on Railway fares and on account of Wealth Tax on agricultural property have been accepted.

The Commission has recommended the payment of grants-in-aid of the revenues of certain States under article 275 (1) of the Constitution aggregating Rs. 2509.61 crores during the five year period commencing from 1974-75, after taking into account the needs of backward States for improvement of standards of essential administrative and social services. This recommendation of the Commission has been accepted. In computing the grants-in-aid of the order of Rs. 2509.61 crores the Commission has not taken into account the net interest liability of the States on account of fresh borrowings and lendings during the Fifth Plan Period. The Commission has recommended that the net interest liability on this account should be computed and the grants-in-aid suitably modified. Necessary action on this will be taken in due course.

The Commission has not favoured the establishment of a National Fund for financing the relief expenditure of the States affected by natural calamities. Instead it has made detailed suggestions in this regard and these will be examined in consultation with the Planning Commission.

The Commission was also required to make an assessment of the non-Plan capital gaps of States on uniform and comparable basis for the five years ending 1978-79 and in the light of its assessment recommend changes in the existing terms of repayment of Central loans outstanding at the end of 1973-74. In the light of the assessment made by the Commission it has recommended debt relief to the States of the order of Rs. 1969.62 crores for the five year period ending 1978-79, as detailed in the summary appended.

The Commission's recommendations fall into three categories (i) those to be implemented by an Order of the President, (ii) those to be implemented by law of Parliament, and (iii) those to be implemented by executive orders. The recommendations under article 270 (relating to income tax) and 275(1) (relating to grants-in-aid) of the Constitution fall in the first category and the necessary Order will be submitted to the President for approval. Recommendations relating to distribution of Union Duties of Excise, additional duties and estate on property other than agricultural land fall in the second category. Necessary legislation will be promoted to implement them. The recommendations relating to distribution of grants to State in lieu of the repealed tax on Railway Fares and grant on account of Wealth Tax on agricultural property and also changes in terms of repayment of Central loans will be implemented by executive orders.

The Commission has made certain general suggestions in the above Report. These do not require any immediate decision and will be considered in due course.

Sd/-

(M.G. Kaul)

Secretary to the Government of India

New Delhi.

11th December, 1973.

Seventh Finance Commission

Report dated 28th October, 1978

The Report of the Seventh Finance Commission, together with this explanatory memorandum as to the action taken on the recommendations of the Commission, is being laid on the Table of the House, in pursuance of article 281 of the Constitution. A summary of the Commission's main recommendations, relating to devolution of taxes. and duties to the States, grants-in-aid under article 275 of the Constitution, financing of relief expenditure and debt relief to the States, is summarised in Chapter 13 of its Report.

A. Shares of Central Taxes and Duties

The Commission's recommendations, covering a period of five years commencing from the first day of April, 1979, relating to sharing of income tax, Union excise duties, additional excise duties in lieu of States' sales tax, estate duty on property other than agricultural land as also payment of grants in lieu of the repealed tax on Railway passenger fares and on account of wealth tax on agricultural property, have been accepted.

B. Grants-in-aid of the revenues of States under the substantive provision of article 275 of the Constitution

(a) Grants-in-aid to cover non-Plan gap on revenue account. Government have accepted the recommendation of the Commission for payment of grants-in-aid of the revenues of certain States, under the substantive provision of article 275(1) of the Constitution, towards meeting their non-Plan revenue gap, as assessed by the Commission, for the five years 1979-84, amounting in all to ₹ 1173.12 crores.

In recommending payment of grants-in-aid amounting to 1173.12 crores, referred to above, the Commission could not compute the net interest liability of the States arising out of their fresh borrowings and lendings during the five years 1979-84. The Commission has recommended that the Central Government should, from year to year, compute in relation to each of the years 1979-84, the net interest liability of the States arising from their fresh borrowings and lendings and that, thereupon, the President should be moved to increase, to the extent required, the amounts of the grants-in-aid recommended by the Commission for the 8 States and, in the case of the other States, the net interest liability so computed should be set off against the surplus as assessed by the Commission and the net deficit, if any, should be given as grants-in-aid to the States concerned by Presidential Order under article 275(1) of the Constitution. Government have accepted this recommendation and necessary action on this will be taken accordingly.

(b) Grants-in-aid for upgradation of standards of administration: Government have accepted the Commission's recommendations for making grants-in-aid to certain States for upgradation of the standards of administration, equivalent to the revenue and capital provisions which the Commission has recommended, subject to the implementation and the monitoring of the upgradation schemes in the manner indicated by the Commission in Chapter 10 of its Report.

(c) Grants-in-aid to compensate States' loss in excise revenue consequent upon introduction of prohibition. Government of India had decided to compensate the States in each of the years 1978-84, by way of grants-in-aid, to the extent of one-half of the established loss of State excise revenue on the introduction of prohibition treating the actual excise revenue of 1977-78 as the base. The decision was communicated to the States in August, 1978 and the Seventh Finance Commission also was informed. The Commission, however, has held the view that, where a State Government implements further measures towards achieving total prohibition in the years from 1979-80 onwards, and thereby suffers a loss in the excise revenue from potable liquor to a figure below that assumed by it for the relevant year, the differences should be made up entirely by the Central Government, by grants-in-aid under Article 275(1) of the Constitution, and has recommended accordingly. The Government of India, however, considered it appropriate that in the matter of introduction of total prohibition, which is in pursuance of the Directive Principles of State Policy, the losses in State excise revenue should be shared jointly by the Government of India and the State Governments concerned. The Government also consider that with the successful implementation of measures towards achieving total prohibition, there is scope for the State Governments to increase their other revenues. Accordingly, Government have decided to adhere to its decision to compensate the States to the extent of one-half of the loss in revenues from State excise, and not accept the recommendation of the Commission in this regard.

C. Alternative criteria of devolution

The Report of the Commission has appended to it a Note of Dissent by one of the Members suggesting an alternative formula for devolution of Central taxes and duties as also statutory grants-in-aid to the States. Government have carefully considered the Note of dissent together with the observations of the majority thereon and have decided that in regard to devolution of resources, which involves a delicate issue of Centre-State financial relations, it would be appropriate to accept the recommendations of the majority.

D. Recommendations on other terms of reference

(i) Financing of relief expenditure: The recommendations of the Commission relating to modifications in the existing arrangements for financing of relief expenditure by the States affected by natural calamities have been accepted by the Government.

(ii) Debt relief: Government have accepted the debt relief, estimated at Rs. 2155.80 crores, recommended by the Commission for the States for the five years 1979-84, but not the recommendations to convert the small savings loans to the States into 'loans in perpetuity'. However, in order not to disturb the order of the debt relief recommended by the Commission for the five years 1979-84, the State Government will not be required to make any repayment during 1979-84 on account of such loans as may be outstanding at the end of 1978-79.

E. Implementation

The Commission's recommendations fall into three categories: (i) those to be implemented by Order of the President, (ii) those to be implemented by law of Parliament, and (iii) those to be implemented by executive orders. The recommendations under articles 270 and 275(1) of the Constitution (relating to income tax and grants-in-aid respectively) fall in the first category and the necessary Order will be submitted to the President for approval. Recommendations relating to distribution of Union duties of excise, Additional duties of excise and Estate duty on property other than agricultural land fall in the second category. Necessary legislation will be promoted to implement them. The recommendations relating to distribution of grants to States in lieu of the repealed tax on

Railway fares and grant on account of Wealth tax on agricultural property and also changes in terms of repayment of Central loans will be implemented by executive orders.

The Government while taking decisions on the recommendations of the Seventh Finance Commission have taken note of the inter-se distribution of resources resulting from the Commission's recommendations. Having regard to the fact that some of the States may not be as favourably placed as others vis-a-vis their developmental requirements, particularly in so far as the minimum needs programme is concerned, Government have decided that modalities will be worked out, in consultation with the Planning Commission, to see that the States with relatively weak financial resource base are enabled to implement adequately the revised minimum needs programme, covering rural water supply, house sites for the homeless, rural roads, rural electrification, rural health care, bonded labour and elementary/adult education.

The Commission had made certain general suggestions in the Report. These do not require any immediate decision and will be considered in due course.

Sd/-
(H.M. Patel)
Minister of Finance

New Delhi
24th November, 1978.

Eighth Finance Commission

Interim report dated 14th November, 1983

'The Interim Report of the Eighth Finance Commission covering the financial year 1984-85 is being laid on the Table of the House. A summary of the main recommendations in the report is appended.

The recommendations contained in the Interim Report have been accepted.'

Sd/-

(Pranab Mukherjee)

Finance Minister

New Delhi
9th December, 1983.

Summary of the Main Recommendations (November, 1983)

1. The Commission has recommended that in respect of the distribution between the Union and States of the net proceeds of Income-tax, Union Excise Duties, Additional Duties of Excise in lieu of sales tax, and Estate Duty the existing arrangements may continue provisionally during the financial year commencing on 1st April, 1984. The Commission has recommended that the State of Sikkim may also receive a share of Union Excise Duties including excise duty on electricity and Additional Excise Duties in lieu of sales tax.
2. The Commission has also recommended that the existing arrangements with regard to grants made available to States in lieu of tax on Railway Passenger fares and wealth tax on agricultural property may continue provisionally during the year 1984-85.
3. The existing arrangements in regard to financing of relief expenditure by the States affected by natural calamities may also be continued during 1984-85.
4. The Commission has recommended that Grants-in-aid under Article 275(1) of the Constitution to cover residuary deficits on revenue account may be paid to the following States for the year 1984-85.

(Rs in crores)

	State	*Sums to be paid as Grant-in-aid*
1.	Assam	38.17
2.	Himachal Pradesh	91.15
3.	Jammu & Kashmir	114.85
4.	Manipur	56.08
5.	Meghalaya	40.27
6.	Nagaland	81.12
7.	Sikkim	11.96
8.	Tripura	53.34
9.	West Bengal	7.89
	Total:	494.83

5. The recovery of small savings loans given to State Governments which was held in abeyance during the period 1979-80 to 1983-84 may be deferred during the financial year 1984-85 also.
6. In its present assessment the Commission has not made provision for expenditure on fresh proposals for upgradation of standards of administration and improvements, if any, needed for the maintenance and up-keep of capital assets and these will be made in the final report.
7. The recommendations contained in the Interim report are provisional and of interim nature and would be subject to such re-adjustment as may be necessary on the basis of the final report.

Report dated 30th April, 1984

The Report of the Eighth Finance Commission covering a period of five years commencing from 1st day of April, 1984 together with the explanatory memorandum as to the action taken on the recommendations of the Commission is being laid on the Table of the House, in pursuance of Article 281 of the Constitution. A summary of the Commission's main recommendations relating to devolution of taxes and duties to the States, grants-in-aid under Article 275 of the

Constitution, financing of relief expenditure and debt relief to the States and other matters, is summarised in Chapter XVll of its Report.

2. As required by its terms of reference, the Commission's recommendations cover the five year period commencing from 1st day of April, 1984. The Commission was requested to submit its report to the President by 31st October, 1983 so that sufficient time would be available to consider its recommendations before framing the Budgets and Annual Plans of the Central and State Governments for 1984-85. However, at the request of the Commission, its term was extended upto 29th February, 1984 (by notification dated 29th October, 1983) and further to 30th April, 1984 (by notification dated 29th February, 1984). The Report of the Commission was submitted to the President on 30th April, 1984 by which time the Budgets and Annual Plans for 1984-85 of the Central and most State Governments had already been finalised.
3. In view of the delay in the submission of the Report, the Commission submitted on 14th November, 1983 an Interim Report covering the year 1984-85, so that the recommendations contained in this Interim Report could be considered prior to the presentation of the budgets for 1984-85. The recommendations made by the Commission were accepted by the government and a memorandum on the action taken was laid on the Table of the House on 9th December, 1983. The budget of the Central Government for the current year, as approved by Parliament, reflects the impact of these decisions.
4. As almost four months of the current year are over and the budgets and Annual Plans for this year are

already in operation, it will cause undue disruption in the economy, if the budgets and plans for the remaining part of the current year were to be changed now. In particular, any change in the formula for devolution of Central taxes and duties in mid year is not considered feasible as it would involve reduction or increase in shares of different States. Taking these considerations into account, the Government have decided to continue with the recommendations of the Finance Commission contained in the Interim Report for the current financial year. The following decisions taken on the Final Report of the Commission and their implementation, therefore, relate to the period 1985-86 to 1988-89.

A. Shares of Central Taxes and Duties

5. For the period of four years commencing from the 1st day of April, 1985, recommendations contained in the final report of the Finance Commission relating to sharing of Income tax, Union duties of excise, additional excise in lieu of State sales tax, estate duty on property other than agricultural land and grant on account of wealth tax on agricultural property have been accepted. In regard to the recommendation of the Commission for enhancing the grant in lieu of repealed tax on railway passenger fares, the recommendation is acceptable to Government but will need to be referred to the Railway Convention Committee. The Government have also accepted the recommendations of the Finance Commission in regard to inter-se distribution of the grant among the States.
6. It may be noted that the Commission has recommended that 5 per cent of the net proceeds of

Union duties of excise (excluding that on electricity) should be set aside and distributed to those States which have deficit after taking into account their shares from the devolution of taxes and duties as proposed by it. This introduces a new principle of directly linking devolution to deficit rather than dealing with them only through grants-in-aid under Article 275. While recognising that there could be different views on the merits of this principle, Government have decided to accept this recommendation of the Commission in the Report but without creating a precedent.

B. Grants-In-Aid of the Revenues of States Under the Substantive Provision of Article 275 of the Constitution

7. (i) Grants-in-aid to cover non-plan gap on revenue account—For the four years commencing from 1st day of April, 1985, the Government have accepted the recommendations contained in the Final Report of the Commission for payment of grants-in-aid of the revenues of certain States under the substantive provision of Article 275(1) of the Constitution towards meeting their non-plan revenue gap as assessed by the Commission.

(ii) The Commission has not computed the net interest liabilities of the States arising out of the fresh borrowings during the period 1984-89. The Commission has recommended that the Central Government from year to year should compute in relation to each of the four years (1985-89), the net interest liability of the States arising out of the fresh borrowings and that, thereupon, the President should be moved to increase, to the extent required, the amounts of the grants-in-aid recommended by the Commission for the deficit States and in the case of other States, the net interest liability so computed should be set off against the surplus as assessed by the Commission. The Government have accepted this recommendation.

(iii) The Commission has not computed the additional burden from 1985-86 arising out of the committed expenditure in respect of plan schemes completed in 1984-85. The Commission has recommended that the Government may compute the requirements of the deficit States on this account taking into consideration the yield from additional resource mobilization measures of 1984-85, and move the President to increase, to the extent required, the amounts of the grants-in-aid. The Government have accepted this recommendation also.

(iv) Grants-in-aid for upgradation of standards of administration, special problems and for financing relief expenditure—The Government have accepted the recommendations of the Commission for making grants-in-aid to certain States for upgradation of standards of administration and special problems for the four years commencing from 1st day of April, 1985, subject to the implementation and monitoring of the schemes in the manner indicated by the Commission in Chapter XII of its Report. The Government have also accepted the recommendations of the Commission that the Centre should contribute annually as grants-in-aid equal to half of the margin money computed by the Commission for financing of relief expenditure.

C. Recommendations on Other Terms of Reference

8. (i) Financing of Relief Expenditure—In addition to the grants-in-aid to the margin money of States for financing of relief expenditure, the Government have accepted the modifications recommended by the Commission to the existing arrangements for financing of relief expenditure.

   (ii) Debt Relief—The Government have accepted the recommendations of the Commission in regard to debt relief for the four years commencing from 1st day of April, 1985.

D. Notes of Dissent

9. The Report of the Commission has appended to it three Notes of Dissent on certain recommendations. The Government have carefully considered these notes and decided to accept generally the recommendations of the majority.

10. The Commission's recommendations fall in three categories:

    (i) Those to be implemented by the Order of the President;

    (ii) Those to be implemented by law of Parliament;

    (iii) Those to be implemented by executive order.

    The recommendations under Article 270 and 275 (1) of the Constitution relating to income tax and grants-in-aid respectively fall in the first category and the necessary order will be submitted to the President for approval. Recommendations relating to distribution of Union excise duties and estate duty on property other than agricultural land fall in the second category. Necessary legislation will be promoted for implementing them. The recommendations relating to distribution of grant to States in lieu of tax on railway passenger fares and grant on account of wealth tax on agricultural property and also changes in terms of repayment of the Central loans will be implemented by executive orders.

11. The recommendations relating to the enhancement in the grant given in lieu of repealed tax on railway passenger fares will be referred to the Railway Convention Committee and implemented if accepted by them.
12. The Commission has made certain other recommendations in the Report. These do not require any immediate action and will be considered in due course.

Sd/-

(Pranab Mukherjee)

Finance Minister

New Delhi
24th July, 1984.

Ninth Finance Commission

First report dated 29th July, 1988

The First Report of the Ninth Finance Commission covering the financial year 1989-90 is being laid on the Table of the House. A summary of the main recommendations in the Report is contained in Chapter XII of the Report.

The recommendations of the Finance Commission regarding devolution of Income Tax, Union Excise Duties, Additional Duties of Excise in lieu of Sales Tax, Grants-in-aid in lieu of tax on Railway Passenger Fares, Financing of relief expenditure, and Debt relief have been accepted. In regard to Grants-in-aid Government accept the recommendations of the Finance Commission with the proviso that the recommendations relating to Grants-in-aid for meeting the requirements of the revenue component of the State Plan may be kept in view by the Planning Commission, while finalising the funding arrangements for the Annual Plans of the States for 1989-90.

The other recommendations of the Commission not relating to immediate devolution, will be considered separately.

Sd/-
(S.B. Chavan)
Finance Minister

New Delhi
2nd September, 1988.

Explanatory Memorandum on the Amendments to the First Report

The First Report of the Ninth Finance Commission and the memorandum on the Government's decision on the recommendations made therein were laid on the Table of the House on 2nd September, 1988. This is to lay on the Table of the House the amendments to that report proposed by the Commission subsequently to correct a few minor computational errors that had crept into the Report. The amendments are—

(i) the share of Union Territories in the net proceeds of income tax earlier fixed at 1.044% (Para 5.30 of the Report) is revised to 1.124%;

(ii) States' share in the net proceeds of income tax earlier indicated as ₹ 2990.38 crores (Col. (i) of Table 9 on page 53 of the Report) is revised as ₹ 2987.94 crores i.e. ₹ 2.44 crores less; and

(iii) as a result of the reduction in the States' share of income tax, the grants given to the following deficit

States, are increased by the amount shown against each—

	(₹ in crore)
Arunachal Pradesh	0.01
Assam	0.05
Goa	0.01
Himachal Pradesh	0.02
Jammu & Kashmir	0.05
Manipur	0.01
Mizoram	0.02
Nagaland	0.02
Orissa	0.05
Rajasthan	0.08
Tripura	0.02

The Government has accepted the amendments in the First Report as proposed by the Ninth Finance Commission.

Sd/-
(S.B. Chavan)
Finance Minister

New Delhi
23rd February, 1989

Second report dated 18th December, 1989

The Second Report of the Ninth Finance Commission covering the five years period commencing from the 1st of April, 1990 together with the Explanatory Memorandum on the action taken on the recommendations of the Commission is being laid on the Table of the House, in pursuance of Article 281 of the Constitution. A summary of the Commission's main recommendations relating to devolution of taxes and duties to the States, grants-in-aid under Article 275 of the Constitution, financing of relief expenditure and debt relief to the States and other matters, is summarised in Chapter XI of its Report.

A. Shares of Central Taxes and Duties

For the period of five years commencing from the 1st of April, 1990, recommendations contained in the Second Report of the Finance Commission relating to sharing of Income tax, Union Duties of excise, additional excise duties in lieu of States' sales tax, have been accepted. The recommendation of the Commission relating to grants in lieu of the repealed tax on railway passenger fares has also been accepted by Government.

B. Grants-in-Aid of the Revenues of States

Under the Substantive Provision of Article 275 of the Constitution

(i) Grants-in-aid to cover non-Plan gap on Revenue Account: The Government have accepted the recommendations contained in the Second Report of the Commission for payment of grants-in-aid of the revenues of certain States under the substantive provision of Article 275 (1) of the Constitution towards meeting their non-Plan revenue gap as assessed by the Commission for the five years 1990-95.

(ii) Grants-in-aid to cover part of deficits on Plan Revenue Account: The Government have accepted the recommendations of the Commission for the payment of grants-in-aid to certain States to cover a part of the deficit of such State Governments on plan account for the five years commencing from the 1st of April, 1990. These grants will be taken into account by the Planning Commission as a resource for financing the States' Plans.

C. Recommendations on Other Terms of References

(i) Financing of Relief Expenditure: The Government

have accepted, in principle, the recommendations of the Commission relating to financing of relief expenditure and setting up of a Calamity Relief Fund in each of the States. The arrangements for the custody and operation of the Fund will be separately worked out in consultation with the Comptroller & Auditor General of India and the Reserve Bank of India.

The recommendation of the Commission on grants to the Madhya Pradesh Government for the Bhopal Gas Leak disaster will be considered as a part of the general scheme for providing interim compensation to gas leak victims.

(ii) Debt Relief: The Government have accepted the recommendations of the Commission in regard to rescheduling/write off of certain loans outstanding against State Governments and elongation of the maturity period of future Central loan for State Plans from 15 years to 20 years with 50 per cent loans enjoying a grace period of 5 years have been accepted. The other recommendations on debt relief requiring in depth examination will be considered in due course.

D. Note of Dissent

The report of the Commission has appended to it a Note of Dissent on certain recommendations. The Government have carefully considered the note and decided to accept the recommendations of the majority as indicated in paras 2, 3, and 4 above.

E. Implementation

The Commission's recommendations fall in three categories:

(i) Those to be implemented by an Order of the President.
(ii) Those to be implemented by Law of Parliament.
(iii) Those to be implemented by executive order.

The recommendations under Article 270 and 275 (l) of the Constitution relating to income tax and grants-in-aid respectively fall in the first category and the necessary order will be submitted to the President for approval. Recommendations relating to distribution of Union Excise duties including Additional Duties of Excise in lieu of sales tax (Under Article 272 of the Constitution) fall in the second category. Necessary legislation will be promoted for implementing them. The recommendations relating to distribution of grants to States in lieu of tax on railway passenger fares and rescheduling of Central Loans will be implemented by executive order.

The Commission has made certain other recommendations in the Report. These do not require any immediate action and will be considered in due course.

Sd/-
(Madhu Dhandavate)
Finance Minister

New Delhi
12th March, 1990

Tenth Finance Commission

Report dated 26th November, 1994

The Report of the Tenth Finance Commission covering the five years period commencing from April 1, 1995 together with the Explanatory Memorandum on the action taken on the recommendations of the Commission is being laid on the Table of the House, in pursuance of article 281 of the

Constitution. A summary of the Commission's main recommendations relating to devolution of taxes and duties to the States, grants-in-aid under Article 275 of the Constitution, financing of relief expenditure and debt relief to the States and other matters is contained in Chapter XVI of the Report of the Commission.

2. Shares of Central Taxes and Duties

For the period of five years commencing from April 1, 1995, recommendations contained in the Report of the Finance Commission relating to sharing of Income tax, Union Duties of Excise, Additional Excise Duties in lieu of States' sales tax, have been accepted by Government. The recommendations of the Commission relating to grants in lieu of the repealed tax on railway passenger fares have also been accepted by Government. The recommendation of the Commission that the receipts on account of 'interest recoveries' and 'penalties' under the Income tax Act should be shared with the States with effect from April 1, 1995, has been accepted by the Government.

3. Grants-In-Aid of the Revenues of States under the Substantive Provisions of Article 275 of the Constitution

(i) Grants-in-aid to cover non-Plan gap on Revenue Account: The Government has accepted the recommendations contained in the Report of the Commission for payment of grants-in-aid of the revenues of certain States under the substantive provisions of Article 275(1) of the Constitution towards meeting their non-Plan revenue gap as assessed by the Commission for the five years 1995-2000.

(ii) Grants-in-aid for upgradation of standards of administration and specific grants to certain States for special problems: The Government has accepted the recommendations of the Commission for making grants-in-aid to States for upgradation of standards of administration and specific grants to certain States for special problems for the four years commencing from April 1, 1996 as recommended by the Commission.

(iii) Grants to States for financing local bodies: The Government has accepted the recommendations of the Commission for making grants to the States for Panchayati Raj Institutions as well as for the Urban Municipal Bodies during the four years period commencing from April 1, 1996. These grants will be treated as part of the Plan of the State Governments, earmarked to be transferred to local bodies.

(iv) Financing of Relief Expenditure: The Government has accepted the recommendations of the Commission relating to the continuation of the existing scheme of Calamity Relief Fund with an enhancement in the corpus of the Calamity Relief Fund. As recommended by the Commission, the existing scheme will be modified in consultation with the States so as to provide flexibility in the choice of avenues for investment. The Government has also accepted the recommendations of the Finance Commission in regard to setting of a Rs. 700 crore National Fund for Calamity Relief (NFCR). The arrangements for the custody and operation of the fund will be separately worked out in consultation with the Comptroller and Auditor General of India and the Reserve Bank of India.

(v) Debt Relief: The Government has accepted the recommendations of the Commission in regard to debt relief including two new schemes of general debt relief for all States, one linked to the fiscal performance of the States and the other linked to the utilisation of proceeds of disinvestment in State Public Enterprises for retiring Central loans.

4. Implementation

The Commission's recommendations fall in four categories:

(i) Those to be implemented by an Order of the President.
(ii) Those to be implemented by Law of Parliament.
(iii) Those to be implemented by executive orders.
(iv) Those to be examined further

The recommendations under articles 270 and 275(l) of the Constitution relating to income tax and grants-in-aid respectively, fall in the first category and the necessary order will be submitted to the President for approval.

Recommendations relating to distribution of Union Excise Duties including Additional Duties of Excise in lieu of Sales Tax (under Article 272 of the Constitution) fall in the second category. Necessary legislation will be promoted for implementing these recommendations.

The recommendations relating to distribution of grants to States in lieu of tax on railway passenger fares and debt relief will be implemented by executive orders.

Other recommendations of the Commission will be considered in due course.

Sd/-
(Manmohan Singh)
Minister of Finance

New Delhi
14th March, 1995.

Eleventh Finance Commission

Interim report dated 15th January, 2000

1. The Eleventh Finance Commission was constituted on 3rd July, 1998 with the mandate to give its report by 31st December, 1999 covering the five year period 2000-2005. On 28th December, 1999, it was given extension of time upto 30th June, 2000 with the direction to give an interim report to enable provisional arrangements for 2000-2001. In pursuance of article 281 of the Constitution, the Interim Report of the Eleventh Finance Commission covering the one year period commencing from April 1, 2000 together with the Explanatory Memorandum on the action taken on the recommendations of the Commission is being laid on the Table of the House.
2. The Commission's interim recommendations relating to provisional arrangements in 2000-01 in respect of devolution of taxes and duties to the States, grants-in-aid under Article 275 of the Constitution and financing of relief expenditure are summarised below.

Shares of Central Taxes and Duties

3. States' share in the net proceeds of personal Income Tax is recommended to be increased from 77.5% at present to 80% for 2000-01. States' Share in the net proceeds of Union Excise Duties is recommended to be increased from 47.5 % at present to 52% for 2000-01. States' Share in the net proceeds of Additional Excise Duties is recommended to be retained at the existing level of 97.797% for 2000-01. These recommendations have been accepted by Government.

Grants-in-Aid of the Revenues of States Under the Substantive Provisions of Article 275 of the Constitution

Grants-in-aid to cover non-Plan gap on Revenue Account

4. The Commission has assessed that the States' would have Revenue Deficit of about ₹ 11,000 crore on Non-Plan account, which needs to be bridged through non-Plan grants from the Centre. The inter-se allocation between States has, however, not been indicated. This will be done in the final report. The Government has accepted the recommendations of the Commission for payment of Rs. 11,000 crore as grants-in-aid of the revenues of certain States under the substantive provisions of Article 275 (1) of the Constitution towards meeting their non-Plan revenue gap as assessed by the Commission for the year 2000-2001 subject to stipulations in para 10 below.

Grants-in-aid for upgradation of standards of administration and specific grants to certain States for special problems

5. The Government has accepted the recommendations of the Commission for making grants-in-aid amounting to ₹ 2,000 crore to States for upgradation of standards of administration and grants to certain States for special problems for the year 2000-2001.
6. The Government has accepted the recommendations of the Commission relating to the continuation of the existing scheme of calamity relief fund with the size of States' Calamity Relief Funds being fixed at ₹ 2,000 crore for 2000-2001 including ₹ 1,500 crore as Centre's contribution.

Grants to States for financing local bodies

7. The Tenth Finance Commission had recommended ad-hoc grants to the States for Panchayati Raj Institutions as well as for the Urban Municipal bodies. For Panchayati Raj Institutions the Tenth Finance Commission had made an ad-hoc provision at the rate of ₹ 100 per capita of rural population (1971 census) amounting to a total of ₹ 4,380.93 crore. For urban local bodies, ₹ 1,000 crore has been provided for the five year period 1995-2000 on the basis of the inter-State ratio of the slum population derived from the urban population figures as per 1971 Census. Eleventh Finance Commission has recommended a 50% increase in the grants to States for Local Bodies with 80% being earmarked for Rural and 20% for Urban Local Bodies. The Government has accepted the recommendations of the Commission.
   Grants in lieu of the Repealed Tax on Railway Passenger Fares

Grants in lieu of the Repealed Tax on Railway Passenger Fares

8. Grant in lieu of tax on Railway passenger fares, which is ₹ 380 crore per annum at present, is recommended to be increased to ₹ 570 crore for 2000-2001.
9. The critical challenge posed by a weakening fiscal situation must be squarely confronted and overcome. A long history of high fiscal deficit has left a legacy of huge public debt and ever-growing bill of interest payments. Although in the current precarious fiscal situation of Centre, it would be very burdensome on Centre's finances to accept these recommendations but the States' finances are also severely strained and, therefore, in the spirit of federalism, Government has accepted these recommendations. While the need of

non-Plan grants to cover the residual Revenue Deficit of States is manifest, the problems that have in the first place caused high revenue deficit need to be addressed. In this context it is pertinent to mention that the challenge of fiscal management is not confined to the Central Government. The financial position of the State Governments has deteriorated sharply in the last few years. Revenue deficits have widened and borrowings are being increasingly used to meet revenue expenditure. Fiscal reform at the State level has acquired great urgency. While we have gone out of our way to help State Government, the determination shown by some States to deal with these issues has also helped enormously. It will be my endeavour to take further collective measures in the next year for promoting fiscal reforms in the States. The final report of the Eleventh Finance Commission will provide valuable inputs for taking policy initiatives in this regard. The Commission has a broader mandate to look into the overall macroeconomic balance. The Commission has indicated in the interim report that it is preparing a scheme of restructuring the government finances so as to restore the fiscal balance

10. Keeping in view the difficult fiscal situation and the collective efforts of the Central and State Governments required in dealing with it, the Government has decided that the Finance Commission should draw up a monitorable fiscal reform programme for the States and the non-Plan grants to cover the assessed Revenue Deficit should be suitably tied up with the progress made in the implementation of the programme.

11. The Government's acceptance of the interim

recommendations is meant to be a provisional arrangement for 2000-2001 only. Necessary provisions have been proposed in Budget 2000-2001. Government will review the decisions in the light of the recommendations of the Commission in their final report and also in the light of the Parliament's decision in respect of the Constitution (Eighty Ninth Amendment) Bill, 2000 introduced in the Lok Sabha on 9th March, 2000 regarding the Alternative Scheme of Devolution recommended by the 10th Finance Commission. Under this scheme, a fixed percentage of the net proceeds of almost all Central taxes, excluding cesses and surcharges, is sought to be assigned to the States w.e.f. 1st April, 1996 in lieu of existing share in Personal Income Tax, Union Excise Duties and Grants in lieu of Tax on Railway Passenger Fares.

Implementation

12. The Commission's recommendations fall in three categories:
    (i) Those to be implemented by an Order of the President.
    (ii) Those to be implemented by Law of Parliament.
    (iii) Those to be implemented by executive orders.
13. The recommendations under Article 270 and 275(1) of the Constitution relating to income tax and grants-in-aid, respectively, fall in the first category and the necessary order will be submitted to the President for approval.
14. Recommendations relating to distribution of Union Excise duties including Additional Duties of Excise in lieu of Sales Tax (under Article 272 of the

constitution) fall in the second category. Necessary legislation will be promoted for implementing these recommendations in a manner consistent with Parliament's decision in respect of the Constitution (Eighty Ninth Amendment) Bill, 2000 introduced in the Lok Sabha on 9th March, 2000 regarding the Alternative Scheme of Devolution recommended by the Tenth Finance Commission.

15. The recommendations relating to distribution of grants to States in lieu of tax on railway passenger fares and debt relief will be implemented by executive orders.

Sd/-
(Yashwant Sinha)
Ministry of Finance

New Delhi
16th March, 2000.

Report dated 7th July, 2000

The Eleventh Finance Commission was constituted by the President on July 3, 1998 to give recommendations on specified aspects of Centre State fiscal relations during 2000-2005. The Commission submitted its Report covering all aspects of its original mandate on 7th July, 2000. Earlier, on 15th January, 2000, the Commission had submitted an interim report for making provisional arrangements for 2000-01. The interim recommendations of the Commission were accepted by the Government and were laid on the Table of the House on 16th March, 2000.

2. The Report of the Eleventh Finance Commission (hereinafter referred to as the Commission) covering the five years period commencing from April 1, 2000 together with the Explanatory Memorandum on the action taken on the recommendations of the

Commission is being laid on the Table of the House, in pursuance of Article 281 of the Constitution. A summary of the Commission's main recommendations relating to devolution of taxes and duties to the States, grants-in-aid under Article 275 of the Constitution, financing of relief expenditure and debt relief to the States and other matters is contained in Chapter XIV of the Report of the Commission.

3. The Finance Commissions are constituted by the President after every five years or earlier under Article 280 of the Constitution to give recommendations on specified aspects of Centre-State fiscal relations. The recommendations of these Commissions are based on a detailed assessment of the financial position of the Central and State Governments and wide consultation with almost all sections of stakeholders. The Commissions usually visit the States, sponsor studies, hold consultations with experts and their recommendations are usually backed up by detailed reasons disclosing methodology adopted by them. The Government has carefully considered some of the main recommendations contained in the above-mentioned Report of the Commission and the action proposed to be taken on these recommendations is detailed below.

Devolution of Share in Central Taxes and Duties to States

4. Under Article 270 of the Constitution, as amended w.e.f. 1st April, 1996 by the Constitution (Eightieth Amendment) Act, 2000, a prescribed percentage of the net proceeds of all Central taxes and duties (except Union surcharge, cess levied for specific purposes under any law made by Parliament and the duties and taxes referred to in articles 268 and 269) is to be

assigned to the States within which that tax or duty is leviable in that year and distributed among those States in terms of Orders issued by the President on the recommendations of the Finance Commission. For the period of five years commencing from April 1, 2000, the Commission has recommended that 28% of the net proceeds of shareable Central taxes/duties may be distributed amongst all such States' where the Central tax/duty is leviable. If in any year during 2000-05, a Central tax/duty is not leviable in a State, the share of that State in that tax/duty should be put to zero and the entire proceeds should be distributed among the remaining States by proportionately adjusting their shares. In addition, 1.5% of the net proceeds of shareable Central taxes/duties in a year may be distributed amongst such States which do not levy sales tax on sugar, tobacco and textiles during that year. The Commission has recommended percentage share of each State in the share of all States and indicated the criteria adopted by them in arriving at those percentage shares in Chapter VI of their Report.

5. The Government has accepted the above recommendations of the Commission.

Grants-In-Aid of the Revenues of States Under the Substantive Provisions of Article 275 of the Constitution

Grants-in-aid to cover non-Plan gap on Revenue Account

6. The Commission has recommended grants-in-aid to be given under Article 275(1) of the Constitution, other than those under the proviso to Article 275 (1), equal to the amount of deficits assessed for each year during the period 2000-05. The amount of the grant for each State, having non-Plan deficits is indicated in Chapter X of their report. The Government has

accepted these recommendations. In view of the coverage of non- Plan revenue deficit of States by these grants, Central Government's total budgetary support on revenue account for meeting the States' non-Plan requirements will be limited to the grants-in-aid recommended by the Commission. The release of these grants will be made in accordance with the next Report of the Commission due to be submitted by 31st August, 2000. Action is, however, being taken to release a part of these grants on an ad-hoc, provisional basis to mitigate hardship to the concerned States.

Grants-in-aid for up-gradation of standards of administration and specific grants to certain States for special problems

7. The Commission has recommended grants totalling to ₹ 4,972.63 crore towards upgradation of standards of administration and special problems of States. The State-wise, year-wise, purpose-wise details of these grants are given in Chapter VII of their Report. The Government has accepted the recommendations of the Commission for making grants-in-aid to States for upgradation of standards of administration and specific grants to certain States for special problems for the five year commencing from April 1, 2000 as recommended by the Commission.
8. The Commission has recommended grants totalling Rs. 10,000 crore for local bodies during 2000-05, to be utilised (except the amount earmarked for maintenance of accounts & audit and for development of database) for maintenance of civic services (excluding payment of salaries and wages). Of this, ₹ 1600 crore p.a. is for rural local bodies and

₹ 400 crore p.a. is for urban local bodies. The inter-State distribution, criterion adopted in arriving at the proposed distribution are given in Chapter VIII of their Report. Of the total grants for local bodies, the Commission has emphasised earmarking of funds in two areas: ₹ 200 crore for development of database on the finances of the Panchayats and Municipalities and ₹ 98.61 crore for maintenance of accounts of Panchayats as the first charge on these grants, be released by the concerned Ministries of the Government of India, after the arrangements suggested by the Commission have become operational. The Commission has also suggested several measures for strengthening of arrangements for maintenance of accounts and audit of local bodies.

9. The Government has accepted these recommendations subject to the following caveats:

   (i) The local bodies should be required to raise suitable matching resources.

   (ii) In cases where elected local bodies are not in place, the Central Government shall hold the share of such bodies in trust on a non-lapsable basis during 2000-05. Central Government may also similarly hold back a part of the recommended share in case of such bodies to whom functions and responsibilities have not been devolved.

   (iii) Earmarking of funds for maintenance of accounts, within the overall recommended level of grants, may be increased to the extent necessary in consultation with the C & AG.

   (iv) Measures to strengthen accounts and audit of local bodies have been accepted in principle. Details will be worked out in consultation with the C & AG.

Financing of calamity relief expenditure

10. The Commission has recommended the continuance of the existing scheme of Calamity Relief Funds in States with an aggregate size of ₹ 11007.59 crore during 2000-05. This includes the Centre's share of ₹ 8255.69 crore, and the States' share of ₹ 2751.90 crore, worked out in the ratio of 75:25. The State-wise distribution and the criterion adopted by the Commission is indicated in Chapter IX of their Report.
11. The Commission has recommended the discontinuation of the existing National Fund for Calamity Relief because a calamity of rare severity is conceptually of such a nature that the intensity and magnitude cannot be anticipated and provided for in advance through the CRF or regular budgetary mechanism. The Central Government's responsibility does not get restricted to the availability of the amount in the Fund as indeed has been shown during 1995-2000 when Central Government released ₹ 2555 crore from NFCR set up with a corpus of only ₹ 700 crores. Instead, the Commission has recommended that the Central assistance to the States in national calamities should be financed by levy of a special surcharge on the Central taxes for a limited period. A surcharge can also instill a feeling of national participation for a national cause. Collection from such surcharge should be kept in a separate fund, to be known as National Calamity Contingency Fund (NCCF), created in the public Account of the Government of India. The Commission has also recommended that Government of India should contribute an initial core amount of ₹ 500 crore to this fund so that funds for initial operations are readily available. However,

drawals from the fund should be accompanied by imposition of the special surcharge so that it is immediately recouped. Any balance left from the collection of the surcharge, after meeting the exigency for which it was collected, should be credited to the fund and not treated as a resource for meeting the budgetary expenditure. In order to ensure that there is no delay in the flow of funds to the States for administration of relief, a legislation enabling the Central Government to levy surcharge may be enacted.

12. The Government has accepted the above recommendations of the Commission. The recommendation concerning National Calamity Contingency Fund will be implemented after necessary legislation is enacted.

Debt Relief to States

13. The Commission has proposed to continue the existing debt relief scheme, linked to improvement in the ratio of revenue receipts of a State to its total revenue expenditure, with enhanced incentive. Details are given in Chapter XI of their report. Besides, the Commission has recommended a moratorium on the payment of installments of debt and interest on the special loans given to Punjab during 1984-94 for combating insurgency and militancy due for repayment from the State of Punjab during the period 2000-05. The Commission has further recommended debt relief to Punjab and Jammu & Kashmir on the basis of specified expenditure incurred on security.

14. The Government has accepted the above recommendations of the Commission.

15. While working out the total quantum of devolution of share in Central taxes/duties to States and grants-in-aid to States, the Commission has considered the trends in total transfers from the Centre to the States on Revenue account and given its recommendations on the basis of the premise that tax devolution and Plan/non-Plan grants from the Centre to the States should not exceed 37.5% of total Centre's revenues, both tax and non-tax. The Government has accepted this ceiling on total Revenue account transfers from the Centre to the States. However, the acceptance does not imply the establishment of a principle of mandatory sharing of a fixed percentage of Centre's revenue receipts with the States.
16. The Commission's recommendations fall in four categories:
    (i) Those to be implemented by an Order of the President.
    (ii) Those to be implemented by Law of Parliament.
    (iii) Those to be implemented by executive orders.
17. The recommendations under articles 270 and 275(1) of the Constitution relating to share in Central taxes and duties and grants-in-aid, respectively, fall in the first category and the necessary order will be submitted to the President for approval.
18. Recommendations relating to setting up of a National Calamity Contingency Fund (NCCF) and enabling the Central Government to levy surcharge for national calamities fall in the second category. Necessary legislation will be proposed for implementing these recommendations.
19. The recommendations relating to debt relief will be implemented by executive orders.

20. Other recommendations of the Commission will be considered in due course.

Sd/-
(Yashwant Sinha)
Minister of Finance

New Delhi
27th July, 2000.

Report dated 30th August, 2000

1. The Eleventh Finance Commission was constituted by the President on July 3, 1998 to give recommendations on specified aspects of Centre State fiscal relations during 2000-05. The Commission submitted its Report covering all aspects of its original mandate on 7th July, 2000. Earlier, on 15th January, 2000, the Commission had submitted an interim Report for making provisional arrangements for 2000-2001. The interim recommendations of the Commission were accepted by the Government and were laid on the Table of the House on 16th March, 2000. The Commission was asked (vide President's order dated 28th April, 2000) to 'draw a monitorable fiscal reforms programme aimed at reduction of revenue deficit of the States and to recommend the manner in which the grants to States to cover the assessed deficit in their non-plan revenue account may be linked to progress in implementing the programme'.

   On 7th July, 2000, the Commission submitted its report covering all aspects of its original mandate except in respect of the additional mandate assigned to it under the President's order dated 28th April, 2000. This report of the Eleventh Finance Commission was laid on the Table of the House on 27th July, 2000 together with an explanatory memorandum as to the action taken by the Government on the recommendations of the Commission.

2. The Commission has now submitted a supplementary report on 30th August, 2000 purportedly under the additional mandate assigned to it under the President's order dated 28th April, 2000. This Report together with the Explanatory Memorandum on the action taken on the recommendations of the Commission is being laid on the Table of the House, in pursuance of Article 281 of the Constitution.
3. This report mainly deals with grants to States in the context of revenue deficit in the accounts of the States. In respect of revenue deficit grants to States, the Commission's recommendations in their three Reports are summarised below—

   - In the Interim Report submitted on 15th January, 2000, the Commission had recommended a lumpsum provision of ₹ 11000 crore in the Central Budget 2000-01 for revenue deficit grants to States without giving State-wise break-up.
   - In the Main Report submitted on 7th July, 2000, the Commission recommended revenue deficit grant of ₹ 35359 crore for 15 States during 2000-2005. The remaining 10 States were revenue surplus in the Commission's assessment. The Commission was asked to draw up a monitorable fiscal reforms programmes and to recommend how to link the release of revenue deficit grants to progress in implementing the programme.
   - Since only 15 States were assessed to be in revenue deficit, the fiscal reforms programme should have normally covered only the 15 States assessed to be in revenue deficit. Instead, in the

Supplementary Report submitted on 30th August, 2000, the majority view in the Commission has recommended monitorable fiscal reforms programmes for all States. It has been recommended that 15% of the revenue deficit grants meant for 15 States during 2000-05 and a matching contribution by Central Government be credited into an Incentive Fund from which fiscal performance based grants should be made available to all 25 States. Release of performance based grants from an Incentive Fund to be set up by withholding 15% of the ₹ 35359 crore deficit grants for 15 States and an equal matching contribution by Government of India with year-wise phasing as follows—

Composition of the Incentive Fund

(*₹ in crore*)

Year	*Withheld portion of the Revenue deficit grants*	*Contribution of the Centre*	*Total fund*
2000-01	1523.06	598.48	2121.54
2001-02	1080.43	1041.11	2121.54
2002-03	994.64	1126.91	2121.55
2003-04	861.74	1259.81	2121.55
2004-05	843.99	1277.55	2121.54
Total:	5303.86	5303.86	10607.72

- The Commission has also recommended that the grants for specific purposes like upgradation, special problems and local bodies, which remain unutilised due to non-observance of conditionalities attached to the release of these grants may also be credited to the Incentive Fund during 2004-05.

4. Important features of the scheme proposed by the Commission in the Supplementary Report are summarised below:

    (i) A group designated as Monitoring Agency may be constituted by the Government of India for drawing up State-specific monitorable fiscal reforms programmes for all States in the context of the broad parameters suggested by the Commission and as accepted by Government of India. The group may include, among other, representatives of Planning Commission, the Finance Ministry of the Government of India and the representative of the State Government concerned.

    (ii) Eighty five per cent of the revenue deficit grant recommended by the Commission and accepted by the Government of India may be released to the relevant States without linking it to performance under the monitorable fiscal reforms programme. Only 15 per cent of the revenue deficit grant to which a State is entitled may be withheld and linked with the progress in performance.

    (iii) The monitorable programme should give equal weight to the raising of revenue and control of expenditure. The areas indicated by the Commission for monitoring are only suggestive; so are the weights. These can be suitably modified while drawing the State specific programme. However, the broad contents of the reform indicated in the Main Report should be kept in view as the ultimate objective is to bring the revenue deficit of the States to zero, in the aggregate, by 2004-05.

(iv) The Incentive Fund should be set up comprising of two parts. The first part of the Fund would comprise 15 per cent of the withheld part of the grants recommended to cover the deficit of the States on non-plan revenue account. Depending on the performance of a State in the implementation of the monitorable programme, the withheld amount would be released to it on a proportionate basis. The second part of the Fund would be created by contribution from the Central Government, equivalent to 15 per cent of the revenue deficit grants recommended by the Commission.

(v) The incentive component is recommended to be provided to all the States. The initial eligibility of the States has been worked out on the basis of the population as per the 1971 Census. The amount will be available to a State in proportion to the level of performance in the implementation of the monitorable fiscal reforms programme for each year.

(vi) If any State is unable to get the full amount initially earmarked for it in any year, such amount will not lapse but will continue to be available in subsequent years to the same State. During the first four years, no amount of this Fund earmarked for assistance/incentive to a State, would be transferred to another State. However, if any State is not able to draw the amount indicated on the basis of the performance of the first four years, the amount undisbursed to a State would form part of the common pool and would be distributed to the performing States in the fifth year on a pro-rata basis in addition to the amounts to which they are initially entitled. The same would apply to the undrawn amount of the withheld portion of the grants to cover non-plan revenue deficit. Every State irrespective of the assessed deficit or not would be entitled to get the assistance on a pro-rata basis related to performance from the additions to the Fund. This additional entitlement can go up to 100 per cent of their initial eligibility indicated for the State concerned. The Fund may be kept separately, preferably in public account.

(vii) The withheld amount of grants. releasable in 2004-05 may be released to the concerned assessed State on the basis of a review of their performance. In case any amount remains unreleased to a State, it would be added to the Fund and would be available to the remaining States. The balance amount in the fund at the end of 2005-06 will lapse to the Central Government.

(viii) The Commission had recommended grants for specific purposes like upgradation, special problems and local bodies in the Main Report. There are certain specific conditionalities for releasing these grants. The progress in the implementation of the identified schemes may be reviewed by the Monitoring Agency. If the Agency is satisfied that a State has not taken effective steps to implement these in the first four years, and is not in a position to utilise the amount either in full or in part, the same may be added to the Incentive Fund in the fifth year.

(ix) In addition to the incentives for better performance, Central Government may also consider the fiscal reforms programme linked assistance by way of extended ways and means advance and additional open market borrowings. The scope and dimension of such facilities should be drawn up by the Central Government bearing in mind the Centre's fiscal position and the macro-economic implications of this facility. This facility should also be extended to all States linked to monitorable fiscal reforms programme drawn up for the State.

(x) The disbursements from the Incentive Fund as well as the utilisation of the grants recommended by the 11th Finance Commission in the Main Report will be subject to review by the 12th Finance Commission.

5. The above recommendations of the Commission have been accepted by the Government in the interest of furthering the cause of fiscal reforms in the States.
6. The recommendations relating to regulation of grants-in-aid under article 275 (1) of the Constitution are required to be implemented by an Order of the President and the necessary order will be submitted to the President for approval.
7. The above recommendations of the Commission substantially alter the recommendations already made in the Main Report and accepted by the Government. Nevertheless, the recommendations have been accepted by the Government in the interest of furthering the cause of fiscal reforms in the States.

Sd/-

(Yashwant Sinha)

Minister of Finance

New Delhi

19th December, 2000

GOVERNMENT OF INDIA
MINISTRY OF FINANCE
DEPARTMENT OF ECONOMIC AFFAIRS

Explanatory Memorandum as to the Action Taken on the Recommendations made by the Twelfth Finance Commission in its Report Submitted to the President on December 17, 2004

1. The Twelfth Finance Commission was constituted by the President on November 1, 2002 to give recommendations on specified aspects of Centre-State fiscal relations during 2005-10. The Commission submitted its Report covering all aspects of its mandate on December 17, 2004.

2. The Finance Commissions are constituted by the President after every five years or earlier under Article 280 of the Constitution to give recommendations on specified aspects of Centre-State fiscal relations. The recommendations of these Commissions are based on a detailed assessment of the financial position of the Central and State Governments and wide consultations with stakeholders. The Commissions usually visit the States, sponsor studies, hold consultations with experts and their recommendations are backed up by detailed reasons disclosing the methodology adopted by them.

3. The Report of the Twelfth Finance Commission (herein after referred to as the Commission) covering the five years period commencing from April 1, 2005 together with the Explanatory Memorandum on the action taken on the recommendations of the Commission is being laid on the Table of the House, in pursuance of Article 281 of the Constitution. A summary of the Commission's main recommendations relating devolution of taxes and duties to the States, grants-in-aid under article 275 of the Constitution, financing of relief expenditure and debt relief to the States and other matters is contained in Chapter 16 of the Report of the Commission.

4. The Government has carefully considered the main recommendations contained in the Report of the Commission and the action proposed to be taken on these recommendations is detailed below.

Devolution of Share In Central Taxes And Duties To States

5. Under Article 270 of the Constitution, as amended w.e.f. 1st April, 1996 by the Constitution (Eightieth Amendment) Act, 2000, a prescribed percentage of the net proceeds of all Central taxes (except Union surcharge, cess levied for specific purposes under any law made by Parliament and the duties and taxes referred to in Articles 268 and 269) is to be assigned to the States within which that tax is leviable in that year and distributed among those States in terms of Orders issued by the President on the recommenda-tions of the Finance Commission.

For the period of five years commencing from April 1, 2005, the Commission has recommended that 30.5 per cent of the net proceeds of shareable Central taxes may be distributed amongst all such States where any such Central tax is leviable. If in any year during 2005-10, a particular Central tax is not leviable in a State, the share of that State in that tax should be put to zero and the entire proceeds be distributed among the remaining States by proportionately adjusting their shares. For this purpose, additional excise duties in lieu of sales tax on textiles, tobacco and sugar are treated as a part or the shareable pool of central taxes. If this tax rental arrangement is terminated and the States are allowed to levy sales tax (or VAT) on these commodities without any prescribed limit, the share of the States in the net proceeds of shareable central taxes shall be reduced to 29.5 per cent. If any legislation is enacted in respect of service tax after the Eighty Eighth Constitutional amendment is notified, it must be ensured that the revenue accruing to a

State under the legislation should not be less than the share that would accrue to it, had the entire service tax proceeds been part of the shareable pool. The percentage share of each State in Union taxes and duties and the criteria for devolution and relating weights assigned to different factors is indicated in Chapter 7 of the Report.

The Government has accepted the above recommendations of the Commission.

Grants-In-Aid of the Revenues of States under the Substantive Provisions of Article 275 of the Constitution

Non-Plan Revenue Deficit Grant

6. The Commission has recommended grants-in-aid to be given under Article 275(1) of the Constitution, other than those under the proviso to Article 275(1), equal to the amount of deficits assessed for each year during the period 2005-10. A total non-plan revenue deficit grant of ₹ 56,855.87 crore is recommended during the award period for fifteen States. The amount of the grant for each State having non-plan deficits is indicated in Chapter 10 of the Report for each of the 5 years starting from the financial year 2005-06.

The Government has accepted this recommendation

Grant for Education

7. The Commission has recommended grants for eight States amounting to ₹ 10,171.65 crore over the award period for the education sector, with a minimum of ₹ 20 crore in a year for any eligible State. The year-wise allocation for each State is given in Chapter 10 of the Report. The grant for the education sector is an additionality, over and above the normal expenditure to be incurred by the States in this sector. Conditionalities governing the release and utilisation of this grant have been specified in Annexures 10.1 to 10.3 of the Commission's Report.

The Government has accepted this recommendation of the Commission.

Grant for Health

8. The Commission has recommended grants for seven States amounting to ₹ 5,887.08 crore over the award period for the health sector, with a minimum of ₹ 10 crore in a year for any eligible State. The year-wise allocation for each State is given in Chapter 10 of the Report. The grant for the health sector is an additionality, over and above normal expenditure to be incurred by the States in this sector. Conditionalities governing the release and utilisation of this grant have been specified in Annexures 10.1 to 10.3 of the Commission's Report.

The Government has accepted this recommendation of the Commission.

Grants for maintenance of roads and bridges and public buildings

9. The Commission has recommended grants amounting to ₹ 15,000 crore for maintenance of roads and bridges and ₹ 5,000 crore for maintenance of public buildings over the award period. The State-wise, year-wise allocations are given in Chapter 10 of the Report. These grants are an additionality, over and above the normal expenditure to be incurred by the States. Conditionalities governing the release and utilisation of these grants have been specified in Annexure 10.4 to 10.6 of the Commission's Report.

The Government has accepted the above recommendations of the Commission.

Grant for Maintenance of Forests

10. The Commission has recommended grants

amounting to ₹ 1,000 crore over the award period for maintenance of forests. The State-wise, year-wise allocation is given in Chapter 10 of the Report. This grant is an additionality, over and above the normal expenditure to be incurred by the States for this purpose .

The Government has accepted this recommendation of the Commission.

Grant for Heritage Conservation

11. The Commission has recommended grants amounting to ₹ 625 crore over the award period for heritage conservation. This grant is to be used for preservation and protection of historical monuments, archaeological sites, public libraries, museums and archives, and for improving the tourist infrastructure to facilitate visits to these sites. The State-wise, year-wise allocation is given in Chapter 10 of the Report. This grant is an additionality, over and above the normal expenditure to be incurred by the State for this purpose.

The Government has accepted this recommendation of the Commission.

Grant for State Specific Needs

12. The Commission has recommended grants amounting to ₹ 7,100 crore over the award period for State specific needs. The State-wise, purpose-wise details of these grants are given in Chapter 10 of the Report.

The Government has accepted this recommendation of the Commission subject to the condition that the grants would be released based on the level of preparedness of the States to utilize the grants for the specific purpose for which they have been recommended.

Grants for Local Bodies

13. The Commission has recommended grants amounting to ₹ 25,000 crore over the award period for local bodies. Of this, ₹ 20,000 crore is for Panchayats and ₹ 5,000 crore is for urban local bodies. The inter-State distribution and the criterion adopted in arriving at the proposed distribution are given in Chapter 8 of the Report. The Commission has emphasized that of the grants allocated to panchayats, priority should be given to expenditure on the O & M costs of water supply and sanitation and that at least 50% of the grants provided to each State for the urban local bodies should be earmarked for the scheme of solid waste management. Besides expenditure on the O & M costs of water supply and sanitation in rural areas and on the schemes of solid waste management in urban areas, panchayats and urban local bodies should, out of the grants allocated, give high priority to expenditure on creation of data base and maintenance of accounts.

The Government has accepted this recommendation of the Commission as per the provisos to recommendations summarized in paras 8.52 to 8.55 of the Report.

Financing of Calamity Relief Expenditure

14. The Commission has recommended the continuance of the scheme of Calamity Relief Fund in its present form with contributions from the Centre and the States in the ratio of 75:25. The size of the CRF for the period 2005-10 is worked out at ₹ 21,333.33 crore. This includes the Centre's share of ₹ 16,000 crore, and the States' share of ₹ 5,333.33 crore. The State-wise distribution of CRF giving the Centre and State's share is indicated at Annexure 9.1 to 9.3 of the Report. The Commission has also recommended continuance or the scheme of NCCF in its present form with core corpus of

₹ 500 crore. The outgo from the fund may continue to be replenished by way of collection of National Calamity Contingent Duty and levy of special surcharges.

The Government has accepted the above recommendations of the Commission.

Sharing of Profit Petroleum

15. The Commission has recommended the sharing of the non-tax revenue of 'Profit Petroleum' arising out of contractual provisions under NELP with the States from where the mineral oil and natural gas are produced in the ratio of 50:50. The details are given in Chapter 13 of the Report.

The Government has accepted the above recommendations of the Commission subject to the condition that this should be within the overall ceiling of transfers recommended by the Commission (38% of gross revenues). This would imply that once the total transfers cross 38% of gross revenues of the Centre sharing of non-tax revenue of Profit Petroleum would not accrue in that year. Further, this should not be considered by the States as establishing a general principle of sharing of the Centre's non-tax revenues.

Debt Relief to States

16. The Commission has recommended that the scheme of Fiscal Reform facility may be replaced by a scheme of Debt Relief over the period 2005-10. The scheme of Debt Relief recommended by the Commission envisages:

(i) The rescheduling of all Central Loans contracted till 31.3.2004 and outstanding as on 31.3.2005 into fresh loans for 20 years carrying 7.5% interest w.e.f. the year a State enacts the Fiscal Responsibility Legislation. Details of the scheme are given in Chapter 12 of the Report.

The Government has accepted the above recommen-

dations of the Commission subject to the condition laid down by the Twelfth Finance Commission that the debt relief (re-scheduling and consolidation and lowering of interest rate) would be admissible on the State enacting the Fiscal Responsibility legislation and would take effect prospectively from the year in which such legislation is enacted. It is also expected that the States would comply with the obligations regarding reduction of Fiscal Deficit and Revenue Deficit imposed by the Fiscal Responsibility Legislation. The Centre would request the next Finance Commission to make appropriate adjustment in case the State availing of the debt relief is not able to comply with the Fiscal Responsibility Legislation.

(ii) A debt write-off linked to reduction in revenue deficit by a State. The quantum of write-off of repayment would be linked to the absolute amount by which the revenue deficit is reduced in each successive year during the award period. In accordance with the recommendation of the Twelfth Finance Commission, the benefit of write-off would be available only if the fiscal deficit of the State is contained to the level of 2004-2005. If in any year, the fiscal deficit exceeds this level, the benefit of write-off, even if eligible otherwise, would not be given. The details of the scheme are given in Chapter 12 of the Report.

The Government has accepted the above recommendations of the Commission.

Central Assistance for State Plans

17. The Commission has recommended that the Centre should release only the grant portion of Central Assistance for State Plan (CPA) and leave it to the State to raise loan portion from any source. For States unable to raise loans from

market, the Centre may act as a financial intermediary but without any subsidisation of cost. The details are given in Chapter 10 of the Report.

This approach has been accepted by the Government, in principle, to be implemented in phases, in consultation with RBI. From 2005-06, the States would be allowed at their discretion, not to draw the loan portion of the CPA.

External Assistance Loans

18. The Commission has recommended that the Centre should pass on external assistance on back-to-back basis to States and manage it through separate Fund in the Public Account. The details are given in Chapter 12 of the Report.

The Government has accepted the recommendation to pass on external assistance on the same terms and conditions on which it was received subject to the condition that the service cost and exchange rate fluctuations would also be passed on to the States under this arrangement.

Accounting Procedure

19. The Commission has recommended a move by the Centre towards introduction of accrual accounting and standardisation of accounting classification down to the object head for all States to improve fiscal management. The details are given in Chapter 14 of the Report.

The Government has accepted this recommendation in principle . The Government Accounting Standards Board in the office of the Comptroller and Auditor General of India would be asked to draw a detailed road map and operational frame work for its implementation.

Miscellaneous

20. The Commission has recommended that the total

transfers (tax devolution and Plan/non-Plan grants) from the Centre to the States should not exceed 38% of gross revenue receipts of the Centre (both tax and non-tax). The details are given in Chapter 7 of the Report.

The Government has accepted this ceiling on total Revenue account transfers, from the Centre to the States subject to the condition that the acceptance does not imply the establishment of a principle of mandatory sharing of a fixed percentage of Centre's revenue receipts with the States.

Implementation

21. The Commission's recommendations fall in the following categories:

(i) Those to be implemented by an Order of the President.

(ii) Those to be implemented by executive orders.

(iii) Those to be examined further.

22. The recommendations under Articles 270 and 275(1) of the Constitution relating to share in Union taxes and duties and grants-in-aid, respectively, fall in the first category and the necessary orders will be submitted to the President for approval.

23. The recommendations relating to sharing of Profit Petroleum, Debt Relief, Central Assistance for State Plans and External Assistance Loans will be implemented by executive orders.

24. Other recommendations of the Commission will be considered in due course.

P.Chidambaram
Minister of Finance

New Delhi
February 26, 2005

GOVERNMENT OF INDIA
MINISTRY OF FINANCE
DEPARTMENT OF ECONOMIC AFFAIRS

Explanatory Memorandum as to the Action Taken on the Recommendations made by the Thirteenth Finance Commission in its Report Submitted to the President on December 30, 2009

1. The Thirteenth Finance Commission (hereafter referred to as the Commission) was constituted by the President on November 13, 2007 to give recommendations on specified aspects of Centre State fiscal relations during 2010-15. The Commission submitted its report to the President on December 30, 2009 covering all aspects of its mandate.

2. The report of the Commission (hereafter referred to as the Report) covering the five year period commencing from April 1, 2010, together with this Explanatory Memorandum on the action taken on the recommendations of the Commission is being laid on the Table of the House, in pursuance of Article 281 of the Constitution. Summary of the main recommendations of the Commission relating to the sharing of net proceeds of Union taxes between Centre and States, grants-in-aid of revenue of States under Article 275, Goods and Services Tax (GST), financing of relief expenditure and roadmap for fiscal consolidation are contained in Chapter 1 of the Report of the Commission.

3. The Government has carefully examined the main recommendations of the Commission. The action to be taken on these recommendations is detailed below.

Sharing of Union Taxes

4. The Commission has recommended that for its award period, the share of States in the net proceeds of Union taxes may be fixed at 32%. The Commission has also recommended

on the inter-se distribution of the States' share amongst the States. The details of the formula for inter-se distribution and the corresponding share of each State recommended by the Commission are indicated in Chapter 8 of the Report. It has also recommended that the total transfers to the States on the revenue account be subjected to an indicative ceiling of 39.5% of the gross tax revenues of the Centre.

The Government has accepted the above recommendations of the Commission.

Grants-in-Aid of Revenues of States under Article 275 of the Constitution

5. The Commission has recommended grants-in-aid of revenues of States for non-plan revenue deficit, elementary education, environment related issues, improving outcomes, maintenance of roads and bridges, local bodies, disaster relief, GST implementation and state specific grants under Article 275 of the Constitution.

Non-Plan Revenue Deficit Grant

6. The Commission has assessed the revenues and expenditure of the States for the period 2010-15 and has projected the deficit for each State after taking into account the amount of share in Central taxes for that State. The Commission has recommended a grant of ₹ 51800 crore to meet this deficit for eight States. The amount of grant recommended for each state year-wise is indicated in Chapter 12 of the Report. The Commission has also recommended a performance incentive grant of ₹ 1500 crore for three special category States of Assam, Sikkim and Uttarakhand that have graduated out of Non-Plan Revenue Deficit. The details of this grant are indicated in Chapter 12 of the Report.

The Government has accepted this recommendation.

Grant for Elementary Education

7. The Commission has assessed the requirement of providing elementary education for each State based on the Sarva Shiksha Abhiyan norms and recommended to provide a grant of ₹ 24068 crore equivalent to 15% of the assessed requirement. The year-wise allocation for each State and the conditionality for release of this grant are given in Chapter 12 of the Report.

The Government has accepted this recommendation.

Environment Related Grants

8. The Commission has recommended three grants under this category of ₹ 5000 crore each aggregating to ₹ 15000 crore. The first grant of each of these ₹ 5000 crore grants is forest grant, the second is for promotion for renewable energy and the third is for water sector. The year-wise allocation for each State and the conditionalities for forest and water sector grants are indicated in Chapter 12 of the Report. The eligibility of each State for the grant for renewable energy is to be decided, as indicated in Chapter 12 of the Report, based on the achievement of each state on this front in the first four years of the award period.

The Government has accepted these recommendations.

Grants for Improving Outcomes

9. The Commission has recommended six grants under this category aggregating to ₹ 14446 crore over the award period. An incentive grant for reduction in infant mortality of ₹ 5000 crore is to be released to States starting 2012-13 depending on the reduction in Infant Mortality Rate (IMR) achieved by the States with reference to the baseline level of 2009-10 figures. Grant of ₹ 5000 crore for improved delivery of justice has been recommended for Lok Adalats and Legal

Aid, Alternate Dispute Resolution Centres, Heritage Court Buildings, State Judicial Academy and training of judicial officers and public prosecutors. The grant for Unique Identification (UID) programme amounting to ₹ 2989.10 crore is to be released based on the number of people covered under the UID database. Two grants of ₹ 616 crore each have been recommended for District Innovation Funds and improving statistical systems at district and State levels. Finally, a grant of ₹ 225 crore has been recommended for setting up database of employees and pensioners.

The Government has accepted these recommendations.

Grants for maintenance of Roads and Bridges

10. The Commission has assessed the requirement of ordinary repairs of roads in a State and has recommended grant of ₹ 19930 crore equivalent to 90% of the assessed requirement for PMGSY roads and 50% of the assessed requirement for other roads, for four years of the award period starting 2011-12. The allocation for each year for each State and the conditionality for this grant are indicated in Chapter 12 of the Report.

The Government has accepted these recommendations.

State Specific grants

11. The Commission has recommended grants aggregating to ₹ 27945 crore for various state specific needs of the States. The details of these grants for each item of grant for each State are indicated in Chapter 12 of the report.

The Government has accepted these recommendations.

12. For monitoring and implementation of all the above grants at the State level, the Commission has recommended setting up a monitoring committee under the chairmanship of the Chief Secretary of the State.

In addition to the grants mentioned above, the

Commission has recommended grants for GST implementation, local bodies and disaster relief which, alongwith the other recommendations relating to these areas, are explained below.

Goods and Services Tax

13. The Commission has recommended a model GST structure that includes features such as single rate, zero rating of exports, inclusion of various indirect taxes at the Central and State level in GST ambit, major rationalisation of the exemption structure, etc. The Commission has recommended a grant of ₹ 50000 crore for implementation of GST as per the recommended model. This grant is to be disbursed initially in the form of compensation for loss due to implementation of GST and residual amount to be distributed amongst States in the terminal year of the award period as per the devolution formula. It has also recommended administrative structure for implementation and monitoring of this grant.

The Government has accepted these recommendations in principle. However, in view of the ongoing discussions between Centre and States on this aspect, implementation of these recommendations alongwith modalities may await the outcome of the discussions.

Local Bodies

14. The Commission has recommended a basic grant and a performance grant for local bodies. Both these grants in any year have been quantified based on a percentage of the divisible pool of the preceding year. For every year of the award period, the Commission has recommended a basic grant amounting to 1.5% of the size of divisible pool in the preceding year. Similarly, for 2011-12 the Commission has recommended a performance grant of 0.5% of the divisible pool of the preceding year and for subsequent years in the

award period, 1% of the divisible pool of the preceding year.

15. It has also recommended a separate special area basic grant of ₹ 20 per capita, carved out of the total basic grant, for every year in the award period for Schedule V and Schedule VI areas and areas excluded from Part IX and IXA of the Constitution. For these areas, it has recommended a special area performance grant of ₹ 10 per capita for 2011-12 and ₹ 20 per capita for subsequent years of the award period.

16. The performance grants are to be released if the States meet conditions specified by the Commission in Chapter 10 of the Report.

17. As per the revenue projections of the Commission, total grant recommended for the local bodies aggregates to ₹ 87519 crore over the award period. The Commission has also recommended distribution of the grants between urban and rural areas and the inter-se distribution between States. The formula and the inter-se shares are indicated in Chapter 10 of the Report.

The Government has accepted these recommendations.

Disaster Relief

18. The Commission has reviewed the existing arrangement of financing relief expenditure in light of the Disaster Management Act, 2005 and has recommended merger of the National Calamity Contingency Fund (NCCF) into National Disaster Response Fund (NDRF) and merger of Calamity Relief Funds (CRF) into State Disaster Response Fund (SDRF) with effect from 01.04.2010 and transfer of the balances in the existing funds into the new funds.

19. The Commission has assessed the relief expenditure requirements of all States and recommended that 75% of the SDRF requirement for general category states and 90% for special category States be met by the Centre through a grant to the States. It has also recommended a grant of ₹ 525 crore

for capacity building. Overall, to meet the Central share of SDRF and for capacity building, the Commission has recommended a grant of ₹ 26373 crore. It has mandated all States to follow the required accounting practices to properly account for relief expenditure.

The Government has accepted these recommendations.

Fiscal Roadmap

20. The Commission has assessed the finances of the Union and States and specified a combined debt target of 68% of Gross Domestic Product (GDP) to be met by 2014-15. It has worked out a roadmap for Fiscal Deficit (FD) and Revenue Deficit (RD) for the award period. For Centre, it has recommended RD to be eliminated and FD to be brought down to 3% of GDP by 2013-14. For States, the Commission has worked out fiscal roadmap for each State depending on its current deficit and debt levels. The States are required to eliminate RD and achieve FD of 3% of their respective Gross State Domestic Product (GSDP) during the Commission's award period in stages, in a manner that all the States would eliminate RD and achieve FD of 3% of GSDP latest by 2014-15. The Commission has also recommended that the borrowing limits of the States should be fixed by the Centre in line with these targets.

The Government has accepted these recommendations in principle. Detailed proposals for amendment of the FRBM Act, as may be necessary, will be taken up separately.

Debt Relief to States

21. The Commission has recommended two debt relief measures to be extended to all States. Firstly, it has recommended that the interest rates on loans from National Small Savings Fund (NSSF) to States contracted till the end of 2006-07 and outstanding as at the end of 2009-10 be reset

at interest rate of 9%. The implication of this relief during the award period is estimated by the Commission to be ₹ 13517 crore. The financial implication over the entire period till the maturity of the last loan covered in this relief measure is estimated to be ₹ 28360 crore. The Commission has also recommended that structural reforms should be brought in the NSSF to make it more market linked.

22. The second debt relief recommended by the Commission is write-off of Central loans to States that are administered by central ministries other than Ministry of Finance outstanding as at the end of 2009-10. The amount of loans outstanding as at the end of 2007-08 was ₹ 4506 crore as noted by the Commission. The Commission has also recommended that any further loans under Centrally Sponsored Schemes should be completely avoided.

23. The Commission has also recommended extension of the debt consolidation facility recommended by the Twelfth Finance Commission to States that have not yet availed this benefit.

24. All the above mentioned debt relief is available to States only if they amend/legislate FRBM Acts in accordance with the recommendations of the Commission. The Commission has also recommended that the States will be eligible for the state specific grants only if they comply with this condition.

> With regard to the recommendation relating to interest rate reset on NSSF loans to the States, the Government has accepted it in principle. However, since the recommendations are comprehensive and cover other structural aspects like interest rate mismatch, tenor mismatch and other administrative matters, Ministry of Finance will constitute a Committee to work out detailed modalities for implementation of this recommendation.

With regard to write-off of the Central loans to States, extension of the debt consolidation scheme recommended by the Twelfth Finance Commission to States that did not avail the benefit till now, and the conditions laid down by the Commission for availing these benefits, the Government has accepted the recommendations of the Commission.

With regard to completely avoiding central loans to states in the future, action will be taken in consultation with the respective ministries.

Other Recommendations

25. In addition to the above, the Commission has made other recommendations that deal with issues including revenue and expenditure reforms at Central and State levels, accounting and budgeting reforms, additional disclosures by the Centre, State and local bodies, etc.

These recommendations will be examined in due course.

Implementation

26. Orders on the recommendations under Articles 270 and 275(1) of the Constitution relating to share in Union taxes and duties and grants-in-aid, respectively, will be issued after obtaining the approval of the President. The recommendations relating to reorganisation of Funds for disaster relief, debt relief to States and borrowing ceilings will be implemented by executive orders. Other recommendations of the Commission will be acted upon in due course.

Pranab Mukherjee
Minister of Finance

New Delhi
February 25, 2010

A brief note on the procedure followed by the Finance Commission for interaction with State Govts.

Before the notification for constituting the Finance Commission is issued, the Govt. of India appoints an officer of sufficient seniority as Officer on Special Duty (OSD). The task of the OSD is to make all logistic arrangements required for the working of the Commission. This includes office space, personnel, office equipment and machinery and other arrangements. This is done in order to ensure that no time is wasted in arranging these things once the Commission is constituted and the Commission starts the work in right earnest. The Commissions in their report highlighted the difficulties faced by the Commission in making arrangements which always delayed the submission of reports.

Apart from the logistic arrangements, the main job of the OSD is to draft the Terms of Reference and "Considerations" for the Commission. The OSD starts the consultative process with the concerned ministries, eminent persons in the field and State Govts. sometimes the consultation with the States is done at the level of Finance Minister but normally this is done at the level of Finance Secretary. This consultation takes the form of meetings with the State Finance Secretaries or correspondence with them. In recent times, the method of correspondence has become common.

It has been the experience that the officer so appointed as OSD becomes the Member Secretary of the Commission but in some cases he is appointed as Secretary of the Commission only without the status of the member.

The Commission formally notifies the rules of procedure to be followed for its working. In addition the Finance

Commission is delegated the powers of "Department" of Central Govt.

Before finalising its recommendations, the Commission starts consultation at various levels. This is done with State Govts., CAG and AGs of the States, ministries of Govt. of India specially Finance, Rural Development, Urban Development, Panchayati Raj, Agriculture etc. It holds discussion with the Planning Commission also though a member in charge of Resources is a member of the Finance Commission. The report of the Thirteenth Finance Commission shows that the Commission consulted 31 ministries.

In addition, the Commission consults economists and economic administrators, meets the Chairman and members of the past commissions, holds workshops and seminars on topics connected with the TORs. It also has consultations with various chambers of commerce and industry. The Thirteenth Finance Commission met the members of the Empowered Committee of Finance Ministers where a joint memorandum on behalf of all states was presented to the Commission.

The Finance Commission also commissions some studies on various subjects in order to have an updated development in the concerned subject which may help the Commission in formulating its views/recommendations. The Thirteenth Finance Commission commissioned 31 such studies on different subjects.

In addition to above, individuals and organizations also meet the Commission to express their views in response to the Public Notice issued by the Commission.

So far as the consultation with the States is concerned, the consultation is very extensive and exhaustive. The process starts with a letter from the Chairman to the Chief Ministers, Lt. Governors of Union Territories and Governors of States under President rule if any. The Chairman, while referring to TOR given to the Commission, solicits the cooperation of the State Govt. in successfully and timely completing the onerous task assigned to it. The Chairman seeks the views of the State Govt. on each and every matter on which the Commission has to give its recommendations.

The letter of Chairman is followed by a detailed letter of the Secretary of the Commission to the Chief Secretary of the States and Union Territories. The Secretary requests the States to give specific views regarding all the matters referred to in the TOR. The Secretary also talks of the information required from the States on their resources and committed liabilities.

The Finance Commission collects detailed information data and other inputs relating to State and Local Body finances through schedules and write ups. The Commission asks for the following information:

(a) Topics on which notes are required for State Finances

(i)	Base and Rates of State Taxes & Duties	-	12
(ii)	Loans due to State Govt.	-	1
(iii)	State Budgetary Position	-	1
(iv)	Natural Calamities	-	2
(v)	State Plan	-	3
(vi)	Economy measures etc.	-	2
(vii)	Subsidies	-	1
(viii)	Norms for maintenance of Capital assets	-	1
(ix)	Management of SRTC	-	5
(x)	Power Sector	-	5
(xi)	Public Sector Enterprises	-	2
(xii)	Debt Consolidation and Relief	-	2
(xiii)	Taxation efforts	-	1
(xiv)	Inter-State Regional Disparities	-	1
(xv)	Quality of Expenditure	-	1
(xvi)	Pension Reform Initiative	-	1
(xvii)	User Charges	-	1

(xviii)	Administrative Reforms	-	1
(xix)	Integrated Financial Management	-	1
	Total:		47

Apart from these topics, the data in the prescribed proforma is also required by the Finance Commission. These proforma run into 45 statement. The period covered is very long. In case of 13th Commission, it covered the period from 2002-03 to 2014-15. This was divided into actuals (2002-2008), RE (2008-09), BE (2009-10) and the projections (2010-15). Preparing the notes on the subject and collecting data for so many items for such a long range of period is a very onerous task. The Statements also include the explanatory notes.

The Finance Commission also asks for separate detailed information on local bodies (ULBs/PRIs) after the 73rd and 74th amendment of the Constitution. Apart from the report of the State Finance Commission, the Finance Commission asks for the notes on the issues raised apart from schedule of financial position on roughly 18 schedules.

In addition, the Commission requires the State Govts. to submit their views on each and every item of TOR and the considerations listed in the notification constituting the Finance Commission. Apart from the subjects notes and schedules, this is the most important part of the memorandum of the State Govt.

On the basis of the notes and schedules furnished by the States, the Commission prepares the status report of each State which it uses at the time of State visit. This is the second part of consultation. The Commission sends detailed guidelines for the visit of the Commission to the States. Apart from the protocol arrangements, the major highlight is the meeting with the Chief Minister along with the other members of the cabinet and State Govt. officials. The Commission indicates the areas and issues on which it would like to hear from the State Govts. This meeting generally lasts for half a day and in the next half, the commission expects a meeting with representatives of political parties, ULBs and PRIs and representatives of trade and industry. The second day is normally devoted to field visits. The Commission indicates the areas to be seen or the State Govt. selects the sites on their own.

With the consultation with the State Govt., public representatives, political parties and trade industry, the Commission formulates its recommendations for the presentation to President before the stipulated time frame.

Bibliography

I. Govt. of India Publications

1. Report of the First Administrative Reforms Commission 1969.
2. Report of the Second Administrative Reforms Commission 2009.
3. Report of the Centre-State Relations Commissions (Sarkaria Commission) 1974.
4. Report of the Centre-State Relations Commissions (M.M. Punchi Commission) 2010.
5. Report of the Tax Reforms Committee 1991
6. Report of the First Finance Commission 1951.
7. Report of the Second Finance Commission 1956.
8. Report of the Third Finance Commission 1960.
9. Report of the Fourth Finance Commission 1964.
10. Report of the Fifth Finance Commission 1968.
11. Report of the Sixth Finance Commission 1972.
12. Report of the Seventh Finance Commission 1977.
13. Report of the Eighth Finance Commission 1982.
14. Report of the Ninth Finance Commission 1987.
15. Report of the Tenth Finance Commission 1992.
16. Report of the Eleventh Finance Commission 1998.
17. Report of the Twelfth Finance Commission 2002.
18. Report of the Thirteenth Finance commission 2007.

II. Economic and Political Weekly

- Special issues of *Economic and Political Weekly*, 2002.
- Ahluwalia, Montek (2000): "Economic Performance of States

in Post Reform Period," *EPW*, May 6.

- Kurain N.J. (1999): "State Govt. Finances," *EPW*, May 8, 1999.
- Lahiri Ashok (2000): "Sub-National Public Finance in India," *EPW*, Apil 29, 2000.
- Rao Govinda and H.K. Amarnath (2000): "Fiscal Correction in India- Illusion and Reality" *EPW*, August 5.
- *Economic and Political Weekly*, Vol. 45, No. 48 - Special Issue on Thirteenth Finance Commission.
- *Economic and Political Weekly*, July 30, 2005 - Special Issue on Twelfth Fiance Commission.
- Godbole Madhav (2001): "Making State Budgets Transparent and User-Friendly," *Economic and Political Weekly*, April 21.
- Rakshit Mihir (2001): "Restoring Fiscal Balance through Legislative Fiat—The Indian Experiment," *Economic and Political Weekly*, June 9.
- Godbole Madhav (2002): "Withering away of canons of Financial Propriety—Maharashtra's Finances," *Economic and Political Weekly*, January 12.
- Karnik Ajit (2002): "Fiscal Responsibility and Budget Management Bill—Offering Credible Commitments," *Economic and Political Weekly*, January 19.
- T.N. Srivastava (2002): "Local 'Self' Government and the Constitution," *Economic and Political Weekly*, July 27.
- Rao M. Govinda (2002): "State Finances in India: Issues and Challenges," *Economic and Political Weekly*, August 3.
- T. Ravi Kumar, Murali Dhar Vemuri (2002): "Centre-State Transfer of Resources—The Population Factor," *Economic and Political Weekly*, August 17.
- Gurumurthi S. (2002): "Twelfth Finance Commission and States' Debt Burden," *Economic and Political Weekly*, October 5.
- G. Thimmalah (2002): "Finance Commission—Decline of a Constitutional Institution," *Economic and Political Weekly*, November 23.
- M. Govinda Rao (2003): "Reform in Central Sales Tax in the Context of VAT," *Economic and Political Weekly*, February 15.
- S. Gurumurthi (2003): "Issues before 12th Finance Commission—Review of Vertical and Horizontal System of Tax Sharing," *Economic and Political Weekly*, February 15.
- R. Kannan, S.M. Pillai, R. Kausaliya, Jai Chander (2004):

"Finance Commission Awards and Fiscal Stability in States," *Economic and Political Weekly*, January 31.

- Nirvikar Singh, Garima Vasishtha (2004): "Patterns in Centre-State Fiscal Transfers—An Illustrative Analysis," *Economic and Political Weekly*, November 6.
- M.A. Oommen (2005): "Twelfth Finance Commission and Local Bodies," *Economic and Political Weekly*, May 14.
- T. Ravi Kumar (2005): "Tax Devolution and Regional Disparities," *Economic and Political Weekly*, May 14.
- N.J. Kurian (2005): "Debt Relief for States," *Economic and Political Weekly*, July 30.
- Jayati Ghosh (2005): "Twelfth Finance Commission and Restructuring of State Government Debt: A Note," *Economic and Political Weekly*, July 30.
- Mihir Rakshit (2005): "Some Analytics and Empirics of Fiscal Restructuring in India," *Economic and Political Weekly*, July 30.
- Archana Dholakia (2005): "Measuring Fiscal Performance of State—An Alternative Approach," *Economic and Political Weekly*, July 30.
- Indira Rajaraman, Debdatta Majumdar (2005): "Equity and Consistency Properties of TFC Recommendations," *Economic and Political Weekly*, July 30.
- M. Govinda Rao, Pratap R. Jena (2005): "Balancing Stability, Equity and Efficiency," *Economic and Political Weekly*, July 30.
- Raja J. Chelliah (2005): "Malady of Continuing Fiscal Imbalance," *Economic and Political Weekly*, July 30.
- Rangarajan C. (2005): "Approach and Recommendations," *Economic and Political Weekly*, July 30.
- Amaresh Bagchi (2005): "Symposium on Report of Twelfth Finance Commission—Introduction and Overview," *Economic and Political Weekly*, July 30.
- G.R. Reddy (2006): "Twelfth Finance Commission and Backward States," *Economic and Political Weekly*, August 12.
- Pratap R. Jena (2006): "Fiscal Marksmanship—Link between Forecasting Central Tax Revenues and State Fiscal Management," *Economic and Political Weekly*, September 16.
- T.M. Thomas Issac, R. Ramakumar (2006): "Why do the States Not Spend ?—An Exploration of the Phenomenon of Cash Surpluses and the FRBM Legislation," *Economic and Political*

Weekly, December 2.

- Subhash Chandra Garg (2006): "Transformation of Central Grants to States—Growing Conditionality and Bypassing State Budgets," *Economic and Political Weekly*, December 2.
- Sarkar P.C. (1994): "Regional Imbalances in the Indian Economy Over, Plan Periods," *Economic and Political Weekly*, March 12.
- Gurumurthi, S. (1998): "Inter-governmental Fiscal Relations," *Economic and Political Weekly*, Vol. XXXIII, No. 35, 36-38.

A

Ahmad Ehtisham (1996): *Intergovernmental Transfers—An International Perspective, in Financing Decentralized Expenditure: An International Comparison of Grants*, edited by Ehtisham Ahmad, Aldershot, U.K., Edward Elgar, Chapter I, cited in S. Gurumurthi (1998).

Ahluwalia M.S. (2000): "Economic Performance in States in Post-Reform Period," *Economic and Political Weekly*, May 6.

Ajit Kumar Singh (Ed.): *Twelfth Finance Commission: Recommendations and Their Implications for the State Finances (2008)*, APH Publishing Corporations, New Delhi.

Amresh Bagchi and Pulin B. Nayak (1994): *A Survey of Public Finance and the Planning Process, Tax Policy and Planning*, edited by Amaresh Bagchi and Nicholas Stern OUP).

Anand M., A. Bagchi and Tapas Sen (2001): *Fiscal Displine at the State Level*, Paper Presented at World Bank, NIPFP Conference, May 2001.

B

Bagchi, Amaresh, J.L. Bajaj and William A. Byrd (1992): *State Finances in India*, Vikas Publishing, New Delhi.

Bagchi, Amaresh (1999): *Tax Assignment in the Indian Federation: A Critique*, in Ahluwalia, I.J. and Little, M.D. (eds.): Essays for Manmohan Singh, Oxford University Press, Delhi.

Bagchi, Amaresh (2000): "Rethinking Federalism," *Economic and Political Weekly*, Vol. XXXV, No. 34, August 9, p. 3034, Bagchi, Amresh (2000a): A note on the Need to Strengthen the Equalising Role of Fiscal Transfers, Report of the Eleventh Finance Commission.

Bagchi, A. (2000): "Trade off between Equity, Efficiency and Autonomy," *The Economic Times*, August 1.

Bird, R.M. (1986): *Federal Finance in Comparative Perspective Canadian*

Tax Foundation.

Bird, R.M. (1986): *Federal Finance in Comparative Perspective,* Canadian Tax Foundation.

Bird, M. Richard (1994): *A Comparative Perspective on Federal Finance, Future of Fiscal Federalism,* edited by Kenneth G. Banting, Douglas M. Brown and Thomas J. Couchene (1994), Queen's University, Kingston, Ontario, Canada).

Brosio, Giorgio and Sanjeev Gupta (1998): *Ethics in Fiscal Federalism in Theory and Practice,* pp. 504-26, cited in S. Gurumurthi (1998).

Brahmananda, P.R. (1999): *Reforms in the Fiscal Relations between Centre and States,* in Gandhi and Subrahamanya (1999).

C

Cassen, Robert and Joshi, Vijay (eds.) (1995): *India—The Future of Economic Reforms,* Oxford University Press, Delhi.

Chelliah, R.J. (1991): *Towards a Decentralized Policy,* Fourth L.K. Jha Memorial Lecture, The Fiscal Research Foundation, New Delhi.

Chaube P.K. (2001): *Evolution of Union-State Fiscal Relations in India: Two Steps Forward and One Step Backward,* Volume of 84th Conference of the Indian Economic Association held at Vellore.

Chaube P.K. (Ed.)(2003): *Fiscal Federalism in India,* Deep & Deep Publications.

Chelliah, R.J. (2001): *Political Economy of Poverty Eradication in India and Essays on Fiscal Reforms,* Safe New Delhi.

Chanda A (1965) Federalism in India, George Allen

D

Development Strategy, Regional Disparities and Centre-State Financial Relations in India, Academic Fundation, New Delhi, 2005.

G

Gandhi, Jagdish P. (2000): *Eleventh Finance Commission: An Opportunity Missed,* Business Line August, 29.

Gandhi, Jagdish P. and Susheela Subrahmanya, (Eds.), (1999): *New Facets of Financial Federalism,* Deep & Deep Publications, New Delhi.

Gandhi, Jagdish P. (2001): *Eleventh Finance Commission: A Critique,* Value of 84th Annual Conference of the Indian Economic

Association held at Vellore.

Gulati, I.S. (1987): *Centre State Budgetary Transfers OUP*, Bombay

Gupta, Paul (Ed.) (1996): *Economic Reforms—The Role of States and the Future of Centre-State Relations*, in Observer Research Foundations, New Delhi.

H

Hemalata Rao (1999): *Federal Fiscal Transfers Criteria: Need for Alternatives*, in Gandhi and Subrahmanya.

Hicks, J.R. (1959): *Essays in World Economics*, Calarendon Press, Oxford.

Hyman, David N. (1999): *Public Finance—A Contemporary Application of Theory to Policy*, The Dryden Press, Harcourt Brace College Publishers.

I

Inman Robert and Daniel Ruined (1997): "Rethinking Federation," *Journal of Economic Perspective*.

J

Johnson, R.A. and D.W. Wichern (1996): *Applied Multivariate Statistical Analysis*, Prentice Hall of India, New Delhi.

K

Kamta Prasad (1999): *Regional Balance and Resource Transfer from Centre to States, Alternative Equilibrium Model*, in Gandhi and Subrahmanya (1999).

Kenneth Kletzer and Nirvikar Singh (1997): *The Political Economy of Indian Fiscal Federalism* (Ed.) Sudipto Mundle Oxfore 1997.

Khan, M.Y. (2001): *Eleventh Finance Commission: North-Eastern States*, Weightage Still Low, Business Line, August 29.

L

Livingstone, N. (1952): "A Note on the Nature of Federalism," *Political Science Quarterly*, Vol. 67.

M

Margin, Vol. 11, No. 2, January 1979, *Quaterly Journal of National Council of Applied Economic Research*, New Delhi.

Mukesh Anand, Amaresh Bagchi and Tapas Sen (2001): *Fiscal Discipline at the State Level*, Paper Presented at World Bank-NIPFP Conference, May 2001.

Musgrave, R.A. (1959): *The Theory of Public Finance*, McGraw Hill Book Co., Asian Edition.

Musgrave, R.A. and P.B. Musgrave (1980): *Public Finance in Theory and Practice*, McGraw Hill IBC, New Delhi.

Mythili, B. (2000): *Mismatch Fixing: The Economic Times,* August 1.

N

Nanjundappa D.M. (1999): More Resources to the States: An Alternative to TFC's Alternative Devolution Scheme, Gandhi and Susheela Subrahyamanya (1999).

National Institute of Public Finance and Policy (1981): Trends and Issues in Indian Federal Finance, Allied Publishers Pvt. Ltd.

P

Planning Commission, Approach Paper to the Tenth Plan, September, 2001, Vito Tanzi (1995): Fiscal Federalism and Decentralization, Paper Presented at Annual World Bank Conference on Development.

Prakash Om (1994): Centre-State Financial Relations in India, Atlantic Publishers and Distribution, New Delhi.

Prest, A.R. (1962): Public Finance in Underdeveloped Countries, Vikas Publishing House, Delhi.

R

Rao, C.H.H. (2005): *Development Strategy Regional Dispontes and Centre State Financial Relations in India Academic Foundation,* New Delhi.

Rao, M.G. and Sen, T.K. (1996): *Fiscal Federalism in India,* Macmillan India Ltd., Delhi.

Rao, M. Govinda and Sen, Tapas K. (1996): *Fiscal Federalism in India—Theory and Practice,* Macmillan, Delhi.

Rao, M. Govinda and Raja J. Chelliah (1996): *Fiscal Federalism in India,* Indian Council of Social Science Research, New Delhi.

Rao, M. Govinda, Ric Shand and K.P. Kalirajan (1999): "Convergence of Income Across Indian States: A Divergent View," *Economic and Political Weekly,* March 27 - April 2.

Rao, M. Govinda (1997): *Indian Fiscal Federalism in Public Finance—Policy Issues for India* (ed.) Sudipto Mundle Oxford.

Rao, M. Govinda & Sen T.K. (1996): *Fiscal Federalism in India,* Macmillion India, Delhi

Rao, M. Govinda (2004): *State Level Fiscal Reforms in India in India's Emerging Economy,* (ed.), Kaushik Basu, Oxford.

Rao, M. Govinda & Sen Tapas (2011): Federation and Fiscal Reforms in India, Vol. 9, No. 84, NIPFP.

Rao, M. Govinda and Nirvikar Singh (2005): *Political Economy of Federalism in India,* Oxford.

Rao, K. Madhava and Duvvuri Subbarao (1996): "Federalism and all that," *The Economic Times*, 30th July, Vol. 36, No. 126.

Rao, Hemlata (1984): "Eighth Finance Panel," *Economic Times*, Vol. XI, 174, September 17, 1984.

Roy, Rathin (1998): *Debates on India Fiscal Policy* in T.J. Byres (ed.): *The Indian Economy*, Major Debates Since Independence, Oxford University Press.

S

Singh, A.K. (ed.), (2008): *Twelfth Finance Commission: Recommendations and Their Impliactions for the State Finances*, A.P.H. New Delhi.

Sinha, K.K. (1972): *Fiscal Federalism and The Transfer Problem*, IEA Conference Volume.

Srivastava, D.K. & Rao Bhujanga (2009): *Review of Trends in Fiscal Transfers in India.*

Subrahmanya, K.N. and Sreekantaradhya, B.S. Eds. (1983): Taxation and Centre-State Financial Relations, Deep & Deep Publications, New Delhi.

T

Taylor, Philip E. (1968): *The Economics of Public Finance*, Oxford, & IBH Publishing House, Third Edition.

Ter-Minassian Teresa (1997): *Inter-governmental Fiscal Relations in a Macro Economic Perspective: An Overview*, in Fiscal Federalism in Theory and Practice, edited by Teresa Ter-Minassian, International Monetary Fund, Washington.

Thimmalah, G. (1998): "Indian Finance Commission," *The Indian Journal of Public Administration*, Vol. XLIII, No. 3, New Delhi.

Themmiah, G. (2000): "Finance Commission Gap Filling Approach," *Economic Times.*

Themmiah, G. (1998): *Indian Finance Commissions*, IJPA, Vol. XLIII, No. 3, New Delhi.

Tripathi, V.P. and Nagar, Saumyha (1984): "Centre State Resource Distribution and Finance Commission," *A Paper Read at National Seminar Organized at Institute of Social Science*, Agra University, Agra.

V

Vithal, B.P.R. and Sastry, M.L. (2001): *Fiscal Federalism in India*, Oxford University Press, Delhi.

W

World Bank Development Report (1998): *Public Finance in Development*, World Bank.

Index